THE
BIOLOGY *of* THE NEGRO

By

JULIAN HERMAN LEWIS, Ph.D., M.D.

Associate Professor of Pathology, University of Chicago; Member of the
Otho S. A. Sprague Memorial Institute for Medical Research
Senior Attending Pathologist, Provident
Hospital, Chicago, Illinois

ISBN: 978-1-63923-849-1

Printed: March 2023

Published and Distributed By:
Lushena Books
607 Country Club Drive, Unit E
Bensenville, IL 60106
www.lushenabks.com

ISBN: 978-1-63923-849-1

THE BIOLOGY OF THE
NEGRO

RESPECTFULLY DEDICATED TO MY TEACHER AND FRIEND

PROFESSOR EMERITUS H. GIDEON WELLS

DEPARTMENT OF PATHOLOGY, UNIVERSITY OF CHICAGO

PREFACE

DISEASE tends to prove the kinship of the different races of man but at the same time clearly demonstrates some of their differences. There is no illness which affects one race that may not also affect every other race, although the manifestations of an illness may vary widely among races, both quantitatively and qualitatively. A disease may, of course, be completely confined to a single race, owing to some specific characteristic of the locale rather than to some optimum relationship between the cause of the disease and the race affected.

Comparative racial pathology is of broad interest. As a measure of the differences and similarities of races, it is of interest to anthropology. The reaction to disease is no less a characteristic of a race than is head form or skin color, and the description and explanation of these racial reactions are just as enlightening in respect to the biological relation between races, to their origin and to their previous history, as are the description and explanation of normal morphology.

The comparison of races in regard to the behavior of disease among them is of considerable importance to medicine. If a disease consistently behaves differently in one race than it does in another, it usually can be assumed that one or more differences in the characteristics of the races are responsible. It may be possible by careful study and comparison of these characteristics to isolate those that account for disease differences, thereby giving useful information concerning the etiology of disease. The characteristics that may differ among races are of two categories. There are those, first, that are biological—being anatomical, physiological, or chemical—of the type by which races are ordinarily distinguished. These are inherent and inheritable and are probably the result of an adaptation to an environment. Then there are those that are environmental in origin and have to do with, among other things, the living conditions, the habits and effects reflecting the mentality of races.

It is difficult to say which of these two types of racial differences is the more important or which one may account for the differences in the effect of a given disease. One must determine first of all in each case if the disease behavior cannot be accounted for by the kind of houses people live in or the kind of work they do or the food they eat.

No organized treatise on racial pathology exists, in spite of its value to at least two important biological sciences. The nearest approach to one is the well-known, but out-of-date three-volume *Handbook of geographical and historical pathology* by August Hirsch. But this is no more than it pretends to be— a medical geography which discusses the distribution of disease among the different countries. Since different countries include different races, the diseases of races are considered, but only incidentally. The same is true of the lesser works on medical geography. In the growing literature concerning *Konstitutions-lehre*, which has to do with the relation of body characteristics to disease, the question of race is involved, since body characteristics vary among races. Most of the information concerning the distribution of disease among races appears in isolated papers and in medical textbooks as a small part of discussions on the etiology of disease.

Comparative racial pathology deserves not only to be the subject of a separate field of investigation and study but also a separate name for its designation. It is suggested that this subject be known as "anthropathology," a word derived in the same way as was "paleopathology" and with the use of the roots that make up the word "anthropology." The term "anthropathology"[1] is derived from the three Greek words, *anthropos, pathos, ologia*, and means the science of the diseases of man. Its comparative meaning is the same as that which is understood in the body of the science of anthropology.

Anthropathology, then, has to do with the comparison of races of man in regard to the expression of disease among them. In keeping with the scope of anthropology, it might also embrace

[1] The new word should more correctly be "anthropospathology," but this is less easily pronounced than "anthropathology."

the comparison in this respect of man and the lower animals, particularly as to the influence on disease of the concomitants of the higher development of man, including such factors as the assumption of the upright position and modern food, living conditions, and artificial modifications of the environment.

A systematic presentation of anthropathology should logically begin with the comparison of diseases in the Negro and the Caucasian, because the literature is more extensive, because many of the biological and environmental characteristics of the two peoples show sharp contrasts, and because a knowledge of the behavior of disease among Negroes has much practical value. Another advantage of such a study of Negroes is the greater possibility of evaluating factors that may influence disease. Groups of Negroes are available who live or have lived under different and known conditions, a situation almost similar to the reproducible and controlled conditions in the laboratory. The essential facts are that a group of primitive people as homogeneous as one can expect, well adapted to an environment, was transferred to different climates and to different social conditions where they interbred with other races, but to some extent remained pure, and where they have become stabilized into groups that show among them the wide social and economic variations that are possible in and characteristic of the American civilization. It is possible, with varying degrees of success, to compare these people under primitive conditions and under civilized conditions, when comparatively pure and when mixed with other races, when enslaved and when free, when affected by poverty and by favorable economic conditions, by illiteracy and education, and in rural and urban life. In no other people is it possible to compare simultaneously such a wide diversity of factors. It is to be admitted that information is not available to the same extent for all these circumstances. For instance, in Africa very little is known about many diseases among the bulk of the Negroes, and it is often impossible to state whether or not some diseases even exist there, much less to give rates of incidence. In those parts of the continent under competent observation it often happens that interest is centered on diseases that are important in that country but of no consequence in America. Again, in this country it is not possible to obtain information about diseases of Negroes during slavery. This is extremely unfortunate, because it would be very interesting and informative to know what the reaction was·of these people to the new diseases they encountered and to be able to trace the development of immunity and adaptation to them.

This book has no thesis to develop or disprove. It pretends to be nothing other than an arranged assembly of the observed and reported facts concerning the biology, including pathology, of the Negro. Originally the plan was to make it as complete as possible, but the material available was found to be so voluminous that it was necessary to stop far short of this and to include only what seemed to be, from the amount of discussion, the most important subjects. Recently there has been a stimulation of interest in the medical and biologic questions concerning the Negro. In 1927 Hrdlička published in the *American Journal of Physical Anthropology* a list of about 250 titles, which comprised most of the accumulated literature on these subjects. In contrast, the *Quarterly Cumulative Index Medicus* alone cited in the single year of 1938, 106 such titles. Publications are appearing too·rapidly to make any review complete at any one time.

It was a sizable problem to determine what people should be included under the term "Negro." In America·it is the custom even in scientific literature to apply this name equally to people of decided African origin and to those who have little or no perceptible amount of Negro blood. Any pigmented race, whether they be Moors, Ethiopians, Arabs, or East Indians, may be grouped indiscriminately in statistics pertaining to Negroes. Some attempts have been made in the literature to distinguish between "mulattoes" and "blacks," but there is no agreement as to what these words mean. In Africa Negroes are a more sharply identified group, although anthropologists speak of "true Negroes" as contrasted to certain other people, like the Bantus, who are considered as intermixtures. In this book the American usage is followed in review of the American literature, and for other literature only that is used pertaining to the Negroid people of the east and west coasts of Africa and of central and southern Africa as well as the intermixtures called "colored" by the English. It is confessed that this word "race" is used very loosely and not with the exactness of the anthropologist, who prefers the word "stocks" or "strains" in referring to what herein are termed "Negro" and "white" races.

Considerable judgment was necessary in the selection of the material reviewed. In addition to the large amount of inconsequential matter that clutters any scientific literature, there is a considerable portion of that concerning the Negro that is so biased and so obviously propaganda that there was no other choice than to disregard it, except when it was desirable to include it in order to illustrate the difficulties in obtaining accurate facts. However, many worthy writings have been omitted, either because of the lack of space or because of oversight.

The author wishes to express his deep indebtedness to Professor Emeritus H. Gideon Wells for his indispensable assistance, guidance, and encouragement at every step in the preparation of this manuscript. His interest in it and his insistence that its completion be expedited are responsible for the conviction that the final product might be well worth the efforts expended. Grateful acknowledgment is also made of the kindness of the following, who have critically read either part or all of the manuscript: Dr. Esmond R. Long, professor of pathology, University of Pennsylvania, and director of the Henry Phipps Institute; Dr. Robert G. Bloch, associate professor of medicine, University of Chicago; Dr. S. William Becker, associate professor of dermatology, University of Chicago; Dr. Midian O. Bousfield, director of Negro health of the Julius Rosenwald Fund, Chicago; Dr. Ulysses G. Dailey, senior attending surgeon, Provident Hospital, Chicago; Dr. Franklin C. McLean, professor of pathological physiology, University of Chicago; and Dr. Allison Davis, Division on Child Development and Teacher Personnel of the American Council on Education, University of Chicago. The author is particularly grateful to the Julius Rosenwald Fund for a grant-in-aid toward the publication of this volume.

TABLE OF CONTENTS

PAGE

LIST OF TABLES xvii

CHAPTER

   I. POPULATION AND VITAL STATISTICS 1

  II. ANATOMY OF THE NEGRO 18

 III. BIOCHEMICAL AND PHYSIOLOGICAL CHARACTERISTICS 82

  IV. MEDICAL DISEASES 99

   V. SURGICAL DISEASES 305

  VI. OBSTETRICS AND GYNECOLOGY 362

 VII. DISEASES OF THE SKIN 369

VIII. DISEASES OF THE EYE, EAR, NOSE, AND THROAT 393

  IX. DENTAL DISEASES 399

AUTHOR INDEX 409

SUBJECT INDEX 425

LIST OF TABLES

TABLE   PAGE

1. Growth of the Negro Population since 1790   5

2. Estimate of Future Decennial Changes in Negro and White Populations   7

3. Distribution of Negro Individuals with Various Amounts of Admixture with Whites and Indians · 29

4. Percentages of Colors Used To Duplicate Color of White Skins 32

5. Percentages of Colors Used To Duplicate Color of Unmixed Negroes 32

6. Percentages of Colors Used To Duplicate Colors of Negroes with Various Degrees of Intermixture with Whites . . . 33

7. Percentages of Colors Used To Duplicate Color of Italians and Mexicans 35

8. Davenport's Theoretical Grades of Skin Color and Their Genotypes 44

9. Theoretical Grades of Skin Color and Their Amended Genotypes 44

10. Ranges of N Corresponding to Genotypes 44

11. Relative Number of Sweat Glands per Unit Surface Area in the Skin of Various Races 59

12. Incidence of the Sickle Cell Trait 235

13. Relative Mortality of White and Colored from Heart Disease, 1931–35 289

14. Relative Mortality of White and Negro from Nephritis, 1930 304

15. Racial Distribution of Gastric Carcinoma 344

16. The Incidence of Abnormal Types of Pelvis in White and Negro Obstetrical Patients 365

17. The Distribution of Abnormal Types of Pelvis in White and Negro Women 365

CHAPTER I

POPULATION AND VITAL STATISTICS

NEGROES in the United States form a sharply deline-
ated but well-integrated racial element of the American population. They are an alien people who have
been remarkably well adapted to an entirely different civilization and climate and in a much better way than other people
have been able to adapt themselves to tropical Africa. A measure of the Negro's success in overcoming the handicaps of a
transplant from his native soil to a contrasting and foreign
country is found in the facts disclosed by his vital statistics.
The population has increased twelve to thirteen times in a century and a half, a resistance to new diseases is increasingly well
developed, and the life-span is continually being lengthened, all
of which indicate, in the words of Holmes,[1] the biological vic-
tory of the black man. At one time the Negro was believed to
be threatened with extinction; but, to the contrary, he is well
established and showing a normal and natural increase without
the aid of a material amount of importation of new blood.

ORIGIN AND GROWTH OF THE NEGRO POPULATION

While the date of the introduction of Negroes as slaves into
this country is 1619, the seed for it was sown over a hundred
years previously by the establishment of slavery in the West
Indies. (For discussions of the early history of slavery in the
New World, see Weatherford,[2] Weatherford and Johnson,[3]
Woodson,[4] and Johnston.[5]) Shortly after the discovery of the

---

[1] *The Negro's struggle for survival* (Berkeley: University of California Press, 1937).

[2] *The Negro from Africa to America* (New York: George H. Doran Co., 1924).

[3] *Race relations: adjustments of Negroes and whites in the United States* (New York
D. C. Heath & Co., 1934)

[4] *The Negro in our history* (Washington, D.C.: Associated Publishers, 1927).

[5] *The Negro in the New World* (New York: Macmillan Co., 1910).

New World by Columbus, Spanish settlers in the West Indies, in need of man power to cultivate the new land and finding the native Indians unsuitable for the purpose, imported Negro laborers from Spain, where African slavery already existed. The first importation, to Haiti, was in 1502. As these new workers were peculiarly qualified for labor in the sugar-cane fields, the demand for them grew rapidly and was supplied at first by the Portuguese, who obtained recruits directly from Africa. The huge profits made in slave trading attracted dealers from practically every European country, including at one time Portugal, Spain, England, Holland, Germany, Denmark, Sweden, and France. Many of these countries had colonies of their own either in the West Indies or in South America, and each of them provided a market of its own for slaves.

The first advent of Negroes on the mainland of America was not in connection with the establishment of the slave trade there but as companions of Spanish explorers.[6] In 1516 thirty of them accompanied Balboa on his explorations. About three hundred Negroes went with Cortez into Mexico in 1522, and an expedition of Paufilo de Narvaez in 1527 to conquer Florida included Negroes, as likewise did the expedition of De Soto. There is an account of a disastrous attempt in 1526 of one Vanques de Ayllon to establish, with the help of Negro slaves, a settlement on the Atlantic coast of this country at what is now Jamestown, Virginia, and later along the coast of what is now South Carolina. All these visits were transitory and probably have nothing to do with the present population of Negroes.

The introduction of Africans into the mainland of America, which actually began slavery there, followed the chance landing at Jamestown of a Dutch vessel in 1619 and is recorded in the well-known sentence taken from the writings of John Rolfe "About last of August came in a Dutch man-of-warre, that sold us twenty negars."

Since a new country always requires more labor than is avail-

---

[6] Wright, *Am. Anthropologist*, 4:217, 1902; J. Rippy, *Negro History*, 6:183, 1921; Browning, "Negro companions of the Spanish explorers of the New World" ("Howard University studies in history, No. 11" [1930]), p. 3.

able, the opening of this new source of supply for workers was not an unwelcome event. Previously the American colonists had made use of indentured servants from England. These were, for the most part, white convicts, who proved unsatisfactory for the work. Moreover, even this source of labor was cut off in 1688. At first the Negroes in Virginia were also used as indentured servants, but this system was gradually changed into slavery, first, by continually increasing the period of indenture and then by legally extending it for life. The final step was the declaration that all the offspring of the Africans should also be slaves.[7]

The cultivation of tobacco in Virginia, of rice in South Carolina, and of cotton in Georgia and other newly developed territory to the south created an immense demand for the slaves, which were supplied chiefly by the British but also by American ships (sailing mostly from Rhode Island and Charleston, South Carolina) and by French and Swedish traders.

Almost from the very first there was a strong opposition to slavery in America, led principally by the Quakers. At the beginning the issue was a moral and social one. Later it became heavily involved with politics and economics. Forces against slavery were responsible for abolition in first one and then the other of the New England states north of Maryland. In 1794 Congress prohibited the participation of American subjects in the slave trade, and in 1808 the importation of slaves was prohibited.

In spite of these federal laws the slave trade between Africa and the states of the union south of the Mason-Dixon line went on with very little interruption of an official kind until the Civil War. It is estimated that in eighteen months—in 1859 and 1860—eighty-five slave ships were fitted out in New York Harbor and that these boats alone transported from 30,000 to 60,000 slaves annually.[8] This illicit trading was carried on particularly in South Carolina, Georgia, and Texas. It is said that

[7] Russell, *The free Negro in Virginia, 1619–1863* (Baltimore: Johns Hopkins University Press, 1913); Weatherford, *loc. cit.*

[8] Dubois, *The suppression of the African slave trade to the United States of America, 1638–1870* ("Harvard historical studies," 1 [New York: Longmans, Green & Co., 1896]).

South Carolina was probably the very last port of the United States that received a cargo of slaves from Africa, although Dublin[9] believes that the last slave ship was the "Lawrence," which ran the federal blockade during the Civil War and landed a boatload of slaves in Mobile in 1862. In 1863 the Emancipation Proclamation abolished slavery completely in the United States.

There have been various estimates of the total number of Negroes brought to America by slave traders. These estimates range from 300,000 to 3,000,000. The following statistics are selected from various authors concerning importations to America and the West Indies:

1666–1766—number of slaves imported by the British alone into British, French, and Spanish-American colonies, 3,000,000

1680–1786—slaves imported into the British-American colonies, 2,130,000, Jamaica alone absorbing 610,000

1716–66—an average of 70,000 slaves per annum imported into the American colonies, or a total of 3,500,000

1752–62—Jamaica alone imported 40,000 slaves

1759–62—Guadeloupe alone imported 40,000 slaves

1776–1800—an average of 74,000 slaves per annum imported into all the American colonies, or a total of 1,850,000 (annual average: by British, 38,000; Portuguese, 10,000; Dutch, 4,000; French, 20,000; Danes, 2,000)

PRESENT POPULATION AND TRENDS

In 1714 there were only 59,000 Negro slaves in America, distributed throughout the colonies. In 1727 there were 78,000, in 1754 there were 293,000, in 1760, 310,000, in 1770, 462,000, in 1780, 582,000, and in 1790, 750,000. Thereafter, and at each decennial federal census, the Negro population, the percentage which Negroes formed of the total population, and the percentage increase each decennium showed over the previous decennium for Negroes and whites are given in Table 1.

It is generally admitted that enumerations of the Negro population are nearly always below the actual number, but in 1870, 1890, and 1920 there were gross undercounts, and estimates of the more probable counts have been made that eliminate to

[9] *Health and wealth* (New York: Harper & Bros., 1928).

some extent the irregularities of the decennial rates of increase.[10] A similar undercount probably occurred in the white population in 1870. Revised counts of Negroes for 1870 and 1890 are, respectively, 5,392,172 and 7,760,000. In 1870 the increases over the preceding ten years would be 21.4 per cent, in 1880, 22.0 per cent, and in 1890, 17.6 per cent. Revised figures for the

TABLE 1

GROWTH OF THE NEGRO POPULATION SINCE 1790

Census Year	Number of Negroes	Percentage of Total Population	Percentage Increase of Negroes during Decade	Percentage Increase of Whites during Decade
1790.	757,208	19.3	. . . .	. . . .
1800.	1,002,037	18.9	32.3	35.8
1810.	1,377,808	19.0	37.5	36.1
1820.	1,771,656	18.4	28.6	34.2
1830.	2,328,642	18.1	31.4	33.9
1840.	2,873,648	16.8	23.4	34.7
1850. . . . . : .	3,638,808	15.7	26.6	37.7
1860.	4,441,830	14.1	22.1	37.7
1870.	4,880,009	12.7	9.9	24.8
1880. . . . . : .	6,580,793	13.1	34.9	29.2
1890.	7,488,676	11.9	13.8	26.7
1900.	8,333,940	11.6	18.0	21.2
1910.	9,827,763	10.7	11.2	21.8
1920. . . . . :	10,463,131	9.9	6.5	15.7
1930.	11,891,143	9.7	13.6	15.7
1940. . . . . : .	12,865,518	9.8	8.2	7.2

whites give 27.5 per cent increase in 1870 and 26.4 per cent in 1880. The Bureau of the Census gives the opinion that the irregular increase from 1910 to 1920 was due to the influenza epidemic, to the World War, and to labor migration, all of which occurred in that decennium. The Bureau admits a probable undercount of 150,000, while Woofter believes the count too low by 150,000–450,000.

The Negro population decreased from 19.3 per cent of the total population in 1790 to 9.7 per cent of the total population

[10] Miller, *Scient. Monthly*, 14:167, 1922; Willcox, *Negroes in the United States* (Washington, D.C.: U.S. Government Printing Office, 1904).

in 1930. This decline resulted from the fact that, with the exception of one decade (1800–1810), the rate of increase among Negroes has always been lower than among whites, owing principally to the immigration but also to a larger natural increase of the whites. From 1910 to 1920 the increase of the Negro population was less than one-half of the white increase, but from 1920 to 1930 the Negro increase was 87 per cent of the white increase. During this latter period immigration was at its lowest, and the white increase was largely due to natural causes. The actual trend in both races is a fall in the rate of increase, which is more rapid in the whites.

A number of predictions have been made of the future population of Negroes. Hoffman[11] believed that the race was headed toward extinction. Regarding this, Woofter says:

A large Negro group will be here for several centuries. Even an increase of 1 per cent every ten years would aggregate eleven and a quarter million Negroes by the end of the century.. On the other hand, if it ever happens that deaths begin to exceed births to such an extent that the population decreases by 2 per cent every ten years, there will still remain, two hundred years hence, a colored population of about seven million; and if this decrease were maintained a thousand years hence the race would still be more numerous than are the Indians today.[12]

Nelson Page[13] thought that before the end of this century the Negro population would be 60–80 million. Booker T. Washington[14] in 1899 said that the next census (1900) would be 10,000,-000. It was, in fact, 8,830,000. Willcox calculated the population for the year 2000 at 24–25 million. Woofter also estimated it at about 25,000,000. Thompson and Whelpton[15] think that the future trends of the Negro and white populations will be represented by such rates of decennial changes as are shown in Table 2. These estimates predict a Negro population of 14,200,000 and a white population of 138,400,000 in 1980. Since

[11] *Race traits and tendencies of the American Negro* (New York: Macmillan Co., 1896).

[12] *The basis of racial adjustment* (New York: Ginn & Co., 1925).

[13] *The Negro: the southerner's problem* (New York: Scribner's Sons, 1904).

[14] *The future of the American Negro* (Boston: Maynard & Co., 1902).

[15] *Population trends in the United States* (New York: McGraw-Hill Co., 1933).

the decrease of the rate of increase is roughly the same in the two races, the proportions will be about the same as at the present. (Concerning the natural increase of the Negro population see Holmes,[16] Holmes and Parker,[17] Whelpton,[18] Woofter,[19] Dublin and Lotka,[20] and Willcox.[21]

Prior to 1910, barely 10 per cent of Negroes lived outside of the South. By 1920 one-seventh lived outside, by 1930, one-fifth. This change was produced by a heavy northward migration from the South. It began in 1914 and was highest in 1920–

TABLE 2

ESTIMATE OF FUTURE DECENNIAL
CHANGES IN NEGRO AND WHITE
POPULATIONS

Census Years	Negro Per Cent	White Per Cent
1940	+8.6	8.4
1950	+6.1	7.5
1960	+3.4	4.9
1970	+1.1	2.6
1980	−0.7	0.9

30, but it is still in progress at the present time. Until 1920 the center of the Negro population was moving southwestward, but now the direction is distinctly northwestward. In 1890, 2.7 per cent of the colored people lived in cities over 250,000. By 1930 it had grown to 19.1 per cent, a larger proportional shift of population to the city than that of any other major group. The Negro population of the North is mostly concentrated in a few large cities. In 1930 there were 233,903 Negroes in Chicago, 327,706 in New York City, and 219,599 in Philadelphia, these three cities alone containing nearly one-third (32.4 per cent) of the total colored population of the North.

[16] Am. J. Sociol., 42:202, 1936.

[17] J. Am. Statist. A., 26:159, 1931.

[18] J. Am. Statist. A., 24:239, 1929.

[19] J. Am. Statist. A., 26: 461, 1931.

[20] Metron, 8:107, 1930.

[21] Quart. J. Econ., 19:545, 1905.

Ever since 1870 there has been a higher proportion of the population in the zero-to-four-year and five-to-nineteen-year age groups among Negroes than among whites, except in the zero-to-four-year age groups in 1920, when they were identical. In general, the proportions in the zero-to-four-year and five-to-nineteen-year age groups among the Negroes have been 10–20 per cent higher than among the whites. The proportion of Negroes in the twenty-to-twenty-nine-year age group was larger than that of whites in 1870, in 1900, and in each census thereafter. The proportions of age groups thirty to forty-four years, forty-five to sixty-four years, and sixty-five years and over have at each census been larger among the whites than among the Negroes. Thompson and Whelpton point out that the trend of the younger age groups is exactly identical in the white and colored and that the proportion among the Negroes will remain larger. The twenty-to-twenty-nine-year group will also remain higher among the Negroes, but the proportion will decline. The trend of the thirty-to-forty-four-year group among Negroes is upward in comparison to the whites, particularly as immigration of whites is declining. The rate of increase of the forty-five-to-sixty-four-year age group is almost the same in the two races. The increase of the age group sixty-five years and over is much less rapid among Negroes than among whites, but it is, nevertheless, increasing.

The younger age groups are concentrated in the rural districts of the South, but recently there has been a marked increase of these groups in cities, especially those of the North. This is due principally to a selective migration of Negroes of the reproductive ages toward the cities of the North. There has been since 1890 a larger proportion of the middle-age groups in the cities than on the farms, and this fact was accentuated in 1930. This is also true of the whites, but the difference between the proportion in the cities and on the farms is not so great among the whites as among the Negroes and has not shown the recent changes that it has among the Negroes. The proportion of Negroes sixty-five years of age and over in the cities is smaller than in the rural areas, and the proportion in the cities is decreasing.

The median age is that age which divides the population into two equal groups, one being older and one being younger than the median. It is affected by the birth rate and by the mortality rate, in that a reduction of the birth rate and a lowering of the death rate raises it, and an increase of births and deaths lowers it. The median age of Negroes has been calculated each decennium since 1820, when it was 17.2 years. It has gradually increased, until in 1930 it was 23.1. This was the highest attained, while the lowest, 16.9 ,was in 1830. In 1820 the median age of the whites was 16.5, and in 1930 it was 26.9.

SEX COMPOSITION

The sex composition of the Negro population was determined for the first time at the census of 1820. At this time, and also at the census of 1830, the males slightly exceeded the females, there being, respectively, 1,034 and 1,003 males per 1,000 females. But at each succeeding census the females were in excess. The ratios of males and females between 1830 and 1930 have been erratic. The excess of females was at its maximum in 1870, when there were 962 males per 1,000 females. This, however, was a defective enumeration, and the next greatest excess was in 1930, when there were 970 males to 1,000 females. The ratio of males to females in the Negro population is similar to the ratios of most European countries, while the ratio among the American whites with an excess of males is like that of the ratios in non-European countries. The Negro sex ratio appears to be a natural one for these people and is determined by the ratio at birth and the differential mortality of males and females.

In rural areas the Negro males exceed the females, while the females exceed in the cities. In 1930 this excess of females was larger in the smaller cities than in the larger ones.

RACE INTERMIXTURE

At the very first appearance of Negroes in America, mating between them and the whites began. It was considered such a problem by the New England colonists that the English and, after the Revolution, the Colonial governments of each state felt called upon to enact legislation against it. Legal marriage was originally practiced but was prohibited by these new laws. Miscegenation resulted, which, if anything, encouraged mating, since legal responsibility was done away with.

The literature has to a large extent been inaccurate concerning the physical and mental effects on the offspring of Negro-white matings. There are those who claim that such offsprings are inferior to either parent when of pure strain; that they inherit only the bad qualities of both races; that they are inferior intellectually and more susceptible to disease. Others, and with equally convincing evidence, attempt to show that the good qualities of the races are inherited; that they are healthier; that the best accomplishments of the Negro race have come from mixed individuals; that the inherited qualities are less significant than the social and economic opportunities; and that there is a favorable selectivity of social factors. These views are more or less personal opinions, and both are supported by biased evidence. Geneticists, who approach the problem more scientifically, usually select some isolated feature, such as skin color (*q.v.*), to study the inheritance by crosses between white and colored.

The terms indicating the degree of intermixture are: mulatto for those with equal parts of white and black, quadroon for those with one-quarter black, and octoroon for those with one-eighth black. These terms are not in popular use in the United States. Everyone who has a discernible or known amount of Negro blood is classed as a Negro, and, of these, those with any obvious amount of white blood are called mulattoes.

The United States Bureau of the Census has made several attempts to enumerate colored individuals who were not black, the first being in 1850 and the last one in 1910. In the 1850 and 1860 censuses the term "black" and "mulatto" appear not to have been defined. In 1850 enumerators were instructed simply in enumerating colored persons to write "B" or "M" in a designated space of the schedule to indicate black or mulatto, leaving the space blank in case of whites. In 1860 no instructions are known to have been given. In 1870 and 1910 enumerators were told to designate as "blacks" those who were evidently full-blooded Negroes, and as "mulattoes" those having some proportion or perceptible trace of Negro blood. No data are available in published reports for the census years 1880 and 1900, and it is known that in 1920 and 1930 no attempt was made to designate people other than as Negro, this term being used in the usual American way.

In the inheritance of skin color, which in the United States is the physical trait by which intermixture is usually determined, blackness may obscure a considerable quantity of white blood which the genes may carry. Because of this and because of the looseness of terms employed, the variations in the instructions to enumerators and differences in discernibility of census-takers, it is obvious that censuses of black and mulatto elements in the Negro population have little significance in determining the amount of intermixture with whites.

The published reports show that in 1850, 11.2 per cent of the Negro population were recorded as being mulatto; in 1860, 13.2 per cent were mulatto; in 1870, 12.0 per cent; in 1890, 15.2 per cent; and in 1910, 20.9 per cent. The white element in the Negro population is increasing and is due to continued miscegenation with whites but mostly to the union of blacks with mulattoes and mulattoes with mulattoes. This increase will continue until the whole Negro population is affected. In certain parts of the country there has been a considerable intermixture of Negroes and Indians.[22]

BIRTH RATE

Statistics concerning birth rates are very unsatisfactory. The Birth Registration Area was formed in 1915 and included only ten states and the District of Columbia. This territory was occupied by just a small part of the total Negro population. By 1929 the Registration Area included most of the southern states,

[22] Herskovits, *The American Negro: a study in racial crossing* (New York: A. A. Knopf, 1928).

in which most Negroes lived, and in 1933 the addition of Texas made the whole United States the Registration Area. But even with uniform laws concerning the registration of births, in some territories there is considerable laxity in their enforcement.

For the periods in which birth statistics are not available, the rates are estimated from the population of children of the low ages and from the known infant mortality. From such data it is found that the crude birth rate, expressed in terms of births per 1,000 population, is usually higher in Negroes than whites. This is also true of the adjusted birth rates expressed in terms of births per 1,000 females at childbearing age, usually from fifteen to forty-four years. Since the number of females at these ages is known accurately only at census years, the adjusted rates are available at present only for 1920 and 1930. Concerning these rates, Thompson and Whelpton[23] say that, although the estimated rates for the United States are the same at ages fifteen–forty-four years for native whites and Negroes in 1920 and one point higher for Negroes in 1930, it is probable that the Negro rates have been relatively larger. The indications are that failure to register births is more common among Negroes than whites.[24] In 1920 about 19 per cent of Negro births were not registered as compared with 6.9 per cent of white births. These adjustments raise the standardized rates of native whites to 103 in 1920 and 82 in 1929 and of Negroes to 119 and 96, respectively, making the Negro figure higher than the white by about 15 per cent in 1920 and 17 per cent in 1929.

The highest birth rate of both white and colored occurs in the rural areas of the South, the difference between the urban and rural rates being about the same for both races. There is a much greater difference between the birth rate for Negroes in the South and North than for whites. In the North Central states the rate is about 25 per cent less for Negroes than it is in the South, and for whites it is about 16 per cent less.

The maximum birth rate for Negroes appears to have occurred during slavery and is described by Dublin. He points out that the maximum of human fertility was probably at-

<hr>

[23] *Loc. cit.;* see n. 15.   [24] Whelpton, *J. Am. Statist. A.*, 29:125, 1934.

tained then and reached the enormous figure of 55 per 1,000 compared with the present rate of about 16. This means that there was an average of nine children per mother, or a child every thirteen months over the whole reproductive period. There was a decline in the birth rate during the adjustment of reconstruction days, then a recovery followed by a more or less steady decline, which is still in progress. There has also been during the same period a fall in the white birth rate. According to the data of Thompson and Whelpton,[25] there was a greater fall between 1920 and 1929 for whites than Negroes. The standardized rate fell 20.4 per cent over this period for whites and 19.4 per cent for Negroes.

In the 1920–29 decennium the white urban rate fell 15.0 per cent and the rural rate fell 19.5 per cent, a difference of 4.5 per cent in the amount of decline. The Negro urban rate fell 8.5 per cent and the rural rate 16.1 per cent, a difference of 7.6 per cent. The decline in birth rates occurred in all divisions of the country and for all ages of women. The only exception was in northern cities for Negro females between ages fifteen and twenty-nine years. The rates for ages fifteen to twenty-four years actually increased, while that for ages twenty-five to twenty-nine years remained unchanged. This is explained by the adjustment of migrated healthy colored women to new conditions after a period of suppression of childbirth.

A discussion of the various factors that may be responsible for the decline in birth rate and the way they operate in Negroes is given by Holmes.

GENERAL MORTALITY

The greatest handicap to a natural increase of the Negro population is his death rate, which is not only high but is particularly effective on the most productive element of the population, that part made up of middle-age and young adult groups.

The history of the Negro's high death rate began with the slave trade to the Western Hemisphere. It has been shown that, on an average, 17 per cent of the Africans died within nine

[25] *Loc. cit.;* see n. 15.

weeks after being removed from Africa and that only 50 per cent of them lived to be effectual laborers. Most of these deaths resulted from cruelties both on the slave ships and on the farms of the New World. Stoddard says in regard to slavery in the West Indies:

The continual dying out of the slave population in a favorable climate created much comment at the time, and many reasons for it were given. In 1764, a Governor attributed it to improper food, undue labor imposed upon pregnant women, and a very high infant mortality. The general opinion seems to have been that the Negroes were worked too hard, and one author asserts this was often deliberately done, as many masters considered it cheaper to buy slaves than to breed them. A colonial writer lays much of the trouble to immorality among the Negroes and to the ensuing ravages of venereal disease. Another writer, perhaps the ablest student of the subject, thinks that much stress should be laid on the great nervous strain imposed by the sudden change from the careless indolence of savage existence, to a life of continuous labor.[26]

In the United States the characteristic shrewdness of the American planter and his utter dependence on Negro labor made him more attentive to his huge investment in human beings, and, for the most part, the barbaric cruelties of the West Indies did not exist. However, the glamour of romance, glory, and pseudo-culture that surrounded the old South tended to obscure the unhappy lot of the slaves. It was not until Harriet Beecher Stowe's semihistorical novel, *Uncle Tom's Cabin*, appeared that the inhumanities were exposed.

But it is of more concern to point out the effect of slavery on the morbidity and mortality of the Negro. In the absence of authentic records, attempts have been made to prove that colored people in slavery were healthier and lived longer than they do now. Such a view is contrary to logic and common sense. It is well known that primitive people coming in contact with the new diseases of the whites meet death and destruction. This can be readily proved by the experience in many of the small islands of the west Pacific Ocean, in South Africa, and in America among the Indians. Whole populations in these countries have been decimated by the white man's diseases, and there is no reason to believe that the Negro newly in America was different, especially as he had the added disadvantage of being

[26] *The rising tide of color against white world supremacy* (New York: Scribner's Sons, 1920).

away from his native country and mode of life. Contrary to opinions expressed otherwise, he must have suffered tremendously from the infections he found in this country.

With the exception of such places as Charleston, South Carolina, and Baltimore, Maryland, mortality statistics first became available to any extent only after the Civil War, when the Negro and the whole South underwent a termendous upheaval reflecting itself in high death rates. From this it is often concluded that freedom as such had a deleterious effect on the Negro's health. In other places no trustworthy data is available on diseases and the mortality of Negroes either for the period of slavery or for many years after emancipation. As a matter of fact, there were almost no accurate mortality statistics prior to 1900. As Whelpton points out, even the 1900–1902 life-tables for Negroes were based on the original registration states only, hence were typical of that comparatively small proportion of the Negro population which was located in northeastern cities. It was not until the life-tables of 1919–20 that Negroes of southern states, with a majority living in rural communities, were adequately represented.

In 1909 the United States Bureau of the Census estimates the mortality per 1,000 for Negroes in the Registration Area as 29.4 and for whites as 17.1. In 1910 the estimate was 25.5 for Negroes and 14.6 for whites. The crude death rate for 1920–24 for Negroes was 16.6 and for native whites 10.4 per 1,000. For foreign-born whites it was 17.2. For 1925–29 the Negro rate was 17.7, the native-white rate 10.1, and the foreign-born–white rate 18.8.

In 1900 the expectation of life for Negro males at birth was 32.5 years and for females 35.0. In 1910 these figures were for males 34.0 and for females 37.7, and in 1920, 40.4 and 42.4, respectively. The comparable white expectation of life in 1900 was for males 48.2 and for females 51.1, in 1910 it was 50.2 and 53.6, and in 1920, 54.0 and 56.4.[27]

The mortality in 1920 was considerably more favorable for Negroes in southern states. The expectation of life for Negro males in the South was 46.4 and in the North, 40.5.

[27] Gover, J. Negro Educ., 6:276, 1937.

At younger ages the white death rate is lower, but at ages above eighty years the Negro rate is lower. The largest relative differences are at ages fifteen to sixty years, the Negro death rates at these ages being over twice those of whites. The age distribution of Negro deaths has three peaks where a relatively great proportion of the total deaths occur: infancy, the period of late adolescence and early maturity, and old age. The distribution of white deaths has only two of these peaks—infancy and old age.

The Metropolitan Life Insurance Company[28] shows that the average death rate for Negro policyholders from 1911 to 1935 for ages one to seventy-four years was 1,578.5 per 100,000 for males and 1,457.9 per 100,000 for females. The rates among whites were 1,128.7 for males and 866.9 for females. The male Negro rate was in excess of 40 per cent over the male white rate, and the female Negro rate showed an excess of 70 per cent over the white female rate. When the mortalities for the period 1911–15 are compared with those for 1931–35, it is found that the colored male mortality declined 28.4 per cent and the colored female mortality declined 31.3 per cent. The white male and female rates declined, respectively, 38.1 per cent and 38.5 per cent. There were 3.5 times as many deaths per 100,000 among colored females fifteen to nineteen years of age as among white females, nearly 3 times as many between ages twenty to twenty-four years, and 2.5 times as many between ages twenty-five to thirty-four years. Colored males showed death rates 2.25 to 2.5 times as high as white males in these same age groups.

The leading cause of death of Negroes as well as of whites in 1935 was, according to *Mortality statistics, 1935*,[29] diseases of the heart. The second largest cause of death of colored people was tuberculosis, while for whites it was cancer. The next four leading causes of death of Negroes were, in order, pneumonia, nephritis, cerebral hemorrhage and softening, and congenital

[28] *Twenty-five years of health progress* (New York: Metropolitan Life Insurance Co., 1937).

[29] U.S. Department of Commerce, Bureau of the Census (Washington, D.C.: U.S Government Printing Office, 1937).

malformations and diseases of early infancy. The next four leading causes of death of whites were nephritis, pneumonia, cerebral hemorrhage and softening, and congenital malformations and diseases of early infancy.

What the Negro gains in a higher birth rate he loses in a higher infant mortality.[30] About 250,000 colored infants are born alive each year in the United States, about two-thirds of whom are born in the rural areas of the South. Of the total births about 22,000 die each year. In every section of the United States the infant mortality rate for Negroes is greatly in excess of that for whites. On a whole, the mortality rates for colored infants are higher in urban than in rural areas, but in several states the rural rates are higher.

In 1934 the white infant mortality rate (deaths under one year of age per 1,000 live births) was 54.5, and the Negro rate was 91.0. More than half of the Negro infants who die during the first year die within the first month. In 1934 the infant mortality rate at one month or less for whites was 36.6 and for Negroes it was 54.1. Natal and prenatal causes were responsible for more deaths than any other cause. Then follow, in order, respiratory diseases, gastrointestinal diseases, and epidemic and other communicable diseases.

The infant mortality rate is rapidly falling. In 1930 the white rate was 59.6 and in 1934 it was 54.5, while the colored rate in 1930 was 99.5 and in 1934 it was 91.0. The rate of fall was about 8.5 per 1,000 births in both races. The Negro infant mortality rate was 132.8 in 1919–20 and 234.1 in 1900–1902.

The percentage of Negro children living to those born to women who bore children in 1934 is 89.5 and for whites it is 92.7. The average number of children ever born to women who bore children in 1934 is 3.6 for Negro women and 3.0 for white. The net gain of children for Negroes (89.5 per cent of 3.6) is 3.2 and for whites (92.7 per cent of 3.0) 2.3 per mother.

[30] Tandy, *J. Negro Educ.*, 6:322, 1937.

CHAPTER II

ANATOMY OF THE NEGRO

THE Negro is ordinarily identified on the basis of obvious anatomical characteristics, such as color of the skin, shape of the nose and lips, the quality of the hair, and the shape of the head and face. In addition to these there are other more or less specific but more subtle morphological features disclosed only by careful measurements or concealed in the internal organs. The anatomy of the Negro has for the most part been established by anthropologists in the study of the relations of the various representatives of mankind. Physicians are generally concerned with the bearing anatomy has on disease, and they have attempted to explain, with varying degrees of success, some of the peculiar manifestations of disease in the Negro on the basis of his anatomy. The prevalence of tuberculosis and pneumonia has been attributed to a small lung and an accompanying low vital capacity, the lack of resistance to certain infectious diseases to a small spleen, an immunity to other pathological conditions to a thick epidermis or some peculiar property of the mesoderm, and the susceptibility to rickets to a dark pigmentation. Some of these correlations seem to exist in fact, but others appear to have no other basis than a last resort to explain phenomena for which there is no other explanation.

The characteristic anatomical features of the Negro are not accidental but are to be considered as an adaptation to a specific environment, a part of which are the diseases with which he has to cope. The efficiency of this adaptation is seen in the success with which he lives in those parts of Africa which are not readily inhabitable by white people. As a matter of fact, Negroes can live much more readily in the countries of Caucasians than the latter can live in Africa, excepting those parts of the continent with climates more or less European in nature. Although the

18

mode of operation of each anatomical characteristic of the Negro as an adaptive mechanism is not always clear, it is so evident in some instances that it may be reasonable to assume that an explanation can be found in all cases.

BODY FORMS

In describing the external anatomic features of the Negro it is imperative to recall that the people included under this name is not by any means a homogenous group. In Africa there are at least four types of Negroes which differ from one another as much as any of them differ from many non-Negro races. In America not only are there more than one of these groups represented, but they have been mixed with varying and oftentimes uncertain amounts of Caucasian and Indian blood. While all Negroes, except those with a preponderance of foreign blood, have certain features in common, no one description can be equally applied to all of them.

Exclusive of the two main non-Negro races of northern Africa, the indigenous races of Africa are divided into the True Negro, the Bushman-Hottentot, the Bantu, and the Negrito (sometimes called Negrillo). By direct and, in some cases, highly speculative evidence anthropologists have established the history of the origin of these people, which consists of a continuous series of invasions of a primitive native substratum by the Hamites and Semites from the north. The inevitable intermixture with the invaders and of various groups of the newly formed people with one another have given rise to the present population, among whom are very few representatives of the original stock.

The delineation of Africans into groups has been made chiefly on the basis of ethnologic evidence, which is much more complete than the physical evidence, but the latter is complete enough to show that the four groups have morphological features that readily distinguish them from one another and from other races. The chief external features on the basis of which races are described are stature, head shape, quality of the hair, character of the face—including the nose, eyes, ears, and mouth

—and the color of the skin. Proportions of various parts of the body to one another expressed by indices have been used, but the racial differences of these indices are often so small and variable that their usefulness is questionable. Head shape is described in terms of the relation of the width to the length and expressed by the cephalic index. If the length approaches the width, the type is termed "brachycephaly," or round-headedness, and the cephalic index is less than 75. The opposite of this is "dolichocephaly," or long-headedness, and the cephalic index is above 80. Between these extremes is "mesaticephaly," with a cephalic index of 75–80. Faces in which the lower part is more prominent are prognathous, while those in which the opposite is true are orthognathous.

The home of the True Negro is in West Africa and extends from about the mouth of the Senegal River, at 16° north, to the eastern border of Nigeria, and south to approximately the equator. These people include among others the familiar Senegalese, Sudanese, the inhabitants of Nigeria and Dahomey, and such well-known tribes as the Ashanti, Mandingo, Kru, Mossi, and Wolof. The main physical characteristics of the True Negro are his very black skin, woolly hair, tall stature—averaging about sixty-eight inches—moderate dolichocephaly, a flat broad nose, thick, often everted lips, and frequently a considerable degree of prognathism. Some of the tribes are very tall, particularly certain ones of northern Dahomey, which average seventy-two inches in height, thus placing them among the tallest races of mankind.

The Bantus comprise the numerous peoples of central and southern Africa. They are grouped together on a linguistic basis, and physically they present a great variety of types, owing to intermixture with various proportions of Hamitic and Negrito blood in the north and Bushman and Hottentot blood in the south. Familiar people among them are the Zulus, Kaffirs, and Ubangi. The average height is sixty-five and three-fourth inches. Their skin color ranges from black to yellowish-brown, the prevalent color being, however, a dark chocolate with a basic reddish tint. The hair is uniformly of ordinary Negro type

—short and woolly—and typically characterized by numerous and often interlocking spirals. The head is generally dolichocephalic; the eyes are usually large, black, and prominent; the nose varies—generally low and broad, it sometimes has a well-formed bridge and relatively narrow nostrils. The face is moderately prognathous, the forehead prominent, cheekbones high, and lips thick and fleshy.

The extremely interesting Negritos are a pygmy people confined to the thickest tropical forests of central Africa. Their stature varies from fifty-two to fifty-seven or fifty-eight inches, with an average of fifty-seven and fifty-four inches, according to sex. The low stature of these people and the high statures of some of the True Negroes make true the statement that among the natives of Africa are both the shortest and the tallest people of the world. The skin of the Pygmies may be reddish, yellowish-brown, or very dark. The body is often covered with a light downy hair. The head tends to brachycephaly. The nose is very broad, with little or no bridge, the eyes rather large and prominent, and the face short, tending to be broad and generally prognathous.

The Bushman formerly occupied the whole of South Africa, but this group is now practically restricted to the central and northern portion of the Kalahari Desert and the northern half of southwestern Africa. The Bushman is distinctive in physical structure from all other Africans except the closely related Hottentot. He is short, averaging about sixty inches, with slightly built well-shaped limbs and small hands and feet. The skin is yellow or yellowish-brown and wrinkles particularly easily. The hair of the head is sparse and, becoming rolled in small tangles, assumes the so-called "peppercorn" appearance. The head is mesaticephalic and low in the crown; the face is orthognathous and flat, with prominent cheekbones, very flat nose, and bulging forehead. The eyes are narrow and slightly oblique, and the lobe may be absent from the ear. Steatopygy is common among them. The Hottentot is supposed to represent an intermixture of the Bushman with the Hamites and is physically closely related to the Bushman. He is somewhat taller, has a longer and narrower head, and more prognathous face. He lives at present in southwestern Africa, north of the Orange River. There has been a great deal of intermixture with the whites of South Africa as well as with East Indians.

STEATOPYGY

This condition of gluteal hypertrophy is partly accounted for by an exaggeration of the normally occurring anterior curving of the lower spine (ensellure), but is chiefly attributable to an unusual accumulation of subcutaneous fat in and around the buttocks. The deposit of fat is not confined to the gluteal regions but extends to the outside and front of the thighs, forming a thick layer reaching sometimes to the knee. This curious development constitutes a racial characteristic of the Bushman, although it is common among the Hottentots and has been stated to occur often among the pygmy Negritos and even sporadically among Negroes all over Africa. It is especially a feature of the women but occurs in a lesser degree among the males. Its development begins in infancy and is fully developed by the first pregnancy.

True steatopygy has not been satisfactorily demonstrated in modern races outside of Africa, although it is probable that it existed at one time in Europe. Carved figures have been found in caves of southern France depicting a condition closely similar to steatopygy.

No completely acceptable explanation of steatopygy has been offered. The condition is often stated to be analogous to comparable conditions in animals, such as the hump of the camel, the caudal fat of certain Galagos (Lemuridae), and of certain desert-inhabiting mammals (marsupials) of central Australia. Huntoon[1] states that steatopygy is probably a functional character acquired through adaptation and transmitted by heredity. He believes its functional character may be referred to environmental conditions involving a regularly recurrent failure of food supply and the consequent alternation of feasts and famines. This possibility assumes that under conditions of

[1] *Harvard African Studies*, 2:83, 1918.

low food supply the fat deposited in steatopygy is utilized as a reserve source of energy. This, however, is contrary to other claims. Deniker[2] states that the fat of the steatopygous masses does not disappear after disease or fasting which has emaciated the rest of the body. Huntoon also suggests the possibility that the condition may have been associated with a hibernation habit in the ancestors of the Bushman and Hottentot. While there is no proof that humans have ever hibernated, reference is made to a closely similar practice of a group of people in Russia. During the winter months, when food and warmth are scarce, these people retire to caves in order to sleep and maintain complete inactivity except for the most urgent necessities. Miller[3] agrees with Huntoon that steatopygy is transmitted by heredity but doubts that the condition can be explained on a teleological basis, since there is no evidence that it helps in famine and since other races without steatopygy can be equally accustomed to scarcity of food. He mentions the facts that fat-tailed or fat-rumped sheep do not resist the evils of a capricious food supply nor do they hibernate. Moreover, hibernating animals do not have fat concentrated in any one region. Miller is of the opinion that steatopygy illustrates the tendency found among animals of one group to carry to an extreme a feature common to all. This extreme development may not in any way be related to usefulness and may even be a disadvantage. In illustration, he cites the fact that the squirrel has a bushy tail, but in the Bornean species (*Reithrosciurus*) the bushy tail is developed to an extreme, almost caricatural. The antlers of deer are out of proportion to the need, but the Irish elk have antlers even more extreme and may be a factor leading to their extinction. In the genus Homo there is a tendency to the accumulation of fat in the gluteal region, especially marked in women. Steatopygy in the Bushman-Hottentot may be the development of this tendency to an extreme. Later Miller[4] advanced the theory that steatopygy may be explained on the ground of a frequently recurring functional peculiarity of the hypophysis or some other

[2] *Races of man* (New York: Scribner & Sons, 1900).

[3] *Am. J. Phys. Anthropol.*, 2:200, 1919.   [4] *Ibid.*, 14:79, 1930.

gland of internal secretion. He was led to this suggestion by the discovery of a white patient who developed a body form strikingly parallel to Hottentot steatopygy in conjunction with true acromegaly. After treatment of the hypophysis with x-ray, the patient reverted to essentially normal proportions, although the osseus acromegalic characteristics remained.

According to Bean,[5] the races of Africa fall into three general anatomic types, which he has designated as hypermorph, mesomorph, and hypomorph. The hypermorphs are slender, with narrow parts, short torso, long extremities, small hands and feet, and elevated shoulders. The hypermorphs are represented by the Bushman, Hottentot, and Bantu. The anatomic form of the mesomorph is broad, stockily built, with a long torso, large hands and feet, short extremities, and drooping shoulders. The mesomorphs in Africa are made up of the True Negroes. These two types of people apparently correspond to Stockard's[6] linear (hypermorph) and lateral (mesomorph) types and are represented among Europeans. The hypomorph, of which there is no European counterpart, is the Negrito of Africa and is described as having a long torso, short extremities, short and broad hands and feet, and broad shoulders.

The principal student of the physical form of the American Negro has been Herskovits. It would be expected from the origin of the present population of colored people in this country that there would be a large diversity of body types among them. Herskovits[7] concludes, on the basis of his study of the amount of variability disclosed in an extended series of measurements, that the Negro is evolving, as the result of certain selective social factors, into a relatively homogenous Negro-White-Indian type with traits that fall between the African Negro, on one hand, and white-Indian people, on the other. It is observed that, on the basis of measurements of height during the Civil War and during the World War, there is little difference in the stature of Negroes and contemporaneous whites but that, like the whites,

---

[5] *Am. J. Anat.*, 33:105, 1924.   [6] *Am. J. Anat.*, 31:261, 1923.

[7] *Anthropometry of the American Negro* ("Columbia University contributions to anthropology" [New York: 1930]).

the stature of Negroes is increasing. The American Negro is taller than the African west-coast peoples, except for the very tallest tribes, but is shorter, in the main, than the East Africans.

Anthropologists have sought to account for the origin of the various human anatomic forms. Such factors as environment,[8] natural selection,[9] racial mixture and mutations,[10] acting singly or together, have been advocated as the determinants of races. It has been pointed out that these theories do not suffice, and in recent years the idea has been advanced that the origin of racial characters is the action of hormones. This idea arose from the knowledge of the role of the glands of internal secretion in such pathological conditions as acromegaly, giantism, dystrophia adiposogenitalis, dwarfism, infantilism, mongolism, and achondroplasia, where there are disturbances of body form and of growth. Keith[11] has been the leader of this view, supported by Stockard,[12] Pfuhl,[13] Bolk,[14] Paulsen,[15] and Berman.[16] Keith says: "The bodily and mental features which mark the various races of mankind are best explained by the theory that the conformation of man is determined by a common growth-controlling mechanism which is resident in a system of small but complex glandular organs." He points out the analogy of various features of Africans to disturbances of internal secretions, such as the dwarfism of Pygmies (pituitary cysts, thyroid deficiency), Mongolian traits of the Hottentot (cretinism), and slender build of the Bantu (castration effects). Pfuhl adds "somatic features as such are not objects of inheritance, but special functional faculties of the endocrine organs are transmitted."

Stockard[17] and Bean[18] are inclined to believe that the anatomy of the True Negroes is due to their nearness to the sea-

[8] Taylor, *Environment, race and migration: fundamentals of human distribution* (Chicago: University of Chicago Press, 1937).

[9] Dixon, *Racial history of man* (New York: Scribner & Sons, 1923).

[10] Huntingdon, *Character of races* (New York: Scribner & Sons, 1924).

[11] *Bull. Johns Hopkins Hosp.*, 33:159, 195, 1922.

[12] *Loc. cit.;* see n. 6.   [15] *Arch. f. Anthropol.*, 18:60, 1920.

[13] *Ztschr. f. Konstitutionslehre*, 9:172, 1924.   [16] *Scient. Monthly*, 21:159, 1925.

[14] *Lancet*, 2:588, 1921.   [17] *Loc. cit.;* see n. 6.   [18] *Loc. cit.;* see n. 5.

coast and the resulting large intake of iodine, which acts as a stimulant to the thyroid. On the other hand, the Pygmies are in the deep forests of central Africa, where there is a dearth of iodine, a fact which may be related to the striking similarity of the features of these people to those of the cretin. Pygmies are likely to be underfed, in general. They are victims of conquests of other African tribes and have been driven into parts of the continent where food is least accessible. The result of repeated generations of underfed people is probably represented by physiques not of normal proportions.

STRUCTURE OF THE SKIN AND ITS APPENDAGES

The skin, as the organ which comes in closest contact with the environment of the individual, possesses marked adaptive characteristics that permit existence under the most favorable circumstances. Also, the skin has functions, both secretory and excretory, that are nicely co-ordinated with the functions of the internal organs. Since the external conditions under which races live vary, and because there are many racial characteristics of internal organs that influence the skin, this organ and its appendages are correlated with race and vary in function and structure as widely as do the races. The skin of the Negro is a remarkable organ and is so constructed as to efficiently meet the demands of the circumstances to which the race is adjusted. Its pigmentation, sweat glands, vascularity, hair, and other features have attributes that share largely in those physical peculiarities that make up this distinct race stock.

PIGMENTATION

The oldest and simplest classification of the people of the earth is that based on the color of the skin, by which they are divided into the white, black, yellow, red, and brown races or, more simply, into the white, black, and yellow races. Skin color, however, is not an accurate basis of anthropologic grouping, because there are wide variations of color within each of the groups and there is an overlapping of colors between them. The inaccuracy is well illustrated by the distribution of pigmentation among Negroes who, although they make up what is called the black race, are far from being uniformly black. While it is true that all Negroes are not black and that all black people are not Negroes, it is also true that the darkest skin color found among mankind occurs in this race. Even among the Negroes of Africa there is a wide variation of color, which ranges from an intense black to a light yellow.

The extremely black people of Africa are said to be found for the most part among the Sudan group that occupies a narrow but much broken strip of territory extending across the continent from 5° south to 17° north of the equator and from the Atlantic to the highlands of Ethiopia. Along with these black people, however, may be found tribes much lighter in color— of a red, copper-colored complexion. In the Congo-Zambezi region the people are, for the most part, very dark but, on a whole, not as dark as the more northern and northwestern tribes. Also among them, and not segregated into tribes, may be found natives lighter in color. In this region, too, live the pygmy people of central Africa who, in contrast to their dark neighbors, have a reddish-yellow complexion. In eastern and southern Africa, the habitat of the large group of Bantu people, the skin color varies from a black almost as dark as that of the northwestern tribes to a light brown. In each locality there is a marked lack of uniformity in pigmentation, but in general there is a tendency toward an increase in depth of color from south to north. The Hottentots, living in southwestern Africa and along the Orange River, and the Bushmen of the Kalahari Desert are the lightest of all African natives. Their skin color is light yellowish-brown approaching very closely that of the Mongolian. Verner[19] states that at least 15 per cent of the entire Negro population of Africa are light colored, a color that he describes as copper-yellow. He says there are as many of these people in Africa as there are Negroes in the United States. Relatively larger numbers were found in the more elevated parts, especially in the headlands about the sources of the Nile, Congo, and Zambezi. His observations are that they are confined, but not exclusively, to the Bantu people.

[19] *Am. Anthropologist,* 5: 539, 1903.

Accounts of early travelers describe fair-skinned tribes in the interior of Africa, but more extensive exploration and observation have not corroborated these reports. It is more probable that the people referred to were groups of albinos (*q.v.*), who are found quite frequently among the natives. A similar situation is the more or less recent announcement of the discovery of white Indians in South America who proved to be albinos grouped together because of interbreeding and the superstitions which ostracized them.

In Ethiopia the color of the population also varies greatly. In the central provinces (Ambara, Gojam) the prevailing color is a deep brown. Northward (Tigré, Lasta) the color is a pale olive, and often fair complexions are found. Southward (Shoa, Kobbo, Amurn) the people are of a chocolate color and often are sooty black. The Nubians of northern Africa are a mahogany brown, a deep bronze, or an almost black shade. In Madagascar the Negroid Sakalavas of the east coast vary in their complexion as do the people of the African continent.

The people in the United States who are classed as Negroes vary extremely in their color. This variation is easier to explain than that in Africa and is due to a widespread intermixture with other races, chiefly with whites and American Indians. It is impossible to estimate how extensive this intermixture has been, either in general or in any one individual. Some idea of it can be obtained from the studies made on Negro populations in Washington, D.C., New York City, and in West Virginia by Herskovits,[20] who shows, in Table 3, the probable amount of intermixture of Negroes, whites, and Indians as determined by genealogical histories of a group of individuals.

Almost every part of the African continent contributed slaves to America, but the chief source was the northwestern coast, that part of the country where the darkest people lived. While there are yet many dark people among the Negroes of America, it is said that their color, even among those supposedly free of intermixture, seldom reaches the maximum blackness of the

[20] *The American Negro* (New York: Knopf, 1930).

original slave stock. Just what role, the change in climatic conditions from those in Africa to those in America has played in producing changes in the Negro's color is apparently not known.

The situation as to skin color of Negroes in the West Indies is somewhat similar to that in the United States, although it seems that intermixture with other races has been less general. This is particularly true of Bermuda, Jamaica, and the Virgin Islands, where the average color of the Negro population is darker than that of the remaining islands and of the United States.

TABLE 3

DISTRIBUTION OF NEGRO INDIVIDUALS WITH VARIOUS AMOUNTS
OF ADMIXTURE WITH WHITES AND INDIANS

Class	Number of Individuals	Per Cent of Total
Unmixed Negro	342	22.0
Negro, mixed with Indian	97	6.3
More Negro than white	384	24.8
More Negro than white, with Indian	106	6.9
About the same amount of Negro and white	260	16.7
The same class, with Indian mixture	133	8.5
More white than Negro	154	9.3
More white than Negro, with Indian	75	5.5
Total	1,551	100.0

MEASUREMENTS OF PIGMENTATION

Anthropologists experience difficulty in accurately describing the various colors met with in human skins. The colors found are not pure spectral colors but are composites of several color elements that defy analysis by mere inspection or comparison with the standards of colors ordinarily used. The skins described as white, black, yellow, red, or brown are at the best but approximations of these colors. The actual colors, with the many slight and subtle variations which are apparent to the eye, are expressed in language with the utmost difficulty. Resort is usually made to comparison with the colors of more or less well-known objects, a method which is admittedly both inaccurate and confusing. In the literature one finds such expressions as jet-black, sooty-black, coal-black (representing, apparently, various shades of black), chocolate-brown, portmanteau-leather color, *café au lait,* saddle color, copper color, olive-yellow, lemon-yellow, rosy-white, swarthy, etc.

In order to obviate such arbitrary designation of skin colors and its inherent errors, attempts have been made to adopt more scientific methods. The first attempt was that of Broca,[21] who assembled a chromatic table in which the colors representing the chief variations of skin pigmentation are given numbers. The original table contained thirty-four different shades, but it was later modified by the Anthropological Institute of Great Britain and Ireland so that the table contained only the ten principal shades of skin color proposed by Topinard. These shades are: (1) pale-white, (2) florid, or rosy, (3) brownish-white, (4) yellowish-white, (5) olive-yellow, (6) dark yellow-brown, chocolate, (9) sooty-black, (10) coal-black. This method, although an attempt at standardization, has the defect of referring to colors capable of wide subjective variations and which do not allow the appraisal of variations of skin colors which might not fall in any one of the above groups. Since then numerous other color standards have been devised, consisting of water-colored paper strips or colored porcelain, wax, or gelatin films. Hintze,[22] who assembled standard colors representing all observed varieties of pigmentation, gave the following essential requirements of color standards for measuring skin pigmentation:

1. Good match of skin color.
2. Color must be permanent.
3. Color must be easily reproduced.
4. Systematic arrangement of colors.
5. Nomenclature must be uniform.
6. Gradations in color should be small.
7. The color standards should be for skins only.

[21] *Instructions générales pour les recherches anthropologique à faire sur la vivant* (2d ed.; Paris, 1879).

[22] *Verhandl. d. deutsch. röntgen. Gesellsch.,* **17**: 56, 1926.

8. Arrangement of colors should be in natural relation of color, tone, and brightness.

9. Standards should be arranged to form a convenient instrument.

Davenport[23] found that in the study of the inheritance of skin color it was necessary to have a still more accurate method of measuring pigmentation. For this purpose he used a color-top to synthetize a color that exactly corresponded with any selected skin color. The colors black, red, yellow, and white, when used as colors of variable sectors of a disk that is rotated rapidly, may be mixed in such proportions as to match any skin color. In actual practice, four circles of paper about 37 mm. in diameter, one each of the above four colors, are mounted through a center hole on the stem of a small wooden top. Each of the disks is cut along one radius so that they may overlap and expose only a portion of the whole surface. The top is then twirled with the fingers on a surface alongside the anterior surface of the arm. The exposed surfaces of the paper disks are varied until the skin color and the color of the spinning top are matched. Certain precautions, such as the character and amount of light, prevention of eye fatigue, and variations in the speed of the top must be observed. The percentages of the entire rotating disk occupied by the sectors of the color disks when the skin color is matched form the color formula for the skin. A later variation uses mechanical means to rotate the disks at a uniform and constant speed. Herskovits[24] showed that in using this method he made as mean observational errors for the four colors: black, 3.21 per cent; red, 2.15 per cent; yellow, 1.19 per cent; and white, 1.44 per cent.

The formulas expressed as percentages of each color in the disk for various white skins as determined by this method are as shown in Table 4.

For eighteen Negroes in Bermuda, Jamaica, and Louisiana who were, as far as could be ascertained, without intermixture with whites, the skin-color formulas were as shown in Table 5.

[23] *Am. Nat.*, 44:641, 1910.   [24] *Am. J. Phys. Anthropol.*, 9:321, 1926.

The formulas for Negroes with various degrees of intermixture, from those who, according to outward appearance, con-

TABLE 4

PERCENTAGES OF COLORS USED TO DUPLICATE
COLOR OF WHITE SKINS

Black	Red	Yellow	White
5	25	20	50
7	40	18	35
2	25	20	53
5	40	18	37
8	31	22	39
5	34	15	46

TABLE 5

PERCENTAGES OF COLORS USED TO DUPLICATE
COLOR OF UNMIXED NEGROES

Black	Red	Yellow	White
75	13.0	2	10.0
71	18.0	7	9.0
78	8.0	5	9.0
77	15.0	3	5.0
50	25.0	8	17.0
75	18.0	4	3.0
45	40.0	7	8.0
58	29.0	6	7.0
60	29.0	6	5.0
46	39.0	8	7.0
52	32.0	8	8.0
47	37.0	12	4.0
54	35.0	6	5.0
37	47.0	13	3.0
43	30.0	12	15.0
45	32.0	13	10.0
40	32.0	13	15.0
70	28.5	1	0.5

tained no white blood to those who apparently contained no
Negro blood were as shown in Table 6.

It is to be noticed that the black factor in the formulas for the
so-called purebred Negroes of Jamaica, Bermuda, and Louisiana

shows a wide variation. While an intermixture with whites cannot with a certainty be ruled out, Davenport[25] states that the variation is similar to that which occurs among the natives of Africa. The Negroes of Louisiana, on a whole, showed less black than the others. When the combination black *plus* red in these formulas is compared, there is comparatively little variation from the mean. Davenport interprets this as meaning that the Negro varies in his skin thickness: that those with thick skins show a greater intensity of black pigmentation than those with

TABLE 6

PERCENTAGES OF COLORS USED TO DUPLICATE
COLORS OF NEGROES WITH VARIOUS DEGREES
OF INTERMIXTURE WITH WHITES

Black	Red	Yellow	White
43	27	12	18
47	32	11	12
46	29	13	12
25	36	11	29
10	48	10	32
8	31	13	48
7	20	16	57
5	47	20	28
5	35	20	40

thin skins, because in the latter the red of the blood is not so greatly obscured. However, no record of actual measurements of skin thickness in Negroes is obtainable. It was noted by Davenport[26] that the aborigines of Australia were darker than the Negroes of Jamaica and Bermuda.

Todd and Van Gorder[27] attempted to improve this method and reduce, as far as possible, its errors. They found that the black, white, and yellow disks used in the color-top were comparable to the color standards of Ridgway. But the red disk contained only 41 per cent of full spectral red, 59 per cent of the color being black. By making this correction of readings, an

[25] *Loc. cit.;* see n. 23.   [26] *Am. J. Phys. Anthropol.,* 8:73, 1925.

[27] *Am. J. Phys. Anthropol.,* 4:239, 1921.

accuracy of 1 per cent can be obtained. The formulas obtained by Davenport must, therefore, be corrected for the impurity of the red, and when so done the variations of the black are markedly reduced. Todd and Van Gorder used the color-top to measure the color of the skin of cadavers. They found that the black factor of the skin is not changed after death and that it is not affected by stretching or wrinkling or by embalming methods or the use of preservatives. The other color factors are less stable under the influence of these effects.

They further pointed out the large amount of black element in the skin of certain non-Negro races. For example, the color formulas for two Italian and three Mexican cadavers are shown in Table 7.

A more elaborate method in which the color wheel is used is that of Memmesheimer.[28] The reflection of a skin area and of a color wheel were brought together in a viewing field by means of a prism. The synthesis of the skin color was based on Ostwald's system of color analysis in which is used a system of standard fundamental colors with modifications depending on various combinations with white and black. The actual operation of the Memmesheimer method consisted of selecting a color sector approximating the skin color and blending it on the color wheel with sectors of white and black. The formula was expressed in terms of parts of black, white, and color. The blended color was then compared with one of the Hintze skin colors.

Another still more complicated but more accurate method of measuring skin pigmentation consists of determining the utilization of light by skin as manifested by its spectral reflection and transmission. Schultze[29] used a photographic-photometric method of recording the light reflected by the skin, further analyzed the results with a Marten's polarization photometer, and plotted curves in percentages of reflected light. He compared in this way various areas of the body of white people but did not use it to compare the skins of different races, although the method is adapted to this purpose. He found that pigmentation tends to

[28] *Arch. f. Dermat. u. Syph.*, 163:201, 1931.   [29] *Strahlentherapie*, 22:38, 1926.

diminish the amount of light reflected by the skin. Dorno,[30] using similar methods, observed variations in the reflection of light by skin as affected by race, age, and sex. He likewise noted general diminution of the light reflected under conditions of increased pigmentation. Sonne[31] estimated that the skin of a normal white individual was capable of reflecting approximately 35 per cent of the visible light falling on it. Sheard and Brunstig[32] used a spectrophotometric method to analyze the light reflected by the skin and recorded skin color in terms of the three attributes of color—brilliance, hue, and saturation. They

TABLE 7

PERCENTAGES OF COLORS USED TO DUPLICATE COLOR
OF ITALIANS AND MEXICANS

Races	Black	Red	White	Yellow
Italians.........	59	29	5	7
	51	32	7	10
Mexicans.......	60	27	5	8
	50	24	15	11
	50	25	15	10

obtained the reflection curves of the skin of various races under different clinical conditions and analyzed them into percentages of fundamental red, green, and violet color value, dominant wave length, and luminosity. From this data can be made estimates of the intensity of pigmentation. They found that the values for the amount of red, green, and violet are maintained at a fairly constant level for all colors of skin. There is little variation in the hue, or dominant wave length, which remains at approximately 590 millimicrons, corresponding to spectral yellow. The brilliance, or luminosity values, however, underwent marked variation and were determined by the amount of pigment in the skin. In other words, the fairest white skin and the darkest Negro skin are indistinguishable except for

[30] *Strahlentherapie,* 22:70, 1926.

[31] *Strahlentherapie,* 25:3, 1927.   [32] *Proc. Staff Meet., Mayo Clin.,* 3:110, 1929.

the relative amounts of light they reflect. A relative luminosity of 7.5 per cent was obtained in an area of skin on the dorsum of the hand of a Negro, while that on the surface of the chest reflected 18.6 per cent of the light falling on it. The relative luminosity of the skin of white blonds ranged from 39 per cent to 46.1 per cent and for white brunets it ranged from 20.9 per cent to 41.7 per cent. For a Chinese the relative figures for different parts of the body were 27.2 per cent, 32.0 per cent, and 33.7 per cent, and for a Japanese, 24.3 per cent and 28.0 per cent. Similar methods were used by Kartschagin,[33] Williams,[34] and Edwards and Duntley.[35]

In addition to being used for anthropological purposes, these more accurate methods for determining skin pigmentation can be used in the clinic. Pathological changes of the color of the skin too slight to be noticed by the unaided eye can be readily diagnosed by these means. Inflammatory reddening of the skin in very dark Negroes, particularly in exanthematous diseases, is often very difficult to determine. Under these conditions a method which would distinguish an increase of the red factor would be very useful.

Davenport[36] points out that in making comparisons of skin color a certain difficulty is introduced by the fact that the color of the skin is not constant throughout the life of the individual. It is generally known that Negro infants are not as dark at birth as they will become later. This is attested to by observers both in Africa and in America as shown by Pruner-Bey,[37] Simonot,[38] Broca,[39] Brodnax,[40] and Schiller-Tietz.[41] Pruner-Bey even claims that it is impossible to distinguish between

[33] *Ztschr. f. physik. Therap.*, **31**:1, 5, 1926.

[34] *Science*, **78**:192, 1933.   [35] *Am. J. Anat.*, **65**:1, 1939.

[36] *Carnegie Inst. Wash., Publ. No. 188*, 1913.

[37] *Bull. Soc. d'anthrop. de Paris*, **1**:293, 1860; **5**:360, 1864.

[38] *Bull. Soc. d'anthrop. de Paris*, **3**:140, 1862.

[39] *Bull. Soc. d'anthrop. de Paris*, **4**:612, 1863.

[40] *Mississippi M. Rec.*, **7**:174, 1903; *M. Brief*, **28**:788, 1900.

[41] *Deutsche med. Wchnschr.*, **27**:615, 1901; *Deutsche Rundschau. f. Geog. u. Statisk.*, **24**:55, 1902.

white and Negro newborns by skin color alone. The opposite
view is held by Robertson,[42] who says that newborn Negroes are
definitely black.[43] Other writers describe the infants as rose-
colored, tallow-white, and bistre-colored. It appears that the
skin color becomes perceptibly darker a few hours after birth,
increasing noticeably during the first few weeks and continuing
to do so during the first year, but does not reach its maximum
until about puberty, after which it diminishes in intensity.
These color changes resulting from age have been followed by
estimating the black in skins with the color-top at different ages
by Davenport,[44] Todd and Van Gorder,[45] and Herskovits.[46]

The tendency of the pigment to be concentrated in certain
parts of the body is generally the same in both Negroes and
whites as far as the location of these darker areas is concerned.
However, Futcher[47] found that in some Negroes there is a sudden transition in the degree of pigmentation in the anterior deltoid region of the upper arm. A darker color on the outer aspect
abuts suddenly on the less deeply pigmented flexor surface
with a resultant linear margin. It was found, always bilaterally,
in thirty-five of two hundred Negroes examined but never anywhere on the body of whites. Once it was found in a Negro bilaterally on the arms, extending to the axillary region, down the
chest in the anterior axillary line, then medially across the chest.
The author saw such a linear arrangement of pigmentation
faintly on the skin of a dark Italian.

Attempts to detect small amounts of Negro blood in otherwise white persons have usually been based on the demonstration of some form of pigmentation. Brodnax[48] says that in people of mixed blood there is a faint but distinct yellow line about
one-half inch wide running from the coccyx to the hair of the
head. In women there is, according to him, a dark line running

[42] *Alabama M. Surg. Age*, 10:413, 1897–98.

[43] *Lancet*, 2:1419, 1898.

[44] *Carnegie Inst. Wash., Publ. No. 188*, 1913.   [45] *Loc. cit.;* see n. 27.

[46] *Am. J. Phys. Anthropol.*, 9:321, 1926.

[47] *Bull. Johns Hopkins Hosp.*, 67:372, 1940.   [48] *Loc. cit.;* see n. 40.

the entire length of the perineum; the vulva also is sometimes dark, and the areola around the nipple is a very dark brown, almost black. Hrdlička[49] claims that pure strains of the colored races will not show a red mark on the skin when the fingernail is drawn over the chest with pressure, but if there is any intermixture with whites at all the redding will be distinct and of some duration and in proportion to the amount of intermixture.

PIGMENTS OF THE SKIN

Since the various colors of normal skin can be synthesized by the visual blending of black, red, yellow, and white, the question arises whether each of these colors represents an actual chromagen in the skin. Davenport was of the opinion that they did. He believed that black referred to melanin, yellow to a lipochrome, red to the circulating blood, and white to the reflection of the more or less opaque skin. On the other hand, Todd[50] treated the various percentages of color in a skin-pigmentation formula as merely quantitative expressions of proportions of arbitrarily chosen colors which when blended by whirling match the skin color and disregarded any implication as to the correspondence of the color-top components to definite substances in the skin, except that he was aware of the black element as representing melanin.

Whether or not blood gives any other value to skin color than those qualities described as "pale," "swarthy," "ruddy," or "healthy" is not definitely known. Vasomotor dilatation due to emotion or drugs and congestion from disease processes are not easily recognized in black skins, but vasoconstriction, anemia, and death impart a peculiar ashy color. There is still more uncertain evidence for the presence in the skin of a yellow lipochrome. No such substance has been isolated, although the distinctly yellow color of some races suggests that there might be a definite yellow pigment. In carotinemia the skin is yellow because of pigment in the underlying fat, but apparently the panniculus adiposus seems not to influence skin

[49] *Am. J. Phys. Anthropol.*, 2:175, 1919.
[50] *Am. J. Phys. Anthropol.*, 11:188, 1928.

color, since there is no correlation with the depth of fat color or the thickness of the layer, both of which are highly variable in degree in the same and between individuals. White in the skin seems to be due to the reflection of light by the cutaneous elements in proportion to the absence of light-absorbing substances. The white melanin described by Spiegler,[51] of some interest here in explaining the white of skin, was shown by Gortner to be unrelated to melanin but a product of keratin decomposition.

The only definitely known pigment occurring in human skin is melanin, a complex amorphous organic substance of high molecular weight that can be isolated chemically from the tissues. It is said that when removed from the skin its color varies from a bright yellow or a reddish-yellow through light and dark brown to black, although these differences in color may be due to chemical alterations incident to isolation or to differences in physical state. The blackness of melanin may be intense, as is testified to by the statement of Abel and Davis,[52] that the entire skin of a very black Negro contained only one gram of the pigment. There has been much discussion of the chemistry of melanin—its origin, the role of enzymes in its production, and the type of cells which produce it, all of which has been ably reviewed by Bloch[53] in a monograph concerning his dopa reaction.

Melanin occurs as fine granules deposited for the most part in the basal cells of the stratum Malpighii of the epidermis but also in the epidermal melanoblasts, the dermal chromatophores, and the dermal melanoblasts. The hue of the skin is determined largely by the pigment in the basal cells and epidermal melanoblasts. All normal human skins, including that of the fairest blonds, contain some melanin. Depending on the color, however, there is a difference in the amount and location of the pigment granules. In blonds only a few cells of the basal layer contain pigment and in a small amount; in brunets more of these cells contain more pigment, and as the skin color increases in darkness more and more of the cells contain granules in larger

[51] *Hofmeister's Beitr.*, 4:40, 1904.   [52] *J. Exper. Med.*, 1:361, 1896.

[53] "Das Pigment," *Handb. d. Haut- u. Geschlechtskr.*, 1:Part I, 1927.

amounts, until in very dark skins the entire basal layer is packed with them. Moreover, the pigment in black skins may be found to extend to and beyond the basal layer into the upper layers of the stratum Malpighii and even into the stratum corneum. The skin of a Negro is very easily identified in microscopic preparations by the large amount of pigment granules, and often degrees of pigmentation can be estimated with some accuracy.

Jordan[54] insists that the color and the size of the melanin granules are the same in all skins, and the entire range of skin color may be accounted for by variations in the number of cells containing pigment and the amount of pigment in each of the cells. On the other hand, Adachi[55] and Becker[56] observed that the shape, size, and color of the granules varied, although they were apparently constant for the individual. Without any other reason to account for the yellowness of Mongolians and certain African natives, it might be that their color is due to these various physical properties of melanin granules.

Edwards and Düntley[57] claim that in addition to melanin there is another closely allied pigment, melanoid, which is a diffused substance present throughout the epidermis. While colored races owe their characteristic colors only to variations in the amount of melanin and melanoid present, there are other pigments common to all skins, namely, oxyhemoglobin and reduced hemoglobin found in the blood vessels of the dermis and carotin, which these authors believe they have demonstrated by spectrophotometric means to be present in the stratum corneum of the epidermis as well as in the fat of the dermis and subcutaneous tissues. Storage of carotin in the stratum corneum and not in the adjacent stratum mucosum is due to the presence of fat only in the former layer and not in the latter, which, although it transports the pigment, cannot retain it.

Karg[58] followed the movement of melanin after transplantation of Negro skin onto white skins and of white skin onto the

[54] Am. Nat., 45:449, 1911.

[55] Ztschr. f. Morphol. u. Anthropol., 6:1, 1903.

[56] Arch. Dermat., 16:259, 1927.

[57] Loc. cit.; see n. 35.

[58] Virchow's Arch. f. Anat., p. 369, 1888.

skin of Negroes. He found that in each case the transplanted skin became the color of the host.

It has been the practice among some Negroes to use cosmetics claimed by their manufacturers to bleach the skin. The majority of these preparations contain some organic combination of zinc and are, in fact, exfoliatives. Because of the deep-seated location and the stable chemical character of melanin, it is unreasonable to expect any change of pigmentation by exfoliation or chemical alteration of the pigment. Severe dermatitis has often resulted from the use of these so-called bleaches.

INHERITANCE OF SKIN COLOR

There is a general interest in the question of inheritance of human skin color, chiefly because of the seemingly capricious manner in which pigmentation is distributed among the children of families with an intermixture of white and Negro blood. In a single fraternity of offspring there may be a very wide variation in color. There is the belief that even very fair mates, who are white to all appearances, will occasionally and unexpectedly produce children with Negro coloration as the result of a forgotten or denied Negro ancestor. The possibility of such an occurrence and the uncertainty of its prediction are sources of dread for those who wish and are otherwise able to escape the social inconveniences allotted to known descendants of Negroes.

Geneticists also have been interested in the inheritance of skin pigmentation in man. In the few studies that have been made, the chief questions that have evolved are concerned with the applicability of Mendelian law to color inheritance and with the composition of inheritable factors which determine skin color. On the whole, the subject is unfortunately in a decidedly unsatisfactory state. The data are meager, and all the papers that have been published need reinterpretation in the light of present knowledge of genetics.

Pearson[59] was convinced that skin-color inheritance did not obey Mendelian laws but that it was a blend—a conclusion which has gained wide acceptance. He obtained his data from a

[59] *Biometrika*, 6:346, 1909.

questionnaire addressed to a medical correspondent in the West Indies who claimed to have observed that the color of the mulatto (from a Negro-white cross) was either brown or yellow, representing a blend of the colors of the parents. The quadroon (mulatto-white cross) was in 90 per cent of the cases lighter than the mulatto, and the offspring of mulatto-Negro crosses was always dark mahogany in color, neither that of a mulatto nor a Negro. Crosses between mulattoes, while giving slight variations in color, never give pure black skins or pure white skins. Pearson claimed that these facts indicated blending. He stated that, according to Mendelian theory, in the case of mulatto-Negro crosses, these would be half mulattoes and half pure Negro offspring, and in mulatto-mulatto crosses, 25 per cent pure white skins, 25 per cent black skins, and 50 per cent mulattoes.

In appraising Pearson's study it must be remembered that it was made in 1909, before the present concepts of genetics were arrived at. When he concluded that skin color does not obey Mendelian laws, he meant a very different thing from what would be meant today by such a statement. It is obvious that he understood by Mendelian heredity merely what is now called one-factor heredity, but his results in no way invalidate the possibility of a more complicated mechanism.

In a more extensive study of the problem, Davenport[60] obtained the pedigrees of 106 different families in Bermuda, Jamaica, and Louisiana in which there were Negro-white crosses. Using the Bradley color-top, he measured the color of all accessible individuals of as many generations as possible in these families; these included 147 matings. He found that the color of the first generation of Negro-Caucasian crosses was always different from that of the parents. It was lighter than that of the Negro parent and darker than that of the white parent. The darkest Negroes produced the darkest offspring. The total range of color in the first generation in terms of percentage of N[61] was 26 points, varying from 20 per cent N to 45 per cent N.

[60] *Carnegie Inst. Wash., Publ. No. 188,* 1913.

[61] Percentage of N is the nomenclature used to represent that proportion of the area of a color-blending disk made up of black in matching a skin color.

In the second generation (children of mated mulattoes and grandchildren of Negro and white pairs) the range of color for all individuals measured was twice as great as in the first generation. Even within one fraternity of offspring the range between the lightest and darkest in the second generation was 1.66 times that in the first generation. The children of mulatto-mulatto crosses may be either much darker or much lighter than either parent. The lightest child of a Negro-white cross had more than twice as much black pigment as the average medium-skinned Caucasian, and the darkest had about three-fifths of the black pigmentation of the darkest Africans. On the other hand, the lightest children of mulattoes were very near the color of the ordinary brunet Caucasian, and the darkest were about two-fifths as dark as the average African.

Davenport believed that the greater range of color in the second generation as compared with that in the first indicated the probability of segregation in color inheritance. That only one-sixteenth instead of one-fourth of the children of mulattoes were fair skinned was evidence that more than one double factor was involved in black pigmentation. From an analysis of his data, Davenport hypothecated that "there are two (double) factors (A and B) for black pigmentation in the full-blooded Negro of the West Coast of Africa and these are separately inheritable." This hypothesis, according to him, called for five conditions of skin color, as shown in Table 8.

It may be pointed out that in the condition where there is one factor for black (Grade 2), Davenport has not taken into account the genotype $aaBb$, and in the condition which calls for two factors for black (Grade 3), the genotype $aaBB$ is omitted. In the actual application of the hypothesis, Davenport treated $aaBb$ as of the same grade as $Aabb$, $aaBB$ and $AAbb$ as like $AaBb$, and $AaBB$ as like $AABb$. When expressed completely, his hypothesis in regard to five grades of pigmentation is as shown in Table 9.

By throwing all the grades of skin color found in Bermuda into a frequency polygon showing the distribution of percentages of skin black, evidence was obtained for the existence of five maximums which were taken to represent the probable ranges of the hypothetical five grades of genotypes. The interpretation given to the grades of genotypes in terms of percentage N is shown in Table 10.

TABLE 8
DAVENPORT'S THEORETICAL GRADES OF SKIN COLOR AND THEIR GENOTYPES

Grades	Genotypes*
1. No factor for black—the Caucasian condition..	*aabb*
2. No *B* factor, the *A* factor simplex—the light-colored..................................	*Aabb*
3. Either no *B* factor and the *A* factor duplex or both *A* and *B* factors simplex—the medium-colored..................................	*AAbb, AaBb*
4. One factor duplex and the other simplex—the dark-colored skin.........................	*AABb, AaBB*
5. Both factors duplex—the black skin...........	*AABB*

* Capital letters (*A, B*) indicate presence of the factor, lower-case letters (*a, b*) indicate absence of the factor.

TABLE 9
THEORETICAL GRADES OF SKIN COLOR AND THEIR AMENDED GENOTYPES

Grades	Genotypes
1. No factor for black (Caucasian).........	*aabb*
2. One factor for black....................	*Aabb, aaBb*
3. Two factors for black....................	*AaBb, AAbb, aaBB*
4. Three factors for black.................	*AABb, AaBB*
5. Four factors for black (pure Negro)......	*AABB*

TABLE 10
RANGES OF N CORRESPONDING TO GENOTYPES

Grade	Per Cent N
1........................	0–11
2........................	12–25
3........................	26–40
4........................	41–55
5........................	56–78

Comparisons of expectation and realization were made by Davenport among 631 offspring whose skin color and pedigree were known. He assumed that there were 26 possible matings among his 5 grades of genotypes, and he illustrates in his family histories 17 of these types. Actually there are 9 genotypes and 81 possible matings. Under the hypothesis of 2 double factors for black, mulatto parents ($AaBb \times AaBb$) should produce the 5 grades in the ratio of 1:4:6:4:1, which is what Davenport assumes when he applies his hypothesis to actual facts. Not all matings between individuals with 2 factors for black would give this result, as Davenport recognizes. Thus $AAbb \times AAbb$, $aaBB \times aaBB$, or $AAbb \times aaBB$ would produce only individuals of the same grades as the parents, and $AAbb \times AaBb$ would produce individuals with 1, 2, and 3 factors for black in the ratio of 1:2:1, etc. Davenport attempts to make an adjustment for these unknown genotypes among the mulattoes and selects 2.8:22:28.5:22:2.8 as the probable expectation ratio for his group. Actually, the ratio 4:18:51:14:1 was obtained.

Criticisms of Davenport's work have been made. Todd[62] and Herskovits[63] pointed out the errors incident to the use of the color-top in measuring skin color. The red disk used was not pure spectral red. It contained 59 per cent black, which should be subtracted from the red readings and added to the black ones. This is probably irrelevant, as it does not materially affect the results of Davenport as long as he always used the same standards. It would be of importance only when his measurements were compared with those of other workers using different standards. Todd found that the correction for black in the red standard reduces the range of black in Negro skins to less than one-half the range in the uncorrected estimates and makes possible the comparison and correlation of skin color with certain measurements of the skeleton.

Barnes[64] criticizes Davenport's emphasis of the bimodality of frequency distribution of color in Bermuda. She finds that when corrections are made for black in the red standard and for age changes in color, his data show no significant traces of bimodality. The peaks of his polygon disappear, and whatever irregularities remain are probably accidental and due to paucity of data.

[62] *Loc. cit.;* see n. 50.

[63] *Loc. cit.;* see n. 24.   [64] *Human Biol.,* 1:321, 1929.

Barnes, herself, studied skin-color inheritance by utilizing the material obtained by Herskovits and his students for his studies of the physical anthropology of the American Negro. The pedigree and skin color were ascertained for 2,391 individuals of 637 families. In addition, 1,612 other individuals, not associated with the families of the study, were studied only for data on age changes in pigmentation.

As evidence of Mendelian segregation Barnes offers, first, the deviation of the color of offspring from the color of parents, expressed in her data as retrogression coefficients of the average color of sons, daughters, or both together, from the average of fathers, mothers, or both together, and, second, the familial and fraternal variability of color.

The question has arisen in popular discussions of color transmission as to whether it is possible to predict the color of children born to mates of given grades of complexion. For an individual child one cannot say in advance what its skin color may be. From Davenport's table the probable range of color among children of a pair may, within limitations, be given, especially if the pedigree of the parents can be established. Among Davenport's families there were 3 with 3 factors of black each for mother and father, which were the darkest mates cited. Among the combined offspring of these families there were 4 who were lighter than any parent, 1 who was much darker than any parent, and 13 who were of the same grade of color as the parents. White fathers (no factors for N) mated with the darkest mothers (4 factors for N) produced among 4 matings no children as dark as the mothers. There were 3 children one grade lighter (3 factors for N) than the mothers, and 14 two grades lighter (2 factors for N). There were none the same color of the father nor any which were one grade darker (1 factor for N) than the father. White fathers and light-colored mothers (1 factor for N) and white mothers and light-colored fathers produced in 22 matings 56 children of the same grade of color as the white parents, 80 children of the same grade of color as the colored parents, and 1 child darker than the colored parents. Matings between very fair-colored persons (with 1 factor for N) produced

in 26 families 24 children who were white (no factor for N), 87
of the same grade as the parents, and 23 who were one grade
darker (2 factors for N). None of two darker grades were produced. Davenport investigated the question of black children
being born to a purebred white married to an extracted white.
Replies received to inquiries concerning this happening in
Jamaica agreed in holding the idea of "reversion to black" to be
mythical. He thought it might have arisen from the fact that
two very light-colored persons might be the parents of a medi-
um-colored child.

Analysis of the inheritance of skin color has been made even
more difficult by the fact that none of the factors for black (or
absence of black) appears to possess the quality of dominance,
in spite of many opinions to the contrary. Data collected by
Barnes give little or no evidence that the average color of children taken in large numbers is nearer the color of one parent
than of the other. The dark children in a family are not predominantly of any one sex, nor does it make any difference in the
distribution of color in children if the father or mother is darker
(Davenport). The latter question was raised by Pearson,[65] who
cited three instances of Negro-white matings in which the mother was white instead of the father, as is usually the case, and in
which the offspring were not mulattoes. The first case, described by Aristotle,[66] was that of a woman in Elis who bore a
white daughter to an Ethiopian, but this daughter had a black
son by a white father. In the second case, described by Parsons,[67] a white woman in York married a Negro and had by him
a distinctly Negro child. The third case, also described by Parsons, was that of a white woman who had a piebald child by a
Negro. The absence of dominance is in part responsible for the
findings which have suggested blending.

The conclusive evidence against inheritance of skin color in
humans by blending is the occurrence of important differences
among children of the same parents, found by both Davenport
and Barnes. In the light of modern genetics human skin color

[65] Loc. cit.; see n. 59.

[66] De generatione animalium, Bk. I, xviii.   [67] Phil. Trans., 55:45, 1765.

can be accounted for neither by blending nor by one pair of Mendelian alleles. There are undoubtedly multiple factors, of which at least two pairs (as suggested by Davenport) may be considered of major importance. It is probable that there are really more than two, as Barnes claims, but the amount of segregation indicates that there cannot be many more of major importance. The combination of multiple factors, with an absence of dominance, is sufficient to account for the known facts, although some of the details are still obscure.

Davenport's observations on the inheritance of hair form, made incidentally to those on skin-color inheritance, led him to conclude that the characteristic woolly hair of the Negro is also a two-factor condition but that skin color and hair texture are inherited separately without any correlation between the two. Black skin color and woolly hair are closely associated in the pure Negro, but the association is, so to say, accidental. The determiners for the two traits dissociate in the germ cells of hybrids and reappear in the next generation in all possible combinations. He cites one of two extracted full black-skinned individuals who had straight hair, and one of three extracted white-skinned individuals who had woolly hair.

SACRAL PIGMENT SPOTS

If the skin of Negro infants is carefully examined there will be found in about 90 per cent of them one or more small bluish-gray pigmented areas situated in the skin of the back. These are known as sacral pigment spots but have also been called Mongolian blue spots, evanescent pigmentation, and mulberry-colored spots. They do not occur exclusively in Negroes but in all other colored races and occasionally in white people (one in 300 or 600). They have been called Mongolian spots because they were at first believed to be characteristic only of Japanese· and Chinese. The sacral spots may be multiple in number and vary in size from a few millimeters to ten centimeters or more. They are most often located in the midline of the sacral region, over the buttocks, shoulders, head or extensor surfaces of the extremities, but almost never on the flexor surfaces.

The spots are present at birth, and it is reported that they may be seen as early as the fourth month of intrauterine life.[68] They are believed never to appear if they are not present at birth. The color deepens at first, then gradually fades, to disappear completely, in most cases, within the first or second year of life, although it may last until puberty and occasionally into adult life.[69]

Brennemann[70] examined forty colored children under one year of age, one-half of them being less than one week old, and found that thirty-five showed well-marked areas of bluish pigmentation. In one child of nine months a mark could no longer be made out with certainty, although shortly after birth there had been a deep-blue sacral spot of considerable size. In four individuals the spots were not present, and they had not previously been observed by the mothers, although Brennemann suggests the possibility that the superficial pigment obscured them. Hermann[71] found the spots in only 25 per cent of the Negro infants he examined.

The significance of the sacral spots is not clear. There are superstitions concerning them among many of the various races. These are recounted by Brennemann. American Negroes have no folklore about the spots, probably because many of them are apparently unaware of their existence. However, in many Negroes the sacral spots are not discernible, except shortly after birth, because of the darkness of the general skin color. Ashmead,[72] with poor supporting evidence and without the agreement of other writers, is of the opinion that the sacral spots in races other than the Negro indicate intermixture with Negro blood.

Through the researches of Adachi[73] and Bahrawy,[74] the histology of the sacral spots is known. The pigment concerned is

---

[68] Baelz, Centralbl. f. Anthropol., 7:329, 1902.

[69] Ashmead, J. Cutan. Dis., 23:203, 1905.

[70] Arch. Pediat., 24:426, 1907.

[71] J. Cutan. Dis., 25:201, 1907.   [73] Loc. cit.; see n. 55; Anat. Anz., 22:323, 1903.

[72] Loc. cit.; see n. 69.   [74] Arch. f. Dermat. u. Syph., 141:171, 1932.

located in cells of the corium, and the optical effects of its deep position are responsible for the blue color in the same way that the dermal deposit of artificially introduced black pigment causes the blue color of tattoo marks. The cells of the sacral spots that contain the pigment are true melanoblasts, since they give a positive dopa reaction (Bahrawy), a test which demonstrates the presence of enzymes believed to be responsible for intracellular melanin formation. Another type of pigment-containing cells found in the corium does not give the dopa reaction and is regarded as chromatophores of connective-tissue origin which obtain melanin by phagocytosis from other sources. The chromatophores, while few in number in normal skins, are concentrated in the skin of the neck, eyelids, anus, genitalia, nipple, and axilla. In normal humans the dermal melanoblasts are found only in the sacral pigment spots. Pathologically, they are the cells that make up the so-called "blue nevus." Except for differences in location and for certain tissue changes associated with the tumor, the blue nevus and the sacral spots are of essentially the same structure; the former being pathological and arising postnatal and the other normal but evanescent and arising prenatal. Since certain melanomas originate in blue nevi, it is presumed that they may also arise in the sacral spots, although no such occurrence has been described. It is of significance that the dermal melanoblasts make up a part of the general pigmentation of certain blue-colored monkeys. In these animals the dermal pigmentation is deep and the epidermal pigmentation scanty. The various colors of other monkeys are believed to be due to the relative amounts of melanin in the corium and in the epidermis. In the higher primates the pigmentation is more analogous to that in the human in that the melanin, for the most part, is in the epithelium. Brennemann[75] and Larsen and Godfrey[76] look upon the sacral pigment spots as a normal human characteristic which is a persistent rudimentary form of what was once a more widespread and functional layer of pigment, such as now exists in certain monkeys. Larsen and Godfrey studied in Hawaii the inheritance of the sacral spots in

[75] *Loc. cit.;* see n. 70.   [76] *Am. J. Phys. Anthropol.,* 10:253, 1927.

crossings of white and colored (Japanese, Chinese, Hawaiians, Filipinos, Negroes, Indians, Puerto Ricans) races and in crossings of colored races with one another. In their theory they assume the activity of two factors—P, a factor for pigment (p, its absence) and o the factor for the presence of the mark (O, its absence). For the mark to be evident, therefore, this latter factor must be homozygous for the o factor, that is, inherited from both parents, represented by oo. An individual, to show the mark, must be $PPoo$ or $Ppoo$. At least one P must be present in the zygotes to make the mark visible, even when the o factor is homozygous. It was further assumed that the different racial types are represented by the following compositions: colored, $PPoo$; white, $ppOo$; Portuguese (who are believed to be considerably mixed with Africans), $PpOo$. This would indicate that colored races always bear the mark along with their other color characteristics; that in the white races, while the mark is not evident, the factor for its presence is carried in the germ plasm; that in the Portuguese there is dilute pigment(Pp) which will make it possible for the sacral spots to show whenever there is oo in the zygotes. The mark should therefore appear sometimes in crosses within the latter race, and this is found to be true. When the results of crossings are estimated on the basis of factor analyses there is a remarkable agreement with the actual inheritance observed.

PIGMENTATION OF THE ORAL MUCOSA

Certain colored people are often seen to have pigmentation extending beyond the true skin into the mucous membrane of the mouth. They are referred to in the vernacular as "blue-gummed" people, and, as this type of pigmentation is most often seen when the complexion is very dark, the expression is generally used to supplement the description of an extremely black skin. Monash[77] examined 220 Negroes of varying degrees of pigmentation and of different ages and showed the existence of pigmented spots in the oral mucosa in 95 per cent (excluding the newborn), which varied in appearance and location.

[77] *Arch. Dermat. & Syph.*, 26:139, 1932.

On the gums in lighter-colored Negroes, they are seen as flat, light-brown, irregularly circular areas, varying in size from 1 to 3 or 4 mm. in diameter, and occupying approximately the center of the gum surface. In the darker subjects these pigmented areas are deeper in color, tend to become confluent, and form a band encircling the central portion of the gum surface. In very dark people, containing 80 and 85 per cent black by the color-top method, not only the central portion but practically the entire gum surface may be covered with a pigmented plaque. In all cases there is a marked tendency for the pigmentation to be symmetrically bilateral. Microscopic examination of these pigmented areas shows a picture identical with that of skin pigmentation. The pigment is found chiefly in the basal cell layer with a tendency to occupy several layers of cells above the basal layer in the more darkly pigmented specimens. Often numerous chromatophores are seen in the papillary body. On the hard palate and on the mucosal surface of the lips pigmentation may be diffuse, resulting in a general darkening of the entire area, or mottled, showing the presence of irregularly circular or elliptical areas of varying size, or a combination of both types may be seen. Very dark subjects show, as a rule, both diffuse and mottled areas, whereas the lighter Negroes usually have only mottling. On these surfaces there is also a tendency for the pigmentation to be symmetrically bilateral. On the soft palate pigmentation may likewise be either diffuse or mottled. In the latter case the pigmented areas are usually small and tend to surround the numerous small blood vessels in this structure. Pigmentation on the cheeks is generally seen in the center, along what is usually considered to be the median raphe, as a flat, brownish, elongated area. The anterior third of this region is the area of predilection. In addition mottled areas may be seen, and in very dark subjects a diffuse pigmentation of the entire cheek may be present. Symmetry is also the rule here.

The tongue is unique in that there is no tendency for the pigmentation on the dorsum to be symmetrical. It is usually observed in the fungiform papillae in the anterior third. One or several of these may show pigmented summits with no other pigmentation observable elsewhere on the dorsum. In darker subjects the number of pigmented fungiform papillae increases. In very dark Negroes, those with 80 and 85 per cent skin pigmentation, pigmented plaques, varying in size from a few millimeters to a centimeter and more in diameter, are often seen. Both the fungiform and the filiform papillae in these areas are pigmented. In older subjects the lateroinferior surface of the tongue occasionally shows a diffuse pigmentation. The plicae fimbriatae are often pigmented. In the floor of the mouth pigmentation is most often limited to the areas about the orifices of the salivary ducts and is generally seen as a pigmented circle surrounding the duct orifice.

Corresponding to the paucity of pigmentation of the skin at birth, oral pigmentation is also slight at this time. It was found by Monash to be present in six of the eighteen infants in his series as light-brown, irregular areas, usually over the palatal and lingual aspects of the gums in the upper and lower incisal regions, with a tendency toward bilateral symmetry. While in infants the pigmentation is first observed on the palatal and lingual surfaces and not on the buccal surface, in adults the latter surface is very often found pigmented with the former surfaces free. This does not mean, according to Monash, that the palatal and lingual gum pigmentation observed in infants disappears in later life but that the infants observed are usually the darker ones in whom pigmented areas will eventually develop on all portions of the gums. In newborn infants oral pigmentation was observed only on the gums. As the age increases the oral pigmentation increases in degree and extent in the following order: inner gum surface, outer gum surface, hard palate, soft palate, lips, cheeks, tongue. The pigmentation is well on its way to completion by the end of the first decade and is practically complete by the end of the second decade. If further oral pigmentation occurs after the age of twenty, it can usually be traced to other than physiologic factors. Of the 5 per cent which showed no oral pigmentation, all were of the lighter group.

Normal oral pigmentation is not confined to the Negro race.

It has been reported in such varied races as the French by Bonnet-Lyon and Lortat-Jacob,[78] Solente,[79] and Milian[80]; in the Filipino by Lortat-Jacob[81]; in the Algerian by Bonnet-Lyon and Lortat-Jacob[82] and Brault Montpelier[83]; in the Arabian, Chinese, and East Indian by Reiche[84]; in the Burmese by Castor[85]; in the German by Jessner[86]; in the Gipsy and Rumanian by Sabareanu[87]; in the natives of Asia Minor by Combes[88]; in the Jews and Lascars by Crouzon[89]; and in the English by Sibley,[90] Hutchinson,[91] Rolleston,[92] and Evans.[93] Becker[94] was able to demonstrate microscopically in German-Swiss, a people not of a particularly dark type, the presence of oral pigmentation, although it was not macroscopically present. Also Adachi[95] found melanoblasts in the buccal mucous membranes of Europeans. In America, Monash[96] found thirty instances of oral pigmentation in Italians, Jews, Greeks, Rumanians, Chinese, Puerto Ricans, Syrians, Peruvian Indians, Hindus, and Ceylonese. The types of pigmentation and areas of predilection were the same as those he found in Negroes, and there was also the same relation to skin pigmentation. When persons of similar shades of any race are examined, there is, apparently, no appreciable difference in the amount or the characteristics of oral pigmentation. Many of the writers cited above point out

[78] *Lyon méd.*, 131:153, 1922.

[79] *Bull. Soc. franç. de dermat. et syph.*, 30:363, 1923.

[80] *Bull. et mém. Soc. méd. d. hôp. de Paris*, 36:297, 1912.

[81] *Bull. et mém. Soc. méd. d. hôp. de Paris*, 33:896, 1912.

[82] *Lyon méd.*, 131:153, 1922.   [84] *Med. Klin.*, 20:204, 1924.

[83] *Provence Med.*, 25:159, 1914.   [85] *J. Trop. Med.*, 15:117, 1912.

[86] *Zentralbl. f. Haut- u. Geschlechtskr.*, 17:272, 1925.

[87] *Lyon méd.*, 131:153, 1922.

[88] *Arch. Dermat. & Syph.*, 16:259, 1927.

[89] *Bull. et mém. Soc. méd. d. hôp. de Paris*, 33:647, 1912; 36:248, 1913.

[90] *Clin. J.*, 8:231, 1896.

[91] *Arch. Surg.*, 7:290, 1896.   [94] *Loc. cit.*; see n. 56.

[92] *Proc. Roy. Soc. Med.*, 3:9, 1909-10.   [95] *Loc. cit.*; see n. 55.

[93] *Proc. Roy. Soc. Med.*, 3:57, 1909-10.   [96] *Loc. cit.*; see n. 77.

that in fair people pernicious anemia and Addison's disease must be excluded before deciding that the oral pigmentation is a normal feature, since in these diseases a similar condition is often found.

PIGMENTATION OF THE NAILS

Another site of extradermal pigmentation seen often, but not exclusively, in the Negro is pigmentation of the fingernails. This occurrence has also been offered as a "giveaway" of colored descent in very fair people, but it is probably another accompaniment of heavy cutaneous pigmentation and can be found in dark people generally if sought for without regard to race. Monash[97] examined the nails of 296 Negroes who varied in age from a few days to sixty-two years and whose skin color was determined by the color-top method. He found that among those whose skin color contained less than 65 per cent black, nail pigmentation was infrequent, about 4 per cent of a group of 89 subjects. Of the group with a skin pigmentation containing 65 per cent and over of black, of which there were 207, 118, or 57 per cent, showed it. If the latter group is divided into two divisions, namely, one with a skin pigmentation of 65, 70, and 75 per cent black and the other composed of the darker ones, namely, those with a pigmentation of 80 and 85 per cent black, the relationship of skin and nail pigmentation becomes further apparent. In the lighter group, of a total of 148 persons, 71, or 48 per cent, showed pigmented nails; in the darker group, of 59 persons, 45, or 76 per cent, showed the same changes. Those of 80 and 85 per cent black and twenty years of age and over showed pigmentation in practically every case. No pigmentation in the nails was observed in children at birth, the earliest case being that of a boy two years and nine months of age. Excluding children of ten days and under, the group below the age of ten years, of which there were 66, 23 per cent showed nail pigmentation. From the ages ten to nineteen, inclusive, 40 per cent showed it. In the third decade, twenty to twenty-nine, inclusive, 70 per cent had pigmentation. In the fourth decade and older, 53 per cent had pigment in the nails.

[97] *Op. cit.*, 25:876, 1923.

Pigmentation of the nails usually occurs in the form of longitudinal stripes running the length of the nail. On each nail there may be single or multiple stripes, and they may vary in width from a thin line to several millimeters. They vary in depth of color in different persons, being generally darker in darker people. They may be present in any portion of the nail but usually occupy the central area or the lateral margins. There is no deeper pigmentation of the nail-bed under these pigmented stripes. In the darker individuals, those with 80 per cent black or more in the skin, there is usually in addition a microscopically diffuse pigmentation of the entire nail substance, even in those parts not showing longitudinal striping.

The first nail to become pigmented is usually that of the thumb, or first finger, and the pigmentation usually proceeds in regular order—the second, third, fourth, and fifth fingers following in sequence. But many cases are observed in which pigmented stripes are first seen on nails of other than that of the first finger and in which the regular sequence of pigmentation is not followed. There is a tendency for the pigmentation to be symmetrically bilateral, appearing on the same nails of both hands, but also this is not true in every case.

Microscopically, the pigmented granules are found to be scattered through the entire thickness of the nail substance, with a tendency for the deeper layers to be more pigmented than the superficial. There is a definite concentration of the pigment in the areas corresponding to the pigmented stripes. The pigment granules take the form of the nail cells and undoubtedly owe their color to the presence of melanin.

Templeton[98] has reported a case of nail pigmentation in a colored woman which appeared when she was nineteen years old. Since the pigmentation began so late in life and consisted of a single longitudinal stripe confined to one hand and one fingernail, it is probable that it is pathological in origin, and it was suggested by Templeton that it is a pigmented nevus of the nail. A section of a paring from this nail showed the general features described above. The case of Ochs[99] of a dark-brown woman with pigmented stripes on all nails since birth seems to be similar to the normal ones described by Monash.

SWEAT GLANDS

The sweat glands are an important part of the heat-regulating mechanism of the body and, like other organs that share this function, show differences among races of people in proportion to the variations in the climates to which the different races are adjusted. The sweat glands secrete water, the evaporation of which from the surface of the body results in a loss of heat. The loss of heat from evaporation is more necessary for those in hot climates than for those in cooler ones, since the loss by radiation and conduction is less adjustable to differences between the temperatures of the body and the surrounding atmosphere. Evolutionary adaptations of the skin to hot climates apparently include the development of a larger number and size of sweat glands. Aron[100] pointed out that pigmented skins, because of the absorption of heat rays, should reach higher temperatures than white skins when exposed to sunlight (a fact verified by Schmidt[101] and Eykmann[102] when black and white skins from cadavers were compared) but that people with dark skins living in the tropics actually showed lower cutaneous temperatures than white people. He claims that the reason for this contradiction lies in the superior efficiency of the sweating apparatus of the natives of the tropics, resulting in a greater evaporation of water and in the loss of more heat. Aron says this superiority is shown by the difference in the manner of sweating rather than in the amount of sweat produced. According to him, the Negrito of the Philippines, upon whom his observations were made, secretes small beads of sweat over the entire body, which soon form a thin film. As the whole surface of the body is covered by this water film, the maximum cooling effect from evaporation is obtained. In the case of the white man, on the other hand, the sweating is practically limited to certain areas of the body sur-

[100] *Philippine J. Sc.*, 6:101, 1911.

[101] *Arch. f. Schiffs- u. Tropen-Hyg.*, 5:207, 1901; *Arch. f. Hyg.*, 47:262, 1903; 65:17, 1908.

[102] *Virchows Arch. f. path. Anat.*, 140:125, 1895.

face. In these areas the sweating is profuse, but, as most of it drops off, comparatively little cooling effect from evaporation is produced. He suggests that the Negrito has a greater number of sweat glands, which are more equally distributed over the entire body. Freer[103] estimates that Malay inhabitants of the Philippine Islands have 12–15 per cent more sweat glands than have whites, Negroes have 7 per cent more, and adult Negritos 26.82 per cent, and Negrito youths 67.54 per cent more. Däubler[104] states that the size of the sweat glands of the native of tropical Africa is much greater than that of the European. Clark and Lhamon[105] counted the sweat glands in the skin of the plantar surface of the foot and of the palmar surface of the hand of 200 American Negroes, 300 American whites, 150 Filipinos, and a large number of Moros, Negritos, and Hindus. His method was to count in a given area the number of openings of sweat-gland ducts seen in enlarged prints of the soles and palms. When the counts were arranged to show the average number of glands per square centimeter of skin area, striking differences between races were disclosed. The results are given in Table 11.

Schiefferdecker[106] has disclosed that there are two types of sweat glands in human skin, having different embryologic origin, structure, secretion, and function. The glands which are in the majority and which secrete the bulk of the sweat are called the exocrine glands and are scattered all over the body. The other type, called the apocrine glands, are, as a rule, found only in certain places, as in the axilla, in the external ear duct, and around the nipples and the anus. The exocrine glands arise embryologically from the free surface of the skin, while the apocrine glands take origin from a hair follicle, although later their ducts may wander to the free skin surface. For this reason they always occur where hair is present at some time of life. The exocrine glands produce a fluid which is formed as droplets

[103] *Philippine J. Sc.*, 7:1, 1912.

[104] *Die Gründzuge der Tropenhygiene* (Berlin).

[105] *Anat. Rec.*, 12:139, 1917.

[106] *Die Hautdrüsen des Menschen und der Säugetiere* (Stuttgart: E. Schiveizerbert, 1922).

within the protoplasm of the epithelial cells of the glands and is
then pushed out into the lumen without any loss of protoplasmic
substance. With the apocrine type, however, a part of the se-
creting cell itself is lost during secretion. This takes place in
such a way that at first the straight free margin of the epithelial
cell is bulged out toward the lumen of the sweat gland, until a
process is formed, which gets narrower and narrower at its base
and, finally, is found isolated in the lumen. The secretion of
these glands is therefore richer in solid substances and is in this

TABLE 11

RELATIVE NUMBER OF SWEAT GLANDS PER UNIT SURFACE
AREA IN THE SKIN OF VARIOUS RACES

Race	Average Number of Glands per Cm.² of Skin Area	Relative Number
American white.............	558.2	100.0
American Negro............	597.2	106.83
Filipino...................	653.6	116.61
Moro.....................	684.4	122.34
Negrito...................	709.2	126.81
Hindu....................	738.2	169.82
General average........	656.8	117.64

respect similar to that of the mammary gland. Schiefferdecker
suggests that they are related to the sex organs and that they
are responsible for body odors which may be specific for individuals, race, or sex. These glands are much larger than the
ordinary sweat glands and very frequently contain iron.[107] Another difference is the greater ease with which the apocrine
glands undergo post-mortem desquamation.

Since the apocrine glands differ in their number among lower
mammalian animals, Schiefferdecker believed that they might
differ among the various human races, a fact which he demonstrated to be true in material from an aboriginal Australian, a
Chinese, two Negroes from Cameroon, and twelve Germans.
Homma[108] extended these observations by comparing the apo-

[107] Homma, *Bull. Johns Hopkins Hosp.*, 38:365, 1926.   [108] *Ibid.*

crine glands of American Negroes and whites. Sections of the skin from the breast, abdomen, mons Veneris, and circumanal region were taken from the cadavers of thirteen male and female Negroes of various colors and twelve male and female white subjects. Interrupted serial sections were made and the sections counted in which apocrine glands were found. Skin from the axilla was not used because of the denseness of the glands in that area. In all four regions studied apocrine glands were found more often in Negroes than in whites. Of the total number of 631 sections taken from colored people, these glands were found in 243 (38.5 per cent), and of 538 sections taken from white people they were found in 62 (11.5 per cent). There are, apparently, on an average, three times more of the glands in the skin of colored people than in that of white people. About 75 per cent more were found in the skin of women than men.

RACIAL CONFIGURATION OF PALMS AND SOLES

Attempts have been made to find in the configuration of the papillary ridges of the fingers and toes patterns of arrangement that would be distinctive for races in the same manner as they are specific for individuals. The first attempt was made by Kollman,[109] who examined the palms and soles of representatives of several races, including Negroes, and found that he could come to no conclusion as to the presence of characteristic configurations among them. Galton,[110] who was the pioneer in mapping the lines of the finger tips for the purpose of description and comparison and on whose work is based the modern method of identification with fingerprints, was likewise unable to show any connection between race and configuration in prints of Englishmen, Jews, Basques, and Negroes. Hepburn[111] examined the feet of a dead Negro and stated that he could find nothing which he could not also find in members of his own race. Schlaginhaufen[112] made fingerprints of Papuans, Negroes,

---

[109] Der Tast-Apparat der Hand der menschlichen Rassen und der Affen (Hamburg and Leipzig: Leopold Voss, 1883).

[110] Finger prints (London: Macmillan, 1892).

[111] Scient. Tr. Roy. Dublin Soc., 5:ser. II, 1895.

[112] Morphol. Arb., 33:577, 1905; 34:1, 1905.

Japanese, Chinese, Indians, Javanese, and Europeans but does not record having found any differences.

Instead of using the papillary lines of the fingers and toes, Wilder[113] used the gross lines of the palms and feet for comparing races and succeeded in demonstrating differences. He pointed out that the palms and soles are transversed by four more or less well-marked bifurcated lines that start with their forked end at the base of the fingers and terminate at the margins of the palms and soles. The lines and their branches, the areas which they inclosed, and various arbitrarily designated points at the margins were designated by letters and numbers. Variations in the configuration of the palms and soles consist of different terminations of the lines, the starting-points being rather constant. Each configuration was described by a formula which consisted of numbers indicating the terminals of the lines and arranged in a definite order. With this technic of describing soles and palms he studied the prints of white people, Maya Indians, American and Liberian Negroes, and Chinese. While no single type of formula occurred exclusively in one race, there was one that predominated in each race. In 52 per cent of the Negro prints and 10 per cent of the white prints the same formula was found, and another formula occurred in 63 per cent of the white prints and 8 per cent of the Negro prints. These were called, respectively, the "Negro formula" and the "white formula." Similar differences were found in both palm and sole prints. Keith[114] showed that the white formulas were more variable than the Negro formulas.

HAIR

The hair is even more characteristic of the Negro than is the color of the skin, because other races may be quite as dark (East Indians), but no other than this race or intermixtures with it has the typical woolly or kinky hair as a stable feature. The character of the hair of the head and beard in the Negro is remarkably constant and behaves as a dominant in inheritance

---

[113] *Am. J. Anat.*, 1:423, 1901–2; *Am. Anthropologist*, 6:244, 1904; 15:189, 1913.
[114] *Am. J. Phys. Anthropol.*, 7:165, 1924.

with wavy and straight hair as recessives.[115] It is easily acquired by other races as the result of small amounts of Negro blood and difficult to lose on breeding Negroes with straight-haired people. While the laws governing its inheritance in Negro-white crosses have not been as thoroughly studied as has been skin color, they are probably Mendelian in character. Woolly and straight hair in intermixtures may be segregated in successive generations and not concomitantly with the segregation of skin color, for it is commonly observed that descendants of Negro-white crosses may be dark and yet have the straight hair of the white, or quite fair with woolly hair. Usually, however, there are gradations between woolliness and straightness that accompany gradations between black and white.

Typical woolly hair may occur congenitally in people identified as white. It is presumptive evidence in these cases that there is an intermixture with Negro unless such a fact can be definitely ruled out. Two of these instances have been described in the American literature by Schokking,[116] and Anderson.[117] Because of the widespread infusion of Negro blood in this country, the type of hair possessed by these individuals cannot with certainty be said not to be due to a Negro progenitor. On the other hand, Mohr[118] described an old family of farmers in Norway, a country where Negroes are a curiosity because of their scarcity, in which all members of three generations inherited typical Negroid woolly hair, although possessing other physical characteristics of Nordics, including fair skin and blue eyes. The hair, though kinky, was blond. Mohr believed, from its inheritance behavior, that this hair was a mutation rather than a heterozygote. Matiegka and Maly[119] have pointed out the prevalence of woolly hair in Europe, and their data give a strong impression of its Negro origin. Wise and Sulzberger[120] relate the interesting case of a Russian Jew who developed over the course of two years a patch of kinky hair in the midst of a

[115] Davenport, *Am. Nat.*, 42:341, 1908.

[116] *J. Hered.*, 25:337, 1934.

[117] *J. Hered.*, 27:444, 1936.

[118] *J. Hered.*, 23:345, 1932.

[119] *Anthropologie*, 7:108, 1929.

[120] *Arch. Dermat. & Syph.*, 25:99, 1932.

luxurious growth of straight, black, scalp hair. Wise[121] cites two individuals who were born with patches of kinky hair among straight hair.

The hairs of the eyelashes and the vibrissae of the nose in the Negro are straight and do not differ materially from those in other races. The coarse body hairs tend to share the characteristics of those of the scalp. The degree of curliness, however, varies, being most marked on the chest and pubes and less so in the axillae. The hair of the mustache and beard tends to be straight until a certain length has been obtained.

The lanugo, or soft body hair, is said by Ziemann and Sklarek[122] to be sparse in the Negro, which accounts for the satin feel of his skin. Fleure[123] states that the body skin of the Pygmies has a fair quantity of lanugo and that among Bushmen it may be found between the scalp hairs.

The degree of hairiness varies among different groups of Negroes. Bushmen and Negroes of the west coast of Africa are quite glabrous, while other groups, such as the Akka and Ashanti, are hairy, although the quality of the hair is about the same. The Negro forms an exception to the rule that seems to apply to other races, namely, that the straighter the hair the more glabrous are the people (Mongols, American Indians) and the more wavy or frizzly the hair the more hairy they are (Melanesians, Iranians). In the glabrous Negroes the mustache and beard are very scanty, the latter being thickest at either side of and below the chin and not approaching the scalp.

There seems to be some correlation between the nature of the hair and its length. Straight hair is, at the same time, the longest, while woolly hair is the shortest. The cosmetic efforts of American Negroes concerning hair, before the days of short-hair styles, had to do with procedures whose purpose was to produce longer hair. That a certain amount of growth was obtained cannot be doubted, but it was probably due to the mechanical stimulation of the scalp from combing and cleansing

[121] M. J. & Rec., 125:545, 1927.

[122] Handb. d. Haut- u. Geschlechtskr., 12:Pt. I, 499, 1932.

[123] Brit. M. J., 2:953, 1926.

rather than to any of the numerous preparations that enjoyed an enormous sale for the purpose.

In the extremely straight-haired races and in the woolly-haired ones there is little sex difference in the length of the hair. Only in types between is the hair of women longer than that of men.

The normal color of Negro hair is black, but it is markedly influenced by intermixture, by applied substances, and by disease (albinism, canities).

Examination of individual strands of woolly hair discloses that they are characterized by spirally arranged narrow rings which have a diameter of from one to nine millimeters. These rings are very near together, numerous, well rolled, and often catch hold of each other, forming tufts and balls. When the hair is relatively long and the spirals sufficiently broad, the whole head looks like a continuous fleece, and it is difficult to separate the interlocked hair strands by combing. This matted fleece-like condition may have been seen occasionally but not very often among American Negroes, partly because of the extensive intermixture with whites but also because of the diligent care most colored people give their hair. The hair of the Hottentot and Bushman is short and consists of very small spirals. It has a tendency, when tangled, to form small tufts which vary in size and are separated by spaces which appear bald, the so-called peppercorn hair. It has been questioned whether the hair follicles in this type of hair were actually spaced in this way to form a sort of mosaic. On investigation, it is found that the follicles are actually uniformly distributed and that when the individual hairs are separated they may become entwined to form new patterns covering the previous bald areas and disclosing new ones. Certain other groups of African Negroes have hair that is not of the extreme woolly type but which is described as frizzly. In this case the spirals of the hair are larger, measuring one or more centimeters in diameter. Sarasin[124] says that new-born Negro infants have straight hair and that the fullest degree of woolliness is not attained until about the sixth year.

[124] *L'Anthropol.*, 35:467, 1925.

Occasionally one observes hair which is very black and glossy and almost Mongoloid in straightness in American Negroes who are very dark and whose features give no indication of inter-mixture with whites. These people are described within their race by words that are a corruption of the word Madagascar, the inference being that their progenitors were brought as slaves from this island rather than from the mainland of Africa.

Rutherford and Hawk[125] found evidences of chemical differences between the hair of Negroes, Indians, Japanese, and Caucasians, as indicated by the proportion of carbon, nitrogen, hydrogen, sulphur, and oxygen. The differences were small, however, and insufficient as a basis either for classifying races or as a means of identification.

The function of the Negro type of hair is said to be one of protection against the heat rays of the sun, although there is no evidence that woolly hair is a better insulator than any other kind. Certainly the peppercorn type of hair, where there is a considerable amount of bald scalp exposed, can offer very little protection.

Numerous classifications of human hair have been proposed. These have been reviewed by Trotter[126] in their chronological order, beginning with Herodotus, who divided the soldiers of Xerxes' army into those with woolly hair and those with straight hair. The classification most used separates hair as: leiotrichi (straight hair), cymotrichi (frizzly or wavy hair), and ulotrichi (woolly hair).

Pruner-Bey[127] is generally credited as being the first to attempt to correlate the gross appearance of the various kinds of human hair with their microscopic appearance, although Browne,[128] an American, preceded him by ten years with his observations on the shapes of cross-sections of hair and his classification of races on this basis. These observers, as well as succeeding ones, showed that hairs varied in roundness, straight ones being more nearly round and woolly ones being

[125] *J. Biol. Chem.*, 3:459, 1907.

[126] *Am. J. Phys. Anthropol.*, 24:105, 1938.

[127] *Op. cit.*, 4:161, 1863.   [128] *Trichologia mammalium* (Philadelphia, 1853).

more nearly flat, with the shape of a lengthened ellipse. Wavy and frizzly hair had cross-section shapes between these extremes. These varying shapes of cross-section are expressed as indices which are the relation of the smallest diameter to the largest. If the major axis of the ellipse be supposed to equal 100, the minor axis will be represented by figures from 40 to 50 for the woolly hair of the Bushman and Hottentot, from 50 to 60 for other Africans, and 85 for the straight hair of Japanese. The hair of Europeans is represented by an index varying from 62 to 72.

Considerable attention has been given to the form of the hair follicle as the factor which determines the cross-section shape of the hair or, by its molding action, bestows the spiral form. The evidence and theories based on it in regard to this influence of the hair follicle are reviewed by Trotter.[129] Most of the work has to do with the angle to the surface of the skin at which the follicles grow and with the shape of the cross-section of the hair follicle.

The accumulated evidence indicates that the shape of the cross-section of the hair and the index that expresses it are not accurate criteria of race. Kneberg,[130] by using a technic that assures sections in a plane at a true right angle to the shaft of the hair, shows that shape of the hair in the three great races of man (Negroid, Caucasoid, Mongoloid) may vary widely within the same race. One specimen of hair may at various levels show many forms—round, oval, elliptical, prismatic, triangular, and kidney-shape. She concludes that the hair index is not reliable as a racial criterion, and its use may lead to fallacious generalizations. Bernstein and Robertson[131] undertook to devise a simpler and more reliable method of differentiating races by hair and proposed the use of weights of identical lengths. They showed that Mongoloid hair weighed the most, Caucasoid hair less, and Negroid hair least. These differences were believed to be due to differences in the area of the cross-section and in the amount of pigment granules and air bubbles. While Negroid

[129] Loc. cit.; see n. 126.   [130] Am. J. Phys. Anthropol., 20:51, 1935.

[131] Am. J. Phys. Anthropol., 10:379, 1927.

hair had the same amount of dense pigment as did the Mongoloid hair, the large amount of air bubbles in the former was chiefly responsible for the low weight. The presence of air bubbles in the shaft of Negro hair may account for another difference noticeable between straight and woolly hair, namely, that the former has a sheen that reaches its extreme in the patent-leather gloss of the Oriental hair, while the latter has a dull appearance. This difference may be due to the diffraction of the air bubbles in Negro hair. It appears not to be due to differences in the scales of the hair, as Hausman[132] found no racial characteristics in the nature of human-hair scales. Kneberg[133] reported, however, that hairs from a single head varied as much as 45 per cent in size, and different parts of the same hair shaft varied as much as 15 per cent even when the tapering tip was avoided. She also says the air and pigment in hair are negligible factors in influencing hair weight.

Trotter[134] summarizes her review of classifications of human hair by saying that, until there is greater certainty as to the histological factors and as to whether they determine form and behavior of individual hair shafts, it will probably be better to follow the more recent general classification based on finer distinctions in the color and behavior of the hairs as observed in its normal state.

Just as whites are interested, for cosmetic purposes, in putting waves and curls in their hair, so colored people are equally concerned in taking them out. Two methods are used: In the first, the curls and spirals are actually ironed out under pressure between heated instruments whose temperature is tempered with oil. This process depends on the same ability of hair to be molded as does the process that results in permanent waves or curls. The second method depends on the chemical action of ointments whose active principle seems to be a high content of alkali. These preparations are applied freely for a very short period and are then washed out, the result being a stiff, straight, glossy hair. The mechanism of this action is unknown, but it is possible that the alkali increases the permeability of the cuti-

---

[132] *Am. Nat.*, 59:529, 1925.   [133] *Op. cit.*, 21:279, 1936.   [134] *Loc. cit.*; see n. 126.

cle of the hair to water and raises the hydration capacity of the hair shaft so that the hair swells and assumes a round shape, the prerequisite for straightness. The effect is transitory and has to be repeated at frequent intervals. Some of these so-called hair straighteners are also simply mixtures of stiff waxes that surround the hair shafts and mechanically hold them straight after the spirals are combed out.

THE SKELETON

There are a number of reasons for the interest of anthropologists and anatomists in the skeleton. It is the real determinant of many of the race-specific characteristics of body form, since it is the framework over which the soft parts are laid. Again, the bones show a progressive development that accompanies the development of animal forms from the lower to higher species, continuing within the human race. The permanence of the skeleton makes it the only means by which the physical form of modern man can be compared with that of prehistoric and extinct forms of mankind. Further is the fact that bones show a relatively low degree of variation within a given race and a large amount of variation between races. Extensive literature on the racial characteristics of the skeleton has accumulated, and much of it concerns the skeleton of the Negro in comparison to that of other races. There is scarcely a bone in the body that has not been the subject of racial comparison, and to discuss all the pertinent observations would require a treatise as complete as a finished text of osteology. In most instances where differences are found the Negro type is pointed out to be more simian in nature, and even where simian relations are not clear it is assumed that since the type occurs in Negroes it must be more primitive in form.

Most of the studies of racial bones are concerned with the skull, because it is the mold for many of the facial features which are distinctive for race, is the housing of the brain, and is the most stable structure within the race. Todd[135] points out that the skull, together with the soft parts of the head, constitutes the

[135] *Human Biol.*, 1:57, 1928.

real entrenched features of the Negro. The characteristics of the Negro skull are such that an experienced craniologist can identify it with ease, although the constant search for new correlations of race and skull morphology indicates that the present information is not entirely satisfactory. The skull, stable as it is, is not without considerable intraracial variation.

In the study of the skull both description and mensuration are used. With the employment of an elaborate and profuse technic of measurement, a large amount of data has been obtained. These are expressed as dimensions of the cranium in various planes, as the size of individual bones, as the content of the cranial cavity, and as angles. The topographical location of foraminae and certain landmarks and the delineation of contours are also included in the descriptive technic. It is impossible to review here all the features of the Negro skull obtained in these ways. Hrdlička[136] has catalogued for the United States National Museum a large number of detailed measurements of craniums of Negroes of South, West, and East Africa, and of America. Todd and Tracy[137] described and compared the front and side views of Negro and white craniums. They found that there were two main types of skulls—the Negro and the white. To the former belonged most of the African skulls and to the latter all the white ones. In between these was another type which differed from the white skull in degree but not in principle. To this type belonged most of the American Negro skulls and a few of those of African Negroes. This is a different finding from that of Hrdlička, who says that not only are the craniums of Negroes from all parts of Africa remarkably similar, but they are faithfully reproduced in the American Negro.

Cameron has applied a large number of mensuration methods, many of which are original with him, to craniums in his comparisons of Negro specimens to those of other races.[138]

[136] Proc. U.S. Nat. Museum, 71:art. 24, 1929.

[137] Am. J. Phys. Anthropol., 15:53, 1930.

[138] Am. J. Phys. Anthropol., 3:63, 1920; 8:143, 1925; 9:334, 345, 1926; 10:275, 280, 286, 1927; 12:155, 164, 176, 182, 192, 1928; 13:91, 335, 344, 1929; 14:33, 284, 293, 1930; 15:508, 520, 1931; 16:237, 243, 248, 1932; 17:99, 1932.

Schulz[139] established the relation of the external nose to the bony nose and nasal cavity. Pruett[140] says there is no appreciable difference in the sella turcica in Negroes and whites. Royster and Moriarty[141] find in children between eight and nine years of age that in a very general way the sella turcica of whites, male and female, is more regular and uniform in contour than that of colored children. The latter show more very large and very small sellae than do white children. Simonton[142] found a variable and slight difference between Negroes and other races in the location of the mental foramen in relation to teeth. Connolly[143] was not certain whether there were significant racial differences in the distance between nasion and glabella. Todd[144] concluded that all measurements of cranial capacity were merely approximations of varying reliability. He found by actual measurement or by mathematical calculation that the average cranial capacity of Negro males was 1,350 cc., of Negro females, 1,221 cc., of white males, 1,391 cc., and of white females, 1,232 cc. Todd and Lyon[145] claim that endocranial suture closure in the Negro presents no fundamental or essential difference in pattern of graph or in age relationship from closure in whites. There is only one modal type of human suture closure, unaffected by race.

Analyses of the racial features of the vertebral column are complicated by the factors of disease, of habits of posture, and by occupation, each of which varies according to race. Recent studies on features of the vertebral column in Negroes, by both descriptive and mensuration methods, have been published by

[139] *Am. J. Phys. Anthropol.*, 1:239, 1918.

[140] *Am. J. Phys. Anthropol.*, 11:205, 1928.

[141] *Am. J. Phys. Anthropol.*, 14:451, 1930.

[142] *Am. J. Phys. Anthropol.*, 6:413, 1923.

[143] *Am. J. Phys. Anthropol.*, 9:349, 1926.

[144] *Am. J. Phys. Anthropol.*, 6:97, 1923.

[145] *Am. J. Phys. Anthropol.*, 8:47, 149, 1925.

Whitney,[146] Ossenfort,[147] Trotter,[148] Todd and Pyle,[149] Shore,[150] Cunningham,[151] Willis,[152] and Lanier.[153]

Racial modifications of the clavicle are of doubtful or insignificant degree. Terry[154] says that in the Negro there is less constancy and slighter development of the conoid tubercle, a possible greater length of the clavicle, and a smaller absolute and relative width of the acromial extremity. Trotter[155] studied the comparative occurrence of synchondrosis and synostosis (bony union) in the joint between the clavicle and sternum in Negroes and whites. Synostosis occurred in 9.8 per cent of colored males and 10.0 per cent of colored females, while they occurred in 11.5 per cent of white males and 26.7 per cent of white females. The similarity of the percentage in colored males and females and the excess in white females are considered a significant race difference. Trotter says synostosis has no relation to age, while most pathologists regard a bony union between the sternum and clavicle as an expression of senility.

The anatomy of the pelvis has received considerable attention in relation to race, principally because of its influence on the general body form, its relation to obstetrics, and its possible influence in molding the head forms that are characteristic of race. The pelvis of Negroes is shown to be narrower and to exhibit less sex differences, but it is questionable as to how much care has been used to eliminate rickets in obtaining the evidence for these statements. Rickets has a marked influence on the form of the pelvis, and this disease is extremely prevalent in colored people. Straus[156] finds the white ilium larger than that of

[146] Am. J. Phys. Anthropol., 8:11, 1925; 9:451, 1926.

[147] Am. J. Phys. Anthropol., 9:439, 1926.

[148] Op. cit., 13:95, 1929.

[149] Am. J. Phys. Anthropol., 12:303, 1928.

[150] J. Anat., 64:266, 1930; 65:482, 1931.

[151] J. Anat., 20:637, 1886.   [153] Am. J. Phys. Anthropol., 25:341, 1939.

[152] Anat. Rec., 26:31, 1933.   [154] Am. J. Phys. Anthropol., 16:351, 1932.

[155] Op. cit., 18:439, 1933.

[156] Am. J. Phys. Anthropol., 11:1, 1927.

the Negro, but all quantitative and qualitative characteristics of this bone that were studied varied so greatly and exhibited such sex and stock-linked overlapping as to be of limited value in determining racial affinities of the pelvis. In a study of the changes in pubic bones associated with age, Todd[157] found, in regard to racial influences, that there were strikingly few differences in pubic metamorphosis between Negroes and whites: Trotter[158] discovered that 50.5 per cent of the whites and 20.7 per cent of the Negroes showed accessory sacroiliac articulations but that these figures are invalidated because the articulations increase with age, and more elderly people were in the white group than in the colored group. Above twenty-four years of age and below seventy-five years the percentage was higher among Negroes, and at other ages it was less. The sacrum of Negroes and whites has been compared in regard to the number of sacral bones, the occurrence of the sacral notch, and the general shape. The sacrum is believed to be narrower in the Negro and its curvature less.

Because the limbs of vertebrates have undergone remarkable changes in their phylogenetic development, physical anthropologists have found it of interest to seek evidences of these changes among the various species of mankind. It is with this background that the bones of the limbs in Negroes are compared with those of whites. In the development of primates into the human, the length of the upper part of the limbs has increased in proportion to the lower part, and when the proportion of the upper-limb bones to the lower bones in Negroes are compared by various indices with that of whites, it is generally found that the humerus and the femur are comparatively shorter than they are in Caucasians. In regard to other anatomical features of the limb bones, Hrdlička[159] says that, while the occurrence of the crista aspera (linea aspera) of the femur and its pilaster show racial differences between Negroes and whites, these differences are of functional origin and are due to the effects of the muscles attached or pressure upon the parts concerned. This

---

[157] *Am. J. Phys. Anthropol.*, 4:1, 1921.

[158] *Op. cit.*, 22:246, 1937.   [159] *Am. J. Phys. Anthropol.*, 19:17, 1934.

variation is mainly individual and ontogenetic in origin rather than hereditary and phylogenetic. Lamb[160] found septal apertures in the humerus in 7.5 per cent of white skeletons and 19.2 per cent of Negro skeletons. Hrdlička[161] found them in 5.2 per cent of white humeri·and 18.4 per cent of Negro humeri, while Trotter[162] found 4.3 per cent and 12.6 per cent, respectively, in white and Negro bones. Terry[163] says the supracondyloid process occurs in about one-twelfth as many Negroes as whites. Ingalls[164] interprets the differences in the anatomy of the cartilages of the femur that he found as indicating that the joints formed by them are of a finer construction and more advanced in development in white people. Theoretically, while the joints of the Negro allow greater freedom of movement, those of whites permit greater stability of posture.

The bones of the feet are said to vary in relation to race, especially the calcaneus, which is longer in the Negro and accounts for the projecting heel in many colored people.

The explanation of the proficiency of Negro athletes, particularly in running and jumping events, has been sought in some characteristic of the anatomy of the lower limbs. The slimness of the legs, the greater length of the legs in proportion to the body length, and the projection of the calcaneus have been suggested. Davenport[165] points out that a proportionately longer thigh is conducive to fast running, and a proportionately shorter thigh is better for jumping.

MUSCULAR SYSTEM

What has been written about the musculature of the Negro has been chiefly from the viewpoint of the anthropologist and the embryologist searching for evidence of the phylogenetic as well as ontogenetic development of man. This evidence consists, for the most part, of the demonstration of anomalies which represent the persistence in man of the musculature of lower forms. It is the consensus that the claim made by some writers of a

[160] Am. Anthropologist, 3:159, 1890.

[161] Anthropol., 10:31, 1932.

[162] Op. cit., 19:213, 1934.

[163] Op. cit., 6:401, 1923.

[164] Am. J. Phys. Anthropol., 9:355, 1926.

[165] Am. J. Phys. Anthropol., 17:333, 1932.

greater frequency of muscle anomalies in Negroes is not supported by convincing evidence. The material offered is too scanty, and the muscular system in man is so labile that there is not enough constancy in any one race for it to be used as a reference of comparison with other races. Most of the textbooks of anatomy list variations of muscles, indicating that they are commonly met with.. Both Bryce[166] and Mall[167] doubt if the myology of the Negro shows a greater relative, frequency of variations which may be regarded as atavistic. The writers who have presented material on this subject, which consists for the most part of the dissection of one or two subjects, are as follows: Turner,[168] Chudzinski,[169] Testut,[170] Giacomini,[171] Michel,[172] Le Double,[173] Virchow,[174] Eckstein,[175] Schultz,[176] Eggeling,[177] Thompson, McBatts, and Danforth,[178] Moore,[179] Lambert,[180] Wells and Thomas,[181] Pöch,[182] Williams, Grun, Wimp, and Whayne,[183] Locchi,[184] Loth,[185] Seib,[186] Hetherington,[187] Barlow,[188] and Binford and Seib.[189]

[166] *J. Anat.*, 31:607, 1897.

[167] *Am. J. Anat.*, 9:1, 1909.

[168] *J. Anat.*, 13:382, 1879; 14:244, 1880.

[169] *Rev. d'anthropol.*, 11:280, 1882; 13:603, 1884.

[170] *Contributions à l'anatomie comparative des races Nègres-Bordeaux* (Paris: Cellini et Cie, 1884); *Monatschr.*, 1:285, 1884.

[171] *Arch. ital. de biol.*, 17:285, 1884.

[172] *M. Rec.*, 41:125, 1892.

[173] *Traité des variations du système musculaire de l'homme* (Paris, 1897).

[174] *Verhandl. d. anat. Gesellsch., München.*, 26:217, 1912.

[175] *Anat. Anz.*, 41:334, 1912.

[176] *Am. J. Anat.*, 23:155, 1918.

[177] *Anat. Anz.*, 54:54, 1921.

[178] *Am. J. Phys. Anthropol.*, 4:205, 1921.

[179] *Anat. Rec.*, 23:307, 1922.

[180] *Anat. Rec.*, 31:193, 1925.

[181] *J. Anat.*, 61:340, 1927.

[182] *J. Anat.*, 63:280, 1929.

[183] *Am. J. Phys. Anthropol.*, 14:45, 1930.

[184] *Compt. rend. Assoc. d. anat.*, 25:21, 1930.

[185] *Anthropologie des partes molles* (Paris, 1931).

[186] *Am. J. Phys. Anthropol.*, 19:229, 1934.

[187] *Am. J. Phys. Anthropol.*, 19:203, 1934.

[188] *Anat. Rec.*, 61:413, 1935.

[189] *Am. J. Phys. Anthropol.*, 24:391, 1938.

INTERNAL ORGANS: WEIGHT, SIZE, AND
OTHER CHARACTERISTICS

In addition to anthropologists who have an academic interest in knowing the comparable physical features of the internal organs of Negroes and whites, pathologists often have the occasion to know whether the same standards of size, weight, and volume can be applied to both races. A few comparative studies of this question have been made, but most of them are valueless, especially those applying to African Negroes, since they concern obviously pathological material, apparently from subjects with tropical diseases. This is particularly true of the data published by Horan[190] and Castor,[191] although they are frequently quoted in the literature.

Chudzinski[192] states that in a small series of African Negroes the volume of the spleen was, on an average, less than in the white race, but no appreciable difference existed in the weight. Bean[193] obtained from autopsy records in New Orelans, Louisiana, Baltimore, Maryland, Charlottesville, Virginia, and elsewhere, the weights of the spleen of 1,341 white men, 1,338 Negro men, 441 white women, and 554 Negro women. The spleen was normal in only 26 white men, 23 Negro men, 15 white women and 7 Negro women. The white male normal spleen weighed, on an average, about 140 g., the Negro male, 115 g., the white female, 130 g., and the Negro female, 80 g. This racial difference in the weight of the spleen was even greater in the pathological specimens and more noticeable between the males. Moon[194] assembled the weights of spleens of 1,000 adult whites and 1,000 adult Negroes from autopsy records in Philadelphia, Pennsylvania. These spleens were admittedly not normal, but care was taken in their selection to discard all cases where there was a record of splenomegaly, malaria, typhoid, acute splenic tumor, acute splenitis or leukemia, or any case where the spleen weighed 350 g. or more. The average weight of the Negro spleen

[190] *J. Trop. Med.*, 13:154, 1910.

[191] *J. Trop. Med.*, 15:17, 1912.   [193] *Am. J. Phys. Anthropol.*, 2:1, 1919.

[192] *Op. cit.*, 16:276, 1887.   [194] *Arch. Path.*, 5:1040, 1928.

was 106.3 g. as against 144.7 g. for the white spleen. In the age period from eighteen to forty-nine the average weight of the Negro spleen was 66.6 per cent of that of the white. Above fifty years it was 68.2 per cent of the white. There were eight Negro spleens weighing 30 g. and less (the smallest weighed 5 g.) and two white spleens weighing 30 g. and less (the smallest weighed 25 g.). No Negro spleen weighed over 325 g., but nine white spleens weighed more than this.

In his series, Chudzinski[195] found the average size and weight of the liver less in the Negro than the average in whites. Bean[196] also states that the liver of Negroes is smaller than that of whites and that the difference is well marked both in normal and in pathological specimens. The white male normal liver was found to weigh, on an average, 1,650 g., while the Negro male normal liver averaged 1,450 g. That of white females averaged 1,400 g. and of Negro females, 1,200 g.

There seems to be little if any difference in the heart and kidney weights due to race.[197] The average white male normal heart weight is 317.6 g., while that of the Negro male is 342.9 g. The white female normal heart weighs 260.0 g. and that of the Negro female, 216.0 g. The average normal kidney weights are: white male, 313.1 g., Negro male, 308.7 g., white female, 287.8 g., Negro female, 305.0 g. Chudzinski's[198] records show that the volume and weight of the kidneys are less in Negroes.

The latter author discusses the relation of the length of the intestines to the stature in the white and black races, respectively, and concludes that the proportion is less in the latter. In Negroes the intestines measured 2.14–6.11 times the stature, while in the white races, as reported by various authors, the proportion varies from 3 to 8 times the stature. It is indicated that the supposedly shorter intestinal length of Negroes is determined by the shortness of the small intestines, for the colon appeared to be absolutely and relatively longer in Negroes.

The genital organs present some differences according to race, but rather in the dimensions of the various parts than in

[195] Loc. cit.; see n. 169.

[196] Am. J. Phys. Anthropol., 2:167, 1919.

[197] Ibid., p. 265, 1919.

[198] Loc. cit.; see n. 169.

their form. The relatively greater size of the penis in the Negro has long been recognized. Duckworth[199] points out that a relatively feeble development of the mons Veneris and labia majora in Negro women has been claimed. The labia minora are variable in their development in the colored races; in some instances they are relatively smaller than in white women, while in others, as among certain people in Ethiopia, they are said to be very large. A curiosity is the so-called "Hottentot apron," which is an exaggerated development of the labia minora among Bush and Hottentot women. This peculiarity, which appears from infancy, is accentuated by relatively small labia majora. The clitoris has been claimed to be larger and the vagina longer in colored women. Turnipseed[200] says that in colored women the hymen is situated 1.5–2 inches farther in the vagina than in white women. This was corroborated by Fort[201] and denied by Hyath[202] and Smythe.[203] The breasts of Negro women, at least those in Africa, are usually conical and piriform in shape, with long nipples. European women have mostly hemispherical breasts, with short nipples. The pendulous breasts of the multipari are markedly accentuated in African women as compared to European women, probably owing to the lack of support which is provided by the clothing of the latter.

THE BRAIN

The brain has been studied more than any other internal organ as to the relation of its anatomy to race. And, while there are some anatomists who give the impression that they are able to distinguish at a glance the brain of a Negro from that of a Caucasian, it is extremely doubtful, according to more conservative writers, that any given brain can, on the basis of its structure, be classified as that of a Negro or white, male or female, genius or individual of average ability. It appears that the zeal

[199] *Morphology and anthropology* (Cambridge University Press, 1904).

[200] *Am. J. Obst. & Gynec.*, 10:32, 1877.

[201] *Am. J. Obst. & Gynec.*, 10:258, 1877.

[202] *Am. J. Obst. & Gynec.*, 10:253, 1877.

[203] *Am. J. Obst. & Gynec.*, 10:638, 1877.

of anthropologists to correlate the structure of the brain with such factors as mental ability or the degree of development of races has in many cases led them to make sweeping generalizations on the basis of data that would be discarded in almost any other biological field. Oftentimes the number of brains examined has been too small. When the sampling is anywhere near adequate, the variation within the group is much too large to justify the very small average difference between groups. Moreover, little or no consideration is given to such factors as stature, body weight, body type, diet and nutrition, and disease conditions, all of which may affect the weight and volume of the brain as a whole or in its separate parts.

There is often a hopeless confusion of purpose in many investigations of the brain, especially that of the Negro. What may appear to be an inquiry into racial anatomic features is more than likely to be an argument of the Negro's inferior intelligence and his low place in the evolutionary scale. Typical of this type of investigation is that of Bean,[204] who, in a profuse number of articles on the racial aspect of the brain as well as other organs, uses each occasion to draw conclusions as to indications in his findings of the Negro's inferiority—conclusions which more cautious observers have interdicted.

The somatic properties that have been used in making racial comparisons of brains are brain volume, including skull capacity, brain weight, character of the convolutions and sulci, and the size of various parts of the brain. Brain volume and brain weight and the pattern of the convolutions have apparently been exhausted as possible indices of race, and their investigation has not yielded adequate data for this purpose.[205] Because a relatively large frontal lobe is a more recently acquired anatomical feature, and since in this part of the brain are supposed to be located the so-called higher centers, a number of investigations of the frontal lobes and their associated parts have been made. Huschke[206] says the Negro brain is of the type of the

[204] *Am. J. Anat.*, 4:353, 1906.

[205] Poynter and Keegan, *J. Comp. Neurol.*, 25:183, 1915.

[206] *Schadel, Hirn und Seele* (Jena, 1854).

European child and woman and that the European woman is a "homo parietalis and interparietalis," while the man is a "homo frontalis." Spitzka[207] states that the area of the cross-section of the corpus callosum, which is associated mainly with the frontal lobe, varies directly with mental ability and claims to have proved it by measuring the area of the cross-section of the corpus callosum of Negroes, white men of ordinary ability, and of several eminent white men. Bean,[208] by measuring the outline of the brain at various angles to the axis, claims to have shown a greater development of the frontal lobes in white people. The lower weight of the Negro's brain, according to him, is due primarily to a smaller frontal lobe. He also finds that the area of the cross-section of the corpus callosum varies with the brain weight, but in the Negro its anterior half is smaller in relation to brain weight than it is in the Caucasian. The area of the genu of the corpus callosum is relatively larger, and the splenium is relatively smaller. Later Bean[209] studied the temporal lobe in white and Negro brains and stated that this lobe is also smaller in the Negro. And since measurements of the lobe that pass below the hippocampus are even less, it is probable that the hippocampus is larger in the Negro. The shape of the temporal lobe is different in the two races also, being slightly more slender in the Negro and almost the same size anteroposteriorly in both races.

In a remarkable publication in 1909, Mall[210] critically reviewed the evidence supporting the claims that there are distinguishing features of the brain for race, sex, and intelligence. It is pointed out that Huschke, in proving sex-specific characters in order to prove race-specific ones, found a difference of only 1 per cent between the averages for the sexes of the proportions which the frontal-lobe weight bears to the total brain weight, although the individual proportions vary from 21.8 per cent to 26.1 per cent. Mall points out that Spitzka, in concluding that there is a relation of the cross-section of the corpus callosum to intelligence, neglected to take into account the

[207] Am. J. Anat., 4: Proc. Am. A. Anat., p. 3, 1906.

[208] Am. J. Anat., 4:353, 1906.

[209] Anat. Rec., 8:479, 1914.   [210] Loc. cit.; see n. 169.

brain weight, and, while the callosum of one of the eminent men (Joseph Leidy) was relatively larger, the callosa of the others were not above the averages for brains of the same weight, and the callosa given for ordinary white men (which are from electrocuted criminals) are much below the average found by other workers. In fact, many Negroes of lighter brain weight, says Mall, have larger callosa than most of Spitzka's eminent men. Mall repeated the measurements that Bean made of the genu and splenium in Negroes and Caucasians and included in his specimens eighteen of the brains that Bean used. He avoided the personal equation by remaining ignorant of the race of the brain until after the measurements were made. He also used a more accurate instrument than did Bean and was able to point out gross errors in the latter's figures. Mall states that his results showed no variation, due to race or sex, either in the genu or in the splenium. He checked the weight of the frontal lobe in Negroes and whites and again found it impossible to detect a relative difference in the weight or size of the frontal lobe attributable to sex or race and states that probably none exists.

Mall also refers to Parker,[211] who stated that the Negro brain bears an unmistakably nearer relation to the ape than does that of the Caucasian and that it was more fetal in character, basing his claims upon observations of the length and form of the fissures of Sylvius and Rolando. Mall says this statement is careless and superficial and is an opinion supported by strong personal prejudice. When he or his colleagues attempted to divide unknown brains into two groups, one with a complex cortical configuration and the other simple, it was found that there was about the same percentage of white and Negro brains in each group.

It is the opinion of Mall "that arguments for difference due to race, sex and genius will henceforth need to be based upon new data, really scientifically treated, and not upon the older statements." Dubois says:

Much has been made of the supposed smaller brain of the Negro race; but this is as yet an unproved assumption, based on the uncritical measurement of

[211] *Proc. Acad. Nat. Sci.* (1878).

less than a thousand Negro brains as compared with eleven thousand or more European brains. Even if future measurements prove the average Negro brain lighter, the vast majority of Negro brain weights fall within the same limits as the whites; and finally, neither size nor weight of the brain seems to be of importance as an index of mental capacity.[212]

Poynter and Keegan[213] recorded the arrangements of the gyri and sulci in a series of thirteen Negro brains. They found that the Negro type established for these brains lies within the limits of individual variation for the Caucasian, hence it is not possible to give a single morphological feature which can be claimed as absolutely characteristic of the race. They did, however, claim to have found the sulcus lunatus in the Negro brains.

Vint[214] examined microscopically the convolutions of various parts of the brains of native Africans and measured the width of the four layers of the cortex. These he compared with similar measurements made by von Economo[215] of European brains. Such a comparison would assume that the histological technic used in both experiments was identical, but no mention is made that this precaution was taken. Vint reports that the cortex of the native brain was thinner than that of the European. This is true of all the individual laminas in the areas examined, except in the lamina zonalis, and in laminas five and six of the visuosensory area. The pyramidal cells of the supragranular layer and the Betz cells of the motor area were smaller in the native brain, but cell counts per unit area were the same in the African and European. Gordon,[216] reporting on Vint's work, says that in the frontal cortex the infragranular layer is 6 per cent wider in the East African brain, the granular layer 1.3 per cent narrower, and the supragranular layer 8 per cent narrower.

In the meninges of most brains, especially the inferior surface of the medulla, there are deposits of varying amounts of black pigment; but it has been observed that in Negro brains and in those of dark-skinned Caucasians, for example, the Mediterranean brunets, this pigmentation is usually marked.

[212] The Negro (New York: Holt & Co., 1915).

[213] Loc. cit.; see n. 205.   [215] Oxford M. Publ. (1929).

[214] J. Anat., 68:216, 1933–34.   [216] Brit. M. J., 1:581, 1932.

CHAPTER III

BIOCHEMICAL AND PHYSIOLOGICAL CHARACTERISTICS

SEROLOGIC SPECIFICITY

IN ADDITION to the physical or anatomical structures, there are also biochemical characteristics that distinguish races, chief among which are certain serological features. During the World War Hirshfeld and Hirshfeld[1] took advantage of the concentration of various nationalities on the Macedonian battlefront to examine the isohemagglutinins of each of five hundred individuals made up of sixteen different races and nationalities. They found that certain people could be grouped together because of a similarity in the distribution among them of the specific blood groups. The European people, including the English, French, Italians, Germans, Austrians, Bulgarians, Serbs, and Greeks, are characterized by the prevalence of group A and a low incidence of group B. An Asio-African group, including Negroes, Madagascans, Annamese, and Hindus, showed a high incidence of group B and a low incidence of group A. In an intermediate group, consisting of Turks, Arabs, Russians, and Jews, the two groups, A and B, occur intermediate to those of the European and Asio-African groups. The Hirshfelds devised a biochemical index which is the ratio of the percentage of agglutinogen A to the percentage of agglutinogen B in a given population and is expressed by the formula $(A + AB)/(B + AB)$. Those races having an index of more than two were assigned to the European type, those with an index of less than one to the Asio-African type, and those with an index between one and two to the intermediate type. Later, Ottenberg,[2] with more information available, extended the number of groups to six and rearranged the races among the groups. The group containing

---

[1] *Lancet*, 2:675, 1919.   [2] *J. A. M. A.*, 84:1393, 1925.

Negroes became the African–South Asiatic type. Both Ottenberg and the Hirshfelds pointed out the anthropological significance of the blood groups, and the latter thought evidence could be produced with this technic which would have a bearing on the origin of races. Their work stimulated a large number of studies of blood groups in people all over the world, and a catalogue of the findings as they accumulated was periodically published by Steffan and Wellisch in the *Zeitschrift für Rassen-Physiologie,* a publication devoted almost exclusively to the study of blood groups.

Much of the data obtained could not be reconciled with the known relationships between races. This was due principally to the use of the Hirshfeld index, which was later declared to be based on unsound mathematics. At least five other indices have been suggested, but the one believed to be most accurate was devised by Bernstein,[3] who advanced the hypothesis that blood groups are inherited as a series of three multiple allelomorphs, A, B, and O, corresponding to the agglutinogens, where A and B are dominant and O recessive. He suggested that the frequencies of these allelomorphs are of more value than the ratio of percentages of blood groups as such and pointed out that if p = the frequency of agglutinogen A; q = the frequency of agglutinogen B, and r = the frequency of O, then $p + q + r = 1$ and p/q represents a correlation of the frequencies of the two dominant mutations.

Snyder[4] presents evidence of the accuracy of Bernstein's conception and indicates that it leads to a more useful anthropological application of the blood-group data. He also formulated four laws governing race classification by means of blood groups. He stated that any people whose blood-group distribution is being studied may be expected to show blood-group frequencies similar to those of other peoples related to it. If any people shows blood-group frequencies different from those to be expected, based on the frequencies of other peoples known to be related to it, the conclusion may be drawn that the former has

[3] *Ztschr. f. ind. Abst. u. Vererbungslehre,* **37**:237, 1925.

[4] *Am. J. Phys. Anthropol.,* **9**:233, 1926.

undergone racial crossing of some sort which the latter have not, or vice versa. Further, if any people shows blood-group frequencies similar to a group of peoples not known to be related to it, the conclusion may be drawn that the former has undergone crossing with the latter group or some similar people. And, if a people lacks one or both of the blood-group mutations as evidenced by an extremely low value of p or q, it may be assumed that the people became isolated from the rest of mankind before the respective mutations took place, or before they spread very far.

The original data which served for the inferences of the Hirshfelds and Ottenberg concerning African Negroes were obtained from the examination of five hundred Senegalese soldiers. The Hirshfeld index for these was 0.8. Since then more than twenty reports of studies of Negroes in various parts of Africa have appeared.[5] The Hirshfeld indices derived from these data range from 2.54 to 0.79 and cannot be reconciled with the known facts of the relation of the different African races to one another and to other races. Application of the Bernstein formula has not been made to all the now available material, but Snyder[6] applied it in a few instances. He plotted the frequencies of p and q on a correlation table and, by inserting the African data in its proper square, found that these people fall into more or less natural groups.

The first study of blood groups in American Negroes was made by Lewis and Henderson[7] who found in 270 subjects 49.0 per cent group O, 26.9 per cent group A, 18.5 per cent group B, and 5.5 per cent group AB, to give an index of 1.35. They suggested that the index of American Negroes is higher than that of African Negroes because of intermixture of the former with whites. The studies of Snyder[8] of 500 American Negroes gave 47 per cent group O, 28 per cent group A, 20 per cent group B, and 5 per cent group AB, to give an index of 1.3. He also examined 144 Jamaican Negroes,[9] who showed 46.5 per

---

[5] Gusinde, *Ztschr. f. Rassenphysiol.*, 8:12, 1936.

[6] *Loc. cit.;* see n. 4.   [7] *J. A. M. A.*, 79:1422, 1922.   [8] *Loc. cit.;* see n. 4.

[9] *Blood grouping in relation to clinical and legal medicine* (Baltimore: Williams & Wilkins, 1929).

cent group O, 29.1 per cent group A, 22.2 per cent group B, and 2.1 per cent group AB. The index was 1.3. In 730 New York Negroes Landsteiner and Levine[10] found 44.2 per cent group O, 30.3 per cent group A, 21.8 per cent group B, and 3.7 per cent group AB, with an index of 1.3.

Following the suggestion of Lewis and Henderson[11] that intermixture with whites has raised the index of American Negroes from the original African index, Pijper[12] tested the Bantu people of South Africa, whose origin is believed to be a mixture of Negro and Hamitic bloods. He found their index to be 1.3, the only native race of Africa which was known at that time to have such a high index. He believed this to be evidence against a Hamitic infusion into a Negro stock, because, although the exact Hamitic index is unknown, it could not be higher than 1.5. If a large infusion of white blood, with an index of at least 3, into American Negroes had raised the original African index to 1.35, it is inconceivable that a slight admixture of Hamitic blood, with an index of 1.5, would have raised the Negro index to 1.35. He stated that the facts pointed the other way and that the Bantu must be looked upon as direct descendants of the Hamitic race, with perhaps a slight intermixture of Negro blood. These conclusions are probably the result of the false evidence given by the Hirshfeld index.

A certain proportion of people secrete the blood-group characteristics into the saliva, gastric juice, and other fluids. Among the whites in Berlin 78 per cent were "secretors,"[13] and in New York 82.4 per cent of the whites were "secretors." On the other hand, 61.2 per cent of the New York Negroes showed this phenomenon. Schiff[14] considers the difference between the above two groups as negligible but the difference between either white group and the Negroes as significant.

Kahn[15] expresses a doubt as to the anthropological value of blood groups. He found among 336 Bush Negroes in South America 83 per cent group O and 17 per cent group B, but none

[10] *J. Immunol.*, 18:87, 1930.   [11] *Loc. cit.*; see n. 7.

[12] *J. A. M. A.*, 95:1927, 1930.

[13] Schiff and Sasaki, *Ztschr. f. Immunitätsforsch. u. exper. Therap.*, 77:129, 1932.

[14] *Am. J. Phys. Anthropol.*, 27:255, 1940.   [15] *J. Immunol.*, 31:377, 1936.

of groups A and AB. These people are direct descendants of natives of the African west coast. There has been little or no intermixture with either the Indians or the whites of South America. They have lived over two hundred years in this country under primitive conditions. Yet their blood group distribution is entirely different from the natives of West Africa and from American Negroes who are, for the most part, descendants of the west-coast stock. Kahn refers to the findings of Grove,[16] who described similar situations among the Asiatic Ainus and among the Moros of the Philippine Islands. Among each of these peoples are two groups living in near-by localities and without any recognizable physical differences but who have very dissimilar blood-group distributions.

Landsteiner and Levine[17] could find no difference between Negroes and whites in the distribution of the immune factor N but did find a slight but definite difference in the occurrence of M. Among 730 Negroes, M occurred in 71.9 per cent, and among 1,709 whites it occurred 80.9 per cent. The difference of 9 per cent is about five times the standard error of difference and is therefore significant. There is about the same racial difference between Negroes and whites in the occurrence of agglutinogen B. Another but less studied immune factor, P, showed also a decided racial difference. It occurred often and reacted stronger in colored people.

Landsteiner and Levine[18] also found that an inheritable agglutinable property detected by a certain abnormal or "extra" hemagglutinin found in certain serums shows a racial difference in inheritance. There is a higher percentage of inheritance of strong reactions and a lower percentage of inheritance of weak reactions in colored families than in whites. There is likewise a racial difference in the inheritance of the subgroups A^1 and A^2. Among eighty-nine Negroes, groups A and AB, 55.1 per cent had the property A^1 and 37.1 per cent had A^2. The corresponding figures for whites were 83.9 per cent A^1 and 13.6 per cent A^2.

Bruck,[19] using an anti-Caucasian serum, claimed that he

[16] J. Immunol., 12:251, 1926.　　[18] Ibid.

[17] Op. cit., 16:123, 1929.　　[19] Berliner Klin. Wchnschr., 44:793, 1907.

could, by means of complement fixation tests, distinguish between the serum of a Caucasian, a Negro, a Malay, a Chinese, and an Arab. Marshall and Teague[20] could not confirm this, using for their comparison the serum of a Caucasian, a Negro, a Japanese, a Negrito, and a Tegalog. Similar experiments by Fitzgerald,[21] using the serum of a Caucasian, a Japanese, and a Negro as antigens, gave negative results. He stated that "the existence of specific (serological) differences has not been proven." Landsteiner and Miller,[22] on repetition of the experiments of Bruck, state that if serological differences exist between Negroes and whites they are much smaller than those between man and the anthropoid apes. The significance of this statement is shown by the difficulty experienced by Nuttall in distinguishing between the primates and man by means of the precipitin test. Landsteiner and Miller were not able themselves to demonstrate serological racial differences, although they believe that it was not impossible that slight differences might be found if individuals of several races, preferably of pure blood, were carefully studied by the serological method in all its modifications.

Fischer and Racquet[23] prepared eight antiserums by immunizing rabbits with serum from either whites or Negroes, and among these antiserums only one showed by complement fixation and precipitin reactions a difference between the serum of the two races. This one antiserum, for white serum, gave an anomalous reaction in that it reacted stronger with Negro serum than it did with the homologous white serum. Absorption of the antiserum with Negro serum did not remove all antibodies for Negro serum, but the absorbed serum did then react more with the white serum than with the Negro serum.

Smith,[24] also using a refined technic for the precipitin reaction, endeavored to distinguish between Negro, Indian, and Caucasian serums. He claims to have obtained results sugges-

[20] *Philippine J. Sc.*, 3:357, 1908.

[21] *J. M. Research*, 21:41, 1909.   [22] *J. Exper. Med.*, 42:841, 1925.

[23] *Ztschr. f. Immunitätsforsch. u. exper. Therap.*, 94:104, 1938.

[24] *Yale J. Biol. & Med.*, 11:629, 1939.

tive of the presence of antigenic components distinctive of these races but admits the lack of proof that the technic is of sufficient delicacy and of adequate reliability to give a method for practical use.

Landsteiner[25] in a review states that the only serological peculiarities observed are those concerning isohemagglutinins, and these are not such as to demonstrate the existence of slight but regular differences by which the race of a single individual could be ascertained but have statistical significance only and deal with the frequency of certain properties. In this respect these serological qualities are comparable to other more or less distinguishing but not always constant attributes of a race, like the color of the eyes or hair or body weight. Wiener[26] also reaches a similar conclusion as to the general failure to disclose race-specific antigens. He states "attempts have also been made to produce sera which would serve to differentiate the blood of different races of the human species. Thus far all attempts have been unsuccessful."

Manoiloff[27] devised a chemical test for the differentiation of races. It depends, apparently, upon oxidation reactions, color changes in dyes serving as indicators. It has been applied in distinguishing Russians, Jews, and Ukrainians, but as far as can be found, it has not been used to distinguish Negroes from other races.

CHEMICAL CHARACTERISTICS

Stone[28] found that different normal values must be set for chemical determinations made on the natives of South Africa. He selected fifty normal adult Bantu natives in southern Rhodesia and made estimations of blood sugar, blood chloride, nonprotein nitrogen, urea, cholesterol, calcium, and phosphorus.

---

[25] *The specificity of serological reactions* (Springfield: Charles C. Thomas, 1936).

[26] *Blood groups and blood transfusion* (Springfield: Charles C. Thomas, 1935).

[27] *München. med. Wchnschr.*, 72:2186, 1925; *Am. J. Phys. Anthropol.*, 10:11, 323, 1927; cf. also Poliakowa, *Am. J. Phys. Anthropol.*, 10:65, 1927; Schapiro, *Ztschr. f. d. ges. exper. Med.*, 63:181, 1928; Grigorjewa, *Ztschr. f. Rassenphysiol.*, 2:92, 1929; Abramavich and Lyn, *Quart. Rev. Biol.*, 5:68, 1930.

[28] *Tr. Roy. Soc. Trop. Med. & Hyg.*, 30:165, 1936.

The blood sugar was lower than the commonly accepted normal values for Europeans. About 80 per cent contained between 70 and 100 mg. per cent, and this is suggested as the normal range for natives. In 12 per cent the value was below 70 mg. per cent, and in 8 per cent it was above 100 mg. per cent. The chlorides were also on the low side of the accepted normals, and this is probably due to excessive sweating. In 86 per cent of the natives the range was between 260 and 300 mg. per cent, which is taken to be the normal native range. The chlorides were above 300 mg. per cent in 12 per cent and below 260 mg. per cent in 2 per cent. Europeans in South Africa also showed a low average for chlorides—275 mg. per cent. Nonprotein nitrogen and urea values depended on the diet. They were higher in natives employed in town where more meat was eaten than in the rural districts. In 94 per cent of the natives the nonprotein nitrogen was between 20 and 40 mg. per cent. Urea in 90 per cent was between 15 and 30 mg. per cent. The cholesterol values showed wide variations ranging from 75 to 190 mg. per cent and could be correlated with the cholesterol content of the food. Serum calcium ranged from 6 mg. to 11 mg. per cent, the largest group showing 9.0–9.9 mg. per cent. Inorganic phosphorus ranged from 1.5 to 4.1 mg. per cent, the largest group showing 3.0–3.5 mg. per cent. These low values are attributable to the diet and do not mean that the normal calcium and phosphorus serum values and the daily requirements are lower in the natives. Stone did not notice symptoms in those with serum calcium values even below 7, and he believes that long deprivation of calcium-containing foods has inured them somewhat to the bad effects of low blood calcium.

Beaudisnet[29] remarked about the low urea content of the blood of natives of the Cameroons sent to the laboratory for analyses. The average was 17 mg. per cent.

Pales and Monglond[30] pointed out the extremely low blood sugar values that may be found in African natives. The largest group among those examined showed from 75 to 90 mg. per

[29] *Bull. Soc. path. exot.*, 30:147, 1937.   [30] *Presse méd.*, 42:765, 1934.

cent. In some cases the blood sugar was as low as 40 mg. per cent and without apparent effect.

For the normal serum calcium of East African natives a large series of examinations has been reported by Kelly and Henderson,[31] who, for forty-two subjects, gave an average of 9.2 mg. per cent in a pre-experimental period, but these, however, had been on a long-term prison diet which was definitely deficient in calcium. A larger series of examinations were later carried out on subjects who were employed on a sisal estate and, in addition to the calcium-deficient maize, which was the main constituent of the diet supplied, they had access to other foodstuffs sold in the district. On three occasions on which the examinations were made, the average serum calcium was 9.74 mg. for thirty-nine subjects, 9.08 mg. for twenty-eight subjects, and 9.77 mg. for twenty-four subjects. The average for these appears to be 9.5 mg. calcium per 100 cc.

Harvey and Vint[32] made calcium determinations of the serum and spinal fluids obtained at post-mortem examinations. When pneumonia was the cause of death, the average serum calcium showed no significant difference either from the 9.5 mg. per cent found as the average normal blood content by Kelly and Henderson or from the average of the pathological cases being described. The average serum calcium when tuberculosis was the cause of death was 9.31 mg. per cent, which is not significantly below what might be regarded as normal in East African natives. There is apparently a correlation between low values of calcium and severity of the disease. A marked increase of serum calcium was observed in the deaths from meningitis, the average being for ten such cases 11.21 mg. per cent. In the other causes of death, comparatively few in number of each, there was little or no reduction or increase in serum calcium. The condition of the kidneys influenced the amount of calcium. In twenty-one cases where there was kidney disease the average was 8.9 mg. per cent and an average of 9.89 mg. per cent in sixty-nine other pathological cases showing no kidney disease. The average for the cerebrospinal fluids was 6.26 mg. calcium per

---

[31] *J. Hyg.*, 29:418, 429, 1930. [32] *Kenya & East African M. J.*, 7:240, 1931.

100 cc. Only in the meningitis group, where 7.45 mg. were found was there any marked deviation from the normal, which, in absence of normal native figures, is accepted to be that found in whites, which is 5–6.2 mg. per cent.

Harrell[33] established in forty-four apparently healthy Negroes that the average blood serum calcium was 10.93 mg. per 100 cc. He states that this is 0.43 mg. higher than the normal blood serum calcium for the white individual, which is 10.5 mg. per cent. In forty-one Negroes with definite or suspected tuberculosis the average serum calcium was 9.8 mg. per cent. In twenty-three of these where the diagnosis was definite, the average was 9.2 mg. per cent, and in six of these who died, the average was 9.1 mg. per cent.

Andes, Kampmeier, and Adams[34] made plasma protein and cholesterol determinations in thirty-one Negroes in New Orleans, one-half of whom were well-nourished young men and the other half of whom were sufferers of various grades of arteriosclerosis. The results were compared with similar determinations in thirty-five healthy white medical students. The cholesterol values in both healthy and arteriosclerotic Negroes showed normal ranges. The total plasma proteins were about the same as in the whites, or slightly increased, but there was a marked difference in the amounts of serum albumin, serum globulin, and fibrinogen. The former was decreased, and the latter two proteins were increased. This resulted in a much reduced albumin/globulin ratio. The findings were similar to those in nephritis and nutritional edema. The authors call the condition a "nutritional pre-edema state" and attribute it to the character of the diet. While most authorities consider nutritional edema to be due to a deficient protein intake, these writers find that in these cases the amount of protein consumed is adequate. However, since the protein is derived chiefly from such foods as beans and potatoes, they believe that the low globulin values are due to a deficiency of these foods in essential amino-acids,

[33] *Am. Rev. Tuberc.*, **19**:350, 1929. (The author uses "grams" throughout his communication when he obviously meant "milligrams.")

[34] *J. Lab. & Clin. Med.*, **21**:340, 1936.

particularly cystin and lysin. There is also an undoubted deficiency in the diet of vitamins A, C, and D. There was no significant difference in the findings in normal and arteriosclerotic Negroes.

In agreement with other writers, Dill, Wilson, Hall, and Robinson[35] were not able to demonstrate any unique physiological characteristic of the Negro which might be related to his capacity for energy transformation. Negroes do have less hemoglobin than whites, and the hydrogen-ion concentration in their blood may be less variable than that of whites, but there is no other evidence for racial peculiarities in serum electrolytes.

An analysis of the blood creatinine levels made by McCord[36] of 209 white and 298 Negro subjects with renal disease showed that higher levels are likely to occur in the Negroes. McCord offers no explanation of this observation. It is likely, however, that the colored patients studied had a higher degree of renal insufficiency and that creatinine as well as other metabolites were elevated to higher levels.

Analyses of human milk from white and colored mothers by Burhans and Smith[37] showed 17 per cent less calcium and 12 per cent less inorganic phosphorus and 30 per cent more chlorides in the colored than in the white.

Williams[38] found a difference between Negroes and whites in the diazo reaction. White patients with typhoid fever and tuberculosis give a positive reaction usually when the prognosis is bad. Negroes also give the reaction in typhoid fever, but not in tuberculosis, whatever the prognosis is.

SPECIFIC RACIAL ODORS

It has often been stated that Negroes have a characteristic body odor that is offensive to whites and, likewise, that there is an odor characteristic of white people which is equally offensive to colored people. Indeed, the existence of body odors specific for a race and disagreeable to others has received some attention in scientific literature and considerable in popular writings.

[35] *J. Biol. Chem.*, **136**: 449, 1940. [37] *Am. J. Dis. Child.*, **26**:304, 1923.
[36] *Tri-State M. J.*, **13**:2689, 1941. [38] *M. Rec.*, **71**:480, 1907.

Adachi,[39] a Japanese investigator, has described the peculiarity of the odor of Europeans, especially of European women, which was often pungent and rancid and altogether unpleasant to Japanese. The odor is chiefly localized in the armpits, where the apocrine sweat glands are most numerous, and is difficult to remove with soap and water. On the other hand, Adachi claims that Japanese are usually free of odor, that if an armpit odor is found in a native, he is disqualified for military service. Günther,[40] as well as several older writers, calls attention to the specific odor of Jews. The odors of colored races have been especially discussed by Andree.[41] In some of the languages of South America there are special words for the odors of Negroes, Indians, and whites. Jaeger[42] believes that all human beings give off odors which are specific for the individual, race, age, sex, and even of mental and emotional states.[43]

Günther[44] says body odors are of two types—inherited and acquired—the latter being more striking and influenced by food (e.g., garlic), occupation, personal hygiene, and locale, while the former is more subtle and is a true racial feature.

The organic substances found in the secretion of the skin are neutral fats, cholesterol, volatile fatty acids, traces of protein, creatinine, aromatic acids, ethereal sulphuric acids, or phenol and skatoxyl, sometimes also of indoxyl, and urea.[45] While the odor of perspiration is said to be due chiefly to the fatty acids, other of the above substances are potent sources of odors, especially when decomposed by bacterial action.[46] If there is any racial specificity of odors, it must be due to the specificity of the

[39] *Globus*, 83:14, 1903. [40] *Ztschr. f. Rassenphysiol.*, 2:94, 1929.

[41] *Völkergeruch, ethnographische Parallelen*, Vol. 2 (Leipzig: Veit & Co., 1889).

[42] *Entdeckung der Seele*, 1:246, 1884.

[43] Havelock Ellis, "Smell," *Studies in the psychology of sex*, 4:59 (1936).

[44] *Loc. cit.*; see n. 40.

[45] Hammarsten, "The skin and its secretion," in *A textbook of physiological chemistry* (New York: Wiley & Sons, 1911); Oppenheimer, *Grundriss der organische Chemie* (Leipzig: G. Thieme, 1916).

[46] Human sweat is devoid of bactericidal properties. On the other hand, it is a good bacterial culture medium (Usher, *Arch. Dermat. & Syph.*, 16:706, 1927). Sweat has been claimed to be both a strong oxidizing and a reducing agent by different writers.

chemical composition of the skin secretions or of the bacterial flora which produces odors by putrefaction. The offensive odors which Negroes and whites attribute to each other are probably the stenches arising from unclean bodies and the result of bacterial decomposition.

FUNCTION OF THE SKIN

Most of the physiologic characteristics of the Negro seem to be those associated with his adaptation to the tropical climates peculiar to Africa. Many of these adaptive mechanisms are inherent in the skin and apparently have for their purpose the protection of the body against the harmful effects of excessive amounts of solar energy, including heat, luminosity, and ultraviolet radiation. The chief protective agent of the skin appears to be its pigmentation, although associated with it and acting in a supplementary fashion toward the same ends are the well-developed sweat glands and subcutaneous blood capillaries. Evidence of the function of pigmentation is furnished by the following facts: first, that natives of various countries are naturally pigmented roughly proportional to the intensity of the sunlight in the places where they are indigenous; second, that Negroes can live unclothed and unaffected under a hot tropical sun where unpigmented people experience much discomfort and even injury, although clothed, hatted, and fitted with tinted eyeglasses; third, unpigmented people exposed to sunlight develop a melanin pigmentation approaching that of the Negro, presumably as protection against the sun's rays.

While it is agreed that melanin in the skin acts as a protective agent against sunlight, it is not at all clear how it functions to this end or against what element of sunlight it is active. Theories have been proposed that postulate the action of cutaneous pigment against each of the forms of solar radiation which are divided according to wave length into radiant energy, luminosity, and ultraviolet radiation. Goldsmith[47] says that the chief function of the pigment is probably to protect the blood from being overheated by absorbing the deeply penetrating red,

[47] *Brit. J. Phys. Med.*, 11:43, 1936.

orange, and yellow rays. On the other hand, Loewenthal[48] points out that blackness is a handicap instead of an advantage in hot climates, since black objects absorb heat and white ones reflect it. Martin[49] showed that the skin of a Negro absorbs 84 per cent of the sun's rays, while the skin of the average blond absorbs 57 per cent. Aitken[50] says pigment is not a defense against either heat rays or ultraviolet rays but is a protection against luminous rays, a view in which he is supported by Hill.[51] For evidence Aitken exposed unpigmented skin to the carbon arc and to the mercury-vapor arc with and without a filter that was supposed to absorb ultraviolet rays. The lights from the two sources contained different amounts of ultraviolet and visible rays. He claims to have shown that protective pigment was formed in least amount when the smallest amount of ultraviolet rays reached the skin and in the largest amount when the quantity of luminous rays falling on the skin was the greatest. The technic of these experiments and the conclusions from them were vigorously criticized by Russel[52] and by Baurvens.[53] The former was of the opinion that pigment protected chiefly against ultraviolet rays, and the latter stated that the Negro under his layer of pigment enjoys the same type of protection from the penetrating thermogenic radiation of the sun as white people do when sitting in the shade on a hot day. Laurens and Foster[54] found that the skin temperature changes in response to varying amounts of energy in the infrared spectral bands were markedly similar in Negro, Japanese, and white subjects. Most writers are of the opinion that pigmentation is most active against the longer wave lengths of ultraviolet rays, a view which is most consistent with the Negro's sensitivity to rickets.[55] As a partial compensation for the shielding effect of pigmentation, the skin of Negroes secretes more sebum, which has a high con-

[48] *J. Trop. Med.*, 39:209, 1936.

[49] *Lancet*, 2:673, 1930.

[50] *Brit. J. Phys. Med.*, 10:30, 1935.

[51] *Brit. J. Phys. Med.*, 9:7, 1934.

[52] *Brit. J. Phys. Med.*, 10:54, 1935.

[53] *Brit. J. Phys. Med.*, 10:54, 1935.

[54] *Am. J. Physiol.*, 118:372, 1937.

[55] Laurens, *M. Rec.*, 150:165, 1939; Miescher, *Strahlentherapie*, 39:601, 1930–31.

tent of sterols that can be activated by ultraviolet rays to vitamin D.

BASAL METABOLISM

Although there may be a racial factor in basal metabolism as shown by McLeod, Crafts, and Benedict[56] and others, it appears that the basal metabolism of Negroes is not so much a function of race as of climate. Thus De Almeida[57] showed that Negroes in tropical Brazil have practically the same basal metabolism and minimal metabolism as whites living under the same condition, indicating that black pigmentation has no effect on heat elimination. The metabolism of both Negroes and whites was about 20.4 per cent less than that of the inhabitants of cold or temperate climates. Steggerda and Benedict[58] found that the basal metabolism of black and brown natives of Jamaica was practically that which was predictable by the Harris-Benedict standards[59] for whites of corresponding age, weight, and height. The similarity of Negroes in Jamaica and whites in America is probably due to the similarities of climates. No metabolism-rate determinations of whites in Jamaica were made.

OTHER PHYSIOLOGICAL CHARACTERISTICS

It appears that other adaptations of the Negro that deal with African climates are the thick woolly hair and the wide roomy nostrils, the former probably acting as a heat and light insulator and the latter offering a better cooling device for hot inspired air than does the narrower nostril of the white.

The observation of Vint[60] that the red blood cells of African natives are macrocytic in size may be in some way associated with climatic conditions, although the great prevalence of parasitic blood diseases in Africa should be taken into account in considering the possible causes of larger red cells. Pijper[61] says

[56] *Am. J. Physiol.*, **73**:449, 1925.

[57] *J. de physiol. et de pathol. gén.*, **18**:712, 958, 1920; **22**:1248, 1924.

[58] *Am. J. Physiol.*, **85**:621, 1928.

[59] *Carnegie Inst. Wash.*, *Publ. No. 279*, 1919.

[60] *East African M. J.*, **16**:295, 1939.   [61] *East African M. J.*, **8**:703, 1934.

that individuals of blood group B have larger red cells than those of group A. Vint could not confirm this and found large cells independent of blood groups.

Other physiological traits of the Negro have been reported that deal·with pulse rate, vital capacity, fertility, and age of puberty and the menarche, but the results are indefinite and uncertain as to whether they are related to race, to climate, or to other environmental conditions.

RESPONSE TO DRUGS

Medical writers of slavery days were apparently under the impression that Negroes responded differently than white people to therapeutic drugs. To this end an almost complete and special pharmacopeia was utilized for the treatment of diseases among slaves. This was probably due partly to a genuine feeling that Negroes were a species distinct from whites and partly to the fact that many unfamiliar diseases were imported from Africa along with the slaves. Modern medicine with its more accurate methods of observation recognize very few differences in the action of drugs in Negroes and white people.

Paskind[62] studied the action of atropine on an equal number of white and colored patients of about the same age and weight. Both groups showed approximately the same ultimate acceleration of heart rate from injection of 1/120 to 1/30 grain of atropine sulphate, but they varied distinctly in the initial depression. In the colored patients the average normal heart rate was 78, while atropine produced an average depression of one beat per minute. In the white group the normal rate was 87; in these cases atropine reduced the rate on an average of ten beats per minute. From these results the Negro appears·to be less susceptible to the central action of atropine than the white man.

Chen and Path[63] compared the pupil-dilating effect of cocaine, euphthalmine, and ephedrine in Negroes, Chinese, and Caucasions, both in diffuse daylight and under controlled artificial illumination, with accurate measurements. Caucasians were

[62] *J. Lab. & Clin. Med.*, 7:104, 1921.

[63] *J. Pharmacol. & Exper. Therap.*, 36:429, 1929.

the most and Negroes the least sensitive to the mydriatic action of these drugs.

A well-known but insufficiently recorded observation is the resistance of Negroes to cathartic drugs. Active substances in doses that produce drastic purgation in white people may have no effect on many Negroes. Niles[64] conservatively states that, on an average, 50 per cent larger doses of cathartics must be given colored people. On the other hand, he claims that smaller doses of anodynes, sedatives, and hypnotics are required for effectiveness in Negroes. There is apparently no difference in the activity of antipyretics in Negroes and whites, while counterirritants are less active in Negroes.

Patton[65] writes about the relative immunity of Negroes to the toxic action of alcohol. He claims that while he observed much drunkenness in colored people, the organic changes in acute and chronic alcoholism are rare.

[64] *South. M. J.*, 6:127, 1913; *J. Florida M. A.*, 5:118, 1919.
[65] *New Orleans M. &-S. J.*, 64:201, 1911.

MEDICAL DISEASES

MANY of the diseases that affect Negroes do so in a way not appreciably different from the way they affect white people. On the other hand, there are conditions that occur among Negroes, at least those in Africa, almost exclusively, not because of a racial predilection but because of the geography of the diseases and because of the intimacy in which these people in their more primitive existence come in contact with their environment. These are of no interest here, where the chief concern is with those conditions in which comparisons can be made and differences, if any, between their manifestations in the two races can be demonstrated. The purpose is not only to point out the differences that may exist between the races but also to seek evidence that will lead to an explanation of the differences. This is the concern of both the physician and the anthropologist.

Attempts have been made to formulate a generalized explanation for the differences of disease patterns among Negroes and whites and have included theories based on such factors as diet, environment, social conditions, genotypic physical characteristics, and the psyche.[1] However, as may be seen from the following discussions, no single reason may be given for the differences in all diseases, and each disease may have several factors that can account for its variation between races.

[1] Walsh and Pool, *Am. J. Med. Sc.*, 196:252, 1938.

TUBERCULOSIS

The seriousness of tuberculosis among Negroes has been known for a long while, but only within comparatively recent years has the fact been turned to the benefit of phthisiology by using it as an approach to the understanding of some of the pertinent problems of the science. The result has been that no disease of the Negro is now being more diligently studied. Every volume of the *American Review of Tuberculosis,* the only periodical in this country devoted exclusively to tuberculosis problems, has for many years contained one or several articles or references dealing more or less directly with tuberculosis in Negroes. That tuberculosis is a different disease in colored people cannot be doubted in view of the evidence, but the various expressions of the differences and their true explanations have not been fully disclosed. The insistence of these academic questions is a greater stimulus of investigation than is the waste of human lives from excessive deaths among Negroes. The more practical fact that the remainder of the American population can never be safe from the disease unless the hazard of infection from this minor group is removed is likewise a potent motive for the study of those characteristics of the disease in Negroes that indicate methods of control.

The vastness of the literature on tuberculosis in colored people and its many viewpoints make it difficult to organize a concise, systematic, and yet anywhere near complete summary. Much that has been written is questionable as to its trustworthiness. One soon learns to identify the reliable sources of information, and among these are the publications of the National Tuberculosis Association, the Henry Phipps Institute, and the United States Public Health Service. One should be able to rely upon trained individuals in universities and sanatoriums who have the facilities to make and record reliable and accurate observations. In addition, several excellent discussions on tuberculosis in Negroes have been published, such as the book by Bushnell on *The epidemiology of tuberculosis,*[1] that by Cummins

---

[1] New York: William Wood & Co., 1920.

on *Primitive tuberculosis*,[2] two serially published papers by Cochrane,[3] and the report of the Tuberculosis Research Committee of South Africa.[4] To these publications credit must be given as the source of much of the data cited herein, especially that concerning Africa.

IN AFRICAN NEGROES

A discussion of tuberculosis in the Negro should begin with Africa. There those features believed to be characteristic of the race are seen in their simplest if exaggerated form. The development of those more or less stabilized modifications of the disease seen in the American and West Indian Negro can be traced through the varying circumstances of existence of the native of Africa.

It is agreed that tuberculosis, unlike some other diseases whose origins can be definitely traced to Africa, was introduced into the continent by invaders from other countries. The first of the invasions was in northern Africa, along the Mediterranean, and is of great antiquity. The length of time tuberculosis has existed there can be measured to some extent by the undoubted tuberculous lesions found among long-buried excavated human skeletons. In more recent times contacts were made with the disease through invasions that spread down the east and then the west coast as far as the extreme end of the continent, where the Union of South Africa now is. Then finally the interior was invaded. With the advent of missionaries, slave traders, explorers, merchants, colonists, and soldiers, there is scarcely a part of Africa that has not been touched by the white man, whose footprints are left in the form of tuberculosis among the natives. There is no question but that even within recent times tuberculosis was completely absent in the more inaccessible parts of the continent. In some cases observers were able to note a lack of it and then to find, after an interval of a few years, unmistakable signs of its appearance.

[2] London: John Bole Medical Publications, 1939.

[3] *Trop. Dis. Bull.*, 34:743, 819, 1937.

[4] *South African Inst. M. Research Publ.*, No. XXX, 1932.

There is a suggestion that some parts of Africa, which appear to have been only comparatively recently settled, particularly on the upper west coast, were in fact explored and used as trading centers at a much earlier period, at which time tuberculosis was introduced. But, owing to the character of the disease in the native, it was not propagated in the absence of the infecting foreigners and consequently died out. This, however, is considered as a remote possibility, since no instance is definitely known where tuberculosis once existing has completely disappeared from a population. At the present time tuberculosis exists in Africa in varying forms and in varying amounts, depending on such factors as proximity of foreigners, the amount of aggregation—as in villages—and the length of contact with the disease.

Tuberculosis in Africans progresses more rapidly, is more fatal, and has a different anatomical picture than in whites of European stock. The explanation of this phenomenon, which is observed not only in African Negroes but to some degree in Negroes wherever they are, involves several of the most debatable problems of tuberculosis. First is the question of race susceptibility to disease. In the old civilized communities of northern Africa, peopled chiefly by non-Negroid races, there has always been a fair number of true Negroes. Like the other people of this area, they have been exposed to tuberculosis a long while. Theirs is the chronic, slowly progressing form of tuberculized people and is seen in the Negroes as well as in the other races. But even with this type of disease tuberculosis in Negroes distinguishes itself by being a little more rapid in progress, a little more acute, a little more fatal. Everywhere the Negro lives he shows the same differences. In some instances these differences are more striking than in others. For this reason the idea has been created of a race susceptibility applicable to Negroes. This tends to show that Negroes, as compared to other races, under the same conditions, have fundamentally less resistance to the disease.

Second, there is the question of the inheritance of susceptibilities or immunities to disease. Negroes seem to have less resistance to tuberculosis than the general run of races. Some races have a higher immunity to the disease than others. These properties are held to be constant and inheritable or are at least very slowly changing features of the races. The relatively immune races are believed to have acquired this characteristic through long experience with tuberculosis, which the non-immune race has not had. How the amount of experience with tuberculosis influences a race characteristic, what the mechanism is that bestows resistance, and the way resistance is transmitted are problems that are studied in the same way as are the problems that concern the acquiring and inheriting of other human characteristics.

Third is the question of the primary infection and its significance in the explanation of tuberculosis in Negroes. Ordinarily tuberculosis, as seen in the adult European or people of similar civilization, involves a series of events beginning with an initial or primary infection, followed by a second infection, the reaction to which, primarily antagonistic to progressive disease, is conditioned by the first infection. The discussion of tuberculosis in the Negro includes such questions as the opportunity for first infections and the ability to deal with them, the development of protective allergy as opposed to a destructive hypersensitivity, and the efficiency of the changed reaction to modify the progressive tendency of the disease.

Finally there is the influence of external or environmental factors. Tuberculosis among natives living under tribal conditions is not nearly so serious an infection as it is when they are transferred to foreign areas to engage in new kind of work and adopt different modes of life.

Previous to 1912 the extent of tuberculous infection among African natives was known only by the clinical evidences of the disease. Since one of the outstanding characteristics of tuberculosis in most natives is the lack of outward signs, even in the presence of massive disease, clinical observation alone is insufficient to determine the extent of infection. It was Calmette who probably more than anyone else popularized the tuberculin reaction. He pointed out its usefulness as a tool both in the practice and in the investigation of tuberculosis and introduced it in making tuberculosis surveys in Africa. He and his colleagues in this way covered most of the French-African colonies and disclosed the variable amounts of tuberculosis in natives and the relation of these amounts to certain factors. Their work was followed by many similar surveys in other parts of the continent.

The results as summarized by Calmette[5] showed that the rates of infection in the French colonies in 1912 varied from 1.8 per cent in French Guinea to 15.1 per cent in Senegal. Mathis and Durieux[6] repeated the tests in the same places eighteen years later and found that the rates had increased tremendously and amounted to as much as 53 per cent. There was a definite relation of the positive reactions to the amount of outside contacts. Natives of the coast, especially those employed on the wharves, had a much higher rate than those in towns in the interior. Mouchet,[7] van den Branden, Fornara, and Staub,[8] and Van Hoof, Clevers, and Donadio[9] tested natives of the Belgian Congo. Mouchet estimated that 7 per cent of all the people were infected. Peiper,[10] Manteufel,[11] Müller,[12] and Kersten[13] found among the German colonies that the rate of infection was 25–30 per cent. Ziemann[14] reported that, among Bantu soldiers recruited from Cameroon, 4.4 per cent were infected, while natives in the highlands showed no infection at all. Of a group of 34 exiled Hottentots, 22 gave positive reactions, and 12 had clinical signs of tuberculosis.

In the South Africa mine areas and in the native territories supplying natives for the mines, the rate of infection was very

[5] Ann. Inst. Pasteur, 26:497, 1912.

[6] Bull. Soc. path. exot., 23:533, 1930.   [7] Bull. Soc. path. exot., 6:55, 1913.

[8] Ann. Soc. belge de méd. trop., 6:235, 1925.

[9] Ann. Soc. belge de méd. trop., 6:183, 1925.

[10] Arch.f. Schiffs- u. Tropen-Hyg., 15:2, 1911; 16:431, 1912.

[11] Arch.f. Schiffs- u. Tropen-Hyg., 18:711, 1914.

[12] Arch.f. Schiffs- u. Tropen-Hyg., 18:690, 1914.

[13] Arch.f. Schiffs- u. Tropen-Hyg., 19:101, 1915.

[14] Centralbl.f. Bakt., Abt. I., 70:118, 1913.

high, mounting in some instances to 100 per cent, varying according to the age group, the elevation of the terrain, the number of repatriated miners, and other factors.[15]

Of the natives of the English controlled colonies—Zanzibar, Tanganyika, and Bahr el Ghazal—tested by Matthews, Wilcocks, and Burrows,[16] those in the populated cosmopolitan island of Zanzibar showed the highest rate of infection, and those in the relatively isolated Bahr el Ghazal showed the least.

It has been repeatedly pointed out that the Hindus, a long and well-tuberculized people, have been a large factor in the spread of tuberculosis among African natives. Musselman and Syrian peddlers have likewise played an important role in infecting the Negroes. These nomadic people, subject to chronic phthisis, with open cavities, scatter tubercle bacilli freely wherever they go.

It is doubtful whether all the tuberculin surveys made among the natives of Africa are comparable, because the same dilution of tuberculin was not used in each case, nor was there a uniform method of carrying out the test. Moreover, old tuberculin deteriorates rapidly in the tropics, and this fact might have vitiated some of the results. Cochrane[17] discusses the possible use of Long's[18] dried purified-protein-derivative (PPD) preparation for tuberculin testing in hot countries.

There is much evidence that, tested in the same way, Africans are more sensitive to tuberculin than are Europeans. For example, Wilcocks[19] points out that in normal Londoners a reduction in strength of tuberculin from 1:1,000 to 1:10,000 resulted in a reduction in positive reactions of 25 per cent. In Tanganyika natives a reduction in strength from 1:5,000 to 1:50,000 resulted in a reduction of positive reactions of only 3 per cent. Likewise, Allen[20] in South Africa showed that a reduction of the dilution of tuberculin from 1:5,000 to 1:10,000 made no differ-

---

[15] *South African Inst. M. Research Publ.*, No. XXX, 1932.

[16] *Tubercle*, 16:(suppl.), 1–87, 1935.

[17] *Loc. cit.*; see n. 3.   [19] *Tubercle*, 16:(suppl.), 31; 1935.

[18] *Am. Rev. Tuberc.*, 30:(suppl.), 757, 1934.   [20] *Loc. cit.*; see n. 4.

ence either in the character of the reactions or in the proportion between positive and negative tests. Actually the proportion of positive reactions was fractionally higher with 1:10,000 than with 1:5,000. With a 1:100,000 dilution the percentage of positive reactors was reduced about 17 per cent. With a 1:1,000,000 dilution there was little difference in the percentage as obtained with 1:100,000, but there was some change in the character of reactions. When the dilution of 1:10,000,000 was used, there was a reduction of 3 per cent from the percentage obtained with 1:1,000,000 and 24 per cent reduction from that obtained with 1:5,000.

Cummins[21] discusses the Negro's type of tuberculin reaction with reference to the significance of allergy in immunity. He says the Negro's reaction is one of "sensitivity-allergy," while that of tuberculized people is one of "immune allergy."

That the clinical form of tuberculosis and its pathological anatomy are unique in the African had occasionally been noted before. Borrel,[22] by the clarity and completeness of his description of the disease in Senegalese soldiers in France, aroused interest in what he called tuberculosis in "primitive" or "virgin" soil. The African troops that were called to French army service during the World War came from a part of Africa where tuberculosis, while not completely absent, was uncommon. In his studies of the interior the natives showed positive tuberculin reactions of 4–7 per cent. In the villages he found 20–30 per cent. In continental France among his own people there was a frequency of 60–90 per cent. At the time of mobilization, the Senegalese soldiers showed a positive rate of 4–5 per cent positive reactions. After being in training-camp for about a year the men rapidly came down with an infection having symptoms entirely confusing to the physicians accustomed to seeing tuberculosis in the French whites. Borrel divided the course of the disease into two periods. During the initial period, lasting from one to three months, there might be at first no outward symptoms or physical changes. At this time enlarged lymph glands may be found in the chest. A lymph gland in the supraclavicu-

---

[21] *Loc. cit.;* see n. 2.   [22] *Ann. Inst. Pasteur,* 34:105, 1920.

lar region could easily be seen or palpated in about 70 per cent of the cases. He emphasized the diagnostic importance of this enlarged supraclavicular gland in an otherwise healthy-appearing individual. Later in the initial period the patient began to show other indications of the infection. There was a change in the happy facial expression characteristic of the well Senegalese. The limbs became soft and flabby, muscle tonus was lost as well as the luster of the healthy skin. There was a loss of weight and a slight fever developed. Borrel called this the lymphatic stage because of a massive involvement of the lymph glands, particularly the tracheobronchial glands. Moreau[23] confirmed this with the x-ray by pointing out the huge densities at the hilum of the lungs, owing to the large size of the hilar glands. The second period was more definitely recognizable as tuberculosis because it followed the usual course of generalized tuberculosis. Pleuritis, peritonitis, and meningitis appeared at times. The outstanding finding was the marked involvement of the lungs with caseous pneumonia. There was little fever, which increased slightly toward the end. Neither was there tachycardia. The sputum was nearly always negative for tubercle bacilli. The second period lasted one to three months, and the disease was uniformly fatal.

Post-mortem examinations proved that the infection was primarily of the lymph glands and secondarily of the lungs. There was never any indication of a fibrous or healing reaction. The sequence of events thus reconstructed was "primary chancre" in the bronchial mucosa, invasion of lymph glands, extension to the lungs, and finally a bacillemia during which, as Borrel picturesquely writes, it "snows" tubercles. A complete lack of resistance is thus indicated, and Borrel rightly compares the condition to tuberculosis in the infant or in experimentally infected guinea pigs or rabbits.

Roubier,[24] Dumas,[25] Traband,[26] Lasnet,[27] Abbatucci and

[23] Bull. Acad. Med., 81:224, 1919.

[24] Gaz. d. hôp., 93:1333, 1920.   [26] Arch. de méd. et pharm. mil., 74:432, 1921.

[25] Lyon méd., 128:180, 1919.   [27] Ann. de méd. et pharm. colon., 20:273, 1922.

Gravellat,[28] Cain and Hillemand,[29] and Paisseau[30] record practically the same findings among the French colonials. They stress the insidious character of tuberculosis in these people, who may be heavily infected, in spite of a prolonged absence of clinical signs. The disease in its later stage, however, becomes generalized, and death quickly follows.

Pott's disease often occurred in these Senegalese soldiers, and in them it behaved differently from that ordinarily seen, according to Castay.[31] The first symptom that usually appeared was a paralysis of the legs without any deformity referable to the spinal column. Pathologically there was a veritable melting-away of the vertebral bodies as a result of rapidly progressing caseation. This caseation began in the center of the bodies, and the outer shell of intact bone prevented deformity. The process was one of tuberculous osteitis instead of the usual osteoarthritis. The x-ray picture was deceiving in that a slight decalcification was all that could be detected.

Bushnell[32] summarizes the features of this primitive tuberculosis as follows: a general involvement of the lymph glands as great pockets of enormously enlarged caseated and suppurating organs; involvement of the lungs with caseous bronchopneumonia; caseous lobar pneumonia or a gelatinous pneumonia; primary involvement of the serous membranes; tuberculosis of the liver, spleen, kidneys, myocardium, pericardium, and often the endocardium; acute intestinal ulcers, and finally terminal miliary tuberculosis of the lungs.

This, then, is the character of the disease in people who have not been previously infected. They become highly allergic in the early stages of infection but do not attain the reactivity that is the basis of resistance.

The lack of an acquired or inherited resistance may not be the whole explanation of the behavior of tuberculosis in the Senega-

---

[28] *Presse méd.* 31:1421, 1923.

[29] *Arch. Med.*, 13:1923, 1923.

[30] *Bull. Soc. méd. d. hôp. de Paris*, 48:1462, 1924.

[31] *Bull. Méd. soc. de radiol. de France*, 22:331, 1934.   [32] *Loc. cit.*; see. n. 1.

lese soldiers. From everyday experience it is known that first infections need not be serious. The period of greatest sensitivity to the tubercle bacillus is in the first few years of life. During this time many individuals receive their initial dose of organisms without any apparent harm. Even primitive Africans may have primary infections without dire results. The deciding factor for the child—European or African—is the size of the initial infecting dose. It may be quite reasonably assumed that the Senegalese troops, in spite of the claims of the French for the hygenic conditions of the continental military camps, were exposed to massive doses of organisms instead of the repeated small doses that safely tide the average individual through the dangers of a primary infection into the comparative safety of the allergic state. These massive infections in virgin soil, together with a disturbed general resistance, hard labor, and exposure in an unadjusted army life, are the causes of this unusual form of tuberculosis.

A thorough and interesting study of tuberculosis among African Negroes has been made in the Union of South Africa by a specially appointed committee headed by Lister and advised by Cummins.[33] The large gold mines of that area, dependent on native labor, were confronted with the problem of a huge morbidity and mortality from tuberculosis among the native miners. The committee, sponsored jointly by the mine interests and the Union government, was selected to investigate and to make recommendations for the alleviation of the reprehensible conditions which exist in the mine fields and in the territories from which the laborers come. The more than four-hundred-page report is, on the whole, a notable contribution to the epidemiology of tuberculosis, although exception must be taken to some of the conclusions that are inconsistent with known facts, particularly those that say life in the mine area is not a cause of the high morbidity rates and that repatriated cases of tuberculosis do not infect other natives. One is led to suspect that these are attempts to absolve the mineowners from blame for their inhumane practices.

[33] *Loc. cit.;* see n. 2.

The industries of South Africa employ annually nearly a million natives. These are drawn from a territory with a population of about seven million, of which two million are employable males between fifteen and fifty years of age. Between three hundred thousand and four hundred thousand are absorbed by the mines and agriculture. The remainder are employed by trades, other industries, the government, as domestics, and by the railways. The natives are almost entirely of Bantu stock and have lived under primitive tribal customs.

Tuberculin surveys of natives in their natural state have already been cited, indicating that they are highly infected. These infections are believed to have begun in 1880, when South Africa became noted as a health resort and many Europeans with tuberculosis went there for cures. While the report gives no statistics as to the amount of active tuberculosis, it does state that in some parts of the native land the disease is very prevalent, while in others it is not so common. Although there are many instances of acute infection, the majority of the cases are chronic pulmonary tuberculosis with a much smaller amount of surgical tuberculosis.

Laborers for the South African industries are obtained from these tuberculized communities by a special organization using a system of "recruiting," which probably amounts to conscription. The natives are sent in lots of three hundred to four hundred twice weekly to Johannesburg, where they are contracted for work in the mines at wages that amount to approximately $125 a year. The very long and strenuous journey results in between 3 and 4 per cent arriving ill enough to be hospitalized. Although they were examined and found healthy before beginning the trip, 23 per cent must be kept from the mines to be rested and fed up because they are physically below par on arrival.

The men at the mines are housed in compounds which provide each occupant with about fifteen square feet, although as far back as 1914, Gorgas,[34] called in consultation to the area, pointed out the inadequacy of living space and recommended

[34] *J. A. M. A.,* 62:1855, 1914.

that at least fifty square feet per occupant be allotted. The food given the miners consists of entrails, heads, hoofs, a certain amount of meat and fat, and certain bones cooked together with vegetables into a stew and issued once a day. Generally three pounds of other meat are given two or three times a week. To this is added other food articles to provide 4,385 calories daily. This diet is listed as containing vitamins A, B, and C.

The working day begins at 4:30 A.M. and ends between 3:00 and 4:00 P.M. Before going to the mines a light meal, consisting often only of coffee or cocoa, is given. The main meal is issued after work, and no food is taken during the approximately twelve hours spent in the mine. The work in the mines consists mainly of drilling, pushing carts, and shoveling ore. While the rock during drilling is thoroughly wetted to prevent dust, a large amount of silicosis occurs. The period of service for each worker in the mines consists of 313 working days, and every day except Sunday is a working day. After this period of service the miner may return home or re-enter into a contract with the same or another mine.

In 1915 the reported morbidity from tuberculosis among the native miners in the Rand was 13.1 per 1,000, in 1916 it was 13.9, the highest rate cited, after which it steadily fell, when in 1930 it was 7.2 per 1,000. The case mortality was 18.7 per cent for the years 1916–20, and for the year 1929–30 it was 17.5 per cent. This, however, applies to case mortality on the mine and merely indicates the speed at which the disease kills, because it is the practice to send all natives home as soon as tuberculosis is diagnosed unless they are *in extremis*, in which case they are hospitalized. No provision is made for treatment either at the mines or in the native territories. If observation of the cases is extended to two years, the case mortality becomes 70 per cent.

It has been possible to correlate the amount of clinical tuberculosis which develops among the miners with the nature of the tuberculin reaction (whether positive or negative) at the time of arrival at the mine. Other factors were the age of the native when he began work in the mines and the length of his mine service.

Twice as many cases developed among those with positive tuberculin reactions as among those who gave negative reactions. Even among those reacting to 1:100,000 and 1:1,000,000 dilutions of tuberculin, more cases appeared than among those giving no reactions, although the difference is not marked, 1.6 times the negatives with the former dilution and 1.5 times the negatives with the latter dilution. This evidence indicates that those already infected are more likely to fall victims of the disease than those who are not.

The data concerning the factor of age are given only for deaths from tuberculosis rather than for cases of the disease. If the mineworkers are divided into three age groups, those under twenty-five years, those between twenty-five and forty years, and those over forty years, it is found that the first group, making up about 20 per cent of the whole, furnished 31.1 per cent of the total deaths. The second group, which makes up 70 per cent of the whole, furnished 39.6 per cent of the deaths. The third group, of whom there are 10 per cent, gave 29.3 per cent of all deaths. The death rate for the youngest group was 2.3 per 1,000, of the middle-age group, it was 29.3 per 1,000, and for the older group, 12 per 1,000.

The first year for the native on the mine area was the period of greatest danger. If he survived and was re-engaged, the risk was much less during the second year and least during the third year. After this the risk rose until it again reached a very high degree after the fifth year. The incidence of disease during the first twelve months of service was 13.4 per 1,000, for the second twelve months it was 3.6 per 1,000, for the third 1.7, for the fourth 2.3, for the fifth 4.2, and the average incidence for those in service over five years was 7.9 per 1,000. It is believed that the increase in incidence after the third year was due to the impairments obtained in mine service, particularly to silicosis.

The clinical form of tuberculosis which was typical of the native mineworker is not the generalized septicemic, or infantile, form but the generalized lymphatic form, or tuberculosis of "school age."[35] This generalized tuberculosis was almost as

[35] Fishberg, *Pulmonary tuberculosis* (2d ed.; Philadelphia: Lea & Febiger, 1919).

much the rule in the positive tuberculin reactors as it was in the negative reactors. Any cases that were diagnosed as chronic tuberculosis arose in the positive reactors and were associated with silicosis, while glandular tuberculosis was fairly common. The clinical type of disease seemed to suggest that the virus of tuberculosis had bestowed a measure of resistance to virulence but lowered resistance to infection.

A series of 600 autopsies on individuals dying of tuberculosis is described. Among them were 300 acute cases in which the cause of death was uncomplicated tuberculosis, 200 chronic cases in which the cause of death was also tuberculosis but in which the disease was associated with silicosis, and 62 cases in which tuberculous lesions were present but death was not actually due to tuberculosis. Of this latter group, 29 showed silicotic lesions in addition to the tuberculosis, 26 had tuberculosis without silicosis and in more or less active form, and 7 had only what seemed to be completely healed lesions.

The cases referred to as acute tuberculosis were neither the completely acute tuberculosis seen in virgin soil nor the modified type of the European adult. It was a progressive disease modified so as to occupy a position between these extremes. On comparing the lesions with those found by Borrel in the Senegalese, a number of differences were observed. While Borrel found the glands, especially the cervical glands, to be usually the site of primary infection and the lungs to be the primary focus in only about 5 per cent of his cases, in these South African miners the primary focus was in the lungs in over 30 per cent of the instances, although there were many examples where there were massive initial caseous lesions in the glands, more especially the tracheobronchials, with secondary spread to the lungs. While caseation in the glands was very common, actual suppuration—characteristic of infantile tuberculosis—although not rare, was uncommon. More often there was some hardening, owing to fibrosis. A considerable number of the cases showed caseous lesions of about equal severity in both the glands and the lungs and, apparently, of equal age. In this group it could not be stated with certainty which was the primary focus. The presence of pulmonary cavities indicated that they occurred in slightly immunized persons.

Tuberculous pneumonia, especially gelatinous pneumonia—a feature of "natural" tuberculosis—was rare in this series. Likewise, the extensive primary involvement of the serous membranes often seen in primary tuberculosis occurred, but not so often.

Unusual features in the acute cases were five instances of tuberculous involvement of the pancreas and two possible cases of primary involvement of the spleen, where the lesions were entirely confined to this organ.

In the 200 cases of chronic types of tuberculosis (really cases of tuberculo-silicosis), there was a marked resemblance to the ordinary fibro-caseous tuberculosis of European adults. There was much more fibrous-tissue formation, and the disease was more often limited to the lungs, although it may have spread to other organs affected with silicosis. More than half the cases showed cavities, and only 37 developed miliary tubercles. While the European adult usually has the ability to prevent tuberculosis from becoming generalized, this is strikingly lacking in the South African native except when associated with silicosis.

Cummins expressed the opinion that the tuberculosis which is so rampant on the Rand is not a newly acquired infection in the mines nor is it due to the regime of the mines of itself. It appears to be an infection obtained in the territories and is "lit up" by the strains and stresses of a new life. The number of positive tuberculin reactors who become ill with the disease and the fact that they develop tuberculosis soon after arriving at the mines are the chief evidences for this conclusion. He states that behind the childhood-type of tuberculosis seen in Africans is a real inborn lack of power to develop the resistance that is commonly observed in Europeans and that it is improbable · that any effort of administrative hygiene can prevent the gradual spread of the already widely disseminated infection. There is hope, he believes, that this spread of infection may bring its own antidote. In settled communities where the disease has long been endemic, tuberculosis tends to exhibit chronic rather than acute types among adults. This helps individuals withstand industrial stress without undue risk of breakdown and to show a steady fall in death rates under relatively prosperous and stable conditions of life.

Matthews[36] says of tuberculosis in the Africans of Zanzibar that, in spite of the elimination of susceptibles, which must have been going on for at least two or three generations, the present permanent population of Africans has no degree of immunity. Possibly continued incursions of fresh stock into their ranks and their poor nutrition are to blame. They appear to be less susceptible than Africans from the mainland, but, when they do fall ill, the disease of those in the towns is almost as acute. Transient Africans who are temporarily in Zanzibar from the mainland have less resistance to tuberculosis than any other section of the population.

In Tanganyika a few of the cases are acute, resembling those in virgin soil. However, the majority seem to be of a nature halfway between such acutely rapid cases and the chronic cases as commonly seen in Europe, and the prognosis is usually bad.[37] In eleven autopsies of natives dying of tuberculosis, six had miliary infection. The tuberculous lesions in these autopsies were not very fibrous, nor was fibrous tissue seen to any extent in the walls of cavities. In one case distinct hard fibrosis was seen, the lesion being apparently healed. There was one instance of calcification in the lung.

According to Burrows,[38] the glandular and subsequent fulminating types of tuberculosis as described by Borrel among the Senegalese were not observed among the Dinkas of Bahr el Ghazal. The disease appears to present the more defined and localized pulmonary and nonpulmonary types. Many chronic cases with a history of five years or more have been observed. Of 145 cases of tuberculosis which have been followed, 57, or 39.3 per cent, have proved fatal, the average length of the history being three years.

[36] *Tubercle*, 16:(suppl.), 48, 1935.

[37] Wilcocks, *Tubercle*, 16:(suppl.), 31, 1935.   [38] *Tubercle*, 16:(suppl.), 16, 1935.

Kahn[39] made an interesting study of an isolated group of Bush Negroes in Dutch Guiana. These people were originally transported from West Africa to the West Indies as slaves and were then taken to the northern part of South America, where they rebelled against their Dutch owners. After a long series of bloody conflicts, a peace treaty was signed in 1760. Today this group of Bush people lives in the wildest and most inaccessible part of Dutch Guiana and have reverted to the customs of their forebears in the forest of West Africa. They have the same blood as many North American Negroes. Kahn believes that as a result of their contact with white people during slavery they must have been infected with tuberculosis, but his survey with tuberculin gives little evidence at present of a widespread infection. He tested 765 individuals with PPD and found 18 who gave positive reactions. All of them belonged to the same family group and lived clustered together within a single village. None of the 18 gave a history of symptoms of tuberculosis except one man who had a cough and a bloody sputum which contained many tubercle bacilli. This person, having spent two years at a distant trading post, was the only one who had been away from the village for any length of time. Apparently, within five months after his return he had infected the others of his family. Kahn questions the theory of susceptibility of Negroes to tuberculosis on the basis of these observations and is more inclined to accept environment as the more powerful factor.

IN AMERICAN NEGROES

In the United States the Negro is so integrated with the population and is so thoroughly a part of the American civilization that his tuberculosis is more like the prevailing type than that which is described in the racially related Africans. Yet there are demonstrable differences and characteristic attributes that are believed to be directly traceable to the American Negro's African heritage. To these are to be added the effects of his present milieu. The proper evaluation of all the factors that may affect tuberculosis among colored people in the United States is diffi-

[39] *Am. Rev. Tuberc.*, 35:36, 1937.

cult. Conservative writers are hesitant to make dogmatic statements. They insist on caution pending the time when more facts are available. Then some of the explanations may become more tenable.

In view of the manifestations of tuberculosis in African natives described above, it is difficult to accept the theory that the disease in American Negroes did not become a serious problem until after the war of the rebellion. There are many writers who claim that slaves had a very low rate of death from tuberculosis and a long span of life as the result of an orderliness of existence, good food, clean living quarters, and adequate medical care. They say further that the disorganization and maladjustment coincident with independence produced hunger, poverty, and insanitary living conditions and marked the beginning of tuberculosis in Negroes in a severe and widespread form.

While there are no mortality statistics as we know them to show the actual facts, several authors deny the above views principally on the basis of their unreasonableness. Slaves were brought to America from a considerable area of Africa, which included the interior as well as coastal regions. It is quite probable that many of them had never before been in contact with foreign people and with tuberculosis. In the new country there must have been multiple opportunities for infection, especially after such debilitating experiences as were associated with the notorious slave ships, the new climate, the breaking-in process on plantations, and the unaccustomed hard labor over long hours. These conditions are analogous to those of the Senegalese soldiers taken to France or of the Bantus recruited into the Rand mines. There is every reason to believe that there was an analogous high rate among the American slaves of malignant tuberculosis such as occurs in virgin soil. Campbell[40] had this opinion, saying that tuberculosis during slavery was not rare among Negroes but was common and existed as acute miliary tuberculosis. It was called "Negro consumption," and often the whole slave population of a plantation was wiped out with the disease. Benjamin Rush made a number of observations on the

[40] *J. A. M. A.*, 27:1188, 1896.

prevalence and virulence of tuberculosis among slaves. He records an instance where several Negro servants were brought into a tuberculous New England family. All of them quickly contracted the disease and died from tuberculosis.

The difficulty in diagnosing the acute primary form of the disease as described by Borrel for the African Negroes is a factor which probably contributed to the opinion of the rarity of tuberculosis among slaves. Accustomed to seeing the chronic productive form of tuberculosis, the antebellum physician may not have recognized the disease in which the patient was apparently well until death was imminent and when the symptoms of a terminal generalized infection appeared.

The earliest accessible reliable records of tuberculosis are those of Charleston, South Carolina, a southern city with an old and large colored population. These records present a practically unbroken series of mortality statistics from 1822 to the present time. The figures show that tuberculosis was by no means a rare disease among Negroes before the Civil War but that it was approximately as common a cause of death among them as it was among the whites. Reyburn,[41] an army physician, examined 7,849 Negro refugees in the District of Columbia and found 290 cases of tuberculosis during the last few months of 1865.

There may be speculation about tuberculosis in the Negro before his emancipation, but there is no question about it afterwards. There are enough statistics, incomplete as they are, to be reasonably sure of the status and trends of the disease from immediately after the Civil War until the present.

Since the Registration Area did not include the whole United States until 1933, the accepted mortality of the Negro was derived by a generalization from data obtained in isolated states and cities with large Negro populations. The original Registration Area, organized in 1900, contained only a small part of the Negro population. In 1915, with the added states and cities, it included only 30 per cent of all colored people. By 1920, however, with the inclusion of Florida, Kentucky, Louisiana, Maryland, Mississippi, North Carolina, Tennessee, and Virginia—states in which a large number of colored people lived—fairly representative mortality statistics were obtainable. Georgia was added in 1922, Alabama in 1925, Arkansas in 1928, and Texas in 1935, which, together with the possessions, included all the United States. Prior to 1933 many areas did not report Negro and white deaths separately. This was a further hindrance to completeness of Negro statistics.

In Charleston, South Carolina, during the period 1822–30, the death rate from tuberculosis was approximately the same in Negroes and whites—in the neighborhood of 450 per 100,000. Likewise, in 1831–40 and in 1841–48 it was the same for the two races but had been reduced during the former period to about 325 per 100,000 and during the latter period to about 260 per 100,000. However, in 1865–74 the Negro mortality was twice that of the white, owing to an increase in the Negro death rate and a decrease in the white death rate. Subsequently the Negro rate continued to rise, while the white rate remained the same, so that in 1900 the Negro rate was about 675 per 100,000, the highest reached there; the white rate at the same time being 200 per 100,000, a ratio of approximately 3.4:1. In the District of Columbia the highest Negro rate—696 per 100,000—was in 1880–84, when the white rate was 317. The maximum recorded tuberculosis death rate in Baltimore, Maryland, is 633 per 100,000, which occurred in 1876–80, the white rate for this period being 299.

It is apparently true, from these accounts, that the death rate of colored people reached its maximum figure in the 1880's, amounting certainly to between 600 and 700 per 100,000 and probably to 900 per 100,000. Immediately after the war, in a disrupted, disorganized South, it was difficult for both whites and Negroes to obtain gainful occupations. The general sufferings of reconstruction days hit the colored people in their most vulnerable spot—their susceptibility to tuberculosis. From the time of these high mortality figures to the present time there has been a remarkable decline in deaths from tuberculosis among Negroes. While the curve of mortality showing this decrease roughly parallels the decline of the curve for whites, there is actually a slight lag in the fall of the colored curve, so that at each year a small increment of increase is added to the breach between the mortality rates of the two races. It has been predicted that this breach will continue to increase until the white mortality curve begins to flatten out as the disease approaches extinction, at which time the colored rates will make greater relative changes.

Prior to about 1925 tuberculosis was the leading cause of death among Negroes. Since then it has been exceeded by heart disease. In white people tuberculosis now stands in sixth place among diseases, being exceeded by heart disease, cancer, nephritis, cerebral hemorrhage, and pneumonia.

The general average death rate in 1934 for Negroes in the United States was 146.4 per 100,000 as compared to 45.1 per 100,000 for whites, the ratio between the two being 3.2:1. There is a considerable variation in the mortality rate of Negroes from state to state and city to city, much more than is the variation of the white rate between the same localities.

The Negro mortality in the northern states[42] was 232.0 per 100,000 in 1934, and in the southern states[43] it was 129.6 per 100,000. This excess of northern mortality over southern mortality is the reverse of what was found among the whites. They had a death rate of 44.0 per 100,000 in the North and 50.1 per 100,000 in the South. Negro tuberculosis is 2.6 times that of the whites in the South but is 5.3 times in the North. The Negro rate has declined more in the South, while among whites the greater decline was in the North. During the period from 1920 to 1933 the rate for colored people decreased 43.5 per cent in the South and 32.6 per cent in the North. Among white people it decreased 56.3 per cent in the North during the same period and 48.9 per cent in the South.

[42] Maine, New Hampshire, Vermont, Massachusetts, Rhode Island, Connecticut, New York, New Jersey, Pennsylvania, Ohio, Indiana, Michigan, Wisconsin, Minnesota, Iowa, Missouri, North Dakota, South Dakota, Nebraska, and Kansas.

[43] Delaware, Maryland, District of Columbia, Virginia, West Virginia, North Carolina, South Carolina, Georgia, Florida, Kentucky, Tennessee, Alabama, Mississippi, Arkansas, Louisiana, Oklahoma, and Texas.

Of the cities, Cincinnati, Ohio, Buffalo, New York, Washington, D.C., and Little Rock, Arkansas, are among those with the highest rates, and Leavenworth, Kansas, Knoxville, Tennessee, Springfield, Ohio, and Monroe, Louisiana, are among those with the lowest.

The amount of difference between the colored and white death rates in various states may vary widely. In Kentucky the Negro rate is only 1.1 times the white rate, while in several northern states it is more than five times greater. There may be several factors to account for this, among which are variations in the accuracy of registrations of tuberculosis deaths and differences between the states in the number of large cities.

Lumsden,[44] in attempting to account for the unequal geographical distribution of tuberculosis in the United States, says that besides poverty, crowding, poor general living conditions—housing, diet, occupation, and social habits—average seasonal temperature, altitude, and frequency and amount of spread of tuberculous infection through personal association, there are factors of as yet unknown nature which influence importantly the regional and racial distribution of tuberculosis mortality in the United States.

The sex and age curves of tuberculosis in Negroes depart from those for whites in several respects. All such curves for the former are on a higher level than any of those of the latter. In both races the average male death rate for all ages exceeds that of females, but the difference between the sexes is less in the Negro than in the whites. The Negro female rate for all ages in 1930 was 95 per cent of the Negro male rate, while the white female rate was 81 per cent of the white male rate. Taken by age groups the female death rates in both races exceeded the male rates at the earlier ages. Later the male rates assumed the ascendancy, beginning with the twenty-to-twenty-four-year group among the colored and with the twenty-five-to-twenty-nine-year group among the whites. A striking feature of sex-age curves for Negroes was the sudden rise in deaths beginning with the ten-to-fourteen-year groups and reaching a maximum

[44] *U.S. Pub. Health Service Bull.*, No. 225, 1936.

among the females with the twenty-to-twenty-four-year group and among the males with the twenty-five-to-twenty-nine-year group. After these maximums there was an almost as sharp decline in deaths among the older age groups, which continued through the sixty-to-sixty-four-year group. After this there was a secondary rise in the sixty-five-to-seventy-year group and a fall in the still older groups. There was a similar rise in the white lower-age groups but not so sudden or so high. The rise continued among the males until the seventy-to-seventy-four-year group, after which there was a slight fall. The white female curve reached a maximum with the twenty-to-twenty-four-year group, remained stationary through the twenty-five-to-twenty-nine-year group, and slowly fell until the forty-five-to-forty-nine-year group, after which it continued to rise throughout the older ages. In 1930 the average white female death rate at all ages was 49.9 per 100,000 and the colored, 188.1, a ratio of approximately 1:3.2. The white female rate for ages twenty-to-twenty-four was 82.4, and the colored female rate for the same ages was 334.1, over four times the white. Thus it seems that much of the excess of the Negro tuberculosis rate over that of the white is to be accounted for by the high mortality of young colored girls, although some of the excess is distributed over the young age groups of both sexes.[45]

The greatest decline in tuberculosis among Negroes has been, at least for the southern states, in the age groups zero to four and five to nine, while among whites the decline was greatest among the age groups ten to fourteen and fifteen to nineteen. For the decennium 1922–32, the decline in each age group was greater among the whites than in the Negroes, except in the group five to nine.

A very obvious fact, then, about tuberculosis in Negroes is expressed by a mortality rate which is, on an average, three to four times that of white people. In addition there are corollary facts which may explain the excessive death rate but which are

[45] Whitney, *Facts and figures about tuberculosis* (New York: National Tuberculosis Association, 1931); Sydenstricker, *Nat. Tuberc. A. Tr.*, 25:262, 1929; Weiner, *Med. J. & Rec.*, 136:26, 1922; Donnelly, *Am. Rev. Tuberc.*, 31:429, 1935.

of themselves interesting and distinctive phenomena. These additional attributes may be best described in their relation to the accepted concept of the natural history of tuberculosis as it exists in our community. The following facts are pertinent: Individuals living in an environment where tuberculosis is endemic are exposed to the possibility of infection in proportion to their opportunity for contact with living cases of the disease. Under ordinary circumstances this opportunity is directly related to the age of the individual and to the density of the population. Adults are more often infected than infants, and residents of cities are more often infected than those of rural areas. Infection may occur at an earlier age and with the same facility in sparsely as in densely populated communities as a result of more direct contact with living cases of tuberculosis, such as occurs within a household or under other conditions of intimacy. The first introduction of live pathogenic organisms into the body—called the primary, initial, or childhood infection—is usually an innocuous event and, under average circumstances, produces no symptoms. But it does produce organic changes that may be identified both in their early and in their late stages. If the number of organisms is great and their virulence is unusually high, or if infection occurs at a very early stage of infancy, this primary infection may produce actual disease which has definite clinical and pathological attributes. The primary infection brings about certain alterations in the defense mechanism of the body that are the basis of a type of reaction which follows the exposure of the tissues to tubercle bacilli or to products of their growth (tuberculin reaction). This changed reactivity is such that a second introduction of living pathogenic tubercle bacilli into the organism produces specific systemic and local reactions that are at one and the same time the cause of disease and a process which tends to heal the lesions. The ultimate outcome of this secondary reinfection, or adult tuberculosis—which is of a type that may be identified clinically and pathologically—depends on many factors but chiefly on the size and virulence of the reinfecting dose of organisms and on what has been broadly termed the "resistance of the host."

A review of the American literature on tuberculosis in Negroes shows that the discussions have been chiefly on the following aspects of the subject:

1. The distribution of infection as determined by surveys using tuberculin
   tests and roentgenological technics
2. The frequency of the association of primary disease with primary infection
3. The nature of the tuberculin reaction as compared with that in other
   people
4. The conditions which bring about differences in frequency of first as well
   as of second infections
5. The clinical characteristics of active tuberculosis as indicators of resistance
   or susceptibility
6. The nature of the pathological changes associated with the disease
7. The comparative effect of the different forms of treatment
8. The causes of differences between Negroes and other races in respect to
   the manifestations of tuberculosis

Surveys of population groups with tuberculin and x-ray have
been made in sufficient numbers to show fairly adequately the
comparative frequency of infection among Negroes and whites.
In general, the difference between the two races has not been
significant. In most cases the Negro rate has been slightly higher than that of whites, but the excess is not of the same order as
the excess of Negro deaths over white deaths.

In New York City, Asserson[46] found that 11.6 per cent of colored infants under two years of age gave positive tuberculin reactions, while 12.2 per cent of white infants of the same ages
gave positive tests. When compared with infants of various
nationalities, it was found that those of Irish parents were infected at the rate of 15.6 per cent, those of Italian parents 12.3
per cent, those of Jewish parents 12.7 per cent, while infants of
native American descent gave a rate of 11.4 per cent. Drolet[47]
assembled the data from various clinics in New York City on the
results of tuberculin tests made on 1,682 colored children under
fifteen years of age and 3,721 white children of the same age.
The colored children gave 47.5 per cent positive reactions and
the white 52.1 per cent. Although there was this small difference in the amount of infection, and in favor of the colored chil-

[46] *Am. Rev. Tuberc.*, 16:359, 1927.   [47] *Am. Rev. Tuberc.*, 30:1, 1934.

dren, the mortality of the latter from tuberculosis was ten times that of the white.

A very extensive study of tuberculosis among the school children of Philadelphia was made by Hetherington, McPhedran, Landis, and Opie.[48] They made tuberculin tests on 4,107 children—1,507 colored and 2,600 white—and x-ray chest examinations of those who reacted positively. Positive reactions were found in 72.9 per cent of the colored children and in 73.9 per cent of the white children, but manifest tuberculosis, discovered by x-ray, occurred approximately four times as frequently in the colored. Latent apical tuberculosis, latent infiltration in the lungs (childhood type), and calcified foci in lymph nodes and lungs were slightly less in the colored.

Aronson[49] made a survey among white and colored school children of Gibson County, Tennessee, white and colored children and colored adults of Lake County, Tennessee, and among colored and white families on plantations in Sunflower County, Mississippi. A larger number of colored children (60.4 per cent) than white children (50.9 per cent) between the ages of five and fifteen years were found to react to 0.01 mg. old tuberculin, and, likewise, more Negro adults (91.2 per cent) reacted than white adults (78.8 per cent). A comparison made of these findings with those of Opie et al. in Philadelphia discloses that the rate of infection is higher in this northern city than in the southern communities. While the Negro rate in Philadelphia is less than the whites there, the reverse is true in the South. Another survey by Aronson[50] in rural communities in Alabama, Florida, and South Carolina also showed a higher percentage of positive reactions among colored. The rate was not only greater than in Philadelphia but was also greater than that in the Tennessee and Mississippi areas. It is noteworthy that the colored people reacted to tuberculin much more intensively, not only qualitatively but also quantitatively. The skin-reaction areas were larger and quite frequently were so intense as to resemble cellulitis. These differences between the nature of the tuberculin re-

[48] *Am. Rev. Tuberc.*, 20:421, 1929.

[49] *Am. J. Hyg.*, 14:374, 1931.   [50] *Am. Rev. Tuberc.*, 28:617, 1933.

action in white and colored were elicited with the smaller doses (0.01 mg.) of tuberculin. With the large dose (1.0 mg.) there was no appreciable difference either in the number who reacted or in the degree of reaction.

The contagiousness of tuberculosis is illustrated by Aronson's comparison of residents on three different plantations in the same county. The corresponding three colored rates of tuberculin reactions were 74.3, 74.2, and 54.7 per cent. Among a white group the rate was 54.8 per cent. The two colored groups with the higher rates had among each a known case of manifest tuberculosis. The group with the low rate harbored no such case, and its rate is practically identical with the white group.

Logie[51] found in Florida that 41.6 per cent of the Negroes and 29.5 per cent of the whites reacted to PPD. A comparison by age groups with Negroes in Alabama showed that in each age group the Florida Negroes gave higher rates of reaction.

In a study of the peculiar tuberculosis problems of Tennessee, Crabtree, Hickerson, and Hickerson[52] made a survey of practically the entire colored population of Kingsport, Tennessee, an industrial town in Sullivan County. Among the 525 tested, 67.4 per cent gave positive reactions to 1.0 mg. old tuberculin. No comparative figure is given for a similar group of whites, but the rates for children are compared in the two races. At each age group the percentage of positive reactions is lower in the colored than in the whites at Kingsport and are also lower than Aronson found in Gibson County and Opie et al.[53] found in Philadelphia. A history of household contact with tuberculosis was given by 27.6 per cent of the 525 people and a history of contact with a manifest case by 20.4 per cent. Of those who had contact with manifest tuberculosis, 73.6 per cent gave positive tuberculin reactions, and of those with no known contact 66.7 per cent gave positive reactions. Peculiarly, those with a history of contact with latent apical tuberculosis gave less reactions than those with no known contact. Tuberculosis in any form—mani-

---

[51] Am. Rev. Tuberc., 39:408, 1939.

[52] Am. Rev. Tuberc., 28:(suppl.), 1-31, 1933.   [53] Am. Rev. Tuberc., 20:421, 1929.

fest, latent, or healed—was much more prevalent in the positive reactors than in the negative reactors. Of the whole group, 5.8 per cent showed either manifest or latent apical tuberculosis, 66.0 per cent showed x-ray evidence of infection without clinical tuberculosis, while 28.2 per cent showed negative tuberculin reactions and no x-ray lesions.

In Williamson County, Tennessee, Gass, Gauld, Harrison, Stewart, and Williams[54] found that 51.8 per cent of the colored and 44.5 per cent of the white school children gave positive tuberculin reactions, although the difference might well be accounted for by the difference in age distribution.

Among 10,232 persons examined by x-ray in Harlem, New York, Barnard[55] found that 2.2 per cent had definite tuberculosis, 4.9 per cent were suspected of having the disease, and 5.2 per cent had healed lesions. In contrast, 976 whites in Brooklyn showed 3.3 per cent definite tuberculosis, 0.9 per cent were suspected, and 5.5 per cent had healed lesions. The Harlem group showed a total of 12.3 per cent infection and that of Brooklyn, 9.8 per cent. Later, Edwards[56] made in Harlem an x-ray survey of 46,625 Negroes and 12,187 whites, all of whom were on home relief and were apparently healthy. Although the mortality from tuberculosis among Negroes was five times that among the whites in this district, the prevalence of chronic pulmonary tuberculosis as determined in the survey was only 3.6 per cent among the colored, while it was 6.1 per cent among the whites. Edwards suggested several factors that might account for these facts, the most important of which was probably the higher case fatality among Negroes, resulting in fewer living cases of pulmonary tuberculosis among them.

In a New York clinic dealing with infants, who, before two years of age, were shown by positive tuberculin reactions to be infected, Brailey[57] studied the type of infection and the mortality from tuberculosis. At one year and at five years after the discovery of infection the percentage of those who had died was

[54] Am. Rev. Tuberc., 38:441, 1938.   [56] Am. Rev. Tuberc., 41:(suppl.), 89, 1940.

[55] Am. J. Hyg., 24:8, 1934.   [57] Am. Rev. Tuberc., 36:347, 1937.

two times as great among the colored as among the white, and at eight years three times as many of the colored had died. Parenchymal primary lesions were found by x-ray in 35.2 per cent of the white infants and in 47.0 per cent of the colored. Among the colored children with such lesions 47.3 per cent had died within eight years, and 25.0 per cent of the white children had died within this time. The mortality from tuberculosis of the colored children was in excess of that of the white, even when there were no parenchymal lesions, the rate being 12.3 per cent as compared to 1.8 per cent. In 77 per cent of the white and 64 per cent of the colored there was intrafamilial contact with a proved sputum-positive case.

Cornely and Allen[58] summarized the results of tuberculin tests made of students in Negro colleges and found little difference between the rate of infection when compared with the results obtained among white college students.

There was no significant difference in the rate of tuberculin reactions among Negro and white school children in Chicago, the former showing 37.0 per cent and the latter 35.2 per cent positive reactions.[59] Bloch, Tucker, and Bryant[60] made fluoroscopic examinations of 9,000 Negroes of various ages in the outpatient clinic of Provident Hospital, Chicago. The incidence of clinically important tuberculosis in the whole group was 3.3 per cent, closely similar to the incidence found by Edwards[61] (3.6 per cent) with the fluoroscope among Negroes in New York City. Among the Chicago group were 1,000 individuals made up of high-school students and Boy Scouts and ranging in age from five to twenty-four years. The incidence of clinically important tuberculosis among these was 0.8 per cent. Including clinically important and unimportant forms of tuberculosis, the total rate of pulmonary disease for the entire 9,000 was 4.3 per cent. The incidence of clinically important tuberculosis (3.3 per cent) among the total of pathological changes (4.3 per cent)

---

[58] *Am. Rev. Tuberc.*, 37:549, 1938.

[59] Novack and Kruglick, *Am. Rev. Tuberc.*, 38:106, 1938.

[60] *J. A. M. A.*, 115:1866, 1940.　　　　　　[61] *Loc. cit.*; see n. 56.

was higher than in the white population, in which the respective figures were 1.2 and 3.5 per cent.

Over a period of nine years tuberculin tests were given to 172,000 white and 32,000 Negro school children of all ages in North Carolina, a very large proportion of both races being from rural districts. Of the whites, 14 per cent reacted positively, while 18 per cent of the colored gave positive reactions.[62] Approximately twice as large a percentage of the positive reactors among Negroes showed demonstrable lesions by x-ray as among whites. They also showed more numerous and more extensive childhood lesions, more caseous lymphatic lesions, and more frequent adult-type lesions. But there was also a large number which showed numerous, or tremendous calcified, presumably healed, lesions.

The entire adult Negro population, amounting to 1,232 individuals, of a small town in Illinois was examined by x-ray by Lindberg.[63] While the mortality of the Negroes was about three times that of the whites, their morbidity was only slightly higher. The tuberculosis discovered was of the productive rather than the exudative type. There was a calcium deposition within the parenchymal and lung-root fields in amount and number greater than among the whites, and in a large share of the Negroes there was a bilateral, apical, extensive fibrosis, indicative of a resistance to tuberculosis infection not unlike that found in the white race. There was a high percentage of parenchymal infection which had not resulted in manifest parenchymal disease. In a later study Lindberg[64] compared the amount and nature of tuberculosis in Negroes, in a white adult group on relief, and in white employed schoolteachers. The findings in the former two groups were almost identical, but both were significantly in excess of those in the employed skilled labor group, thus indicating the role of economic status in morbidity.

Various PPD surveys made in thirty-one states and summarized by Whitney and McCaffrey[65] are of interest because of the

[62] McCain, *Am. Rev. Tuberc.*, **35**:24, 1937.   [64] *Am. Rev. Tuberc.*, **39**:666, 1939.

[63] *Ann. Int. Med.*, 8:1421, 1934–35.   [65] *Am. Rev. Tuberc.*, 35:597, 1937.

large and representative areas covered. The data include tests made on 41,493 whites and 7,823 Negroes during 1934–36. The percentage of positive reactions among whites, adjusted for age, as averaged from all tests was 46.5 per cent. The average Negro rate, similarly adjusted, was 47.8 per cent. The Negro infection rates were higher than the white rates in almost every age group up to twenty years and over, where the white rate was higher. The trend of infection among the Negroes tested increased with age up to age twenty at an average of 0.5 per cent for every year of life as compared with an average increase of 1.0 per cent for every year of life among white persons. A previous report by Whitney and McCaffrey[66] on a similar survey with tuberculin MA-100 in eighteen states showed that among 906 colored persons tested 38.4 per cent gave positive reactions, while 24.8 per cent of 10,876 white persons gave positive reactions. The percentage of positive reactors among whites during the first four years of life was higher than that in the colored group. During the fifth year of life and at each age thereafter, with few exceptions, the proportion of positive reactors to MA-100 was considerably greater among the colored tested than among the whites.

Members of the Henry Phipps Institute, which has long been concerned with problems of Negro tuberculosis, have, as a part of their general investigations on the epidemiology of tuberculosis, made studies on the character, frequency, and mode of spread of the disease in Negro families. Opie[67] pointed out that the healed childhood lesions of the lung as well as the chronic and latent forms of pulmonary tuberculosis were less frequent in the Negro than in white people but that acute miliary tuberculosis of the lymph nodes was more frequent. In explanation of this he was of the opinion that the American Negro is less tuberculized than is the white race and for the reason that the acute forms of tuberculosis are not adapted to scatter tubercle bacilli. The various tuberculin surveys cited above have shown, however, that the Negro is not only tuberculized but, in most instances, more so than are white people. Also the availability

[66] *Ibid.*, 33:78, 1936.   [67] *Am. Rev. Tuberc.*, 10:265, 1924; 22:603, 1930.

of bacilli for tuberculization is not lacking, since counts of organisms in the surface dust and clothing in the homes of colored
people and in the sputum of infected individuals show larger
numbers than are found under similar circumstances with
whites. While data may show acute cases of tuberculosis
more common among Negroes, the occurrence of long-lasting
open cases is not precluded. In addition, the short life of acute
cases, with its limiting action on the spread of the disease, is
compensated for by a larger number so that the germ-scattering
effect is just as effective.

McPhedran and Opie[68] compared tuberculin tests and the results of roentgenological examinations of Negro families in
which there were cases of tuberculosis with tubercle bacilli in
the sputum, those with no tubercle bacilli in the sputum, those
in which there was suspected tuberculosis, and those in which
there was no tuberculosis. The most significant difference between these families was in the percentage of those infected in
the earlier years of life. By the fifteenth year of life practically
100 per cent of the members of the families were infected in the
homes where there was tuberculosis, whether the sputum of the
diseased individuals contained tubercle bacilli or whether the
disease was suspected or actual. Members of families with no
tuberculosis were also infected, but in a smaller percentage, until the fiftieth year, when all individuals were infected. As far
as the data permit comparison the figures concerning all except
members of families with no tuberculosis closely resembled those
for white families under similar conditions. In Negro families
with no family exposure to tuberculosis the number who reacted
to tuberculin in the age period zero to four years is less than the
whites, but at the age period five to twenty-nine years the number is more. In subsequent years it is less. The number of lesions demonstrable by x-ray in Negro families exposed to tuberculosis is slightly greater than in similar white families, but the
two races differ markedly in the nature of the lesions. Manifest
lesions of the childhood type, indicating failure of the childhood
infections to heal, were more frequent in the Negroes, while cal-

[68] *Am. J. Hyg.*, 23:494, 1936.

cified nodules in the lungs and lymph glands were less. While tuberculosis of the childhood type is seldom recognized in white adults, it is not uncommon in colored persons of the same age. The incidence of manifest tuberculosis of the adult type is about the same in the two races, but latent apical tuberculosis is much less frequent in Negroes. No tuberculosis was found in Negroes giving negative tuberculin reactions, while tuberculous lesions (calcified) were found in 5 per cent of the whites who reacted negatively to 1 mg. of tuberculin. In Negroes who reacted to 0.1 or 0.01 mg. of tuberculin, 40–47 per cent had demonstrable lesions, and 21.1–35.5 per cent had infiltrating lesions. In whites who reacted to 0.1 or 0.01 mg. tuberculin, 41.5–68.7 per cent had lesions, and 25–57.4 per cent had infiltrating lesions. The mortality of Negroes from tuberculosis, like morbidity, rises following household exposure to the disease and far exceeds that of the general Negro population. The excess is present at each age. Since an increased death rate following exposure occurs after fifteen years of age, the disease is regarded as the result of an exogenous infection and not one acquired in childhood.

Wells and Smith[69] and Flahiff[70] studied tuberculosis as it existed among the Negroes of Jamaica, who live under circumstances quite different from those of the Negroes of America. In 1930 Opie and Isaacs[71] called attention to some of the features of the disease on this island, particularly to its high prevalence, its rapidly fatal course, the large number of tubercle bacilli eliminated in the sputum, the anatomical characteristics of the disease,[72] and the nature of the living conditions which were so conducive to its spread. Wells and Smith made tuberculin tests of 5,554 individuals in Kingston, the capital of Jamaica. These people were divided into four groups according to their location in the city, but also representing four different economic and social groups. They were, in addition, classified according to color and designated as black, dark brown, and

[69] *Am. Rev. Tuberc.*, 34:43, 1936; 37:625, 1938.

[70] *Am. Rev. Tuberc.*, 37:560, 1938.   [71] *Am. J. Hyg.*, 12:1, 1930.

[72] Opie, *Am. Rev. Tuberc.*, 10:265, 1924; 22:603, 1930.

light brown. The greatest factor in affecting the rate of infection was the amount of contact with active cases of tuberculosis.
Where there was the greatest crowding (largest number per
room) and where there was at the time of testing a case of tuberculosis in the household, the number of positive reactions was
the highest. There was no definite relation of positive reactions
to color, although there was a slight downward trend of the percentages of positive tests from the blacks to the light browns.
The blacks showed 84.4 per cent positive reactions, the dark
browns 81.3 per cent, and the light browns 79.5 per cent. The
desirability of the living conditions, however, decreased in the
same way that these figures increased. Wells and Smith were
led to doubt if the white race possesses any inherent quality, inherited or acquired, which when mixed with other races may influence the effect of tuberculous infection in so far as such information is recorded through the tuberculin reaction. They
compared their results with those of Opie *et al.* in Philadelphia
and found that the infection rate of those having contact with
tuberculosis in Philadelphia was higher than those with a similar
history in Kingston. The infection rate of those with no contacts was higher in Kingston than in Philadelphia. In the cities,
towns, and rural areas of the remainder of Jamaica there was no
difference in infection or disease among those of different color
or of different sex. In the large towns the infection rate was
71.8 per cent, in the small towns it was 58.1 per cent, and in the
rural areas it was 47.1 per cent. In Kingston manifest tuberculosis was found in 1.4–1.87 per cent of the population in the poor-
est districts, in 0.95 per cent of those in the intermediate districts, and 0.5 per cent in the prosperous districts. Latent apical
tuberculosis was most prevalent in the prosperous areas and
least in the poor ones. Latent childhood infection was least in
the prosperous and most in the poor districts. In the large and
small towns manifest tuberculosis was of about the same prevalence—1.4 per cent of the population—while in the rural areas
it was 0.5 per cent. Latent infections were about the same—
3–6 per cent—in the towns and rural areas.

It has often been pointed out that the course of tuberculosis in American Negroes is much more rapid than it is in white persons. Brock[73] found in his experience that the duration of the disease in colored patients averaged 4 months, while in whites it averaged 10 months. Rogers[74] reported that for 75 Negroes the average duration of fatal tuberculosis was 1 year and 1 month. For 75 whites it was 1 year and 6 months. Pinner and Casper[75] found the disease fatal for 47 Negroes with an average of 324 days, while for 96 whites they found it fatal on an average of 995 days. McPhedran and Opie have called attention to the rapid character of the disease in some Negro families. The whole course from onset to fatal termination sometimes lasted only 4 months, with several members of a family passing from health to fatal issue within the period of a year. The common and characteristic picture of tuberculosis in the Negro is that described by Ornstein[76] who says the disease is primarily an acute exudative infiltration of the lungs with caseous pneumonia. Necrosis and destruction of the pulmonary tissue occur rapidly, and the necrotic tissue is quickly expectorated, leaving in its place multiple cavities which quickly merge into single or multiple large cavities. These cavities act as excellent culture flasks for the growth and rapid multiplication of tubercle bacilli, and the sputum becomes heavily laden with the organisms. The formation of cavities in the lungs, with the accompanying propagation of tubercle bacilli, makes these patients a constant threat to themselves and also to their contacts. Unfortunately, after the patients have expectorated their necrotic lung tissue, they lose their toxemia and feel much improved. The temperature frequently subsides, their appetites pick up, strength returns, and they are led to believe that they have overcome the disease. Weight is often added very rapidly during this period.

Another study of the type of clinical disease in Negroes was made by Israel and Payne,[77] who compared the clinical course and x-ray findings over a period of five and one-half years of Negro and white adults diagnosed as having tuberculosis at the

[73] *Am. Rev. Tuberc.*, 28:767, 1933.

[74] *Am. Rev. Tuberc.*, 4:669, 1921.

[75] *Am. Rev. Tuberc.*, 26:463, 1932.

[76] *J. Negro Educ.*, 6:303, 1937.

[77] *Am. Rev. Tuberc.*, 41:188, 1940.

Henry Phipps Institute. Contrary to the usual reports in the literature, racial differences in the extent of disease at the time of diagnosis were relatively slight, but the lesions in two-thirds of the Negro patients appeared exudative in character. In the majority of white patients lesions were predominantly proliferative or fibrotic. The type of symptoms the patients described and the duration of illness prior to diagnosis were correlated with type of disease rather than with race. Negroes gave accurate histories of their illness, and the reason they were more often found with advanced disease was not because of negligence, but because their lesions were more acute in evolution. The authors point out that there was no correlation between length of illness and extent of disease, and early diagnosis does not insure detection of minimal lesions. They show that death from tuberculosis occurred more frequently and more rapidly among Negro patients than among white patients with similar lesions, although they state that prognosis of the individual patient appeared to depend more upon the type of infiltration present than upon his race. Acute miliary tuberculosis was equally uncommon in both races. A small number of the Negro patients had tuberculosis with characteristics of childhood-type lesions, but no white patients had disease of this type. Negro patients reacted more strongly to tuberculin than did white patients with similar lesions, which was in agreement with other observers. Severe reactions were more common in patients with minimal disease. Weak reactions were more common in patients with advanced disease. The Negro patients less often gave a history of recent intimate contact with tuberculosis and had a lower incidence of calcified childhood lesions. Basal tuberculosis and complicating heart disease were more common in the Negro than in white patients. Differences between white and Negro patients in age and weight at the time of diagnosis, in incidence of tuberculous complications and of diabetes and in the results of sputum examination, were slight or inconstant.

While more Negroes suffer from the acute and rapidly fatal form of tuberculosis, it must not be inferred that the chronic apical pulmonary infections with fibrotic cavitation do not also occur. This is a fact that is not sufficiently emphasized in the literature. The result is that, unless one has had direct experience with many Negroes under widely varying circumstances, the impression is gained from the various publications that all Negro cases of tuberculosis are of the acute form and that all white cases are of the chronic phthisis type. According to reports, the high frequency of the acute fulminating form among African natives is obvious. Casual observation may distinguish the differences in behavior of tuberculosis in these people and in people of European stock. But in America the difference between Negroes and Caucasians is not so easily seen but is usually determined statistically and with the aid of careful x-ray, physical, and post-mortem examinations. Interesting in this respect are the observations of Ulmar, Ornstein, and Epstein[78] at the Sea View Hospital for tuberculosis in New York, where the majority of the nurses are colored, as well as many of the patients. They found the character of the disease in the nurses, which is looked upon as an occupational disease, markedly different from that occurring among the Negro patients. The lesions were usually minimal and consisted of the small nodules of the acinous-nodose variety described by Aschoff,[79] or the chronic productive form, or the small subapical exudates which rapidly resolve. Even those cases which were caseous and broke down with cavity formation simulated the "isolated phthisis" of whites described by Pinner and Casper.[80] Here is a large group of adult colored females who did not show the characteristics believed to be typical of tuberculosis in Negroes.

It is difficult to estimate the case fatality and average duration of fatal tuberculosis for several reasons. People vary in their sensitivity and knowledge about the early symptoms of the disease. Ofttimes many do not seek medical advice until their condition is far advanced, and it frequently happens that cases of tuberculosis are discovered only by accident, as the re-

[78] *Quart. Bull., Sea View Hosp.*, 2:49, 1936; *J. Negro Educ.*, 6:303, 1937.

[79] *Lectures on pathology* (New York: Hoeber, 1924), p. 55.

[80] *Loc. cit.*; see n. 75.

sult of a routine physical examination. Moreover, physicians do not always agree as to what constitutes an active or a latent infection. There is also a wide variation in different localities and among physicians in the promptness with which definitely recognized cases of tuberculosis are reported. Then, too, most of the published data concerning the clinical as well as other features of the disease issue from tuberculosis institutions where there is a large selective factor applying to the patients.

According to the Framingham standards, it is recognized that for every annual death from tuberculosis there are eight living cases of the disease. This ratio had been challenged, and proportions of six and seven active cases have been suggested. There is an agreement, however, that for Negroes the ratio of annual deaths to living cases is much smaller than it is for whites, being estimated as from two to four cases per annual death, the reason for this being that the duration of disease before termination in death is much less. Roth[81] obtained from army statistics a white ratio of one annual death to 8.75 living cases, a close approximation to the Framingham standard. Under the same conditions he obtained a ratio for Negroes of 2.63 cases per annual death.

Mortality, case fatality, and duration of fatal cases are closely connected with treatment, particularly with the facilities and methods for treatment, the stage of the disease at which treatment is begun, and the ability to respond.

It is well known that the number of hospital and sanitorium beds available for colored patients is woefully insufficient. Adequate hospitalization requires at least one bed for each annual tuberculosis death. In the report of the Committee on Tuberculosis among Negroes[82] it is shown that in 1934 there were 21,099 Negro deaths from tuberculosis in the United States, while there were only 3,334 beds for colored tuberculous patients. In 13 southern states, where 75 per cent of the Negroes live, there were 11,385 Negro tuberculous deaths, indicating a require-

[81] Am. Rev. Tuberc., 38:197, 1938.

[82] A five year study and what it has accomplished (New York: National Tuberculosis Association, 1937).

ment of the same number of beds for treatment, while there were actually only 1,666 beds. There is an even greater deficiency in the North, where beds are seldom set aside for Negroes, and other races are given preference for available beds.

Since early diagnosis and treatment are of prime importance in the prognosis of tuberculosis, and since the seriousness of the disease among Negroes demands all the advantages which can be brought to bear, many writers deplore the fact that so often colored patients are first seen only in the late stages of the disease, when there is less likelihood of desirable results. Several explanations have been offered for this delay in recognition of tuberculosis in Negroes. First is probably the lack of adequate case-finding programs among colored people.[83] Second, as shown by Israel and Payne, is the suddenness of onset which characterizes the disease in many Negroes. Third is the lack of an appreciation of the significance and seriousness of the early symptoms of tuberculosis. This is a characteristic common to the uneducated—white and colored—who make up the bulk of the dispensary class. Fourth is the psychological attitude of the Negro, which is primarily fear of disability. Finally the economic status of most of these people is such that an interruption of employment means complete indigency. The tendency is to work as long as they are physically able.

The various appraisals that have been made of the efficacy of the different forms of treatment have been handicapped because many of the cases studied were in far-advanced stages. At one time it was believed that once tuberculosis in a colored person was diagnosed the prognosis was hopeless. It is now known that prognosis depends on the stage at which the disease is discovered. When comparable stages in white and colored patients are compared, the effect of treatment is about the same.[84] This applies not only to the standard method of rest in bed but also to the different types of collapse therapy.[85]

[83] Bloch, *Am. Rev. Tuberc.*, 37:174, 1938.

[84] Bogen, *Am. Rev. Tuberc.*, 24:522, 1931.

[85] For discussions of treatment of tuberculosis in Negroes see Ballard, *J. Nat. M. A.*, 24:30, 1932; Brock, *op. cit.*, 24:436, 1931, 28: 767, 1933; Carter, *J. Outdoor Life*, 19:9, 1922.

Discussions of the bearing syphilis has on the occurrence and prognosis of tuberculosis concerns Negroes because of the high frequency among them of both these diseases. Many of the reports of the mutual effects of syphilis and tuberculosis refer directly to experiences with colored people. There appear to be no definite conclusions as to whether syphilis adversely influences the course of tuberculosis or whether syphilis can without danger be adequately treated in the presence of active tuberculosis.[86]

Sicklemia, another condition found frequently in Negroes, apparently has no bearing on the occurrence of tuberculosis. Dolgopol and Stitt[87] found sicklemia in 5.2 per cent of colored patients with tuberculosis and in 6.5 per cent of colored persons without tuberculosis. A chronic anoxemia, owing to diseased lungs, apparently is not a factor in sicklemia.

Negroes have a characteristic distribution of blood groups,[88] but since there is no evidence of greater or less susceptibility to tuberculosis in individuals belonging to the different groups,[89] the blood-group index of Negroes is unrelated to their reaction to tuberculosis.

The role of monocytes and lymphocytes in tuberculosis led Brock and Black[90] to study these cells in the peripheral blood of Negroes with tuberculosis, especially those with the acute exudative form, which is more commonly seen than in whites. The monocyte was found to be constantly elevated above the normal level and showed no fluctuation above and below the normal line, as is the case in chronic progressive disease. This

1922; Chadwick, Markoe, and Thomas, *Am. Rev. Tuberc.*, 28:759, 1933; Cutler, Rodgers, and Cippes, *Am. Rev. Tuberc.*, 30:80, 1934; Donnelly, *South. Med. & Surg.*, 98:75, 1936; Gaines and Kellar, *Am. Rev. Tuberc.*, 28:779, 1933; Nash, *Dis. of Chest*, 2:24, 1936; Simington, *M. Bull. Vet. Admin.*, 11:29, 1934; Fisher, *Am. Rev. Tuberc.*, 35:62, 1937; Beatty, *Am. Rev. Tuberc.*, 32:41, 1935; Hruby, *Am. Rev. Tuberc.*, 40:255, 1939; Kettlekamp, Murphy, and Trumpe, *Am. Rev. Tuberc.*, 38:458, 1939.

[86] For discussions and literature see Guild and Nelson, *Am. Rev. Tuberc.*, 33:31, 1936; Padgett and Moore, *Am. Rev. Tuberc.*, 33:10, 1936; Warring, *Am. Rev. Tuberc.*, 40:175, 1939.

[87] *Am. Rev. Tuberc.*, 19:454, 1929.   [89] Sasano, *Am. Rev. Tuberc.*, 23:207, 1931.

[88] Cf. chap. iii, n. 7.   [90] *Am. Rev. Tuberc.*, 24:136, 1931.

indicates continuous spread, with no evidence of an arrested phase. Elevation of the lymphocytes in tuberculosis is definitely associated with the arrested phase and is a manifestation of the immunity process. It is believed that the lymphocyte acquires a qualitative change following continuous reinfection throughout the preadult period and thereby aids in preventing growth of bacilli in the body and also in causing their disintegration. Since the lymphocytes in the peripheral blood of Negroes with acute exudative tuberculosis is high in spite of any evidence of an arrested phase, it is suggested that in them the lymphocytes fail to acquire this qualitative change, owing to a possible lack of repeated infection in early life. The nature of this change is not discussed, nor is any evidence given that lymphocytes may undergo qualitative alterations.

Harrell[91] found the normal serum calcium 0.43 per cent lower in Negroes than in whites, whose average value is 10.5 mg. per 100 cc. of blood, the difference probably being accounted for by the Negro's diet and lack of exposure to sunlight. In tuberculosis the serum calcium in colored people is lowered to an average of 9.1 mg. per 100 cc. of blood, but no figure is given for serum calcium in white consumptives.

In order to find the difference between colored and white people in their reactions to tubercle bacilli under controlled conditions, Levine[92] inoculated 74 white, 38 Negro, and 24 Puerto Rican children with identical amounts of living attenuated bovine tubercle bacilli (BCG). Necrosis of the local lesion on the thigh occurred more rapidly in Negro children than in white. Inguinal abscesses developed in more children and more rapidly among Negroes and Puerto Ricans than among whites. When the effect of such variables as age, previous exposure to tubercle bacilli, economic status, and nutrition were taken into account, there still remained a racial factor that is related to the more severe reaction in Negroes and Puerto Ricans.

Several excellent pathological studies of necropsied material from tuberculous Negroes have been made. These have cor-

[91] *Am. Rev. Tuberc.*, 19:350, 1929.
[92] *Am. J. Dis. Child.*, 51:1052, 1936.

roborated and extended the information obtained clinically, although the significance of the data from necropsies is limited, because it concerns fatal tuberculosis and because the material is usually selected, having come from tuberculosis institutions. The tissue reactions, being the real basis of clinical phenomena, are of much more importance in revealing racial variations than are morbidity and mortality statistics, which may often be misleading in their implications. Probably the most extensive report is that of Pinner and Casper, who describe the lesions in 303 necropsies of colored and 219 necropsies of white patients dead of tuberculosis in charity institutions of Chicago and Detroit. The material was analyzed principally according to method of spread of the disease in the body, the presumption being that the amount and mechanism of spread are measures of resistance, since resistance tends to confine and localize lesions. There are four types of propagation recognized—lymphogenous, hematogenous, direct extension, and intracanalicular (along preformed natural channels). Since generalized miliary tuberculosis might be considered just a mechanical accident and not related to the defensive powers of the body, these cases were excluded, although attention is called to the fact that at every single decade of life there were at least 30 per cent more instances of miliary tuberculosis among the colored, except at the ages above fifty, when the difference was insignificant. Among the remaining cases hematogenous spread of the infection, as determined by gross lesions in distant organs, occurred over twice as often in Negroes as in whites (84.2 per cent as compared to 40.0 per cent), although in the first decade of life this type of spread occurred at the same rate in both races, and in the second decade there was only a small difference. The frequency of lymphatic metastases in Negroes, determined by gross lesions in lymph glands, was over six times that in whites (66.8 per cent as compared to 10.8 per cent), although during the first decade of life lymphatic spread in whites was double that in the colored. Both lymphatic and hematogenous metastases occurred in the same individual about eight times as frequently in Negroes as in whites. Practically all organs were much more often the seat of metastases in Negroes than in whites, the lymph nodes showing in this respect the greatest difference.

While lymph- and blood-borne metastases occurred both in Negroes and in whites, but with different frequencies, and while all types of lesions occurred in both races, but with different frequencies, there were some lesions which Pinner and Casper believed to be practically diagnostic of tuberculosis in Negroes, although these findings did not occur exclusively in them. They are (a) massive lymph-node caseation, (b) massive exudative lesions which do not respect the normal anatomical boundaries of organs, and (c) a type of generalized tuberculosis without the formation of miliary tubercles but with irregularly scattered nodular, exudative foci. A very important observation was the occurrence in Negroes of calcified lesions, representing healed primary infections, among lesions which appeared to be, and probably have been called by others, a childhood type of tuberculosis. But they represent to these authors a type of tuberculosis in persons of low resistance typical of Negroes, in which there are multiple completely caseated lymph nodes, with rapidly caseating pneumonia, or massive hematogenous and lymphogenous spread, including cases dying from generalized miliary tuberculosis.

The interpretation and significance given to these observations by Pinner and Casper will be discussed further on.

Everett[93] likewise found widely different anatomical characteristics of tuberculosis in Negroes and whites. He described a series of necropsies on 402 individuals, 172 of which were colored and 230 white. Pulmonary tuberculosis was the cause of death of 44 of the colored and 21 of the white persons, and tuberculous peritonitis caused the death of 2 of the colored. Among the remaining, there were 12 Negroes and 17 whites in whom no tuberculosis was found, and 187 whites and 109 Negroes in whom there were latent lesions. Of the 21 whites dying of tuberculosis, 2 showed the childhood type of disease and 19 the adult type, while among the 44 instances of fatal tuberculosis in Negroes, 22 were of the childhood type and 22 of the adult type. On the

93 *Am. Rev. Tuberc.*, 27:411, 1933.

basis of a racial comparison of the occurrence of tuberculous pneumonia, excavation and fibrous-tissue formation in both childhood and adult forms, Everett concluded that tuberculosis pursues a more rapidly fatal course in the Negro than in white people, that widespread tuberculous pneumonia with rapid excavation of the lung is more frequent, and that formation of fibrous tissue is less conspicuous in the colored than in the white. On the other hand, latent apical tuberculosis is found considerably less frequently in the Negro than in white adults. In more than half of the Negro adults (13 of 21) with childhood-type tuberculosis, the lesion had its origin in the apex of the lung. Of the 2 white cases of childhood-type tuberculosis, 1 arose in the apex and 1 at the base.

Rogers,[94] in a report of necropsy lesions in 75 colored and 75 white bodies dead of tuberculosis, says there was no essential difference in type or extent of pathological changes in the two series.

Opie[95] described the findings in two series of necropsies on Negroes, one in St. Louis and one in Jamaica, both of which were too small to give significant results.

In necropsies on 113 Negroes dying of tuberculosis in Jamaica, Wells[96] found 67.3 per cent of them were of the adult type and 32.7 per cent of the childhood type. The average age of the cases with childhood-type tuberculosis was 21.5 years and of those with adult type it was 32.4 years. The amount of fibrous-tissue reaction in the series of adult-type tuberculosis varied with the duration of the disease. In 32 of 76 cases fibrous-tissue formation predominated, in 35 instances fibrosis associated with caseous infiltration was found, and in 9 instances the pulmonary lesions were almost exclusively caseous. No comparisons were made of lesions found in the whites of Jamaica.

Rodriquez-Pastor[97] refers to the findings of Koppisch,[98] who observed that in Puerto Rico the anatomical characteristics of

[94] *Am. Rev. Tuberc.*, 4:669, 1921.

[95] *Op. cit.*, 10:265, 1924–25; 22:613, 1930.

[96] *Am. Rev. Tuberc.*, 39:796, 1939. [97] *Am. Rev. Tuberc.*, 35:13, 1937.

[98] *Puerto Rico J. Pub. Health & Trop. Med.*, 11:492, 1936.

the tuberculous lesions in the whites and mulattoes do not differ from those in well-tuberculized people, and the percentage incidence of lethal, subsidiary, and doubtful tuberculous lesions in Negroes was nearly the same as in whites and mulattoes, although the mortality of the colored was 13 per cent higher than the whites.

Fisher[99] is of the opinion that chronic fibrotic tuberculous lesions are now being seen more often in Negroes, although he is not certain but that the cause is that the better educational and field-work facilities have brought to the clinics some of the more chronic survivors. Long[100] calls attention to the variation among the hospitals of Philadelphia in the post-mortem findings of chronic tuberculosis among Negroes, which he attributes to the selection involved in obtaining permission for necropsy.

A few pathological studies of extrapulmonary tuberculous involvement among Negroes have been made. If the organs are arranged in the frequency of their involvement in white and colored necropsies reported by Pinner and Casper, the order is about the same for the two races, with a greater frequency of lesions in every organ among the colored. The skin was not involved in any of the white cases but was in 1.5 per cent of the colored. There is some indication that Boeck's sarcoid, affecting the skin as well as internal organs, occurs more frequently in Negroes.[101] The relation of sarcoidosis to tuberculosis is not clear, but the relative frequency in Negroes of this comparatively benign condition, with a low or absent hypersensitivity to tuberculin, is not in keeping with the usual expression of tuberculosis in these people. Some writers are of the opinion that sarcoid is a form of tuberculosis that does not caseate. Disintegration of the tissues and caseation is an outstanding feature of tuberculosis in Negroes.

Auerbach[102] found 45 instances of aneurysms of the pul-

[99] Loc. cit.; see n. 85.   [100] Op. cit., 35:1, 1937.

[101] For discussion and literature on Boeck's sarcoid in Negroes see Nomland, Arch. Dermat. & Syph., 30:59, 1934; Pinner, Am. Rev. Tuberc., 36:706, 1937, 37:690, 1938, 39:186, 1939; for discussion of relation of sarcoid to tuberculosis see Longcope, J. A. M. A., 117:1321, 1941.

[102] Am. Rev. Tuberc., 39:99, 1939.

monary artery, 11 of the cases being in Negroes and 34 in whites. This is a smaller proportion of Negroes than is indicated by the ratio of 3 Negroes to 5 whites in the hospital population. Since the aneurysms are associated with cavitation in chronic pulmonary tuberculosis, Auerbach believes that the lesser occurrence in Negroes is due to their more acute form of the disease.

Tuberculoma of the brain apparently occurs more often in Negroes.[103]

Flippin and Smith[104] indicated that Addison's disease caused by tuberculosis of the adrenals is not as rare among Negroes as formerly believed. The difficulty of recognizing the pathological pigmentation of Addison's disease in Negroes is probably the basis of the opinion of rarity in colored people.[105]

Adequate explanation of the behavior of tuberculosis in Negroes is an extremely difficult subject, but this has not deterred the proffer of several different theories in which their champions emphasize one or the other of the various factors.[106] These theories may be divided into those which deal with environmental influences and those which have to do with consitutional factors. A similar debate persists on the relative importance of these two factors in many diseases, but in none of them is it more strenuously argued than in relation to tuberculosis in Negroes.

The view of Opie that the status of tuberculosis among colored people is due to their escape from primary infection in early life is generally believed not to hold, since tuberculin surveys show that the incidence of infection of Negroes at all ages closely

[103] Anderson, *Arch. Neurol. & Psychiat.*, 20:354, 1922; Ferris, *J. A. M. A.*, 92:1670, 1929; Scott and Graves, *Am. Rev. Tuberc.*, 27:171, 1933; Lewisohn, Freilich, and Ragins, *Arch. Int. Med.*, 7:1141, 1937; Jaffé and Schultz, *Am. Rev. Tuberc.*, 33:302, 1936.

[104] *Am. J. Med. Sc.*, 192:756, 1936.

[105] For other reports of Addison's disease in Negroes see Scheult, *Lancet*, 2:94, 1907; Lemann, *New Orleans M. and S. J.*, 78:814, 1926; Evans, *Am. J. M. Sc.*, 176:499, 1924; Sala and Jacobi, *Arch. Int. Med.*, 46:375, 1930; Welty and Robertson, *Am. J. Med. Sci.*, 192:760, 1936; Gordon, *Interstate M. J.*, 22:550, 1915; King and Mulholland, *Virginia M. Monthly*, 58:455, 1931.

[106] See West, *Ann. Rev. Tuberc.*, 41: (suppl.), 114, 1940, for a discussion of the racial factor in the epidemiology of tuberculosis.

approximates that of white people. Moreover, Pinner and Casper[107] point out, first, that delayed primary infection occurs also in white people, and when it does it proceeds just as mildly as it does in childhood; second, that the typical type of tuberculosis in Negroes is not a nonallergic process; and, third, that the type of disease in adult Negroes, generally called childhood-type tuberculosis, is in fact not that type but one that simulates it, since healed calcified lesions can often be found.

Of the other theories, stressing either environmental conditions or the lack of sufficient defensive powers, owing to failure to inherit immunity or to an innate racial susceptibility, the latter is apparently the more readily accepted one, despite the cautious examples of Long,[108] Opie,[109] and Bushnell.[110] The chief advocates of the idea of racial susceptibility, whose conclusions are quoted most freely, are Pinner and Casper. After discarding other theories with unwarranted facility, they say that "there exists a true racial (genotypic) difference between the two races (entirely mysterious in character), which confers high resistance on one and low resistance on the other race," although they are credited with more positiveness than they themselves admit, since they simply offer this view as a postulate and say: "We are impressed by the necessity of considering the likelihood of true genotypic differences."

If by genotype Pinner and Casper mean a fundamental hereditary constitutional character controlled by a combination of genes, of the same type as are skin color and hair texture, then a genotypic low resistance to tuberculosis should have the same constancy as do other genotypic traits. This, however, is not true of the Negro's reaction to tuberculosis, because in many cases the type of tuberculosis is of the same fibrotic type as seen in the majority of white people. In their own series of necropsies, Pinner and Casper remark that there is an overlapping of the two races in the centers between the two extremes of strictly

[107] Loc. cit.; see n. 75.

[108] Kentucky State M. J., 34:124, 1936.   [109] Loc. cit.; see n. 95.

[110] The epidemiology of tuberculosis (New York: William Wood & Co., 1920).

isolated fibrotic tuberculosis at one end and massive exudative lesions at the other.

Genotypic traits are not as rapidly modified as is the Negro's reaction to tuberculosis. From the extraordinary high-mortality rate in the 1880's, the tuberculosis mortality of colored people has shown a remarkable drop. While this change in mortality may not mean a change in reaction but a response to effective antituberculosis efforts, modifications of mortality rates may be just as striking in the absence of campaigns against the disease, as has been the case in Mexico City.[111] But there is unmistakable evidence of a change in body reaction, concerning which Long says: "Apparently as time goes by the range of variation in racial resistance in man is narrowing. The tuberculosis of Negroes, Polynesians, Eskimos and other groups with former astounding tuberculosis mortality, appears to be far less acute, in general, in its anatomical type today."[112]

The type of tuberculosis found in the Negro is not characteristic of that race, since it is found in several races. Pinner and Casper included eleven Mexicans among their series of Negroes, since their type of reaction to tuberculosis is essentially similar to that of the Negro. The same type is likewise found in Marquesans, Polynesians, Tahitians, Hawaiians, and Eskimos. In Constantinople Deycke[113] did not find among the whites the prevalence of ulcerative phthisis beginning in the apexes, which is common in other parts of Europe. The predominant form was disseminated miliary tuberculosis, pulmonary tuberculosis without cavity formation, tuberculosis of lymph nodes, and tuberculous peritonitis.

It is universally true that those people who have been in contact with tuberculosis a long time show principally a chronic type of disease, and those who have been in contact with it a short while show principally an acute type of disease. It is therefore rational to suspect some causal relation between length

[111] Alarcón, *Am. Rev. Tuberc.*, 35:6, 1937.

[112] *Tr. Nat. Tuberc. A.*, 31:308, 1935.

[113] *Beitr. z. Klin. d. Tuberk.*, 4:(suppl.), 142, 1913.

of experience with the disease and resistance to it, although the mechanism by which they are related may not be understood. The ideas of "survival of the fittest" and of "inheritance of acquired immunity" have been offered as the methods by which changes in resistance are accomplished. The evidence for and against them are not peculiar to tuberculosis but are common to the problems of inheritance of other human traits.

The chief argument against environmental conditions as an explanation of tuberculosis among Negroes is that it is not clear how external factors can influence the qualitative features of the disease. Pathologists have no hesitancy in recognizing that the balance between resistance of host and virulence of the invader greatly influence the qualitative type of response in other infections. A peritonitis produced by a highly virulent streptococcus in an individual that has been debilitated by disease gives an entirely different anatomical picture than a similar infection with a low-grade organism in an otherwise healthy person. It might well be that people who for most of their lives have been subjected to such conditions as undernourishment, overwork, insufficient rest, inadequate clothing and shelter, and dissipation react qualitatively in a different manner to tuberculosis than those who have lived a more hygienic life. While it is true that debilitating factors lower resistance to tuberculosis, it is difficult to understand how they produce this effect other than by altering the type of defense. If the defensive mechanism is the same in a debilitated person as in one who is not, the resistance to the disease should be the same.

Massive infection is one of the possible sequences of poor living conditions, and Long[114] suggests that in a relatively resistant person it might lead to approximately the same anatomical result as moderate infection in one of high susceptibility. On the other hand, Pinner and Casper doubt that such is the case. They cite the experiments of Santo[115] and Schminke and Santo,[116] who showed that metastatic involvement in guinea pigs and rabbits

[114] *Kentucky State M. J.*, 34:124, 1936.

[115] *Beitr. z. Klin. d. Tuberk.*, 76:191, 1931.

[116] *Verhandl. d. deutsch. path. Gesellsch.*, 26:275, 1931.

artificially infected with tuberculosis is not related to the size of the infecting dose and that the anatomical character of human tuberculous lesions is unrelated to their bacillary content. Repeated infections in animals also do not always depress the defense reactions.

Attempts have been made to compare the reactions to tuberculosis of Negroes and whites living under similar and controlled conditions. Roth[117] compared soldiers living in an army encampment; and Clark[118] compared veterans in government hospitals. The obvious fallacy in these comparisons is that the fate of the subjects in regard to tuberculosis may well have been determined long before they were placed under observation. It is doubtful if in this country a comparison can be made of a group of white people and of Negroes who live and have always lived under similar external conditions.

In the light of the facts that have been accumulated, predictions have been made of the ultimate fate of Negroes in regard to tuberculosis. Previous attempts have shown that such predictions are hazardous. It was believed at one time that these people would be eliminated from America as the result of their diseases, particularly of tuberculosis. But the actual facts are that they have dealt with them successfully enough to even allow a moderate increase in population. There are communities of Negroes in which there is no tuberculosis problem, where the colored people, for some unexplained reason, do not react in the same manner as do the mass of colored people, thus indicating the possibility of the whole Negro population in dealing adequately with the disease.

A genotypic low racial resistance, if this is the true explanation of the Negro's tuberculosis, dooms him to a continual high morbidity and mortality except for the changes that can be brought about by improvement in living conditions and by lesser exposure to infection. On the other hand, a mechanism that permits by experience an increased immunity ultimately but slowly will result in a better ability to successfully deal with tuberculosis in spite of, or even because of, his present con-

[117] Loc. cit.; see n. 81. [118] Tr. Nat. Tuberc. A., 28:226, 1932.

dition. The white race has been tuberculized so long that no other stage of the disease is known among them than that which is represented by the present type of reaction. It is difficult to account for the assortment of resistances among them, ranging from the high resistance of Jews to the much lower resistance of the Irish, except in the light of their actual experience with the disease. Human races are enough alike to expect that similar experiences will bring about similar results.

The most adequate and the simplest explanation of the variation of the effect of tuberculosis among races is the theory of natural selection. With tuberculosis, as with other diseases, those who succumb are the weakest of the race, and those who survive are the strongest. The qualities which the strong possess, without the necessity of accounting for them, are transmitted to the progeny, and in due course all members of the group will have inherited the constitutionally fixed ability to resist the disease. The relative amount of such resistance among races will depend upon the relative length of exposure to the infection. Negroes and other races who have known the disease a comparatively short time have not yet had the opportunity to acquire the full resistance that the forces of natural selection have brought to most of the white races. The changes that are accomplished by this mechanism must be measured in terms of generations and are of necessity slow in being established, yet in the comparatively short history of exposure of Negroes to tuberculosis a marked alteration in the type of disease can be clearly demonstrated. As Pinner points out, there is no way to estimate how long such a selective process must go on to cause sizeable changes. He refers to Anderson,[119] who, on the basis of mortality rates and age incidence in the racially mixed population of Mauritius, concludes that a race unexposed to tuberculosis and which then had a continued contact with tuberculosis "begins to acquire resistance within thirty years, has already acquired it to an appreciable extent in fifty years, and in more than one hundred and less than two hundred years has developed resistance to the full degree" (according to English standards). Pin-

[119] *Tr. Roy. Soc. Trop. Med. & Hyg.*, 21:463, 1928.

ner believes that the example of the American Negro is more than sufficient to repudiate such statements and is inclined to invalidate the importance of natural selection as it applies to the Negro and tuberculosis. On the other hand, Long accepts it as the mechanism for the development of racial immunity as measured by the change of tuberculosis from a generalized type to the localized pulmonary form. Using scrofula as the example of generalized tuberculosis, he says:

Today we appear to be observing a last stand of scrofula in the Negro race. Again we are confronted with an overlapping of causes in the relatively high incidence of the scrofulous type of tuberculosis in this race. In the first place the Negro is far closer than the white man to the period of first introduction of tuberculosis. The factor of natural selection toward the more chronic localized type has not operated over as long a period as in the white. Equally or more significant, however, is the fact that pulmonary tuberculosis is far more common in Negroes than in whites. If scrofula is four times as common in Negroes, it must not be forgotten that pulmonary tuberculosis, which may lead to generalized tuberculosis of lymph nodes, is three to four times as common also. When the rate for pulmonary tuberculosis in the Negro reaches the relatively low rate of the white population today, it will be surprising if there is not a corresponding decrease in the scrofulous form of the disease. . . . . The races of the world are in different stages of a process loosely called racial immunization, which is in a large measure really natural selection toward chronic localized rather than generalized tuberculosis. Most of the white race has long been exposed to tuberculosis and probably already derived what benefit it may expect on this score.[120]

SUMMARY

The consensus from the mass of data shown is to the effect that tuberculosis in Negroes is a far more serious disease than it is in white people. The chief evidence of this is the large excess of Negro mortality over white mortality. In addition, there are pathologic and clinical attributes that indicate a lesser resistance by the tissues of the body to the progress of the disease when it attacks the Negro and which help explain the more frequently and rapidly fatal issue in these people.

Neither these statements nor any other generalizations about tuberculosis can be applied uniformly and unrestrictedly to all Negroes, since there are groups within the race that have the same type of disease and end result as within any other race.

[120] *Bull. Hist. Med.*, 8:819, 1940.

But taking Negroes as a whole, it may safely be said that, in comparison to most branches of the white race, they show as a basic attribute of the organism either the absence of a factor that increases resistance or the presence of a factor that decreases resistance. It is also to be recognized that there are certain external or environmental conditions that oppose or accelerate such a factor and which, while not specific for race, may operate differentially between races, usually to the disadvantage of the Negro.

If as Negroes are included all the people of African descent in America who have been a part of a tuberculized community for over three hundred years, along with the natives of Africa who have had different degrees of contact with tuberculosis ranging from none at all to constant exposure in European colonized districts, there can be found within the race all forms of the disease that can occur in the human race. The most malignant form is that often found in certain African natives who, without the benefit of tuberculized progenitors and without having before been exposed to the tubercle bacillus, receive their first infection in relatively large doses. This combination of circumstances leads to the type of infection aptly described as the "virgin soil" type. It is of a definitely characteristic clinical and pathologic form, is rapidly progressive, short-lived, and uniformly fatal. It indicates the minimum of resistance. In contrast to this is the slowly progressing phthisis which may be found in African natives of long residence in the older civilized areas of North Africa and in some of the Negroes of America. However, the bulk of Negroes in both hemispheres suffer with a form of disease between these extremes. In the main, it is an exudative type that quickly develops and shows a tendency to caseous pneumonia and generalization.

The excess of infection and the excess of morbidity among American Negroes are not of the same order as the excess of mortality. In fact, the amount of infection as disclosed by tuberculin surveys may be less in some communities, although the mortality from tuberculosis is several times that of the white people in the same community. And the number of cases of active disease discovered by roentgenological methods may not exceed the number discovered among comparable groups of white people. The explanation of this may be relatively simple: namely, that the ubiquity of the tubercle bacillus in most communities offers approximately equal opportunities for both races to become infected. The infection is more likely to lead to disease in Negroes, but, since the disease develops more rapidly and leads more often to death, an accumulation of those who are ill is less likely than in white people, among whom the disease has a tendency to last a long time.

These and other features of tuberculosis in Negroes, especially in those of the United States, where more accurate observations are possible, can be tabulated as follows:

1. The mortality may be as much as five times the mortality in white people.
2. Tuberculosis is the second largest cause of death among Negroes, while it is the seventh largest cause among white people.
3. The excess of Negro tuberculosis deaths is greater in the North than in the South, in the cities than in rural districts.
4. Active tuberculosis begins at earlier ages in Negroes. The maximum death rate is at younger age levels. Young Negro females are particularly susceptible to the disease.
5. The annual decline in tuberculosis mortality is at a slower rate among Negroes.
6. On the whole, tuberculous infection and morbidity are greater in Negroes but do not show the excess that the mortality does.
7. The tuberculosis found in the majority of Negroes is of the exudative type, with caseation, generalization, and a small degree of fibrotic reaction.
8. Negroes show a hypersensitivity to tuberculin, a condition probably associated with the exudation and caseation characterizing their disease.

Although there is agreement on the major facts of tuberculosis in colored people, there is by no means a concurrence of opinion as to their explanation. Two schools of thought vie with each other for acceptance. The first assumes susceptibility to tuberculosis to be an inborn inheritable racial trait, and the second emphasizes the role of external factors, including accessibility to primary infection, natural selection, and living conditions. In favor of the first theory is the similarity and constancy of the type of reaction to tuberculosis of the bulk of Negroes no matter where they live. Against it is the fact that the same type of disease may be found among other and diverse races, such as

Eskimos, Hawaiians, South Sea Islanders, and isolated primitive groups of Russians. In the United States the people classed as Negroes are a heterologous group composed of various degrees of intermixture of African and white blood ranging from an imperceptible amount of white blood to apparently full-blooded Africans. The term "Negro" applied to all these people has no racial significance but does indicate a definite social position. The statistics of tuberculosis among Negroes apply to the whole group and do not clearly show that there is any difference between those who are mostly white and those who are mostly African. This would indicate that the tuberculosis said to be characteristic of Negroes is not at all characteristic of a race but of a social pattern, since this is the sole attribute that is common to the whole group.

The type of tuberculosis that is said to be constant for Negroes applies only to a given time, because there is evidence that the form of tuberculosis is shifting, with a tendency to be more chronic—indicating more resistance.

With proper consideration of all facts concerning tuberculosis in Negroes and of tuberculosis in general, it is believed that the most acceptable theory for the explanation of the behavior of the disease among these people is that which takes into account the fact that they have not been in contact with tuberculosis long enough to develop a racial immunity through the forces of natural selection. But any explanation must also take into account the hazards of the living conditions of the large part of the Negro population.

SYPHILIS

Much of the American literature on syphilis is concerned with the Negro. It deals chiefly with its prevalence and the peculiarities of its clinical and anatomical effects as compared with white people. In a great many respects the natural history of syphilis is similar to that of tuberculosis. Both have a typical reaction in "virgin soil," both are modified in the course of time as a community resistance is developed, and both are intimately related to environmental conditions. Syphilis apparently began in white people about the last part of the fifteenth century. Since then, when the disease was known as the "great pox," marked changes in its manifestations have taken place. Originally there were great epidemics of syphilis when the symptoms were acute and florid ulcerating lesions of the skin and destructive gummas of internal organs were common clinical conditions. Today among white people ulcerative skin lesions and gummas are unusual, but neurosyphilis has gained in frequency. It is believed these changes represent the development of an immunity. Symmers[1] wrote about "syphilis as a disease of diminishing severity" and compared the relatively mild effects seen at the present time to the more severe reactions recorded as characteristic of the original disease. Pathologists with twenty-five or more years' experience have themselves been able to witness in the morgue some of these changes in the type of syphilitic reaction.

Syphilis was not introduced to all races of people simultaneously. With a considerable degree of accuracy, the time of the first infection can be correlated with the type of disease reaction, especially with the amount and nature of neurosyphilis, and by arranging nations and races in the chronological order of their first experience with syphilis, a kind of "stop-motion" picture of the evolutionary phases of the disease can be seen.

Differences have been established between the Negro and the white man in regard to both the prevalence of syphilis and its clinical and pathological manifestations, but it is questionable

[1] *Social Hyg.*, 3:197, 1917.

whether these differences are fundamentally racial in nature or whether they are due to differences in the histories of the races in regard to contact with the disease and in the operation of external, chiefly social, factors. Similar differences may be found between groups within the white race and between the white race and races other than Negroes. It appears that syphilis was introduced to African Negroes by white people approximately three or four hundred years after their first experience with it, and the basis of the difference between the two races is perhaps that white people have a longer lineage of syphilitic ancestry than have colored people. It is doubtful that Negroes are ten times more promiscuous or ten times more ignorant than the white people they live so close to, as in the South, to account for ten times more syphilis, as has been claimed for some groups of colored people. But the disease is rapidly changing in colored people. Neurosyphilis is apparently increasing, bone and visceral syphilis seem to be decreasing, syphilis of the cardiovascular system will probably diminish, and a general resistance to invasion by spirochetes should develop, resulting in a lowered prevalence of the disease. As the disease grows older in all races there may be a tendency to the establishment of a universal uniformity in type. Kanner[2] pictured a cycle in the development of racial immunity in syphilis in terms of neurosyphilis in which three different stages are represented by Negroes, white people, and American Indians: The early stage in the Negro, where neurosyphilis is relatively uncommon but increasing; a later stage in white people, where neurosyphilis is at its maximum and decreasing; a still later stage in the American Indian, where neurosyphilis has again reached a minimum after having passed through the earlier stages, since the disease is much older in this race than any others.

PREVALENCE

Many attempts have been made to fix at some numerical level the amount of syphilis among colored people. The methods used have ranged from pure guesses to the Wassermann

[2] *Am. J. Syph.*, 11:23, 1927.

testing of whole communities. The results obtained have reflected the diversity of the methods employed and have indicated the operation of highly variable factors that make it impossible to say with any exactitude just how prevalent the disease is. Criticisms of the methods and the fallacy of applying specific results to the whole race have been made.[3] Jason pointed out that estimates of the prevalence of syphilis in Negroes have ranged from 12 to 74.1 per cent (even wider limits have been given) and that imperfections in serological tests, lack of uniformity in technics used, the number of tests made on each individual, variations in the age, sex, marital status, number, geographical distribution, and, most of all, the socioeconomic level of the different groups profoundly affect the results. Hazen divided the surveys of syphilis into nine different type groups and showed the inherent errors of each. He concluded that there is none that is not open to objection. Belding and Hunter also showed that the social and economic status markedly influences the incidence of syphilis and that when whites and Negroes are grouped together in the same socioeconomic groups the presence of the Negro in each group has no influence on the results. They likewise observed that the statistics concerning the northern and southern Negro are markedly different, the syphilis rate of the latter being 2.5 times that of the former and 3.5 times greater than that of the foreign-born (West Indies) Negro in the North. They pointed out that occupation is another important factor. The rate among occupational groups in Boston, Massachusetts, varies from 7.6 per cent for those in domestic and personal service to the high figure of 55.5 per cent for chauffeurs. Belding and Hunter say:

It is a prevailing opinion among southern physicians that syphilis is so common in the Negro that the majority of adults are infected. This generalization, though possibly true for certain sections, is too sweeping when applied indiscriminately to the entire race. Until further Wassermann surveys have been made on representative groups, taking into consideration social standing, education and intelligence, the actual extent of syphilis in the whole race cannot be actually determined.

[3] Jason, *Am. J. Syph.*, 19:313, 1935; Hazen, *Am. J. Syph.*, 20:530, 1936; Maxcy and Brumfield, *South. M. J.*, 27:891, 1934; Belding and Hunter, *Am. J. Syph.*, 8:117, 1924; Lemann, *South. M. J.*, 27:33, 1934.

Maxcy and Brumfield say that "familiarity with the pathology of syphilis leads to a realization of the impossibility of an exact statement of its degree of prevalence in any population group." Lemann has pointed out that all statistics on Negroes are based upon the poorer class.

The surveys of syphilis among American Negroes have, for the most part, been made in hospitals, clinics, penal institutions, military posts, and among various labor groups. In recent years use has been made of the so-called one-day census of patients who are under treatment for syphilis, as an indication of the amount of the disease. There is a great selective factor in the results obtained under all these conditions, and a fallacy is involved when they are applied to the general population. Probably the most accurate surveys are those of entire communities, such as have been made in certain areas in the South under the sponsorship of the Julius Rosenwald Fund and by the United States Public Health Service and local health administrations.[4] However, these represent no more than what they are: namely, surveys of a particular class of Negroes in communities which, unfortunately, are characteristic of many parts of the deep South and which for the most part are made up of ignorant, oppressed, uninhibited sharecroppers on cotton plantations among whom syphilis varies with the degree of physical and financial victimization by plantation owners and the availability of treatment facilities.

The most recent comparison of the incidence of syphilis in Negroes and whites was made by Vonderlehr and Usilton[5] on the basis of physical examinations and serologic blood tests of the first million volunteers and selectees called for classification under the Selective Service Act of 1940. A rate of 45.2 cases of syphilis per 1,000 persons examined was found. While no figures are given separately for Negroes and whites, the authors state that the rates for syphilis among Negroes were consistently higher than those for white men in all the states. For the coun-

[4] Clark, *The control of syphilis in southern rural areas* (Chicago: Julius Rosenwald Fund, 1932).

[5] *J. A. M. A.*, 117:1350, 1941.

try as a whole, the prevalence of syphilis among Negro selectees and volunteers was thirteen times that among the whites. In 20 states and the District of Columbia the Negro rate was in excess of ten times that of the white rate. There are indications that high rates among Negroes are coincidental with high rates among whites. The 13 highest rates among the states are in southern states, including the District of Columbia. All cities showing a prevalence of syphilis of more than 100 per 1,000 are southern states.

In nearly every case where a comparison has been made with the contiguous white population, the prevalence of syphilis among Negroes has been found to be higher. The excess has been so high in some instances as to arouse the suspicion of the operation of certain extraneous factors such as the great prevalence of malaria and tuberculosis, to which the Negro is apparently highly subject, that might invalidate the accuracy of the Wassermann test by giving false positive reactions.

The excess of syphilis among Negroes is not only in the adult population but also in children in the form of congenital syphilis. Further evidence of excessive syphilis is given in the high rates of stillbirths, abortions, and premature births.

Information concerning syphilis in Africa is scanty and incomplete. Hirsch,[6] writing in 1885, says the disease was imported by Europeans and was almost entirely confined to the coastal regions. Central Africa, if not entirely free of it, had syphilis only to a slight degree. The disease was particularly prevalent on the east coast and in the East African islands of Mauritius and Reunion, Madagascar, Mozambique, and Zanzibar. In these places it was estimated to exist in five-sixths of the whole population. Hirsch says further that the disease was rare among the Hottentots and still rarer in the Bechuana tribes. Livingstone found the people in the central regions of South Africa to be absolutely exempt from the disease. Into Abyssinia, where the number infected is estimated at nine-tenths of the population, syphilis was imported by the Portuguese in the fifteenth cen-

[6] *Handbook of geographical and historical pathology* (London: New Sydenham Society, 1885), Vol. 2.

tury. In the whole of northern and western Africa syphilis is said to have had an enormous diffusion among the African natives. During the fifty years since Hirsch wrote, there has been a much greater penetration of the whites into the interior of Africa. This, together with the movement of infected natives back and forth between areas of endemic syphilis and virgin fields, has guaranteed that there is hardly a place on the continent where the disease is unknown. Chesney[7] lists the number of cases reported in various parts of Africa, as well as in Haiti, Jamaica, Virgin Islands, and the Dominican Republic, but does not attempt to give rates. The question of the distribution of syphilis in these countries is complicated by the presence of yaws, which is claimed to be indistinguishable from lues. The debate whether they are the same disease or distinct but similar diseases which can or cannot be distinguished has created a considerable literature. It is certain that both diseases give the same serological reactions, and Wassermann surveys are of little use in ascertaining the prevalence of syphilis in countries where yaws is endemic.

Hewer[8] says the incidence of syphilis in the Sudan may be judged by the fact that the blood of 420 prisoners, apparently in good health, showed a positive Kahn reaction in 31 per cent. He points out that congenital syphilis is surprisingly rare. On the other hand, McArthur[9] says that in the natives of Bechuanaland congenital syphilis is the commonest form of the disease and that acquired syphilis is rare. Third-generation syphilis may often be found in whole families. Gordon[10] writes about the difficulty of differentiating yaws and syphilis. He refers to the diseases together as "spirochetosis." In the British colony, Kenya, yaws is believed to be decreasing and syphilis increasing. Only two tribes out of forty, or four hundred thousand out of three million natives, are reported free of both diseases. The

[7] *A geography of disease* (St. Louis: George Washington University Press, 1935), p. 417.

[8] *Brain*, 55:537, 1932.

[9] *Brit. J. Dermat.*, 35:411, 1932.   [10] *Proc. Roy. Soc. Med.*, 27:245, 1933-34.

m'anifestations of congenital syphilis (Hutchinson's teeth and scars of interstitial keratitis) are rare. In a series of Kahn tests cited by Gordon, 69 per cent were positive. Heim,[11] writing about syphilis in the German colonies, says that syphilis has an incidence less than in Germany. He estimated that in German East Africa the incidence was 0.013 per cent, in the Cameroon 0.004 per cent, in Togoland 0.007 per cent, and in southwestern Africa it was 0.182 per cent.

THE PRIMARY LESION

Although Morison[12] states that induration of the chancre is more pronounced in the Negro, Zimmermann[13] was not able to note such a difference. Heim[14] finds that in the natives of German East Africa the initial lesion is persistent but rarely becomes phagedenic; on the other hand, Lambkin[15] says that in the natives of Uganda the chancre often becomes phagedenic. Tarayre[16] finds in the West Indian Negro that the initial lesion almost always shows a mixed infection and tends toward phagedena, with resulting cicatricial disfigurement of the genital organs. In most instances the inguinal glands on both sides are involved and usually ulcerate. Heim notes that in African natives the chancre is not often seen, because they are unaware of its significance and do not seek treatment. McArthur[17] also remarks about the rarity of chancres in the natives of South Africa. There are many instances of syphilis where there is no discernible or known portal of entry of the spirochetes, the condition known as syphilis d'emblée.

Attention has often been called to the rarity of extragenital chancres in colored people. Morrison,[18] Thompson,[19] and Zeisler[20] have, among others, commented on this. Among the

[11] *Arch. f. Dermat. u. Syph.*, 118:165, 1913.

[12] *Tr. Am. Dermat. A.*, 12:29, 1888.   [13] *Arch. Dermat. & Syph.*, 4:75, 1921.

[14] *Loc. cit.*; see n. 11.

[15] *A system of syphilis* (London: Oxford University Press, 1914), 2:237.

[16] *Arch. de méd. et pharm. mil.* 90:749, 1929.

[17] *Am. J. Syph.*, 7:569, 1923.   [18] *Loc. cit.*; see n. 12.

[19] *Syphilis: diagnosis and treatment* (Philadelphia: Lea & Febiger, 1928).

[20] *J. A. M. A.*, 67:1546, 1917.

syphilitics in Johns Hopkins Hospital, Zimmermann[21] found 6.6 per cent of the chancres in white people to be extragenital and only 1.4 per cent in colored patients to be so. In a series of 6,149 consecutive cases of syphilis in the Negro, Hazen[22] reports only 8 instances of extragenital chancres. Of these 2 were tonsillar, 5 labial, and 1 digital. Zeisler[23] reported multiple chancres of the lip in a colored woman. Lofton[24] and Atkinson[25] noted a tendency to multiple chancres in the Negro. Turner[26] says that in his material extragenital chancre in white people is about three times more frequent than in colored patients. The rarity of extragenital chancres in Africans also has been pointed out by McArthur and Thorton,[27] Vos Hug,[28] and Frasier.[29]

Reasoner[30] is of the opinion that the chancre is a local defense mechanism possessed by the skin and mucous membrane but which is absent in these tissues of the Negro except in those of the genitalia.

SECONDARY LESIONS

Zimmermann[31] says the glandular reaction in secondary syphilis is more marked in the Negro than in the white, frequently to such an extent that the cervical, epitrochlear, even pectoral and preauricular lymph glands are visibly enlarged. He also found that arthralgia, myalgia, periosteal and osteocopic pain were severe in 21 of 279 colored patients in the secondary stage, while only 7 of 228 similar white patients were severely affected by such symptoms. Not infrequently in early secondary syphilis the Negro presents symptoms of an intense reaction on the part of the bones and joints: namely, pain with severe nocturnal exacerbation, multiple circumscribed areas of exquisite tenderness, and at times, in a few, marked effusion in

[21] Loc. cit.; see n. 13.

[22] Loc. cit.; see n. 4.

[23] Loc. cit.; see n. 20.

[27] South African M. Rec., 9:25, 1911.

[28] South African M. Rec., 13:123, 1915.

[29] South African M. Rec., 13:151, 1915.

[24] Am. J. Dermat., 7:203, 1903.

[25] Maryland M. J., 1:135, 1877.

[26] Bull. Johns Hopkins Hosp., 46:159, 1930.

[30] J. A. M. A., 67:1799, 1916.

[31] Loc. cit.; see n. 13.

the joints. Baetz[32] also remarks about the pain of secondary osseous syphilitic lesions in the Negro, and Turner[33] refers to the racial predisposition of bone and joint pains in early syphilis in the proportion of 5 Negroes to 1 white.

Baetz[34] and Carter[35] agree that syphilitic lesions of the mouth and throat are appreciably less frequent in the Negro than in the white. Zimmermann found secondary lesions of the mouth in 42.1 per cent of the white patients and 27.2 per cent of the colored. Stokes, Cole, Moore, O'Leary, Wile, Clark, Parran, and Usilton[36] say mucous patches are 10 per cent more frequent in white patients. Hazen[37] thinks, on the other hand, that they are more frequent in the Negro and particularly stresses the hypertrophic mucous patches near the commissure, which he says are certainly more numerous in the Negro.

Zimmermann[38] found that 1.8 per cent of the white and 12.9 per cent of the colored syphilitic patients had acute iritis. Atkinson[39] found 11 cases among 100 Negroes with primary and secondary lesions. Stokes et al.[40] found the excess in Negroes to be most marked on comparison of Negro and white females, the rate in the former being 3.4 times the rate for the latter. Keratitis and keratoiritis are very rare in the secondary stage, but Stokes found 10 such cases among colored patients. Turner[41] found secondary lesions of the eye in 2.9 per cent of the white and 6.8 per cent of the colored patients who had secondary lues. These lesions also recurred more often in the colored.

It appears that condylomas are very frequent in the Negro, especially in the female, although the claim of Hazen[42] that all colored syphilitic women have them is an overstatement of the fact. Zimmermann found that the incidence for male syphilitics was 11.8 per cent white, and 17.7 per cent colored, while for fe-

[32] *New York State J. Med.*, 100:820, 1914.   [33] *Loc. cit.*   [34] *Loc. cit.*

[35] *Report of supervising surgeon general, Marine Hospital* (Washington: U.S. Government Printing Office, 1883).

[36] *Ven. Dis. Inform.*, 13:165, 1932.

[37] *Syphilis* (2d ed.; St. Louis: C. V. Mosby Co., 1928).

[38] *Loc. cit.*; see n. 13.   [40] *Loc. cit.*; see n. 36.

[39] *Loc. cit.*; see n. 25.   [41] *Loc. cit.*; see n. 26.   [42] *Syphilis.*

males it was 26.3 per cent white, and 52.2 per cent colored. Stokes[43] says condylomas in colored females are 3.5 times more common than in white males, 3 times more common than in colored males, and 2 times more common than in white females. Among native Africans Heim[44] says condylomas are the dominating form of secondary lesion.

Perhaps the most striking difference between white and colored syphilitics in the secondary stage is in the skin lesions, as described by Fox,[45] Stelwagon,[46] Hazen,[47] and others. The most characteristic eruptive lesion of the Negro is the annular papular syphilide, first described by Atkinson[48] under the name of syphiloderma papulatum circinatum and later emphasized by Gilchrist[49] and Fox. Hazen says two distinct types of eruption are included under this heading: first, lesions arising from the grouping of several papules and, second, those arising from a single papule. Thus they may arise from grouped follicular lesions, either large or small papules, either discoid or lenticular, and from the papulosquamous lesions. These syphilides are most frequent upon the face. They are distinctly rare upon the limbs. They are occasionally found upon the mucous membrane of the mouth. Annular lesions are found in congenital as well as in acquired syphilis, although they are less frequent. Fox found 11 annular syphilides among 193 colored syphilitics and none among 72 white syphilitics. Zimmermann found them twice among 228 white patients and 40 times among 279 colored patients. In a series of 2,844 cases of secondary syphilis in the colored, Hazen[50] found 478 instances of the annular syphilide. In a series of 2,000 white patients he found no such lesions.

The papular and pustular syphilides are much more frequent in the Negro, according to Zimmermann and Hazen. Zimmermann says a common clinical syndrome in the Negro consists of

[43] Loc. cit.

[44] Loc. cit.; see n. 11.   [45] J. Cutan. Dis., 26:67, 109, 1908.

[46] Diseases of the skin (Philadelphia: W. B. Saunders, 1914).

[47] Loc. cit.; see n. 4.   [49] Maryland M. J., 42:1200, 1909.

[48] J. Cutan. Dis., 1:15, 1882.   [50] Arch. Dermat. & Syph., 31:316, 1935.

a profuse folliculopapular syphilide, definite syphilitic arthritis (usually of the ankles), marked polyadenitis, and iridocyclitis. This, he says, is not a mere coincidence, although at present their significance is speculative. Recurrent secondary skin lesions in those who have been inadequately treated are found oftener in white subjects. Stokes claims that colored females present fewer skin manifestations than white or colored males or white females. Alopecia is more frequent in white females than in white males and almost twice as frequent in the white female as in the colored female. In white males alopecia is slightly more frequent than in colored males, and in the colored males and females the incidence is approximately the same according to Zimmermann.

Secondary lesions in the natives of Uganda[51] were characterized by intense and confluent eruptions, ulcerations of the mucous membrane of the mouth and throat, laryngitis, iritis, periostitis, and joint affections. Heim noticed that in German East Africa secondary manifestations are not often observed in the secondary stage, but when they are seen the reaction is many times more severe, with a tendency toward frequent recurrences. Glandular enlargement is often so extreme as to recall trypanosomiasis. Heim mentions the findings of another observer, Schroedter, who states that roseola occurs in the natives, appearing as an intensification of the normal skin color. Hewer[52] says florid secondary lesions of the skin and mucous membranes are almost the rule among the Sudanese.

The lesions of the central nervous system characteristic of the secondary stage are described under "Neurosyphilis," pages 170–78.

TERTIARY SYPHILIS

In his series of syphilitic patients at Johns Hopkins Hospital, Zimmermann found tertiary syphilides of the skin in 17.5 per cent of the whites and in 14.5 per cent of the colored. The most common cutaneous lesion among the white patients was the nodular syphilide—10.9 per cent as compared with 3.6 per cent

---

[51] Lambkin, *A system of syphilis.*   [52] *Loc. cit.;* see n. 8.

in the colored—while in the Negro the gumma was the most common—11.1 per cent as compared with 7.1 per cent in the white. Hazen[53] found cutaneous gummas nearly six times more frequently in Negroes than in whites, while nodular lesions were about the same. He also calls attention to the paucity of late palmar or plantar syphilides in colored patients, although lesions of the soles and palms are not at all infrequent during the secondary stage. Turner[54] did not observe any striking difference in the incidence of late syphilitic lesions between the two races except that they were more advanced in the colored when seen.

Zimmermann and Hazen refer to the experiments of Finger and Landsteiner,[55] who showed that nodular and gummatous lesions do not represent merely different localizations of the same process in the cutaneous tissue but are due to fundamentally different biologic processes. They inoculated the syphilis virus into patients with nodular syphilides and into those with skin gummas. In the former, nodular lesions formed and in the latter, gummas.

Hazen points out that certain skin complications occurred in Negroes with tertiary syphilis observed by him. They were syphilitic dyschromias, atrophia cutis maculosa luetica, dermatitis from discharges of broken-down gummas, and chronic urticaria, the latter conditions being very rare in the white.

The mucous membranes seem to share with the skin a lessened susceptibility to disease.[56] Fox[57] points out the rarity of leucoplakia both in his experience and in that of others whom he questioned. Zimmermann found it in 9 of 421 white syphilitics and in 2 of 466 colored syphilitics. In 1 of the latter it was associated with carcinoma of the tongue. Hazen says that leucoplakia of the severe type, involving the tongue, is distinctly rare in the colored race. He did frequently see gummas of the

[53] *J. A. M. A.*, 63:463, 1914.

[54] *Loc. cit.*; see n. 26.

[55] *Die allgemeine Pathologie der Syphilis: Handbuch der Geschlechtskrankheiten,* 2:944 (Wien and Leipzig: A. Hölder, 1912).

[56] Carter, *loc. cit.*   [57] *Loc. cit.*; see n. 45.

tongue and enormously enlarged lips, owing to lymphatic obstruction and perforated palates. Paullin, Davidson, and Wood[58] found 4 cases of syphilis of the larynx among 662 colored syphilitics. Turner,[59] on the other hand, found no striking difference in the incidence of late syphilitic lesions of the skin and mucous membrane between white and Negro patients, except that in the latter these lesions when seen were more advanced and destructive than in whites.

Osseous lesions are about twice as frequent in the Negro as in the white. According to Zimmermann, they are the commonest form of tertiary syphilis in colored people. Turner and Hazen agree with these statements. Zimmermann rarely observed syphilitic arthritis but stated that it occurred oftener in the Negro patients. Gumma of the sternoclavicular joint is believed by Hazen[60] to be more frequent in the colored.

In a group of 399 untreated Negro syphilitic patients studied by Vonderlehr, Clark, Wenger, and Heller,[61] 11.5 per cent gave evidence of late involvement of the bones, joints, and skin. Of these, 9 per cent showed periostitis, osteitis, or Charcot's joint. Less than 1 per cent presented late syphilis of the skin, and 2 per cent had both a late skin and a bone or joint involvement.

Concerning syphilis of the respiratory tract, there seems to be little information. Hazen and Turner say there is little difference between the two races. The same is true regarding visceral syphilis, including syphilis of the stomach, liver, and salivary glands. Zimmermann considers orchitis to be about three times as common in the Negro as in the white, and Hazen is inclined to put the difference still higher. A great deal has been written about the high prevalence of syphilitic stricture of the rectum in colored women,[62] but following the recent advances in the pathology of lymphogranuloma inguinale, it is generally

[58] Boston M. & S. J., 197:345, 1927; Tr. A. Am. Physicians, 42:48, 1927.

[59] Loc. cit.; see n. 26.

[60] J. A. M. A., 63:463, 1914.   [61] J. A. M. A., 107:856, 1936.

[62] Jones, J. A. M. A., 42:32, 1904; McNeill, Syphilis and public health (Philadelphia and New York: Lea & Febiger, 1918), p. 91; Zimmermann, loc. cit.; Hazen, J. A. M. A., 63:463, 1914.

admitted that this disease rather than syphilis is the cause of the strictures.[63]

As in early secondary syphilis, the Negro is especially prone to develop iritis as a late manifestation. Of 40 cases of iritis among nearly equal numbers of white and colored patients, Zimmermann found that 29 were of the latter race. Turner, however, found that the difference in the incidence of primary affections of the uveal tract, choroid, and retina, and of vascular keratitis in the race groups with late syphilis is not as striking as in early syphilis. The ratio was 2.1 per cent white and 3.1 per cent colored. Moore[64] claims that in early or late syphilis iritis is twice as common in colored people.

Hazen[65] believes lymphadenopathy is more frequent in the Negro but also states that enlarged lymph glands are present in almost all Negroes, whether or not infected with syphilis. This is especially true, according to Moore et al.,[66] for laborers whose extremities are subject to trauma. Gummatous lymphadenitis is apparently practically confined to the Negro race, according to Hazen. Turner makes the same statement, saying that the cervical lymph glands are by far the most frequently involved and that the resemblance to tuberculous lymphadenitis is often very striking.

There is little information about tertiary lesions in the natives of Africa. The late stages of syphilis and yaws are said to be particularly difficult to distinguish. Lambkin says tertiary syphilis is manifested as rupial syphilides, osteoarthritic involvement with severe nocturnal pains, periostitis, and osteomyelitis. McArthur says there is an absence of visceral syphilis. In a large number of post-mortems he has never seen a gumma of the viscera. Brock[67] described a particular pulmonary fibrosis among about 35 per cent of the syphilitic workers in the Rand

---

[63] Cole, *J. A. M. A.*, 101:1069, 1933; Bloom, *Surg., Gynec. & Obst.*, 58:827, 1934; Sulzberger and Wise, *J. A. M. A.*, 99:1407, 1932; Stannus, *A sixth venereal disease* (London: Bailliere, Tindall & Cox, 1933).

[64] *Am. J. Ophth.*, 14:110, 1931.

[65] *Am. J. Syph.*, 20:530, 1936; *J. A. M. A.*, 63:463, 1914.

[66] *Ven. Dis. Inform.*, 13:317, 1932.   [67] *Lancet*, 1:1270, 1912.

gold mines, which he attributed to the syphilitic process. But McArthur was not able to confirm this. He did find much tuberculosis, the development of which is favored by syphilis, and which is the nature- of the pulmonary lesions described by Brock. McArthur emphasizes the chronicity of tertiary lesions in natives of South Africa. Nasopharyngeal ulceration of many years' duration, showing little more than a very slowly progressing tissue destruction, are of common occurrence. Another manifestation frequently met with, according to McArthur, is a grouping of various forms of pustular syphilides about the elbows, knees, thighs, and buttocks. The latter is a particularly favored situation, and the pustules are generally implanted in a mass of gummatous tissue. These lesions are so slightly progressive as to be almost stationary. They give rise to little inconvenience, and bodily health is unimpaired. Still another condition frequently seen is a syphilitic condition of the scalp called locally "wit-kop" and which closely simulates favus. It begins as a small indurated papule, and by the coalescence of many such papules the scalp becomes completely covered with white heaped-up crusts.

In the German colonies Heim emphasized the ulcerating gummatous processes involving the leg, arms, skull, and face, producing contractures, when joints are involved, and destruction of cartilaginous structures. He cites from reports of physicians in various posts in the colonies, all of whom stress the occurrence of gummas which readily break down and ulcerate.

LATENT SYPHILIS

There is evidence that latent syphilis, in which there is no clinical activity of the disease, makes up a larger proportion of a population of colored syphilitics than white. In the Rosenwald surveys large numbers of individuals with positive Wassermanns were found who showed no evidence of disease and who were actively engaged in heavy manual labor. Turner found that 41.1 per cent of white people in the late stages showed latency, while 56.6 per cent of the colored showed the same. Latency was more prevalent in females than in males, but the

excess of females was more in the colored. Moore and his col-
laborators[68] analyzed a group of 1,290 white and 646 colored
patients with latent syphilis from 4 co-operating clinics and
found that 80.1 per cent of the whites and 68.0 per cent of the
colored showed no physical signs of syphilis. Of the whites, 6.0
per cent showed generalized lymphadenopathy and 20.1 per
cent of the colored showed this. Suggestive but not diagnostic
signs of cardiovascular syphilis were found in 2.1 per cent of the
white and 4.6 per cent of the colored. Suggestive but not diagnostic signs of syphilis of the central nervous system were found
in 13.5 per cent of the white and 12.1 per cent of the colored.

NEUROSYPHILIS

Studies of the comparative racial incidence of neurosyphilis
have been made both as it occurs in the early stages and as it
occurs in the late stages. Moore[69] examined the spinal fluids of
syphilitics in all stages of the disease after various amounts of
treatment and determined the amount of neurosyphilis in the
absence of gross evidence of injury to the nervous system. Of
the whole group, 12.7 per cent showed abnormal fluids, but of
the whites 15.9 per cent and of the colored 8.3 per cent showed
by changes in the spinal fluids that asymptomatic neurosyphilis
is about twice as prevalent in white syphilitics as in colored
syphilitics. In another report Moore[70] disclosed that not only is
there a wide difference between the white and colored races in
their susceptibility to early neurosyphilis, as indicated by 25.6
per cent for the former and 15.4 per cent for the latter, but also
that the defense reactions of the central nervous system in the
Negro enable him to deal with invasion, so that, judging from
the spinal fluid changes, his neurosyphilis is consistently milder
than is that of the white. Turner[71] says that perhaps in the
majority of all patients the central nervous system is invaded at
the time of the general dissemination of organisms in the early
stages of syphilis, although in relatively few patients does the
clinical or serologic picture of acute meningitis appear. Al-

[68] *Loc. cit.*

[69] *J. A. M. A.*, 76:769, 1921.

[70] *Bull. Johns Hopkins Hosp.*, 33:231, 1922.

[71] *Loc. cit.;* see n. 26.

though all the factors that determine the production of symptoms in one patient and not in another are unknown, it appears that race is one of them. Turner found that neurosyphilis in early syphilis is more than twice as high in whites as in Negroes. Neurorecurrences, which appear in patients having had insufficient treatment, occur more than three times as frequently in white as in colored patients, indicating again that there is a profound difference in the vulnerability of the central nervous system of the two races as regards infection with the spirochetes of syphilis. Levine[72] found among syphilitic soldiers that 23.7 per cent of the whites and 12.2 per cent of the colored had abnormal spinal fluids.

Stokes and his colleagues[73] found among 2,269 white and colored patients with early secondary syphilis and before any treatment had been given definite clinical evidence of central nervous system involvement in 1.7 per cent. This involvement was, without exception, an acute syphilitic meningitis, either with or without cranial-nerve palsies, and was of the type that yields readily to treatment. The racial distribution of this type of lesion was 1.9 per cent of the white males, 0.7 per cent of the white females, 4.7 per cent of the colored males, and 0.5 per cent of the colored females. The incidence of neurosyphilis without clinical symptoms, the diagnosis being made by spinal fluid examination, was 38.1 per cent of white males, 32.6 per cent of white females, 23.1 per cent of colored males, and 19.7 per cent of colored females.

An even more outstanding difference between neurosyphilis in the white and colored races is the incidence of the late lesions, especially of tabes dorsalis and general paresis. It was a matter of common belief among the older writers that these two conditions were very unusual in Negroes. However, more recent observers have pointed out that, while striking racial differences do still exist, they are not of the extent as formerly recorded and that neurosyphilis is increasing in the Negro and decreasing in the white, although the factor of recent availability of better diagnostic facilities for Negroes must be taken into account.

[72] J. Lab. & Clin. Med., 5:93, 1919.   [73] Loc. cit.; see n. 36.

Von Leyden[74] quotes Buri as sponsor for the earliest statement that "tabes occurs very rarely in the large number of Negroes." The American literature, beginning about forty to fifty years ago, contains many reports of from one to five cases of tabes in Negroes, each one stressing the unusualness of the condition.[75]

Pollock,[76] calculating the racial incidence of general paresis among the general population in New York State from the number of admissions to the New York State hospitals, concluded that the rate was three times as high among Negroes. It is probably an error to assume that the relative occurrence of a disease among Negroes and whites in a hospital represents the same relative occurrence of the disease among the two races in the general population.

In Panama, Wender and Sampson[77] found that in a hospital devoted to the care of the insane, 23.4 per cent of the admissions of West Indian Negroes were for neurosyphilis, while 8.2 per cent of North Americans (white), 12.2 per cent of the Panamanians, and 19.5 per cent of the Chinese were for neurosyphilis. There were twice as many nonparetics as paretics among the Negroes, about equal numbers among the Panamanians, and 2.5 times as many paretics as nonparetics among the North Americans. Hubbard[78] is of the opinion that, if neurosyphilis in the Negro has ever been less than in whites, it is not so any longer, since he found among 1,000 white and 500 colored insane women in Washington, D.C., that 45.7 per cent of the white and 47.5 per cent of the colored had some form of neurosyphilis. Of the total colored admissions, 6.6 per cent had general paresis,

---

[74] *Tabes Dorsalis. Die Erkrankungen des Rückenmarkes, Nothnagel System* (Wien and Leipzig: A. Hölder, 1897).

[75] McConnell, *J. Nerv. & Ment. Dis.*, **16**:212, 1889; Burr, *J. Nerv. & Ment. Dis.*, **19**:278, 1892; Lloyd, *Philadelphia Hosp. Rep.*, **3**:172, 1896; Pearce, *Therap. Gaz.*, **22**:654, 1898; Francine, *Am. J. M. Sc.*, **119**:543, 1900; Hecht, *Am. J. M. Sc.*, **126**: 705, 1903; Lucke, *J. Nerv. & Ment. Dis.*, **43**:393, 1916; Maloney, *Locomotor ataxia* (New York: Appleton & Co., 1918); Hindman, *Am. J. Pub. Health*, **5**:218, 1915; Zimmermann, *loc. cit.*

[76] *Ven. Dis. Inform.*, **5**:112, 1924.   [77] *J. Nerv. & Ment. Dis.*, **58**:525, 1923.

[78] *Arch. Neurol. & Psychiat.*, **12**:198, 1924.

while it was found in only 1.8 per cent of the white admissions. Of the colored syphilitic women 40.2 per cent were paretic, and 30.5 per cent of the white syphilitic women had general paresis. Turner[79] determined the amount of neurosyphilis among 6,562 colored syphilitics and 3,438 white syphilitics. Of the colored, 10.5 per cent had some form, while 33.0 per cent of the whites had some form. General paresis, tabes dorsalis, tabes with optic atrophy, tabes with Charcot joint, taboparesis, paraplegia, optic nerve atrophy, and unclassified were all more prevalent in the white. Tabes with Charcot joint and taboparesis were each ten times more prevalent. However, eighth nerve lesions, epilepsy, and syphilitic cerebral vascular lesions were slightly in excess in colored patients.

Lemann[80] points out that tabes in the Charity Hospital, New Orleans, is 2.17 times more prevalent in the white than in the colored. Vonderlehr, Clark, Wenger, and Heller[81] found that 26.1 per cent of 399 untreated syphilitic Negro males had either clinical or serologic evidence of central nervous system involvement. Definite clinical evidence of neurosyphilis was found in 7.8 per cent of these patients, while in 18.3 per cent the diagnosis was based on serologic evidence only. The 7.8 per cent which had clinically active neurosyphilis was made up of 3 per cent with a relatively benign parenchymatous type and 4.8 per cent with all other forms of central nervous system involvement. In the latter group the most serious type was the vascular form. The benign parenchymatous type did not appear to run the classical course of general paresis or tabes dorsalis. The manifestations which were common included positive reactions in the spinal fluids and changes in the pupillary reactions and tendon reflexes. No typical cases of general paresis or tabes dorsalis were found, but one case of simple dementia was observed. In the Alabama hospital for insane Negroes Ivey[82] found that not a single Negro over twenty-five years of age was confined because of syphilis of the central nervous system. Peterson[83] points out

[79] Loc. cit.; see n. 26.
[80] Loc. cit.; see n. 3.
[81] Loc. cit.; see n. 61.
[82] M. Rec., 84:712, 1913.
[83] The patient and the weather (Ann Arbor, Mich.: Edwards Bros., 1934).

that the Negro who migrates north is more likely to develop tabes dorsalis or general paresis.

Deadman and Morgan,[84] in Vanderbilt Hospital, Nashville, Tennessee, found that, while the ratio of white to Negro in the luetic clinic was 1 white to 3 Negroes, the ratio of the incidence of neurosyphilis was 3.81 whites to 1 Negro. However, the ratio of the various forms of neurosyphilis varied markedly. The largest difference between the two races was in the occurrence of general paresis, which was 55.1 per cent and 18.9 per cent, respectively, in white males and females, and 24.1 per cent and 1.7 per cent, respectively, in colored males and females. In no form of involvement was the incidence higher in colored females than in white females, but in the vascular forms of neurosyphilis, in neurorecurrences, cranial nerve involvement, meningitis, epilepsy, and meningovascular syphilis the uncorrected rates were higher in the Negro.

Quite contrary to the general opinion that general paresis is less in the Negro than in the whites is that of Foster,[85] who claims that, from his experience in Louisiana, the disease is more frequent in colored people, that the neurological changes are well marked, that there is a difference in the mental picture, that the remissions are less often found, but that the course is more rapid than in the white race.

Jeans and Cooke[86] showed a striking and constant difference in the incidence of neurosyphilis in congenitally syphilitic white and colored children. In the white infants up to two years of age two-fifths had neurosyphilis, and in one-fifth of these there occurred clinical evidence of activity in the nervous system, or active neurosyphilis in one-twelfth of all white syphilitic infants. In colored infants, on the other hand, only one-fifth had neurosyphilis, and only one-fifth of these showed clinical signs of neurosyphilis, or active neurosyphilis in one twenty-fifth of all colored syphilitic children. In older syphilitic children the difference was still more marked. Older white children had neurosyphilis in one-third of all infections, and of these over one-half

[84] *South. M. J.*, 26:809, 1933.   [85] *Am. J. Psychiat.*, 5:631, 1925–26.

[86] *Prepubescent syphilis* (New York: D. Appleton & Co., 1930).

had marked clinical involvement, or one-sixth of all older white syphilitic children had serious neurologic lesions. In older colored children only one-eighth had neurosyphilis, and of these only one-eighth had clinical manifestations, or one sixty-fourth of older syphilitic children had clinical neurosyphilis. In 7 of 416 older white children the infection was apparently latent, since fixed or sluggish unequal pupils were the only evidence of neurosyphilis. In no colored child was such pupillary abnormality observed. Of 301 white children of all ages who did not have spinal fluid examinations, 18 had typical clinical neurosyphilis. Of 211 similar colored children without spinal fluid examinations, none had clinical neurosyphilis.

A number of theories have been proposed to account for the differences between Negroes and whites in regard to neurosyphilis. A theory, popular at one time but apparently completely abandoned now, was to the effect that white people used their brains more than Negroes, and the fatigue resulting from overwork lowered the resistance of the organ to the syphilitic virus. In the first place it is extremely doubtful if conscious intellectual effort adds little more than an infinitesimal amount to the total work done by the central nervous system. Second, the difference in neurosyphilis of the two races applies also to the spinal cord and peripheral nerves, which are not involved in mental processes. Third, it is just as rational, or more so, to say that the facts about neurosyphilis indicate that the brain of the Negro is better able to withstand invasion by syphilis because it is a stronger and better organized organ than it is in white races. Finally, the work of Jeans and Cooke shows that the racial differences in neurosyphilis is manifested in early infancy, before the development of intellectual processes.

Three other theories, worthy of more serious consideration, are: (1) the races are infected with two different strains of spirochetes, the Negro with a dermotropic strain and the whites with a neurotropic strain; (2) the invasion of the central nervous system is modified by a high incidence of malaria; and (3) there is a fundamental racial difference in the susceptibility of the nervous system in the two races.

The idea of neurotropic and dermotropic strains of spiro-chetes is supported by experimental evidence obtained with animals artificially infected with syphilis,[87] but there are also many clinical data that are opposed to this conception. The original infection of Negroes came from white sources, and there is yet considerable transmission of the disease from one race to the other, so the likelihood of a specific strain of spirochetes be-ing confined to one race is very small. The organisms that in-fect Negroes do not lack neurotropism, because the investiga-tion of Moore, Turner, and others shows that the difference in initial invasion of the central nervous system is not nearly so great in the two races as is the permanency of such invasions; also, there have been a number of cases similar to the one of Sézary,[88] where a white man acquired syphilis from a colored woman in an area where there were no white women and where neurosyphilis was very rare among the natives. Although the strain acquired was, according to usage, a dermotropic one, the white man developed neurosyphilis.

Since malaria is widespread among the large bulk of Negroes, especially those living in the South, and since malaria has a known beneficial influence on syphilis of the central nervous system, some credence must be given the theory that malaria has some relation to the low incidence of neurosyphilis in col-ored people, especially since other races living in other heavily infested malarial countries have also a low rate of neurosyphilis. Many countries in which this form of syphilis is unusual are tropical or subtropical. Thus in Sicily, the African Levant, and Turkey it is stated to be infrequent. Among uncivilized races in Africa it is almost unknown. That these countries have also a high incidence of malaria is well known. Bercovitz[89] wrote from Hainan, China, where syphilis is the commonest disease among the natives, that it is estimated that 50–60 per cent of the people are infected and that all stages of the disease can be seen. How-ever, neurosyphilis is very rare. Bercovitz believes that this

[87] Levaditi, *Ann. Inst. Pasteur*, 37:189, 1922.

[88] *Bull. Soc. franç. de dermat. et syph.*, 40:1344, 1933.

[89] *J. A. M. A.*, 82:1713, 1934.

scarcity of neurosyphilis is due to the prevalence of malaria. He states that practically every native in Hainan harbors the malaria parasite and that approximately 90 per cent have one or more attacks each year. Merzbacher and Bianchi[90] are of the opinion, from investigations in several Argentine provinces, that malaria modifies the evolution of syphilis in a favorable way. Merzbacher[91] further states that in certain provinces in which malaria is prevalent neurosyphilis is almost unknown. Rosenberg[92] stated that a previous attack of malaria was noted to have a beneficial effect in cases of neurosyphilis in tropical villages. André,[93] after three years' experience in Paraguay, noted that neurosyphilis was rare, and, although he did not mention malaria as the reason, it is known that this latter disease is rampant there. Kerim[94] stated that in Turkey neurosyphilis is rare and malaria is common. Kirschner and Van Loon[95] pointed out that in Java neurosyphilis is three times as common in the Europeans as in natives and that those who develop general paresis are immune to malaria induced by inoculation. Lutrario[96] says that the incidence of neurosyphilis in malaria-infested regions of Italy is low and is high in those regions that have no malaria. Needles[97] showed that, although 31.8 per cent of 6,823 natives in the interior of the Amazon Valley gave positive Kahn reactions, there was only one case of neurosyphilis. On the other hand, the average percentage of the occurrence in the blood of the natives of one or more species of malaria parasites was 38. Needles thought it possible that the high rate of malaria was responsible in part for the rarity of neurosyphilis, since most of the natives acquired malaria in infancy or childhood and, because treatment was inadequate, suffered from

[90] *Arch. argent. de neurol.*, **2**:252, 1928; *Bol. Inst. de clin. quir.*, **4**:181, 1928.

[91] *Deutsche Ztschr. f. Nervenh.*, **113**:1, 1930.

[92] *Arch. f. Schiffs- u. Tropen-Hyg.*, **33**:463, 1929.

[93] *Lyon méd.*, **139**:683, 1929.   [94] *Wien. klin. Wchnschr.*, **39**:915, 1924.

[95] *Klin. Wchnschr.*, **3**:2001, 1924.

[96] *Bull. Office internat. d'hyg. pub.*, **25**:1769, 1933.

[97] *Arch. Neurol. & Psychiat.*, **34**:618, 1935.

chronic malaria with recurring acute exacerbations throughout life.

Malaria is not the sole factor in influencing the occurrence of neurosyphilis. Its importance in this regard is lessened by the observation of Nägelsbach[98] that in the mountainous districts of western Abyssinia, where malaria is unknown, syphilis behaves just as it does in the Sudan, where parasyphilitic lesions do not occur. Furthermore, there is also considerable evidence that the coincidence of malaria with syphilis does not protect the subject from subsequent general paresis. Mandl and Puntigam[99] gathered sixteen cases from the literature where general paresis or tabes dorsalis had occurred in patients who had spontaneous malaria at various periods after their primary syphilitic infection. They report a further four cases of general paresis, two of taboparesis, and nine of tabes similarly occurring.[100]

That there is anything racially characteristic about the manifestation of neurosyphilis can be denied because of similar manifestations in other entirely unrelated races. The low incidence of neurosyphilis in Bosnia, Herzegovina, Turkey, certain parts of Italy, Russia, China, in South America, and in Africa is associated with some other common factor than race. As has been pointed out, this common factor is probably the age of the disease in the race.

SYPHILIS OF THE CARDIOVASCULAR SYSTEM

The cardiovascular system of the Negro seems to bear the brunt of his syphilitic infection. It appears that the well-known predilection of the spirochete of syphilis for the heart and blood vessels is accentuated in this race, and the advantage he gains from a relative immunity of the central nervous system is lost in the damage done to the circulatory system. While most of the difference between the white and the colored race in syphilis of the cardiovascular system is apparently due to differences in

---

[98] *Arch. f. Schiffs- u. Tropen-Hyg.*, 30:121, 1926.

[99] *Zentralbl. f. d. ges. Neurol. u. Psychiat.*, 133:196, 1931.

[100] See also Gougerot, *Bull. Soc. franç. de dermat. et syph.*, 34:234, 1927; Richter, *Deutsche med. Wchnschr.*, 54:222, 264, 1928; Schwartz, *München. med. Wchnschr.*, 71:618, 1924.

the degree of acquired racial immunity because of differences in the length of exposure of the two races to the disease, it is prob-able that an added factor is the fact that Negroes for the most part do heavy manual labor, whereby the heart and blood ves-sels become a *locus minoris resistentiae* for the syphilitic virus and yield to the strain on the tissues, with the resulting lesions characteristic of cardiovascular system.

The higher incidence of syphilitic aortitis, aneurysm, and heart disease among Negroes has been pointed out by many investigators.[101]

Cason is of the opinion that the current belief that the spiro-chetes of syphilis have a predilection for the heart and blood vessels of the Negro is incorrect and is due to the facts that Ne-groes come under observation with older lesions than whites and that they do heavier work. When white and Negro syphilitics with the same duration of the disease and who do the same type of labor are grouped together there is little difference in the in-cidence of cardiovascular disease.

Information about cardiovascular syphilis in African Negroes is scant. There is no reason to believe that wherever syphilis is found among them effects on the heart and blood vessels may not also occur. Substantiation of this statement are the ob-servations of Heimann, Strachan, and Heyman[102] in a series of necropsies and clinical studies of heart disease in South Africa. There were thirty-three cases of cardiovascular syphilis among Kaffirs, Hottentots, and mixed natives. Among these were ten aneurysms. The commonest condition was aortic regurgitation, which was found in more than half the cases. Syphilitic cardio-

---

[101] Janeway, *Boston M. & S. J.*, 174:925, 1916; Wyckoff and Ling, *Am. Heart J.*, 1: 440, 1926; Wood, Jones, and Kimbrough, *Am. J. M. Sc.*, 172:185, 1926; Osler and McCrae, *Principles and practice of medicine* (New York: D. Appleton & Co., 1927); Stone and Vanzant, *J. A. M. A.*, 89:1473, 1927; Lamb and Twine, *Nelson's loose leaf system*, 4:337, 1927; Davison and Thoroughman, *South. M. J.*, 21: 465, 1928; Smith and Kimbrough, *South. M. J.*, 21:634, 1928; Hopkins, *Arch. Dermat.*, 22:232, 1930; Martland, *Am. Heart J.*, 6:1, 1930; Cason, *Am. J. Syph.*, 15:527, 1931; Schwab and Schulze, *Am. Heart J.*, 7:223, 1931; Glaser, *Am. Heart J.*, 7:6, 1931; Laws, *Am. Heart J.*, 8:608, 1933; Lillie and Pasternack, *Ven. Dis. Inform.*, 15:39, 1934; Hedley, *Pub. Health Rept.*, 50:1127, 1935; Tildon, *Med. Bull. Vet. Admin.*, 13:144, 1936; Hazen, *Am. J. Syph.*, 20:530, 1936.

[102] *Brit. M. J.*, 1:344, 1929.

vascular degeneration apart from aortic insufficiency was also common, and there was one case of syphilitic cerebral thrombosis. Dennison[103] had different findings from those of Heimann, Strachan, and Heyman. He states that, while syphilis is common in the East African, syphilitic heart disease is rare. Heim,[104] who wrote about the manifestations of syphilis in the natives of the German colonies, did not refer to cardiovascular syphilis.

CONGENITAL SYPHILIS

The racial features of congenital syphilis, other than the incidence, have not been emphasized. Jeans and Cooke, who have written extensively on hereditary syphilis, have little to say about the comparative appearance of the disease in the two races. In 1920 Jeans[105] reviewed the literature but cited nothing as having been written on this subject. In their book, *Prepubescent syphilis*, they do mention three characteristic features of congenital syphilis in colored children. In early congenital lues they found that serpiginous types of late secondary skin eruptions are much more common in colored than in white infants. In fact, they noted the marked examples only in colored infants. The characteristic feature is irregular lines of infiltrated skin slightly raised above the surface and without ulceration or loss of substance. These lines sometimes present a bizarre configuration but generally in the form of irregular concentric circles. Another feature of congenital syphilis in Negro children is the low incidence of neurosyphilis, which has been discussed. The third feature concerns dental hypoplasias, which have been much more common in the white syphilitic children than in the colored. They observed that most of the typical deformities, especially those of the upper central incisors, have occurred in white children, and characteristic Hutchinson's teeth have only occasionally been seen in the colored children.

TREATMENT

The questions have been asked whether, as a whole, syphilis is a milder or severer disease in Negroes than in white people

[103] *Brit. M. J.*, 1:478, 1929.

[104] *Loc. cit.;* see n. 11.   [105] *Am. J. Dis. Child.*, 20:55, 132, 1920.

and whether it yields to treatment more easily or with more difficulty. The consensus is that there is no significant difference either in the severity of lesions or in the response to antisyphilitic treatment.[106]

Heim[107] points out the extreme sensitiveness of Africans to mercurialism. Walsh and Stickley[108] suggest that arsphenamine poisoning occurs oftener in the colored, especially women. They reported fourteen cases of the acute condition, eleven of which were in colored women. They believe an instability of the hematopoietic system to be the explanation as well as the stoicism of colored women, which prevents them from confiding warning symptoms of the first injection of arsphenamine and which would thereby prevent a fatal outcome from subsequent injections. On the other hand, Yampolsky[109] declares it is rare to have untoward symptoms in the Negro following the use of antisyphilitic arsenicals.

Cole et al.[110] state that the favorable influence of pregnancy on syphilis is accentuated in colored women and also that colored women respond to antisyphilitic treatment better than do whites.

Since most colored people in the South are resistant to tertian malaria, Branche[111] conceived the idea of using quartan malaria for the treatment of general paresis in Negroes instead of the generally used tertian strain. This procedure, now in wide use, gives excellent therapeutic results. In his latest report Branche[112] claims 94 per cent takes after quartan inoculation into 346 Negroes. While agreeing with the advantages of the method, Fong[113] obtained only 53.2 per cent takes in Negroes.

Many reports have been made of the beneficial results of treatment in Negroes, but, on a whole, these differed little from those obtained in whites.

[106] Hazen, *J. A. M. A.*, 63:463, 1914; Heim, *loc. cit.*

[107] *Loc. cit.*

[108] *Am. J. Syph.*, 19:323, 1935.   ·   [111] *J. Nerv. & Ment. Dis.*, 83:177, 1936.

[109] *Am. J. Dis. Child.*, 48:81, 1934.   [112] *Am. J. Psych.*, 96:967, 1940.

[110] *Ven. Dis. Inform.*, 15:83, 1934.   [113] *Am. J. Syph.*, 24:133, 1940.

SUMMARY

The peculiarities of syphilis in Negroes appear to consist chiefly of a larger amount of infection among them and in the lability of the cardiovascular system to syphilitic lesions. There is, in addition, a questionable difference between white and colored people in the occurrence of syphilitic lesions of the central nervous system. The greater tendency of Negroes to develop annular syphilides has been emphasized by several writers.

Moral laxity, ignorance, poverty, and the unavailability of clinical facilities have been claimed to be the chief factors in the high rate of syphilis among Negroes. The United States Public Health–Rosenwald Fund investigations have shown an important relationship of economic status and the amount of syphilis in a community. With better incomes there are better schools and less ignorance, better moral standards and less exposure, more efficient hospitals and clinics providing greater facilities for treatment, all of which have a decided lowering effect on disease rates.

The susceptibility of the heart and blood vessels of Negroes to syphilis is marked. The reason for this is not clear. Differences in the strains of the spirochetes attacking white and colored people, qualitative characteristics of the makeup of the blood vessels, and relative amounts of severe physical labor done within the two races have been suggested.

While the older literature indicated that there was a marked difference in the occurrence of syphilis of the central nervous system, to the effect that it was rare in colored people, more recent writers deny the existence of any difference and even claim that it is more prevalent in Negroes. Those who insist that Negroes are less affected suggest the same type of factors that are given to explain the differences in cardiovascular syphilis; namely, the tissue affinities of the infecting spirochetes—neurotropic strains more often invading white people—qualitative variations in the structure and properties of the central nervous system, and differences in the amount of mental and nervous activity in the two races.

There is a possibility that there is a more basic cause for the racial characteristics of syphilis which is analogous to the suggested cause of the racial differences in tuberculosis. Syphilis, like tuberculosis, is greatly influenced by tissue immunity, which is usually directly acquired but which may also be acquired in some degree by inheritance. Negroes have not been in contact with syphilis as long as have most white races, and there probably has not been the opportunity to develop the same racial resistance through the forces of natural selection.

YAWS

The literature on yaws is very extensive, but most of it has to do with the much-debated question as to whether it and syphilis are the same or different diseases, and little of it is concerned with the differences, if any, in its effect on various races. It is very evident from the many statistics and case reports in the literature that yaws is chiefly a disease of Negroes, seemingly not because of an unusual predilection for these people but chiefly because of the geographical distribution of the disease. It is a tropical and subtropical infection and practically never invades temperate zones. Of the Negro countries, it is common in tropical Africa, the West Indies, and in those parts of Central and South America with similar climates. It is rare in the United States, and most of the cases found here, according to Fox,[1] are seen in the northern Atlantic seaports in white sailors who have been in tropical countries. In those countries where the disease is endemic it is not uniformly distributed, for which various explanations have been given, such as indigenous hygienic habits, facilities for treatment, the concomitant amount of syphilis, rainfall, altitude, and the presence of certain insect vectors. Among the West Indian islands it is very prevalent in Haiti, the Dominican Republic, Jamaica, and Martinique, while it is practically absent in the Virgin Islands, the Bahamas, Barbados, and Bermuda. There is also a wide variation in its distribution in Africa. In certain parts, such as Liberia, West Africa, French Equatorial Africa, it is very prevalent, the majority of the population showing evidences of infection. On the other hand, in other parts it is unusual or absent. Butler,[2] an ardent advocate of the unitarian hypothesis of yaws and syphilis, believes that what is called yaws is a massive infection of new races with untreated syphilis. According to him, tropical countries with a low incidence of yaws signify that syphilis is under control or that it has not been introduced into the general population.

[1] *Arch. Dermat. & Syph.*, 6:675, 1922.

[2] *Am. J. Clin. Path.*, 9:1, 1934; *U.S. Nav. M. Bull.*, 35:6, 1937.

Butler[3] presents evidence that yaws existed in North Carolina during the early days of slavery. It was brought to this country by slaves from Guinea and transmitted to the whites by cohabitation. It was called "country distemper" and had all the symptoms of syphilis, though no scandal was attached to the disease. It was not affected by mercury.

Because yaws attacks white people relatively infrequently, some writers have interpreted this as signifying that the disease has a selectivity for colored races. Those who have had the opportunity of comparing the infectivity of Negroes with other races say there are no variable racial susceptibilities. Thus, Turner and Saunders[4] say that in Jamaica the black, white, brown, and yellow races may be equally easily infected, although they point out that children of white and Negro crosses have a greater resistance than those of either of these two races or of East Indians. Pardo-Costello[5] found that in Cuba, where 41.5 per cent of the population is Negro, the white and colored are equally infected, and there is no difference in the development of lesions and in the clinical symptoms found.

Since syphilis in the Negro has a characteristic clinical and pathological appearance, particularly as to the type of skin lesions and in the effects on the cardiovascular and nervous system, investigators have sought similar characteristics in the effects of yaws as a source of evidence for or against the theory of the unity of the diseases. Fox,[6] who is familiar with syphilis in the American Negro, studied yaws as it appeared in the rural districts of Haiti. He found that the cutaneous lesions resembled those of syphilis in many respects but differed in others, though perhaps not fundamentally. Striking features were extragenital mode of infection (unusual for syphilis in Negroes), the keratotic lesions of the soles, the absence of lesions of the mucous membranes in the early stages, and the clinical identity of tertiary manifestations with those of syphilis. In addition to

[3] *Arch. Dermat. & Syph.*, 32:446, 1935.

[4] *Report of the Jamaica Yaws Committee* (Kingston: Government of Jamaica, 1933).

[5] *Arch. Dermat. & Syph.*, 40:762, 1939.   [6] *Op. cit.*, 20:820, 1929.

the classic granulomatous lesions, a miliary papular eruption was not infrequently seen as an early manifestation, which at times closely resembled lichen scrofulosorum. Yaws of the scalp was noted and also an instance of severe paronychia. In one case showing a scaling, macular eruption of the palms, which was indistinguishable from that of secondary syphilis, the patient presented undoubted evidence of yaws. Parenchymatous involvement of the brain and spinal cord in yaws, which is infrequent in syphilis in Negroes, does not occur, although nontabetic lesions are found in yaws as well as in syphilis. Fox mentions a series of 722 consecutive autopsies in Haiti, among which there were 10 cases of yaws, 8 of which showed aneurysms of the aorta. There was an absence of lesions in children similar to the stigmata of congenital syphilis. It is not clear what conclusions Fox arrived at as to the relation of yaws to syphilis on the basis of these observations.

Turner,[7] who also has had much experience with syphilis in the Negro, compared syphilis as found among the colored people in Baltimore with yaws in the rural districts of Jamaica and with yaws and syphilis as found in the city of Kingston, Jamaica. He concluded that there are easily recognizable differences between the two diseases which cannot be explained on the basis of differences in factors, such as race (since all observations were made on Negroes), age of the person at time of infection, the portal of entry of the organisms, or the social and economic status of the infected individual. From these findings, as well as from experiments with animals, he believes, first, that *Treponema pallidum*, the causative agent of syphilis, possesses pathogenic properties which differ from those of *T. pertenue*, the causative agent of yaws, and, second, that the differences noted between yaws and syphilis in man are due at least to inherent differences in the causative agent of each disease.

Weller examined microscopically the lesions from cases of yaws in Haiti and found in the aorta[8] and in the viscera[9] changes

[7] *Am. J. Hyg.*, 25:477, 1937.

[8] *Am. J. Syph.*, 20:467, 1936.   [9] *Ibid.*, 21:357, 1937.

which were not unlike those which are usually considered characteristic of syphilis.

Harley[10] examined 5,597 cases of yaws in Liberia, where about 80 per cent of the people have the disease, and where venereal syphilis apparently does not occur. He tabulated the frequency of occurrence of what he calls the cardinal symptoms of yaws in order to identify all the cases as being this disease. He also gave evidence that such locally occurring disorders as goundou, gangosa, and juxta-articular nodes, formerly believed to be separate disease entities, are, in fact, manifestations of yaws. Goundou and gangosa are nasopharyngeal localizations of tertiary lesions, while juxta-articular nodes are the fibrotic tumors situated over the olecranon and lower part of the femur, occurring in the tertiary stage of both yaws and syphilis. He came to no definite conclusions as to the relation of syphilis and yaws but proposed to use his findings as the basis of a statistical comparison of the lesions of the two diseases that would indicate a definite answer as to their identity or difference.

[10] *J. Trop. Med.*, 36:217, 1933.

LYMPHOGRANULOMA VENEREUM

Lymphogranuloma venereum,[1] a disease formerly believed to be associated with the tropics and with the colored races indigenous to such countries, is now known to be widespread, affecting most countries and most races. This newer concept of its distribution is due, first, to the realization that several diseases previously considered as distinct entities are, in fact, a part of lymphogranuloma venereum, whose manifestations are influenced by sex, portal of entry, and age of lesion, and, second, to the discovery of the Frei test, which makes available a ready and fairly accurate means of diagnosis.

Basically, lymphogranuloma venereum is an adenitis and periadenitis of the local lymph glands, following the introduction of a filterable virus at the site of the primary lesion, usually situated on the genitalia. The inflammation, suppuration, and necrosis in and about the inguinal lymph glands in the male constitute the buboes of the disease, and the subsequent cicatrices often produce a blockage of lymphatic drainage that results in elephantiasis of the penis and scrotum. In the female the primary lesion is believed to be usually located on the vulva or posterior wall of the vagina, and, while there may or may not be inguinal buboes, the lymphatic structures deep within the pelvic girdle are involved. This often results in elephantiasis and ulceration of the vulva—the so-called esthiomene—or in stricture of the rectum. Before these processes were unified as stages of a single disease, they were designated under a variety of different names, including such terms as climatic bubo, strumous or scrofulous bubo, elephantiasis pudendorum, esthiomene vulvae, and anorectal syphiloma. Indeed Stannus[2] lists forty-three designations of the disease which have been used by different writers in various languages.

During the course of the infection an allergy develops which forms the basis of the Frei test used for the diagnosis of lympho-

[1] For a more thorough review of the disease see Stannus, *A sixth venereal disease* (London: Bailliere, Lindall & Co., 1933); Frei, *J. A. M. A.*, 111:1653, 1938; Jones and Rome, *New Internat. Clin.*, 2:178, 1938.

[2] *Loc. cit.;* see n. 1.

granuloma venereum. Pus aspirated from a bubo or, in some instances, the extract of the brain of a mouse or of chicken embryonic tissue inoculated with the virus of the disease forms the antigen. Injected intracutaneously the antigen produces a local inflammation in patients having lymphogranuloma venereum.

Although Klotz[3] fifty years ago reported 120 cases of climatic bubo, presumably among whites in the United States, recent interest in the disease was aroused in this country by the introduction here of the Frei test by Sulzberger and Wise,[4] DeWolf and VanCleve,[5] and Cole.[6] These authors applied the test in clinics in Cleveland and disclosed, as has been corroborated by studies in various parts of the country, that lymphogranuloma venereum is not an uncommon disease. Most of the evidence, however, shows that it is much more prevalent among the Negro population than among the white. D'Aunoy and von Haam[7] emphasize that it is "widespread in New Orleans, particularly among the Negroes," and that in one clinic 461 cases were observed. DeWolf and VanCleve[8] saw twice as many colored men as white with the disease in Cleveland. In St. Louis, according to a series of 790 tests made by Gray, Hurt, Wheeler, and Blache[9] on a mixed population, the incidence of lymphogranuloma venereum in the whites was found to be 3.4 per cent and in Negroes it was 40 per cent. In Philadelphia Martin[10] stresses the higher frequency in Negroes without giving actual figures. Robinson[11] found the Frei test positive in 1 per cent of the whites examined in Baltimore and in 60 per cent of the Negroes. Goldblatt[12] likewise found that 60 per cent of the Negroes reacted in Cincinnati. Brandt and Torpin[13] say that a large number of positive Frei reactions in Negroes is not accounted for by symptoms or a history of the disease. They believe that such reac-

[3] *Berl. klin. Wchnschr.*, 27:132, 153, 175, 1890.

[4] *J. A. M. A.*, 99:1407, 1932.

[5] *J. A. M. A.*, 99:1065, 1932.

[6] *J. A. M. A.*, 101:1069, 1933.

[7] *South. M. J.*, 29:911, 1936.

[8] *Loc. cit.*; see n. 5.

[9] *J. A. M. A.*, 106:919, 1936.

[10] *J. A. M. A.*, 101:1551, 1933.

[11] *J. A. M. A.*, 108:31, 1937.

[12] *J. A. M. A.*, 108:31, 1937.

[13] *Am. J. Syph.*, 24:632, 1940.

tions may be due to (*a*) nonspecific factors, (*b*) coreactions (other diseases), or, (*c*) unrecognized disease in the past. The most striking racial differences are found in the incidence of stricture of the rectum, a disease whose etiology was definitely determined only after the development of the Frei test. Previously it had most often been attributed to syphilis and was usually called anorectal syphiloma. Gonorrhea and amebic dysentery had also at times been thought to cause rectal stricture. Although inconsistencies in attributing these diseases as causes have been repeatedly pointed out, it was not until Frei and Koppel[14] applied the Frei test to patients with rectal stricture and in whom all other probable causes had been ruled out that the real nature of the process was disclosed. They proved thereby that lymphogranuloma venereum was definitely the cause of rectal stricture, and their findings have since been corroborated many times.

Rectal stricture occurs preponderantly in females, but it is in Negro females that the disease is particularly frequent.[15] Some authors used this latter fact unjustly as evidence of the syphilitic nature of the strictures. Rosser[16] believed that the great frequency and severity of rectal stricture in the Negro is due to a so-called fibroplastic diathesis. However, with the demonstration that lymphogranuloma venereum is the cause of rectal stricture, the frequency of the strictures in colored people is explained by the frequency in them of lymphogranuloma venereum, although the explanation of why they are infected with the virus of lymphogranuloma venereum more often is lacking.

D'Aunoy and Schenken[17] believe that many of the chronic pelvic infections that are common in colored women are due to lymphogranuloma venereum. They cite a case in which the extirpated Fallopian tubes appeared grossly to be chronic sal-

---

[14] *Klin. Wchnschr.*, 7:2331, 1928.

[15] Martin, *loc. cit.*; *Tr. Am. Proct. Soc.*, 36:91, 1935; Aley, *Tr. Am. Proct. Soc.*, 35:150, 1934; Lee and Staley, *Ann. Surg.*, 100:486, 1934; Gray *et al.*, *loc. cit.*; Vander Veer, Cornia, and Ullery, *Am. J. M. Sc.*, 190:178, 1935; Matthewson, *J. A. M. A.*, 110:709, 1938.

[16] *J. A. M. A.*, 84:93, 1925.　　　　　[17] *J. A. M. A.*, 110:799, 1938.

pingitis nodosa but which on microscopic examination showed the picture of lymphogranuloma venereum. Paulson[18] suggests that some of the cases of ulcerative colitis might be due to a virus similar to that of lymphogranuloma venereum. He prepared an antigen from the scrapings or washings of the mucous membrane of the affected bowel and found that it gave positive reactions in patients with ulcerative colitis.

Although long associated with tropical countries and known to be especially prevalent among colored people, there is surprisingly little factual information about the occurrence of lymphogranuloma venereum among Negroes in Africa. Chesterman,[19] using the Frei test, found foci of the disease in urban centers and rural districts in the Belgian Congo. He describes cases of bubo in the male and of rectal stricture in the female. Gray[20] reported five cases of rectal stricture in Nigeria, one in a white male and four in native women. Stannus[21] recalls in retrospect having seen several cases of esthiomene in east-central Africa but did not at that time recognize the true nature of the condition.

[18] *J. A. M. A.*, 109:1080, 1937.

[19] *Tr. Roy. Soc. Trop. Med. & Hyg.*, 31:585, 1938.

[20] *Brit. J. Ven. Dis.*, 8:114, 1932. [21] *Loc. cit.;* see n. 1.

MALARIA

Out of the large volume of literature on malaria in Negroes there is little that can be culled which applies specifically to these people. The importance of malaria to the Negro is by virtue of the fact that he lives in those parts of the world— Africa, the West Indies, and South America—which, among others, form the great reservoirs of the disease. There is no evidence that race per se is a factor in the existence or perpetuation of malaria.

There is one phase of the malaria problem, however, where the Negro as a race figures prominently. Even in this relation the assumption of a racial factor is believed to be wrong, although in attempting to establish this, important facts about the disease have been disclosed. This particular angle referred to has to do with immunity in malaria. It has been long thought that the Negro is immune to the disease, the basis for which is the well-known fact that white settlers in parts of Africa where malaria is endemic rapidly succumb to the disease, while the natives flourish, seemingly without ill effects from it. The study of this resistance of the African disclosed the paradox that he is at one and the same time immune and yet is heavily infected with parasites—facts which, nevertheless, are not inconsistent when compared with some other disease, like tuberculosis, in which active infection is the basis of immunity. Taliaferro[1] points out that the meaning of immunity as applied to malaria is ambiguous, as it may refer to immunity to the parasites or to the toxins produced by the organisms. The Negro is certainly not immune to the parasites, because in those areas in Africa where the disease flourishes practically every infant, before it is six months old, becomes infected and remains so throughout life. In this first infection the child becomes ill, the spleen enlarges, and parasites in large numbers are found in the blood. With a history of recovery and reinfections, the disease becomes latent, the organisms disappear from the circulation, and the spleen regresses in size. The latency is evidenced by the disease

---

[1] *The immunology of parasitic infections* (New York: Century Co., 1930).

becoming active when there are debilitating conditions. But in the absence of such factors the individuals remain well, owing to the immunity to the toxins of the parasites which are present.

In addition to this acquired immunity there is said to exist a natural immunity demonstrable on rare occasions. This, when it occurs, is an individual characteristic and is in no way related to race.

The relation of race to the immunity of the Negro is summarized by Wilson and Wilson,[2] who, on the basis of their own comparative observations in Africa and in India, refuted the claims of Schüffner, Swellengrebel, Annecke, and DeMeillon[3] that there are racial differences in the immune mechanisms in Africa. Wilson and Wilson also state that there can be no clear-cut racial distinctions in the immune reactions to malaria. They were quite unable to distinguish first infections in African infants from endemic areas, in adult Africans from nonendemic areas, in Indians, or in Europeans, either by their clinical severity, or by the parasite count, or by the morphology of the parasites seen. Frequent reinfections are necessary for the development and maintenance of complete immunity under natural conditions, and this applies to any country and to any race. The immune status of a community is dependent on the infected anopheline infestation of the locality, and the immunity obtainable in any community by one race is obtainable by any other race.

On the other hand, Ashford[4] reviewed certain writers on the subject of immunity in malaria and came to the conclusion that racial or inherited immunity to malaria, while relative, definitely exists as a result of generations of exposure of the indigenous population. This form of mass immunity is specific for the several species of parasites as it is in individual immunity, so that the natives of a malarial region are relatively least immune to the species last introduced into their native land or to those of new lands into which there is migration. It appears that, be-

[2] Tr. Roy. Soc. Trop. Med. & Hyg., 30:431, 1937.

[3] Publ. South African Inst. Med. Research, 4:245, 1931; Centralbl. f. Bakt., Abt. I, 125:1, 1932.

[4] Am. J. Trop. Med., 16:665, 1936.

cause of this racial immunity, malaria has a relatively low mortality and relatively low morbidity among the native adults. The efficiency of the acquired immunity of African natives seems to be due to the fact that first infections and reinfections are allowed to run their full natural course. Europeans developing malaria in Africa are usually treated early with quinine and the disease is aborted. No immunity is developed, yet because of the lack of an inherited immunity it is dangerous for them to risk the disease without treatment.

The endemicity of malaria in an area is thought to be adequately determined by surveys of the incidence of spleen enlargement and the incidence of parasites in the circulation. The accuracy of such surveys has been questioned. It is obvious that, in order to give any indication at all as to the occurrence of the disease, the examinations must be made early in life. Clark[5] expressed the opinion that race is an important factor in determining whether or not the spleen will become enlarged in malarial infection. Carley and Balfour[6] attributed to race the difference in "spleen rates" in Negro and white children in the Mississippi Delta, living under the same chances of malarial infection. They found in Panama children also[7] that splenomegaly, as a sign of malaria, is more constant in the mestizo (mixtures of Negro, Indian, and white) than in the Negro. An enlarged spleen is more likely to be accompanied by parasites in the peripheral blood in a Negro child than in a mestizo child.

The intensity of the malarial infection of the West Indies and Central and South America has been known since the time of Columbus. In these places, as in Africa, the apparent immunity of the Negro subsequent to his heavy infection is high. Striking evidence of this was seen during the construction of the Panama Canal, which was made possible by the imported labor from the West Indies. The contrast in the mortality from malaria between these West Indian laborers and the American whites was remarkable.

[5] United Fruit Company, seventeenth annual report (Boston, 1928).

[6] South. M. J., 22:377, 1929.   [7] Am. J. Trop. Med., 12:467, 1932.

In the United States, malaria, while a great health problem among Negroes, again shows no race discrimination. Although the clinically active disease in many areas affects colored people more than it does white people in the same area, it is probably because the living conditions of the former are more conducive to more extensive and severe infection. The general mortality statistics for malaria show that the death rate among colored people is approximately eight times that among white people. These figures, however, do not give an adequate picture either of the extent of malaria in this country, since malaria is not an important cause of death, or of its relative occurrence in the two races, since the majority of the Negroes live in the southern states, where the largest endemic areas are, while the majority of the whites live in northern states, where there is little malaria.

In that part of the South where malarial infection is the heaviest, namely, in the lower valley of the Mississippi River,[8] there is not much difference in the infection rates of white and colored. What difference exists is due to the fact that Negroes live under conditions more favorable to the disease. Most of them live in rural districts where there are more open ponds and swamps, their houses are more open and less screened, their occupations expose them more freely to mosquitoes, and antimalaria information and control measures are less available to them. Furthermore, the larger excess of debilitating causes—tuberculosis, syphilis, malnutrition, fatiguing labor—activate latent malarial infections into active disease.

The apparent immunity of the Negro is much less evident in America than in Africa, the reasons for which are understood if the modern conception of immunity in malaria is acceptable. While practically 100 per cent of the Africans receive their first infection before the sixth month of life, the highest rate of first infection among Negroes at any age in American malarial districts is about 24 per cent. Also the possibility for repeated reinfections which permit retention of immunity is less, owing to control measures.

[8] Dowling, *Am. J. Trop. Med.*, 4:461, 1924.

A number of writers have advanced the hypothesis that malaria was more accountable for the downfall of the Greek and Roman empires than any other factor. Ross, in the Introduction of a book by Jones[9] on this subject, points out that such evils as superstition, war, misgovernment, and vices to which intellectual decadence is often attributed may not be the primary cause but, like the national deteriorations, are secondary to disease as the primary cause. It is not the acute epidemic diseases that are important in this relation. These may even leave a people stronger, because the weak are killed off. The effective factor is those endemic diseases, like malaria, which, when once introduced, oppress a nation forever. If malaria is such a potent agent in destroying civilizations it can be equally potent in preventing the development of a nation. It seems that the backwardness of the African people, an adequate reason for which has been sought, might be accounted for by the retarding action of malaria and other endemic diseases, like sleeping sickness. Evidence has been disclosed that malaria existed in Africa at least since 2100 B.C. If malaria can be thus incriminated, it is probable that the salvation of the African people lies not in schools and churches, important as these may be, but in screen doors and quinine.

[9] *Malaria: a neglected factor in the history of Greece and Rome* (Cambridge, Eng.: Macmillan and Bowes, 1907).

LEPROSY

Because Africa is one of the oldest endemic centers of leprosy, Negroes have been closely involved with the history of the disease. Particularly they have been cast in the role of conveyors of the infection to the New World, where they were taken as slaves. While much has been written about the geographic distribution of leprosy, little can be gleaned from the accumulated information as to what extent differences in racial susceptibilities have been a factor in the extremely variable amounts of the disease found in different countries. Hirsch[1] writes about the special liability of Negroes in places where there are mixed populations. He states that in the West Indies, in South America, and in South Africa, where Negroes and white people live together, the disease is much commoner among Negroes and among those mixed with Negro blood than among white people to whom it is relatively, or even absolutely, rare. This statement is not borne out by more recent and accurate information. In the first place, there is a great variation in the distribution of leprosy among Negroes in the West Indies and among the colored natives of Africa, a fact that is against the idea of a uniform higher racial susceptibility of Negroes. The disease is common in the Negroes of Cuba, Jamaica, the Barbados, Trinidad, Bahamas, Guadeloupe, and Madagascar, while it is much less common in the Virgin Islands, Haiti, the Dominican Republic, and Bermuda. Likewise, in parts of Africa, especially in certain regions of the interior, the disease is believed to be unusual or absent, although it is probable that defective medical information might be responsible for this impression.

In the United States there is also a variation of opinion as to the relative occurrence of leprosy in white and colored people. Hopkins and Denney[2] state that statistics from the United States National Leprosarium in Carville, Louisiana, show that the disease occurs twice as often among white people as among

[1] *Handbook of geographical and historical pathology* (London: New Sydenham Society, 1885).

[2] *J. A. M. A.* 92:191, 1929.

Negroes. A more recent informal statement from the medical officers of that institution indicates that the proportion of white and Negro patients confined there is about the same as the pro- portion of whites and Negroes in the general population.

There has been some suggestion that the nodular form of leprosy is more often found in Negroes than in whites, but there is no reliable evidence that this is true. Cozenanette[3] reported a rather high incidence of mental diseases among lepers which did not differ in nature from that occurring in non-lepers except in the tendency to progress more rapidly to deterioration. The psychoses that develop may be either depressive or delusional in form. An opinion expressed about these views indicated that the depression resulted from a reaction to the rigorous isolation rather than from organic changes associated with leprosy, and that racial differences in the incidence of depression are deter- mined by the differences in ability to adjust to confinement in a leprosarium. Delusional psychoses in leprosy occur in those predisposed to such conditions and have no racial selectivity other than that which is found in the general population.

[3] *J. A. M. A.*, 89:1496, 1927.

ACUTE INFECTIOUS DISEASES

DIPHTHERIA

All available statistics for Negroes, whether in Africa or in America, indicate that these people are much less susceptible to diphtheria than are white people.[1] Medical writers have been especially impressed with the rarity and mildness of the disease among the natives in certain parts of Africa and have been led to inquire if their immunity is a natural one or if it is acquired. Kleine and Kroo[2] state that in East Africa diphtheria is completely unknown. They performed Schick tests on 101 natives, 95 of whom were children ranging in age from six to fifteen years, the remaining 6 being adults. Not a single positive reaction was obtained. Since slight reactions are difficult to detect in black skins, they sought to check the Schick tests with titrations of antitoxin in the blood serum. Extraordinarily high titers of antitoxin were disclosed in the serum of 11 individuals. More than 1 unit per cc. of serum was found in 2 instances, 0.5 unit per cc. in 3, 0.1 unit per cc. in 2, and 0.05 unit per cc. in 3. In accounting for these findings Kleine and Kroo believed there might be latent infections among the natives, although they considered the possibility of heterogenous antigenic stimulation of antibody formation or simply a physiological secretion of antibodies without the action of antigen. Fischer,[3] who also had neither seen nor heard of a case of diphtheria in East Africa among the natives, made Schick tests on 283 children from seven to thirteen years of age and found only 3 positive reactions. Titration of the antitoxin content of 83 serums disclosed that 73 per cent of these contained 0.05 unit or more of antitoxin per cc. No instance of 1 unit per cc. was found. The finding of even this small number of positive reactions indicated to Fischer that the immunity of natives was not absolute. Grasset

---

[1] Hirsch, *Handbook of geographical and historical pathology* (London: New Sydenham Society, 1885); Clemow, *Geography of disease* (Cambridge, 1903); Hoffman, *Race traits and tendencies of the American Negro* (New York: Macmillan Co., 1896).

[2] *Deutsche med. Wchnschr.*, 56:46, 1930.

[3] *Ztschr. f. Immunitätsforsch. u. exper. Therap.*, 74:244, 1932.

and Perret-Gentil[4] made similar examinations in an entirely different community. They tested 276 Bantu Bush Negroes in Portuguese East Africa and 287 urban Bantus in Johannesburg. Ages from four months to advanced old age were represented. The primitive Bush people gave 6.16 per cent positive Schick reactions and the urban natives 10.45 per cent. Antibody titration of serums showed that the largest number (38.95 per cent) contained more than 0.2 and less than 0.5 unit per cc., although 2.32 per cent contained more than 1 unit per cc., and 7.56 per cent contained less than 0.02 unit per cc., which is the lowest limit of antibody concentration that permits a negative Schick reaction. These authors think that diphtheria infection actually occurs among the natives. They find that 96 per cent of the females twenty years of age have negative Schick reactions. This immunity is conveyed passively to their infants, who give a very high percentage of negative reactions the first few months of life. Cauchi and Smith[5] state that the natives are immunized actively by what appears to be subclinical diphtheria. In Nigeria they tested 1,753 individuals ranging in age from one month to twenty years. For the whole group 19 per cent gave positive Schicks. Those one to twelve months of age gave 32.6 per cent positive tests, those one to ten years 21.7 per cent, ten to fifteen years 2.0 per cent, fifteen to twenty years 2.0 per cent.

While Negroes in the United States suffer from diphtheria more than they do in Africa, they nevertheless show much less liability to the disease than do whites. It must be remembered, however, that all comparative statistics for diphtheria in this country must be considered in the light of the many factors that may influence the rate of infection, the case fatality, and the mortality. The differences that are usually associated with race may also be due to differences in density of population, hygienic habits, the availability of and the readiness to accept artificial immunization, and the accuracy and promptness of antiserum administration. In none of the studies made of racial differences in regard to diphtheria are these factors adequately evaluated.

4 *Compt. rend. Soc. de biol.*, 113:1457, 1460, 1933.   5 *Lancet*, 2:1393, 1934.

Crum[6] points out that in thirty southern cities during the five years 1909–13, the average annual death rate of the white population from diphtheria and croup was 13.7 per 100,000 against an average rate of only 8.1 for the Negro population. The morbidity rates, according to statistics from Washington, D.C., from 1908 to 1915, were likewise less in Negroes. The white morbidity rate for all ages in that city was 16.6 per 10,000 population, while the Negro rate was 9.6. The white morbidity rate for each age group was higher, except that of the ten-to-nineteen-years group, which was 1 per cent higher in the Negro. On the other hand, it appears that the case-fatality rate is greater in Negroes. The Washington figures show that from 1896 to 1915 the average case-fatality rate for the whites was 9.4 per cent and for Negroes it was 17.4 per cent.

Black,[7] impressed by the very small proportion which Negroes contributed to the cases of diphtheria observed in a fairly extensive epidemic in Mississippi, inquired if this was a local or a general phenomenon. He found that in the United States from 1915 to 1924 Negroes quite generally suffered a lower mortality from diphtheria than did whites, the only exception to this rule being found in certain large cities during certain years. This relative exemption of Negroes from diphtheria is effective principally during the period from one to ten or fifteen years of age. During the first year of life and during adult life the Negro rates are slightly higher. These same characteristics also apply to the differences exhibited in morbidity. Black made Schick tests in Mississippi, Tennessee, and Baltimore on Negro and white children and found no appreciable differences in immunity if corresponding ages are compared. On the other hand, the responsiveness to immunizing injections of toxin-antitoxin mixtures was higher in Negro children than in white.

In rural Alabama, Chason[8] found that the mean percentage of immunity among Negroes was higher and increased more rapidly until the eleventh year of age than it did among whites.

[6] Am. J. Pub. Health, 7:445, 1917.

[7] Am. J. Hyg., 13:734, 1934.   [8] Am. J. Hyg., 23:539, 1936.

A change in the Schick reaction from positive to negative occurred in 24 per cent of the Negro children in 67 days and in only 11 per cent of the white children in 91 days. At six years of age 68 per cent and at ten years of age 92 per cent of the white children were Schick negative, while at seven years of age 92 per cent of the colored children were negative.

Further corroborating evidence of the lesser effect of diphtheria on colored people are the statistics of the Metropolitan Life Insurance Company[9] which show that from 1911 to 1935 the white male death rate was 44.0 per 100,000 and the white female death rate 42.1 per 100,000, while the colored male rate was 25.8 and the colored female rate 24.1. However, the mortality among whites has decreased much more rapidly than it has among Negroes. For the years 1911–15 the mortality among white children was double that for the colored, but in the period 1931–35 the excess of white over colored mortality at ages one to fourteen years was only 7 per cent among males and 24 per cent among females.

The findings of Zingher[10] were at variance with results of most investigations in that he observed a high percentage of positive reactions in Negro children in the public schools of New York City and in two orphan asylums. He gave no figures but states that the data were unexpected, since these people lived in congested areas.

Doull and Fales[11] found in Baltimore a slightly lower diphtheria-carrier rate among Negro children than among whites.

LOBAR PNEUMONIA

The opinion is firmly established in the literature that the Negro is far more susceptible to pneumonia than is the white, although occasionally this view is questioned. Reiman says:

The reports of the relative susceptibility of different races are unreliable. Until studies are made of the incidence of different types of pneumococci in causing pneumonia, conclusions cannot be drawn. Such susceptibility may

[9] *Twenty years of health progress* (New York: Metropolitan Life Insurance Company, 1937).

[10] *J. A. M. A.*, 77:835, 1921.   [11] *Am. J. Hyg.*, 3:604, 1923.

not be racial in nature but merely evidence of the lack of previous exposure or lack of specific immunity to infection. The probabilities are that no true racial differences exist in regard to susceptibility to pneumococcus lobar pneumonia.[12]

Bullowa,[13] working on problems of pneumonia in Harlem Hospital, where 80 per cent of the patients are Negroes, is less convinced of the higher susceptibility of Negroes from his own experience than from the reports in the literature.

The Negro is a victim of most of the circumstances that are factors in a high incidence of pneumonia—severe labor, exposure, inadequate nourishment, poor housing, rural habitation, and so forth. While statistics invariably show a higher rate for colored people, in appraising them due consideration is rarely given these factors.

Apart from the question whether or not there is a true racial susceptibility to pneumonia, there have been three events that focused attention on the high death rates from pneumonia among Negroes. These instances were the construction of the Panama Canal, the operation of the Rand mines in South Africa, and the World War. Pneumonia occurred in severe epidemics and was responsible for thousands of deaths. The studies made of these epidemics not only showed the reaction of the Negro to the disease but gave important information concerning the behavior of the disease in general.

The bulk of the labor used in the construction of the Panama Canal was supplied by Negroes brought from the West Indies, mostly from Jamaica and the Barbados. In 1906 there was in Panama a force of 22,989 Negroes; in 1907 there were 28,600 Negroes; and in 1913 there were 46,000 Negroes. Concomitant with the importation of these people there was a rise in the death rate from pneumonia, which began in October, 1905, and reached its maximum in July, 1906, when there were 84 deaths among 22,989 Negroes, giving an annual death rate corresponding to 43.41 per 10,000. The annual death rate for the whole of 1906 was 18.74, and for 1907 it was 10.61 per

[12] *The pneumonias* (Philadelphia: W. B. Saunders, 1938).

[13] *The management of the pneumonias* (New York: Oxford University Press, 1937).

10,000. By 1908 it was 2.6; after that there was a gradual decline, until in 1913 the rate was 0.42. Gorgas[14] studied the conditions responsible for these high rates. He found them to be,
first, a nonimmunity of the newly arrived people and, second,
the crowding of the laborers into barracks. The exposure of the
nonimmunes to cases of pneumonia resulted in the establishment of immunity or infection, but most usually the latter. The
opportunities for contact with pneumonia were very high in the
crowded barracks. Altitude, season, sleeping in wet clothes or
in a draft, seemed to have no effect on the incidence of the disease. The greatest factor was the length of time the laborers
had been on the Isthmus. Statistics showed that the same number of men over three months on the Isthmus who furnished two
cases of pneumonia would give nine cases if they were men who
had less than three months of service. At first the men were
housed in the barracks, which allowed only thirty feet of floor
space. But in 1907 the men were permitted each to build his
own hut, with a small cultivatable piece of land, and to bring
over his family. Gorgas believed that this scattering of the men
was the chief cause of the sudden and permanent drop in
pneumonia.

A closely similar condition existed in the Rand mines of South
Africa. The miners were recruited from natives in the interior.
They were housed in crowded barracks, and among the newly
arrived there was a high incidence of pneumonia, giving a mortality in 1912 of 26.3, while at the same time among those natives who had had more or less contact with the white man's
civilization, the mortality rate was only 8. The mortality of the
recruits during the first six months at work was 15.83 per 1,000,
9.01 during the second six months, and 5.31 during the third six
months. Laborers obtained from central Africa were more
susceptible than those coming from the east coast. As on the
Isthmus of Panama, it was recognized that the disastrous effect
of this nonimmunity could be counteracted by isolation of the
men in small housing units. Another interesting experiment was
carried out with these laborers of the Rand mines. Sir Almroth

Wright recommended that they be vaccinated against pneumonia, and this was carried out, but the results were contradictory. In one instance the death rate was markedly reduced, and in another the death rate was no different from the controls. Various reasons have been offered to explain this difference, but opinion is in favor of the explanation that it is due to differences in the organisms used for the vaccines in the two experiments or a disparity between the vaccine organism and the infecting organism in the unsuccessful experiment.

In the World War a large number of cases of lobar pneumonia occurred, but the value of the statistics is reduced because it was not at all times possible to differentiate accurately between the various types of pneumonia. The Surgeon General's report shows that during 1918 in the entire army the incidence rate for pneumonia of all kinds, including the cases complicating measles and influenza, was nearly three times as high for the colored as for the whites. It is not justifiable, however, to draw any conclusions regarding susceptibility to lobar pneumonia from this statement, for the reasons given above. In the volume on *Medical and casualty statistics*, issued by the Surgeon General and embracing the whole period of the war, from April 1, 1917, to December 31, 1919, for the entire army in all countries, the death rate of white troops as given for lobar pneumonia was 1.96 per 1,000 strength, while for the colored troops it was 7.75 per 1,000 strength. There was a wide variation in the mortality rates reported from the various camps, the highest being 61.62 per 1,000 strength in Camp Beauregard in Louisiana and the lowest being 1.25 per 1,000 strength in Camp Hancock in Georgia. Other high rates were 49.03 in Camp Wheeler, Georgia, and 36.49 in Camp Devens, Massachusetts. The highest white rate, 9.00 per 1,000 strength, was in Camp Wheeler and the lowest, 0.11, in Camp Forrest, Georgia. In Camp Beauregard the white rate was 3.37, and in Camp Devens it was 8.42. The army experience corroborated the observations made in Panama and in the Rand mines, namely, that the nonimmune new recruits from rural regions were extremely susceptible to pneumonia, especially in overcrowded barracks.

For the whole United States in 1935 the estimated mortality rate for pneumonia among the whites was 41.25 per 100,000 and 74.11 per 100,000 for the Negro population. The white male death rate was 49.2, and the Negro male death rate was 94.08. The white female and Negro female rates were, respectively, 33.14 and 54.91 per 100,000.

According to Dublin and Lotka,[15] the death rate for lobar pneumonia among insured Negroes—both males and females—was more than double that for white persons in the five-year period 1931–35. Moreover, the lobar pneumonia death toll among Negroes far exceeded that among white persons throughout life. There was a substantial drop in mortality among Negroes between 1921 and 1935, but it did not keep pace with the decrease among white persons.

It seems that, while the Negro is more likely to contract lobar pneumonia, his chances of dying from the disease are no greater or even less than those of whites. Chatard,[16] who analyzed the cases in Johns Hopkins Hospital over a period of sixteen years (1889–1905), shows that of the white cases 30.14 per cent died and of the colored cases 31.2 per cent died, this being only a small difference in the case mortality. He pointed out that the mortality was much higher among the laborers, especially those with outdoor occupations. Kelly,[17] in describing a series of 6,500 cases of lobar pneumonia in the Cook County Hospital, Chicago, states that from 1917 to 1924 the case fatality was 39.2 per cent for 3,749 white males and 34.7 per cent for 818 white females; 30.6 per cent for 1,876 colored males and 31.9 per cent for 388 colored females. Each year the case fatality in the male Negroes was 5–13 per cent below that of the male whites, with a difference of 8.8 per cent for the entire seven and one-half years. The female Negro case fatality was 4.6 per cent less than that of white females. Musser communicated to Holmes[18] some of the statistics from the Charity Hospital in New Orleans. He re-

[15] *Twenty-five years of health progress* (New York: Metropolitan Life Insurance Company, 1937).

[16] *Johns Hopkins Hosp. Rept.*, 15:55, 1910.

[17] *J. Infect. Dis.*, 38:24, 1926.   [18] *Human Biol.*, 3:203, 1931.

ported that in 1926 out of 101, cases of lobar pneumonia among the colored patients 33, or 32.7 per cent, died, while out of 65 cases among whites 30, or 46.2 per cent, died. In 1929 the case mortality was slightly higher in the Negroes. Musser stated that, while Negroes are especially prone to contract pneumonia, "we have never considered that after the Negro has developed pneumonia he is more likely to die than the white man."

There have been reported no racial differences in the symptoms or pathological findings[19] except that empyema was relatively more frequent in the colored.[20] Neither was there any connection between race and the grade of leukocytosis in pneumonia.[21]

Much more information about pneumonia has been acquired since the publication of most of the data concerning pneumonia in Negroes, and it would be interesting and informative to study the disease in them in relation to these newer facts, such as the type of organisms that infect them, the frequency of bacteremia and its relation to their mortality, and the efficacy of antiserums in their treatment.

SCARLET FEVER

The prevalent belief that scarlet fever is uncommon in the Negro is based chiefly on the data afforded by the general mortality statistics, statistics of the United States Army, and the experience of the Metropolitan Life Insurance Company—all of which apparently indicate that colored people suffer less than white people from the disease. Cornely[22] challenges this opinion on the basis of an analysis of mortality and morbidity statistics for southern and northern areas. He obtained statistics from northern and southern cities and from southern states and compared them with reference to the relative morbidity and mortality from scarlet fever among white and colored. He disclosed that, while there are great differences between the two races in the South, where most Negroes live, there is in the northern

[19] Fabyan, *Johns Hopkins Hosp. Rept.*, 15:81, 1910.

[20] McCrae, *Johns Hopkins Hosp. Rept.*, 15:167, 1910.

[21] Chatard, *op. cit.*, p. 89, 1910.   [22] *Am. J. Pub. Health*, 29:1003, 1939.

cities very little inequality in the rates for scarlet fever among colored and white populations. Cornely states that, if the Negro were highly resistant to the disease, as he is believed to be, even though his mortality and morbidity in the North and South might not be similar, the disparity between the two races would be just as great in the North as in the South. This is not true, however, according to his data. Moreover, the results of the Dick-test surveys made by Pevaroff and Hindman[23] in Cleveland, by Smythe and Nesbit[24] in Gary, and Dyer and Sockrider[25] in Washington, D.C., have shown that there is no significant difference between reactions of white and Negro children to the Dick test.

Cornely is of the opinion that the recorded low mortality and morbidity from scarlet fever in Negroes in the South may be explained on two facts: (1) the occurrence of very mild and subclinical cases which are not recognized and not reported and (2) on the very poor reporting of typical cases and deaths in the rural areas of the South, where almost 70 per cent of the Negroes are to be found. Mayer and Davison[26] have shown that, although in North Carolina the number of cases reported was less than half that in New York City, the mortality from scarlet fever was about the same, and the rate of susceptibility, indicating the amount of previous infection, was much lower than that found in various other comparable groups in the United States. This probably indicated that in North Carolina there was as much scarlet fever as in New York City but that more cases escaped diagnosis.

Cornely shows that more cases and deaths were reported from southern cities than from southern states, to which he attributes the lack of medical facilities in the rural districts as compared with the cities. The inefficient reporting of deaths and cases has been attested to.[27] The failure to diagnose scarlet fever in Negroes can easily be understood in view of the deep pigmentation which obscures the rash upon which diagnosis often depends.

[23] *Am. J. Hyg.*, 19:749, 1934. [25] *Pub. Health Rept.*, 40:593, 1925.
[24] *J. Prev. Med.*, 2:243, 1928. [26] *South. M. J.*, 22:835, 1929.
[27] Gover, *Pub. Health Bull.*, 235:39, 1937; Puffer, *Am. J. Pub. Health*, 27:603, 1937.

Most writers agree that scarlet fever occurs very infrequently in the natives of Africa, while some even say that in certain parts of the country it is never found. Junge in Liberia, Crichton in Lagos, Nigeria, Remy in French Duala, Villaverde and Suarers in Spanish colonies, and Jennings in Freetown, Sierra Leone, deny, according to Borman,[28] the existence of scarlet fever in these countries. Bötticher[29] quotes Bruen and Cook as saying that there is no scarlet fever in central Africa, Senegambia, the Gold Coast, Cameroon, and the Congo. Gillespie, Duff, and Howells[30] say scarlet fever may be found in Accra (Gold Coast) but is generally unrecognized because of the pigmentation and is usually diagnosed as angina. Moulin[31] denies an immunity of native Africans.

Fischer[32] made Dick tests on 376 natives in Tanganyika, where there is little or no scarlet fever, or, at least, never in epidemic form. He observed that it was difficult at all times to be sure of a positive reaction and was compelled to use swelling instead of reddening and swelling as the criterion. There was an undoubted positive reaction in 1.8 per cent of the natives as compared to one-third of Europeans. He believes that there is no absolute immunity of the Negro and that the lack of epidemics is due to the lack of contact with Europeans ill with the disease. Cauchi[33] tested 1,752 natives in Nigeria and found 19 per cent to give positive tests. Of the children under one year of age 30 per cent gave positive reactions. Up to ten years of age 10 per cent were positive. From then on there was almost complete immunity. Borman[34] tested 27 children from nine months to fourteen years of age on the west coast of Africa and found 21 to be positive and 6 negative. There was a decrease in the percentage of reactions as age increased. In Europe and America it is also true that immunity increases with age. This is be-

[28] *Deutsche med. Wchnschr.*, 62:7, 1936.

[29] *Diphtheria and scarlet fever in tropical and subtropical countries and in foreign races* (inaug. diss., Tübingen, 1934).

[30] Borman, *loc. cit.*

[31] Böttischer, *loc. cit.*

[32] *Münchén. med. Wchnschr.*, 77:1749, 1930.

[33] *Lancet*, 2:1393, 1934.

[34] *Loc. cit.*

lieved to be due to contacts with the disease as the individuals grow older. But since in Africa, where the natives have little contact with scarlet fever, the immunity increases in the same way, it may mean that it is due to the natural development of immunity processes with age rather than to an actively acquired one.

YELLOW FEVER

The Negro has been a conspicuous figure in the history of yellow fever. Around him has centered the centuries-old debate on the place of origin of the disease. Whether or not the Negro brought yellow fever to the Western Hemisphere, the fact remains that many of the epidemics in this part of the world were closely associated with the movement of slave ships. The most severe and numerous epidemics in the United States appeared to be related to the slave trade, in that the ports of call of the slave ships were the places most affected, and when the importation of slaves became illegal there was a marked drop in the number of cases of yellow fever. These facts were not necessarily evidence that Negroes were responsible for the introduction of yellow fever, for they may indicate the filthy conditions of the slave ships, which provided excellent opportunities for the transportation and breeding of the disease virus both in the bodies of the crew as well as the human cargo and in the mosquitoes carried in the hatches and water tanks of the ships.

One of the best-established facts in the epidemiology of yellow fever is that the Negro shows a resistance to the disease not shown by any other race. This remarkable resistance has been demonstrated in many epidemics and particularly those in the southern part of the United States. Fenner wrote: "It is a well established fact that there is something in the Negro constitution which affords him protection against the worst effects of yellow fever; but what it is I am unable to say."[35] Carter[36] mentions a French expedition sent into Mexico in 1862, accompanied by a troop of African soldiers which came from an area

[35] *History of the epidemic yellow fever at New Orleans in 1853* (New York: Hall, Clayton & Co., 1854).

[36] *The early history of yellow fever* (Baltimore: Williams & Wilkins, 1931).

that had not been in contact with yellow fever in historic times. The Africans, nevertheless, enjoyed an almost absolute immunity from yellow fever when in Mexico, while the whites of the expedition, similarly circumstanced, suffered severely. In the last epidemic in the United States, that of 1905 in New Orleans, only 19 of 434 deaths were colored. In the southern United States the easily acquired immunity of colored people during the frequent and severe epidemics enabled them to be of great service in the care of others ill with the disease. During the Spanish-American War, a regiment of Negro "immunes" was organized for service in the yellow fever swamps of Cuba.

In Africa, where the disease is endemic, the attacks of yellow fever in the natives are usually so mild that it is often difficult to determine if they are really yellow fever. And if the attacks occur in children, which they often do, the symptoms are even milder and more difficult to diagnose because of the tendency of yellow fever to be lighter in childhood. Until recently, when more accurate methods were employed, the only indications that yellow fever was endemic in parts of Africa were the attacks of the disease among white people, who were very susceptible and suffered severely in contrast to the natives.

It seems that the resistance of the Negro is not so much a resistance to invasion by the yellow fever virus as a resistance to the effects of its toxin. He seems to contract the disease as readily as do whites but to suffer from it less severely and with much less mortality.[37] Marchoux, Salimbeni, and Simond[38] and Augustin suggest, but without sufficient proof, that the yellow fever mosquito feeds on Negroes less readily than on whites. It has been claimed that intermixture with even a small amount of white blood makes the Negro just as susceptible as whites to yellow fever.

In addition to a natural racial resistance, Negroes may acquire an active immunity by recovery from an infection. Since the infection is ordinarily mild and recovery is likely to occur, this fact is of great practical importance in those parts of Africa

[37] *Ibid.*; Augustin, *History of yellow fever* (New Orleans: Searcy & Pfaff, 1909).

[38] *Ann. Inst. Pasteur*, 17:665, 1903.

where the disease is endemic. It is probable that in Africa infection is acquired in early childhood and survival results in a lifelong immunity. It has been pointed out that the characteristic endemicity of yellow fever in Africa is the result of a proper balance among the native population between immune and susceptible people. The supply of susceptibles, chiefly in the form of newborns, but also supplemented by immigrants from noninfected areas, is just sufficient to keep the disease going. If there is a proportionately large influx of susceptibles, either whites or natives, the infection may reach epidemic proportions. On the other hand, if the immunes greatly increase, in proportion to the susceptibles, the disease may undergo "spontaneous elimination because of the failure of the human host."[39]

The coast of West Africa is the part of the continent that has been most involved with yellow fever and today is one of the last strongholds of the disease. The exact boundaries of the area in which the disease exists are not known, but the British Yellow Fever Commission[40] gave the view that in the portion of West Africa that extends from Senegal in the north to the French Congo in the south there are always some areas in which the infection is temporarily manifesting itself. It is probable that there are also areas in which the infection is more permanent or from which it is never wholly absent.

It is now possible to use much more accurate methods than were hitherto available for the survey of countries as to the presence of yellow fever. Stokes, Bauer, and Hudson[41] have established that the causative agent of yellow fever was a filterable virus and that the disease could be transmitted to monkeys by the injection of blood from patients with yellow fever. Later Theiler[42] showed that mice could also be infected by intracerebral injections of patients' blood. The serum of patients recently recovered from the disease will protect both monkeys and mice against infection. With these two methods it is possible to definitely locate yellow fever in an area or to outline the path

[39] Carter, *loc. cit.*; see n. 36.

[40] *Fourth and final report* (London: Churchill, 1917).

[41] *Am. J. Trop. Med.*, 8:103, 1928.   [42] *Ann. Trop. Med.*, 24:249, 1930.

of a previous epidemic.[43] In addition to these methods Klotz[44] established the technic of viscerotomy, which consists of the removal of a bit of liver from the bodies of those suspected of having died from yellow fever and examining it microscopically for acute yellow atrophy, which is specific for yellow fever under the conditions of the test.

Opinion is about equally divided between two theories as to the actual origin of yellow fever. One theory is that it arose in the Western Hemisphere,[45] probably around the coast and central part of Mexico. It has been suggested that the downfall of the once elaborate Mayan civilization is attributable to yellow fever. The rival theory is that the disease originated in Africa and was brought West either by slaves or by members of the crews of slave ships.[46] Manson-Bahr[47] says that it is impossible to choose between these two theories. Hudson, Bauer, and Phillips[48] found that the serum from immune people in the Western Hemisphere as well as in Africa protected monkeys against West African fever virus, from which it is concluded that the virus in both parts of the world is identical. Theiler and Sellards,[49] using mice as test animals, and Sawyer, Kitchen, Frobisher, and Lloyd,[50] using monkeys, came to the same conclusions. Klotz and Belt[51] find that the quality of the lesions arising in yellow fever in Africa is similar to that of the lesions occurring in American cases (Brazil, British Honduras, San Salvador, and Louisiana). Furthermore, the incidence of various types of changes in different tissues is broadly the same, with differences only in a few reactions, which may be accounted

[43] See Beeuwkes, Bauer, and Mahaffey on the use of monkeys in a survey of an area in southwestern Nigeria (*Am. J. Trop. Med.*, 10:299, 1930), and a series of papers by Sawyer, Bauer, Whitman, Burke, and Soper concerning the distribution of immunity in North, Central, and South America, the West Indies, Europe, Asia, and Australia and the verification of a suspected epidemic in Brazil (*Am. J. Trop. Med.*, 17:137, 1937).

[44] *Am. J. Trop. Med.*, 7:271, 1927; 9:241, 1929; see also Hoffmann, *Am. J. Trop. Med.*, 8:563, 1928.

[45] Augustin, *loc. cit.*; see n. 37.   [46] Carter, *loc. cit.*; see n. 36.

[47] *Manson's tropical diseases* (Baltimore: Wood & Co., 1936).

[48] *Am. J. Trop. Med.*, 9:1, 1929.   [50] *J. Exper. Med.*, 51:493, 1930.

[49] *Ann. Trop. Med.*, 22:449, 1928.   [51] *Am. J. Trop. Med.*, 10:299, 1930.

for by the technic used. From these facts they conclude also that the pathological processes arising in yellow fever in Africa are identical with those in American cases.

SMALLPOX

Africa vies with the Orient in the claim of being the oldest seat of smallpox. At least it is known that the disease there is of great antiquity. This applies only to certain portions of Africa, because the introduction of smallpox into parts of the continent comparatively recently invaded by outsiders has been observed by modern writers and described by Hirsch.[52]

Smallpox is said to break out in Africa in the form of epidemics, but, for the most part, the disease is endemic and usually seen in the form of the mild variety known as alastrim. The American disease was introduced by the early Spanish explorers and not by African slaves, although the latter did introduce alastrim, which still remains in endemic form in the West Indies, South America, and to some extent in the southern United States.

At the present time, when the prevalence of smallpox is, for the most part, a measure of the extent of preventive vaccination, the statistics on the distribution of the disease indicate less the influence of racial susceptibilities than the readiness of people to accept vaccination. But during the era of large epidemics, among the unvaccinated it was observed that Negroes were somewhat more susceptible to smallpox than were white people. This was expressed both by morbidity and by mortality returns.

Although the large epidemics of the nineteenth century no longer occur, it is a fact that, of the twenty-six countries reporting smallpox morbidity to the League of Nations from 1921 to 1930, the United States showed the highest attack rate, with the exception of British India. Hedrick[53] shows that the origin of these cases is principally in the northwestern states. The southern states, where most Negroes live, are among those with the lowest rates.

[52] Loc. cit.; see n. 1.   [53] Pub. Health Rept., 51:363, 1936.

In 1930, of the states giving separate mortality returns for Negroes and whites (all southern states), there was a total of 66 deaths from smallpox, 41 of which were among the whites and 15 among the colored. The Metropolitan Life Insurance Company showed for 1911–35 a white male mortality rate of 0.2 per 100,000, white female rate of 0.1 per 100,000, Negro male rate of 0.6, and Negro female rate of 0.4.

MEASLES

Holmes[54] points out the sources of errors in making racial comparisons in regard to the incidence of measles. The disease has a distinct geographical distribution and has a low incidence in the South, where most Negroes live. The relative number of children in the two races is likewise of considerable importance in the interpretation of general mortality statistics as applied to the differential effect of the disease.

It appears, however, when due consideration of all factors is made, that measles, like most other exanthemata, affects Negroes less than it does whites. Adjusted rates for the registration states of 1920 show that during 1920–27 the mortality rates were lower for colored people each year, except for 1923 and 1924, when the Negro rates were higher. During these years there was a large increase of measles in the South. The white rates were increased also for these years, but since a larger proportion of the Negroes live in the South, the effect was more marked on the colored rates. The statistics of the Metropolitan Life Insurance Company show that for 1911–35 the white male mortality rate was 6.0 per 100,000, white female 4.6, Negro male 3.4, and Negro female 2.9.

Measles is widely known in Africa. McKinley[55] lists in a general way the present status of the disease in different colonies. There is not a single place cited where measles is designated as being absent, but the amount of infection as judged from the number of cases reported is very variable. In most communities the disease is not considered as an important health problem.

[54] *Human Biol.*, 3:71, 1931.

[55] *A geography of disease* (Washington, D.C.: Washington University Press, 1935).

The exceptions were the British Gold Coast, Basutoland, and French West Africa, the largest number of cases reported being in the latter colony. In Somaliland measles is said to be rare, and in South Africa, where there are many Europeans, and in the Belgian Congo it appears to be common. Since there are apparently no accounts of epidemics of malignant measles, such as have occurred in some of the recently infected South Sea Islands, it is probable that measles is not a new disease in Africa.

PERTUSSIS

Negroes seem to be much more susceptible to whooping-cough than are white people. This is evidenced by both morbidity and mortality rates. Crum[56] refers to the morbidity statistics for Washington, D.C., for the five-year period 1908–12, which show that the attack rate was higher for the colored than for the white population at ages under one year and also at ages one to four years. These ages are the periods when whooping-cough is most contagious and most fatal. At ages above five years the attack rate for Negroes was less than that of whites. When all ages were combined, there was little difference in the morbidity of the two races. For representative southern cities at ages under one year the average Negro death rate was nearly three times as high as the white death rate, and at ages one to four years the average death rate was five times as high. Whooping-cough is usually complicated in fatal cases with bronchopneumonia, to which Negroes seem to succumb more easily than do whites. The higher susceptibility of Negroes to whooping-cough is also borne out by the returns of the Metropolitan Life Insurance Company. For each age group cited, the average annual mortality from 1911 to 1935 was higher in the colored, but the excess was most marked for the group one to fourteen years of age. For the whites in this group the average annual death rate was 9.1 for males and 13.0 for females. The colored rate to correspond was 30.5 for males and 37.4 for females.

[56] *Am. J. Pub. Health*, 5:996, 1915.

Statistics on influenza among colored people during the pandemic of 1918 teaches more about the characteristics of influenza in general than about their relative susceptibility to the disease. Since influenza of itself is rarely fatal and death usually results from complicating conditions, of which the most frequent is pneumonia, the differential mortality of colored people from influenza is to be interpreted as due to the differential mortality from complicating conditions, and consideration of the statistics cannot be separated from those of pneumonia. Influenza, like many other infectious diseases, depends on the presence or absence of immunity to the disease, which, in turn, is influenced greatly by the opportunity for contact with large numbers of people, such as is afforded in large cities as opposed to rural areas. Also, the chances for contact with the disease, and, consequently, the chances for infection are higher under conditions of overcrowding than otherwise. If there were a greater incidence of and mortality from influenza and its complications, they could more easily be explained by the facts that colored people are, first, preponderantly rural and, second, that they usually live in overcrowded houses rather than by the assumption of a difficult-to-prove inherent racial susceptibility, as has been made by some writers.

Among the earliest observations on influenza in Negroes was that of Opie *et al.*[57] at Camp Pike, Arkansas, during the first few months of the epidemic which began there in September, 1918. Of 41,778 white men, 24.6 per cent developed influenza, while 13.3 per cent of 10,773 colored men developed the disease. It is suggested that this difference is not a racial one but is due to a difference in the time spent in camp. A group of 1,860 of the above colored troops was transferred in the midst of the epidemic to Fort Root, where there already were 2,130 Negroes who had been in camp six weeks or longer and among whom there had been no influenza. During the epidemic 43.6 per cent of the transferred men developed the disease, and only 7.6 per cent of the old group developed it. In Camp Pike 12.7 per cent

[57] *J. A. M. A.*; **72**:556, 1919.

of the whites developed pneumonia, and 19.8 per cent of Negroes developed this complication. The rate of fatality from pneumonia was slightly higher in the white men with influenza than in the colored, 31.7 per cent of the former dying and 28.2 per cent of the latter.

Howard and Love[58] point out that white soldiers from the South had much higher admission and death rates from influenza, pneumonia, and other respiratory diseases than white soldiers from other sections. The lowest rates for these diseases were among white soldiers from the Pacific and the Rocky Mountain states. They state that Negroes stationed in the United States had, for the country at large, lower admission rates for influenza than all the whites and much lower than those from the South. The death rates for all pneumonia infections were more than twice as high for colored troops as for white troops. The case mortality for all pneumonias was, on the other hand, 20 per cent lower for the colored troops than for the white troops.

For the whole United States Army during the period of mobilization for the World War—extending from April 1, 1917, to December 31, 1919—the admission rate for influenza for colored enlisted men was, according to *Medical and casualty statistics* issued by the Surgeon General, 207.5 per 1,000 strength, and for white enlisted men it was 186.5 per 1,000 strength. In the United States the rates for colored and white men were 266.5 and 242.6, respectively, per 1,000 men, while for the army in Europe it was 152.1 for colored soldiers and 119.9 for white soldiers. The mortality rate for all colored enlisted men was 8.0 per 1,000 and for the whites 5.8 per 1,000. In the United States the rates were 10.7, colored, and 7.4, white, and in Europe 5.2, colored, and 3.9, white. The case fatality was for all colored enlisted men 3.8 per cent, for all white enlisted men 3.1 per cent. In Europe the colored fatality rate was 3.4 per cent and the white 3.3 per cent, while for the army in the United States 4.0 per cent of the colored influenza cases died, while 3.1 per cent of the white cases died.

[58] *Mil. Surgeon*, 44:522, 1920.

Among the civilian population the same difficulty in differentiating influenza and pneumonia infections and deaths existed as among soldiers in service. Frost[59] surveyed for the United States Public Health Service several localities for the attack rates of influenza among colored and white. He found that the incidence rates among the colored were uniformly lower than the white, the differences persisting after adjustment of the rates to a uniform basis of sex and age distribution.

Dublin and Lotka[60] point out that in the years before the epidemic the colored death rates from influenza and pneumonia among insured people were higher than those of the whites but that during the epidemic the ratio was markedly reduced, owing to the fact that the excess of colored deaths over normal deaths was much less than the white excess. The death rate for colored persons in 1918 actually dropped below that of whites in the age ranges between twenty and fifty-five years among males and twenty and forty-five among females.

In Chicago Robertson[61] says that in all age groups the increase in deaths from influenza and pneumonia during the epidemic was much less in the Negro.

ACUTE POLIOMYELITIS

Information concerning the racial aspect of poliomyelitis is meager, yet that concerning Negroes is more complete than that for any race other than white, although the data are open to criticism. While rules for reporting cases of the disease are stringent, particularly during epidemics, the reports from places where epidemics occur most often and are most severe have not, until recently, been carefully segregated as to race. In the southern states, where the bulk of Negroes live and where official morbidity and mortality returns have for a long while been separated for white and colored, major epidemics of infantile paralysis do not often occur. Most of the information on polio-

[59] *Pub. Health Rept.*, 35:584, 1920.

[60] *Twenty-five years of health progress* (New York: Metropolitan Life Insurance Company, 1937).

[61] *An epidemic of influenza in the city of Chicago during the fall of 1918: a bulletin from the Chicago Board of Health.*

myelitis in Negroes comes from special investigations made by individuals or groups, and even these most often either casually mention the occurrence in colored people or give impressions instead of reliable figures on its prevalence.

Harmon[62] obtained data upon the incidence and fatality of poliomyelitis from 8 southern states—North Carolina, Louisiana, Tennessee, Maryland, Virginia, Alabama, Mississippi, and South Carolina—and from 2 large northern cities—Chicago and New York—where there are large colored populations. While epidemics are unusual in the South, Harmon finds that the yearly case rates of the disease are comparable to those of interepidemic years in the northern states. In the states in which the case rates per 100,000 population of both races are given— North Carolina, Alabama, Mississippi, and Maryland—the annual incidence of the disease among whites was from 2 to 6 times that in Negroes. During the epidemic year of 1916 in Maryland the case rate for Negroes exceeded that of whites. In Chicago, during the 12 years for which comparative data are available, the white case rate also exceeds that of the colored except for 1 year (1930), when the Negro rate was higher, and another year (1928), of low total rate, when the rates for the 2 races were about equal. The figures for the 1937 epidemic in that city, as well as in neighboring cities which were involved, are not available, but it is the impression in medical circles that, in Chicago at least, very few colored people were attacked. For New York City during the epidemics of 1916, 1931, and 1933, the only years for which comparable data are obtainable, the white case rates were, respectively, 1.6, 2.1, and 2.7 times higher than the Negro rates. During an earlier epidemic in 1907 there were only 2 cases in Negroes out of a total of 752 cases in New York City, although, if they had been in proportion to the population, there would have been 14. The Negro rate, therefore, was oneseventh of the white rate.

Watkins and McKenzie[63] reported that in 1924 there were 300 cases of infantile paralysis in Detroit, among which were only 5 cases in Negroes, although these people made up one-twelfth

[62] *J. Infect. Dis.*, 58:331, 1936.   [63] *Ann. Clin. Med.*, 4:149, 1935.

of the population. Francis[64] reports an outbreak in Texarkana in 1913 where there were 124 cases in whites and 19 in Negroes, although the white population was about 2.5 times that of the Negro population. In Fort Worth, Texas, in the 1927 outbreak, Crouch[65] reports that of 58 cases none was noted among the colored population. In a recent epidemic in North Carolina, Root[66] gives the white case rate as 19.6 per 100,000 and the Negro rate as 13.5 per 100,000.

The evidence is, therefore, that poliomyelitis attacks colored people to a less extent than it does white people. The mortality of Negroes from the disease in relation to the total Negro population is also less than it is for whites. For the whole country during 1934 the mortality rate for Negroes was 0.59 per 100,000 and for whites 0.74 per 100,000. When the statistics are broken down into age groups, it is found that the morbidity and mortality rates in Negroes are lower in every age group. A striking exception is the higher case rate in 1934 in North Carolina for Negroes under one year of age.

However, when the case fatality of the disease in colored people is studied, it is found that once they become infected they are more likely to die than are whites. This is shown in the published statistics of Alabama, Mississippi, and Maryland, where case fatality was higher in Negroes thirty-seven times and less fifteen times. In the three epidemics in New York City, the case-fatality rate in Negroes twice exceeded that in whites.

Various opinions have been expressed to explain the difference between the comparative case rates and the case-fatality rates. It is difficult to conceive a reactive immune process that protects against an initial infection and yet which does not modify the course of the disease after infection. It may be possible that the physical barriers of the body against infection which, according to the best evidence, are those of the nasal mucosa, more effectively restrain the entrance of the virus of poliomyelitis into the Negro's system, but after infection is established the immunochemical processes aroused are less efficient. Other ex-

[64] *Pub. Health Rept.*, 28:1693, 1913.

[65] *Texas State J. Med.*, 4:149, 1927. [66] *South. M. J.*, 29:184, 1936.

planations offered are that less opportunities for contact with sources of infection exist among colored people, while poorer medical care, less detection of early cases, or incomplete reporting might explain the higher fatality rates.

Little is known about the occurrence of the disease among the natives of Africa. Strong and Shattuck[67] on an African expedition to Liberia and the Belgian Congo encountered cases of probable poliomyelitis in these places. Hudson and Lennette[68] state that an inquiry into the occurrence of the disease led to no satisfactory results as far as Liberia is concerned. Since cases in natives were reported from neighboring West African colonies, it is quite possible that the infection also occurs in Liberia. They tested the serums of twenty Liberian natives working inland on the Firestone Rubber plantations as to their ability to neutralize the poliomyelitis virus. Using the serums undiluted, they found that eighteen of them neutralized the virus, one did not, and one remained undetermined, because one test animal died early of an intercurrent infection. Shaughnessy, Harmon, and Gordon[69] obtained positive virus neutralizing tests with serums of natives of the Virgin Islands, where the disease seldom occurs. It is disputed whether the presence of neutralizing substances in the blood depends on contact with the disease and represents a degree of specific immunity or whether they arise as a result of unspecific stimulation and therefore give no information as to previous exposure to the disease.

In a treatise on the geography of disease, giving a survey of the incidence and distribution of tropical and other diseases, McKinley[70] summarizes observations on the incidence of poliomyelitis in various parts of the world. Among the natives of the various British African colonies there was a total of fifty-five known cases together with a record of questionable cases in others. He quotes a Belgian correspondent, who cites an epi-

[67] *The African Republic of Liberia and the Belgian Congo* ("Contributions for the Dept. of Trop. Med. and the Inst. for Trop. Biol. and Med.," No. V [Harvard University Press, 1930]).

[68] Quoted in International Committee for the Study of Infantile Paralysis, *Poliomyelitis* (Baltimore: Williams & Wilkins, 1932), p. 118.

[69] *J. Prev. Med.*, 4:157, 1930.   [70] *Loc. cit.*; see n. 55.

demic of infantile paralysis in 1922 in the Belgian Congo. In Haiti five cases are cited, and in the Virgin Islands none had been observed.

RHEUMATIC FEVER

It is difficult to be certain about the status of rheumatism among Negroes because of the small amount of statistical data available and because those which have been published are at variance. It is repeatedly stated in textbooks of medicine that rheumatic heart disease in Negroes is unusual because rheumatic fever among them is uncommon. Harrison and Levine[71] say that acute rheumatic fever, chorea, and mitral valvular disease resulting from rheumatism are rare in the South but occur equally in the two races. Gleick[72] gives figures to show that rheumatic fever is a common disease in New York City but that it occurs very much oftener in white people, although colored people live under conditions that are conducive to the disease. Roy[73] cited a case of chorea in a Negro as an oddity.

On the other hand, the statistics of the Metropolitan Life Insurance Company show deaths from acute rheumatic fever to be more numerous among its colored policyholders. From 1911 to 1935 the white male death rate was 3.9 per 100,000, the white female rate also 3.9, the colored male 5.7, and the colored female 7.1. It is probable that none of the information concerning rheumatic fever in Negroes is reliable because of the vagueness of the disease and the tendency of it to simulate other conditions.

TYPHOID FEVER

Negroes seem not to have been excessively affected by typhoid fever, although they have by no means been free of it. The disease has been reported in most parts of Africa. Attention has in most instances been called to the infection there by outbreaks among Europeans. Discussions have arisen as to whether these outbreaks originated from endemic disease among the natives or from sources imported by the whites. Duke[74] re-

[71] *South. M. J.*, 17:914, 1924.

[72] *Arch. Pediat.*, 44:326, 1927.

[73] *M. Rec.*, 40:215, 1892.

[74] *Lancet*, 1:897, 1924.

views the evidence concerning this question and quotes the annual medical report for northern Nigeria for 1915, which states: "It is well-nigh certain that typhoid was originally imported by Europeans, and that a number of native carriers have consequently developed since. . . . . The indigenous native seems to be less susceptible to intestinal disease than is the average European, and this probably explains why native outbreaks have not attended every European case." The report from the same source for 1917 says: "West African natives constitute a particularly dangerous type of dysenteric and enteric carrier; they are themselves so tolerant of abdominal affections that they not infrequently can carry on easily whilst in a condition which would inevitably frustrate any European." Instances are described of finding in Kenya Colony typhoid lesions post-mortem in natives where the disease was not suspected clinically. Typhoid very often, especially in the tropics, runs an atypical course, with a mild continued fever that cannot be distinguished from one of the many unclassified types of fevers that are met with there.[75] From these reports it is evident that typhoid fever occurs in various parts of tropical Africa and that the local medical opinion credits the natives with greater powers of resistance than the Europeans possess. Duke points out, however, that the case fatality of the disease among natives is fairly high, probably owing to the fact that only severe cases are recognized. Manson-Bahr[76] is of the opinion that the relative exemption of the native races in Africa is due to the immunizing effect of living in constant contact with typhoid or to an attack in childhood. This is borne out by Widal tests on serums of natives who are apparently not ill with typhoid fever. Such examinations have been made in the Sudan,[77] Southern Rhodesia,[78] British Guiana,[79] and Kenya Colony.[80] Positive reactions were obtained by the latter in from 0 to 34.2 per cent of

[75] Crombie, *J. Trop. Med.*, 1:128, 157, 1898.

[76] *Manson's tropical diseases* (Baltimore: William Wood & Co., 1936).

[77] Hargan, *J. Hyg.*, 32:523, 1932.   [78] Alves, *South African M. J.*, 10:6, 1936.

[79] Giglioli, *J. Hyg.* 33:379, 1935.

[80] Dowdeswell, *Tr. Roy. Soc. Trop. Med. & Hyg.*, 31:364, 1937.

the serums tested with H antigen and from 7.0 to 31.4 per cent when tested with O antigen. Duke, in the Uganda Protectorate, found that 3 of 272 serums from patients in the hospital gave positive Widal tests. He states that the evidence suggests that typhoid organisms exist in the native populations of the country but that, under normal conditions of life, the balance between the organisms and their native hosts is well adjusted. Alterations in environment—particularly changes in diet, crowding, and close contact with strangers (white and colored)—may disturb this equilibrium, and the organism may then assert itself in its classical European form.

Cluver[81] estimates that 2 per cent of South African natives may be typhoid carriers. Typhoid Vi agglutinins were found by Davis[82] in 7.47 per cent of 657 normal African natives in a titer of 1:5–1:12.5. This specific type of agglutinin was also found in 10 per cent of normal natives by Horgan.[83] In 60 normal natives the titer was 1:40–1:60, and in 58 it was 0 to 1:40, according to Lewin.[84] On the other hand, Pijper and Crocker[85] found no Vi agglutinins in the normal serums of South African natives.

While there is no large literature on the comparison of Negroes and whites in their reaction to typhoid fever in the United States, it appears that, in general, the interracial variations are not different from those described by Howard[86] in an account of the natural history of typhoid in Baltimore from 1851 to 1919. Howard points out that the curves showing the course of the death rates of colored people over these years are much less regular than those for the whites. During some of the years the Negro rate fell below the rate of the whites, and in other years it was above. The highest rate for the whole series of years is the colored rate for 1890, which reached 90.13 per 100,000 population, while the highest rate for whites reached 69.93 per 100,000 in the same year. Over the whole period of

[81] Quart. Bull. Health Organ., League of Nations, 5:153, 1936.

[82] J. Hyg., 40:406, 1940.   [83] Op. cit., 36:368, 1936.

[84] South African Inst. M. Research, Publ. No. 41, 7:413, 1937.

[85] J. Hyg., 37:332, 1937.   [86] Bull. Johns Hopkins Hosp., 31:319, 1920.

years the mortality of the colored was somewhat higher than that of the whites. Howard was unable to report on the relative morbidity of Negroes and whites in Baltimore except for the years 1918 and 1919, when the morbidity of the Negro was much less than that of the white. The incidence of the disease was not only greater in the white race than in the colored but was greatest in the white male and greater in the white female than in either colored males or females. The statistics also showed that the case fatality of typhoid fever was greater in the colored; that the risk of dying from clinically recognized typhoid is twice as great for the colored as for the white, somewhat greater for white males than for white females, and twice as great for colored males as for colored females.

The mortality returns of the Metropolitan Life Insurance Company show, similarly, a greater liability of Negroes to fatal typhoid fever even in recent years, when the disease has become a minor public health problem. For the five-year period 1931–35 the death rates among white persons were 1.6 per 100,000 for males and 1.2 for females; among the colored they were 5.2 and 3.6, respectively.

The interpretation of these data should be made in terms of the nature of typhoid fever. It is pre-eminently a disease of filth and always indicates a contamination of material taken into the mouth with material excreted from the intestinal or urinary tract. The occurrence of the prerequisite contamination is a measure not so much of race as it is of ignorance, living conditions, occupation, social habits, and food and water supply. While case fatality may be an indication of the relative resistance of races to typhoid fever, it also represents how early and how accurately the disease is diagnosed, the availability of adequate treatment, and the comparative health background of the races.

DISEASES OF THE BLOOD

PERNICIOUS ANEMIA

There are divergent opinions about the frequency of pernicious anemia in the Negro. Carr[1] found in Cook County Hospital, Chicago, records of 148 cases of the disease among all patients between 1912 and 1920. Of these, 6 were in Negroes. This was less than 5 per cent of the total cases, while the Negro admissions, according to the author, were more than twice this rate. Traut[2] found in the same institution between January, 1921, and August, 1926, records of 256 cases of the disease, among which were 8 in colored patients. This number is also out of proportion to the colored admissions, which at that time amounted to approximately 33 per cent of all admissions. During 5 years (1918–22 inclusive) Wilson and Evans[3] found 8 colored cases among 111 cases of pernicious anemia in the Johns Hopkins Hospital. At Peter Bent Brigham Hospital there were 500 cases of the disease among 80,145 total admissions from April, 1912, to November, 1932.[4] The percentage of total cases of pernicious anemia to total admissions was 0.62. There were 4,503 colored admissions, and among them were 3 cases, or 0.07 per cent of the colored admissions. The percentage of colored cases of total cases was 0.06 per cent, while the percentage of colored admissions of total admissions was a little over 5 per cent. Matthews[5] reports 2 cases of pernicious anemia among 4,940 colored patients in the United States Veterans' Hospital at Tuskegee, Alabama. Kampmeier and Cameron[6] obtained their data in the State Charity Hospital in New Orleans for the decade 1926–36. During this period liver therapy for pernicious anemia was used, and this served as an additional means of diagnosis. For the decade there were 247,239 colored admissions and 277,324 white admissions. Among the former were 14 au-

[1] *Am. J. M. Sc.*, 160:737, 1920.

[2] *Illinois M. J.*, 51:322, 1927.   [3] *Bull. Johns Hopkins Hosp.*, 35:38, 1924.

[4] Friedlander, *Am. J. M. Sc.*, 187:634, 1934.

[5] *U.S. Vet. Bur. M. Bull.*, 5:494, 1929.   [6] *Am. J. M. Sc.*, 192:175, 1936.

thentic cases of pernicious anemia, and among the latter were 98 authentic cases. While the admissions were approximately equal, the disease occurred seven times more frequently in the white patients. Entirely different results were obtained by Jamison in the same city. While colored patients made up 25 per cent (49,188) of the total of 122,524 admissions to the Charity Hospital of New Orleans, 29 per cent (12) of 54 cases of pernicious anemia were in the colored patients. Jamison concludes that the disease is fairly frequent in Negroes.

Most writers are under the impression that the rate of the disease in Negroes is elevated in proportion to the amount of intermixture with whites. Cornell[7] quotes Longcope as saying that pernicious anemia seldom, if ever, occurs in the full-blooded Negro.

No essential differences have been brought out between the expression of the disease in Negroes and in other people, except that the classical lemon-colored skin is, of course, not seen in colored people, nor is there any equivalent color change seen. Willson and Evans obtained evidence that the disease was milder in colored people, but Carr could not corroborate this.

SICKLE CELL ANEMIA

In 1910 Herrick[8] examined the blood of a young Negro from the West Indies and found in the stained smear a type of poikilocytosis he had never before seen. The patient presented a group of symptoms and clinical findings that were so typical of the condition that their description by Herrick has been little modified by the many writers who described subsequent cases. Since this publication a large number of similar cases have been reported and a large literature created describing the symptoms, pathology, and treatment of the condition. Considerable attention has likewise been given to the mechanism of the sickling phenomenon and to a search for the elusive underlying cause.

As information accumulated concerning the condition referred to as sickle cell anemia, it became evident that it was

[7] *Pernicious anemia* (Durham, N.C.: Duke University Press, 1927).

[8] *Am. J. M. Sc.*, 6:517, 1910.

necessary to distinguish between three distinct clinical conditions that have in common the fact that normal-appearing erythrocytes in freshly drawn blood will, when kept in *vitro* under suitable conditions, assume certain bizarre shapes commonly referred to as sickling. There is, first, a large group of individuals who may be in perfect health, or at least without symptoms referable to their blood defect, but whose erythrocytes readily sickle in wet, sealed preparations. There is no anemia, and no sickle cells are demonstrable in the circulation. There is a second and much smaller group in which sickle cells occur in the circulation in varying numbers but whose blood will develop additional sickle cells from normally shaped erythrocytes in wet preparations. These individuals show a more or less characteristic group of symptoms, which include an anemia, icterus, abdominal and joint pains, and pathological findings that are chiefly centered in the spleen and bone marrow. Still another group is made up of those who may or may not have sickle cells in the circulation but who do show them in wet preparations. While they are not definitely ill, they have vague complaints and give a history of past attacks with symptoms like those of the second group. The pathological findings in these patients who die of other causes are similar to those of the second group.

Since the first group is entirely free of anemia, it is a misnomer to refer to the condition as sickle cell anemia. For this reason Cooley and Lee[9] suggested the name "sicklemia" for the phenomenon of the sickling trait, and although it is a hybrid word, it is descriptive and simple. Steinberg[10] defines, then, sicklemia as applicable only to "those whose blood preparations on standing for from several to twenty-four hours show sickle erythrocytes, while the health of these persons is apparently normal, their blood without abnormalities and their previous history free of symptoms and signs of anemia." It is the condition that is usually disclosed in the several surveys of large groups of Negroes, the results of which are often erroneously referred to as the incidence of sickle cell anemia. Hahn and

[9] *Am. J. Dis. Child.*, 32:334, 1926.   [10] *Arch. Path.*, 9:876, 1930.

Gillespie[11] suggested the term "drepanocytemia" for the same condition, and Graham and McCarty[12] introduced the word "meniscocytosis," neither of which names has been generally accepted, probably because of their cumbersomeness. The second and third groups are true sickle cell anemia cases. The two groups are based on the fact that the disease readily shows remissions and relapses. When the disease is active, as shown by symptoms, physical signs, and the blood picture, including an anemia and the presence of circulating sickle cells, it is called "active sickle cell anemia." When there is a known remission or a history of attacks of a more active state, and at the time of examination there are indefinite symptoms, physical signs and changes in the circulating blood, the condition is known as "latent sickle cell anemia." This latter term, however, has been erroneously applied to sicklemia under the impression that the latter sooner or later becomes the full-blown sickle cell anemia, an impression for which there is no convincing evidence.

The chief interest here is the fact that sickle cell anemia, as well as sicklemia, is a condition that is almost, but apparently not completely, confined to Negroes or those mixed with Negro blood. The first case was observed in a Negro, and subsequent ones until 1925 were found in this race alone. After about twenty-two cases had been described in American colored people, the publication of cases appeared that created a doubt that sickle cell anemia occurred exclusively in these people. Castana[13] reported an instance of an Italian child with semilunar gigantocytes, anemia, and jaundice. Archibald[14] described a bona fide case in a ten-year-old Arab boy born in the Sudan. Another case was reported in a Cuban[15] and one in a Greek.[16] Lawrence[17] found sickle cells in the blood of a white woman, her brother, a

[11] *Arch. Int. Med.*, 39:233, 1927.

[12] *J. Lab. & Clin. Med.*, 12:536, 1927.   [13] *Pediatria*, 33:431, 1925.

[14] *Tr. Roy. Soc. Trop. Med. & Hyg.*, 19:389, 1926.

[15] Stewart, *Am. J. Dis. Child.*, 34:72, 1927.

[16] Cooley and Lee, *op. cit.*, 38:103, 1929.   [17] *J. Clin. Investigation*, 5:31, 1927.

sister, and a niece; and on examination of one hundred and two other white people found sickle cells in the blood of three of them. Sights and Simon[18] added to the literature a well-marked case in a man of Scotch-Irish blood. Rosenfeld and Pincus[19] described sickle cell anemia in an Italian boy in whose family were four others in three generations who showed the sickling trait. Clarke[20] cites two other cases in an Italian. A Mexican woman and her two daughters were shown by Wallace and Killingsworth[21] to have the sickling trait. Cardoza[22] likewise found a case in a Mexican boy. Cooke and Mack[23] presented two children of a typical white midwestern American family who had sickle cell anemia and whose father showed sicklemia. Two Sicilian sisters with the disease are cited by Hayden and Evans.[24]

On the other hand, Sydenstricker[25] examined the blood of one thousand white people in the South for sicklemia without disclosing a single case. Miyamoto and Korb[26] tested in the same way one hundred whites in St. Louis, and Diggs, Ahmann, and Bibb[27] tested three hundred and nine whites in Memphis, and in no instance was a positive reaction found in wet preparations.

Rosenfeld and Pincus[28] critically analyzed the reports of sickle cell anemia in whites in the literature and came to the conclusion that most of them should be eliminated as not acceptable cases. They did not accept the case of Castana,[29] first, because there were no illustrations given; second, because there was no mention of the behavior of the patient's red cells in sealed, wet preparations—an essential test for sickle cell anemia; and, third, and most important, Castana's description of the semilunar or sickle-like gigantocytes and his references to these cells by other authors definitely identified them as *corps en demilune*

[18] *J. Med.*, 11:177, 1931.

[19] *Am. J. M. Sc.*, 184:674, 1932.

[20] *Nebraska M. J.*, 18:376, 1933.

[21] *Am. J. Dis. Child.*, 50:1208, 1935.

[22] *Arch. Int. Med.*, 60:623, 1937.

[23] *J. Pediat.*, 5:601, 1934.

[24] *Arch. Int. Med.*, 60:133, 1937.

[25] *South. M. J.*, 17:177, 1924.

[26] *South. M. J.*, 20:912, 1927.

[27] *Ann. Int. Med.*, 7:769, 1923.

[28] *Loc. cit.*; see n. 19.

[29] *Loc. cit.*; see n. 13.

of the French. Such cells represent degenerative erythrocytes and not true sickle cells.[30]

The case reported by Archibald[31] in an Arab boy was a typical sickle cell anemia illustrated by convincing photographs. Both parents were Arabs, and their blood showed no evidence of sickling. Nothing is stated of the possible presence of Negro blood in the family, nor is any mention made regarding the appearance of the features of the patient or his parents. Since the residence and place of birth of the patient are in the Sudan, a region where the inhabitants are predominantly Negro and where interbreeding is common, the probability of an admixture with Negro blood in this case is very strong.

The facial characteristics of the Cuban boy reported by Stewart[32] indicated clearly a mixture with Negro blood, which is common in Cuba. Although there is no admitted history of a Negro in that part of the family that could be traced for three generations, such an occurrence cannot be eliminated under the circumstances. The blood of the mother and sister of the patient showed the sickling trait. The same possibilities, if not more so, of intermixture apply to the Mexicans reported by Wallace and Killingsworth[33] and by Cardoza.[34]

The photomicrographs of the erythrocytes of Lawrence's[35] six white cases showed not the morphological characteristics of true sickle cells but of the peculiar red-cell deformity described by Dresbach[36] as "elliptical cells." Lawrence[37] later included these cases in a report on "elliptical erythrocytes," an entirely different condition.

Although there was no evidence of Negro blood in the direct families of the Greek patient observed by Cooley and Lee,[38] the three Italians reported by Rosenfeld and Pincus,[39] and the two

[30] Schilling, *The blood picture*, trans. Gradwohl (St. Louis: C. V. Mosby Co., 1929); Lambin and Leto, *Rev. belge sc. med.*, 2:246, 1930.

[31] *Loc. cit.;* see n. 14.

[32] *Loc. cit.;* see n. 15.

[33] *Loc. cit.;* see n. 21.

[34] *Loc. cit.;* see n. 22.

[35] *Loc. cit.;* see n. 17.

[36] *Science*, 19:469, 1904.

[37] *Am. J. M. Sc.*, 181:240, 1931.

[38] *Loc. cit.;* see n. 9.

[39] *Loc. cit.;* see n. 19.

Sicilians reported by Hayden and Evans,[40] these cases cannot be used as evidence to prove that the Negro influence is not necessary for the occurrence of sickle cell anemia, since anthropologists have pointed out that in the past there has been a large infusion of Negro blood in the so-called Mediterranean races.

It would seem, therefore, that there remain only three cases that have occurred in pure Caucasians—that of Sights and Simon[41] in a white native American of Scotch-Irish descent and that of two children[42] whose father is of a family that has lived for several generations in Illinois, Ohio, and Missouri and whose mother has forebears from Virginia and Kentucky. However, Stewart says of the former case that "the absence of racial and geographic study of other members of the patient's family to exclude the possible admixture of Negro blood decreases considerably the value of this case from an ethnologic viewpoint."[43] The same can be said of the latter two cases, particularly since the maternal branch of the family originated in former slave states.

Thus it appears that the burden of proof in presenting cases of sickle cell anemia or sicklemia in white people is to show, first, that they are true instances of the conditions and not other types of red-cell deformity and, second, that the progenitors of the patient are entirely free of Negro blood, a task that may be difficult, owing to disappearance of obvious Negro features on dilution with white blood and to the tendency under such circumstances to deny Negro forebears.

It is difficult to make an accurate estimate of the incidence of sickle cell anemia in colored people, because the condition is often overlooked. In centers where clinicians see large numbers of Negroes and are acquainted with the disease, they are on the lookout for it and consequently see the largest numbers. Those not alert to its occurrence are likely not to recognize even severe cases with characteristic symptoms and signs, much less mild cases with less definite diagnostic findings. If the diagnosis of sickle cell anemia is made solely on the presence of a slight

[40] Loc. cit.; see n. 24.   [42] Cooke and Mack, loc. cit.; see n. 23.

[41] Loc. cit.; see n. 18.   [43] Loc. cit.; see n. 15.

anemia and sicklemia, the incidence of the disease is likely to be overrated because of the tendency of colored children to have a moderate anemia,[44] irrespective of the presence of sicklemia. The rate of occurrence of sicklemia has been determined rather definitely by surveys of colored populations in various parts of the country. The accuracy of such surveys is subject to several factors which may account for the different results obtained. There is a well-known vagary about the occurrence of sickling in moist preparations of the blood of a given individual. At one examination a large number of sickle cells may develop, while subsequent tests will disclose little or no sickling. Whether this is due to an actual variation in the sickling properties of the individual's blood or to an unrecognized but variable factor in the technic is not clear. It is known that purposeful manipulations of the technic will give results that vary from a rate of 4–15 per cent. The original method of sealing a drop of blood under a cover slip with vaseline or paraffin has been improved: first, by sealing with asphaltum, then by sealing under paraffin oil in a test tube, by mixing certain dyes or chemicals with the blood, and by using blood taken in a certain way. These changes have been made in keeping with certain principles that had been established for the sickling process and which will be discussed farther on.

In Table 12 is given the incidence of sicklemia obtained by different authors for various localities. Probably none of these figures represent the full rate of occurrence of the sickling trait.

Sydenstricker[45] estimated that in colored hospital patients the ratio of sickle cell anemia to sicklemia was 1:9. In a survey of school children he found the ratio to be 1:50 and adds that "among children admitted to the hospitals and outpatient clinics the number is, of course, greater." Diggs, Ahmann, and Bibb[46] recognized during a thirty-month period fourteen cases of sickle cell anemia in the medical and pediatric wards of the Memphis General Hospital. Estimating the number of patients with the sickle cell trait as 7.4 per cent of the total number of

---

[44] Cooley and Lee, *loc. cit.*; see n. 9; Miyamoto, *loc. cit.*; see n.26.

[45] *Op. cit.*, 25:620, 1932.   [46] *Loc. cit.*; see n. 27.

admissions to the hospital during the same period, they find that the ratio of sickle cell anemia to sicklemia is 1:40 and state that if these figures are approximately correct they indi-

TABLE 12

INCIDENCE OF THE SICKLE CELL TRAIT

Investigators	Place	Number Examined	Number Positive	Per Cent
Sydenstricker, Mulherin, and Houseal*............................	Ga.	300	13	4.3
Cooley and Lee†..................	Mich.	400	30	7.5
Miyamoto and Korb‡.............	Mo.	300	19	6.3
Wollstein and Kreidel§.............	N.Y.	150	13	8.6
Josephs‖.........................	Md.	250	16	6.4
Smith¶...........................	La.	100	5	5.0
Dolgopol and Stitt**..............	N.Y.	77	4	5.2
Levy††...........................	N.Y.	213	12	5.6
Graham and McCarty‡‡............	Ala.	1,500	122	8.1
Brandau§§........................	Texas	150	10	6.7
Sydenstricker‖‖......	Ga.	1,800	99	5.5
Diggs, Ahmann, and Bibb¶¶	Tenn.	2,539	211	8.3
Ahmann***........................	Fla.	674	65	9.6
Wallace and Killingsworth†††.......	Texas	1,205	65	5.3
Beck and Hertz‡‡‡...............	Pa.	100	13	13.0
Cardoza§§§.......................	Ill.	1,263	120	9.4
Hausen-Pruss‖‖‖‖.................	N.C.	100	15	15.0
Total........................	....	11,121	832	7.48

* *Am. J. Dis. Child.*, 26:132, 1923.
† *Am. J. Dis. Child.*, 32:334, 1926.
‡ *South. M. J.*, 20:912, 1927.
§ *Am. J. Dis. Child.*, 36:998, 1928.
‖ *Bull. Johns Hopkins Hosp.*, 40:77, 1927.
¶ *Tr. Roy. Soc. Trop. Med. & Hyg.*, 210:410, 1934.
ᵃ⁰ *Am. Rev. Tuberc.*, 19:454, 1929.
†† *Ann. Int. Med.*, 3:47, 1929.
‡‡ *J. Lab. & Clin. Med.*, 12:536, 1927.

§§ *Am. J. M. Sc.*, 180:813, 1930.
‖‖ *South. M. J.*, 25:620, 1932.
*** Diggs, Ahmann, and Bibb, *Ann. Int. Med.*, 7:769, 1923.
††† *South. M. J.*, 29:941, 1936.
‡‡‡ *Am. J. Clin. Path.*, 5:325, 1935.
§§§ *Arch. Int. Med.*, 60:623, 1937.
‖‖‖‖ *J. Lab. & Clin. Med.*, 22:311, 1936.

cate that sickle cell anemia is much more frequent than is commonly believed and that the number affected in the United States alone probably numbers in the tens of thousands.

What bearing the sickle cell trait has on the development of sickle cell anemia is a matter of controversy. Some writers believe that sickle cell anemia affects only those with sicklemia, which is thought to be always present at birth, if at all, and that for this reason every case of sicklemia is potentially one of sickle cell anemia. Some unknown factor is supposed to initiate the processes which are responsible for the anemia and other features of the disease. One theory assumes that the sickle erythrocyte is an abnormal cell and is readily susceptible to hemolysis or phagocytosis. It is not clear whether this theory refers to all erythrocytes in a sicklemic person or only to erythrocytes that have sickled in the body, because in the latter instance the theory would be less rational, since, as far as is known, sickling does not occur *in vivo;* at least sickled cells are never found in the circulation of sicklemic persons. If sicklemia is converted into sickle cell anemia some explanation must be given for the conversion in the body of potential sickled cells into actual sickled cells.

Others state that there is no evidence that sicklemia ever becomes active sickle cell anemia.[47] The sickle cell trait is not incompatible with good health and the attainment of old age.[48]

The statement is generally made that sicklemia is congenital and hereditary. Huck,[49] after studying its distribution in two families for three generations, concluded that the condition is transmitted according to the law of Mendel as a dominant characteristic. That the sickle cell trait is congenital is easily verified by the finding in the umbilical cord erythrocytes that readily sickle. But Steinberg[50] questions the logic of the claim that it is inherited as a Mendelian dominant, when supported only by the available evidence, which consists for the most part of a demonstration of the condition in the parents and their children of a few families.

Cooley and Lee[51] suggested the possibility of an African tribe characterized by sickle cells as the normal erythrocyte, and that, by intermixture, introduced it into other groups of Negroes and other races. However, no evidence of the existence of such a tribe has been disclosed, but few or no investigations have been

[47] Anderson and Ware, *Am. J. Dis. Child.*, 44:1055, 1932.

[48] Diggs, Ahmann, and Bibb, *loc. cit.;* see n. 27.

[49] *Bull. Johns Hopkins Hosp.*, 34:335, 1923.

[50] *Loc. cit.;* see n. 10.　　　　　　[51] *Loc. cit.;* see n. 9.

made in Africa. Smith[52] reported three cases in natives, one from Lagos and two from Nigeria. The cases were not seen clinically but were located by finding sickled cells in smears of the spleen obtained from previous autopsies and preserved in formalin. Russell and Taylor[53] found a case in a native of the Gold Coast.

The numerous investigations concerning the factors that influence sickling both *in vitro* and *in vivo* have led to the accumulation of many isolated facts, none of which appear to give any clue as to the causes of the process.[54]

Cardoza[55] has been interested in the immunology of sickle cell anemia. Since isoagglutinins are a phenomenon concerned with erythrocytes, are inherited, and have a distinct racial distribution, facts which are also true of the sickling trait, he investigated the relation between isoagglutinins and the sickling trait. Further indications were, first, the fact that Guthrie and Huck[56] found an anomalous isoagglutinin in a sickle cell patient, and, second, that Landsteiner[57] found a specific racial immune agglutinogen in Negro bloods. However, Cardoza's experiments showed that the sickling trait is not confined to individuals of any one of the isohemagglutinin or immune agglutinogen groups. Nor was he able to locate an anomalous isohemagglutinin among his group of sicklemics that corresponded to the one discovered by Guthrie and Huck.[58] Erythrocytes from a sicklemic patient agglutinated with an isoagglutinating

---

[52] *Tr. Roy. Soc. Trop. Med. & Hyg.*, 210:410, 1934.

[53] *West African M. J.*, 5:68, 1932.

[54] Hahn and Gillespie, *loc. cit.*; see n. 11; Beck and Hertz, *Am. J. Clin. Path.*, 5:325, 1935; Hausen-Pruss, *J. Lab. & Clin. Med.*, 22:311, 1936; Cardoza, *loc. cit.*; see n. 22; Diggs and Ching, *South. M. J.*, 27:839, 1934; Sydenstricker, *M. Clin. North Amer.*, 12:1451, 1929; *J. A. M. A.*, 86:12, 1924; Alden, *Am. J. M. Sc.*, 173:168, 1927; Cooley and Lee, *loc. cit.*; see n. 9; Wollstein and Kreidel, *Am. J. Dis. Child.*, 36:998, 1928; Mason, *J. A. M. A.*, 79:1316, 1922; Hargrove and Matthews, *J. Lab. & Clin. Med.*, 19:126, 1933; Diggs, *J. Lab. & Clin. Med.*, 17:913, 1932; Eastland and Higgins, *Bull. School M. Univ. Maryland*, 14:178, 1930; Schriver and Waugh, *Canad. M. A. J.*, 23:375, 1930; Dolgopol and Stitt, *Am. Rev. Tuberc.*, 19:454, 1929; Yates and Hansmann, *Am. J. M. Sc.*, 191:474, 1936; Anderson and Ware, *loc. cit.*; see n. 47.

[55] *Loc. cit.*; see n. 22. [57] *J. Immunol.*, 27:469, 1934.

[56] *Bull. Johns Hopkins Hosp.*, 34:80, 1933. [58] *Loc. cit.*; see n. 56.

serum and washed are still able to sickle, and cells already sick-led can, according to Cardoza, be agglutinated by the proper agglutinating serum. A tendency toward autoagglutination *in vitro* has been observed by Sydenstricker[59] and Diggs and Ching.[60]

Of the various clinical symptoms of sickle cell anemia, anemia is the most important feature of the active disease. The red blood cell count varies considerably between patients and in individuals, but there is a tendency to a progressive decrease that is interrupted with remissions and relapses. Anderson and Ware[61] state that the average count is between 2,000,000 and 2,500,000, although occasionally it is as high as 3,500,000 and may be as low as 600,000.[62] While death in sickle cell anemia is usually due to intercurrent infection, it may be from the anemia itself.[63]

The hemoglobin content varies with the red cell count and averages 40–50 per cent with a low of 10 per cent. Diggs[63a] has summarized the blood findings in seventy-four cases. He says there are signs of red blood cell destruction, such as poikilocy-tosis, degenerative forms, microcytes, increased serum bilirubin, a negative direct and positive indirect van den Bergh test, urobilinuria, and phagocytosis of erythrocytes by large mono-nuclear leukocytes. There are in the blood signs of increased regenerative activity on the part of the bone marrow—megalo-blasts, intermediary forms, nucleated red cells, nuclear frag-ments of all types, a diffuse basophilia, macrocytes, increased reticulocytes, a leukocytosis with nuclear changes as indicated by Arneth's shift to the right and left, and increased platelets. The average red blood cell in sickle cell anemia is smaller than normal. The cell volume is decreased out of proportion to the

[59] *South. M. J.*, 25:620, 1932.

[61] *Loc. cit.;* see n. 47.

[60] *South M. J.*, 27:839, 1934.

[62] Campbell, *Arch.* Surg., 31:607, 1935.

[63] Ryerson and Terplan, *Folia haemat.*, 53:353, 1935; Wollstein and Kriedel, *loc. cit.;* see n. 54; Corrigan and Schiller, *New England J. Med.*, 210:410, 1934; Yater and Mallori, *J. A. M. A.*, 96:1671, 1931; Hamman, *South. M. J.*, 26:666, 1933; Jaffé, *Virchows Arch. f. path. Anat.*, 265:452, 1927; Steinfeld and Klauder, *M. Clin. North America*, 10:1561, 1927. Franklin and Schwartz say 50 per cent of sickle cell anemia patients die with tuberculosis (*J. Lab. & Clin. Med.*, 15:519, 1930).

[63a] *J. Lab. & Clin. Med.*, 17:913, 1932.

decrease in the red blood and hemoglobin. The color index is variable but usually below one.

In sicklemia there is apparently no anemia that is related to this condition. Cooley and Lee[63b] and Miyamoto and Korb[64] point out that the so-called normal red cell count of colored children is usually lower than that of white children, whether or not sicklemia is present.

Bunting[65] found that sickled erythrocytes from patients with sickle cell anemia or with the sickle cell trait did not form rouleaux and remained almost entirely unsedimented after one hour's time, while nonsickled cells from the same patients formed rouleaux and sedimented.

According to Singer,[66] in two of three cases of sickle cell anemia the red cells showed a high resistance to hemolytic action of lysolecithin, the substance formed from lecithin by the action of lecithinase.

There is usually a jaundice expressive of excessive destruction of red cells and said to be represented in Negroes by a greenish-yellow tinge of the sclerae, although it must be remembered that many healthy colored people, especially very dark ones, have a slightly yellow color of the sclerae. This yellowish color had been thought to be the only physical sign of sicklemia, but Diggs, Ahmann, and Bibb[67] investigated this question and concluded that the color of the sclerae cannot be used as a diagnostic aid in the detection of sicklemia.

There has been much interest in the ulcers of the leg often found in sickle cell anemia and described in the first case by Herrick.[68] These ulcers have been believed to have a typical form and are diagnostic. Anderson and Ware[69] found that they had occurred in 40 per cent of the reported cases, but there is no information as to their incidence in a group of colored people without sickle cell anemia. Some writers believe that the ulcers are due to a lowered resistance from the anemia in which leg in-

[63b] *Loc. cit.*; see n. 9.

[64] *Loc. cit.*; see n. 26.

[65] *Am. J. Med. Sc.*, 198:191, 1939.

[66] *Am. J. Med. Sc.*, 199:466, 1940.

[67] *Loc. cit.*; see n. 27.

[68] *Loc. cit.*; see n. 8.

[69] *Loc. cit.*; see n. 47.

juries do not readily heal. Others think they are related to the pathological conditions in the underlying bone found in sickle cell anemia. Still others say they have no connection whatever with sickle cell anemia and are incidental to the habits and mode of life of many colored people, such as going barefoot in fields, working in certain occupations, and sitting before hot fireplaces and stoves. Diggs, Ahmann, and Bibb[70] selected a group of Negroes with scars of leg ulcers, such as are described in sickle cell anemia, and found that the incidence of the sickle cell trait in them was practically the same as among those without the trait.

The size of the spleen, in view of the pathological findings in this organ that have been described, is of interest. It seems that in the early stages of the disease, and therefore most often in younger individuals, the spleen is enlarged. But as the disease progresses or its duration increases the spleen becomes smaller, until it is no longer palpable. This correspondence of the size of the spleen with the stage of the disease and the resulting variability in palpability caused a disagreement as to the reliability of spleen size as a diagnostic aid. Huck[71] believed that the absence of splenomegaly served to differentiate sickle cell anemia from congenital hemolytic icterus. Sydenstricker[72] and Hahn[73] stated that splenomegaly occurred in 15 per cent of the cases. It is agreed now that only in the late stages the spleen may become so small that, as in one case, it is impossible to find it on opening the abdomen at operation.[74]

A peculiar and poorly understood group of symptoms said to be characteristic of sickle cell anemia are the abdominal and joint crises, accompanied with severe localized pain. The abdominal manifestations have been clearly described by Campbell.[75] He points out that the acute pains are accompanied by fever, mild jaundice, and leukocytosis. The pain may be in the

[70] Loc. cit.; see n. 27.

[71] See Sydenstricker, South. M. J., 17:177, 1924.

[72] J. A. M. A., 83:12, 1924.

[73] Am. J. M. Sc., 175:206, 1928.

[74] Ching and Diggs, Arch. Int. Med., 51:100, 1933.   [75] Loc. cit.; see n. 62.

left upper quadrant, suggesting splenic infarcts, or in the epigastrium and right upper quadrant, simulating cholecystitis or hepatic tenderness from other causes, or even gastric or duodenal disease. Again, there may be a cramplike pain, either generalized or localized, in the epigastrium associated with nausea, vomiting, obstipation, and distension and strongly suggestive of intestinal obstruction. Instances are known in which acute appendicitis has been mimicked and mistakenly operated, and on occasions acute salpingitis has been erroneously diagnosed. The symptoms and signs may vary in the same person from day to day, so that more than one abdominal condition is portrayed.

The cause of the pain is unknown. Infarcts in the spleen, perisplenitis, embolus of the liver, changes in the spinal cord or nerve roots, owing to bony changes, have been suggested, but none of these ideas has complete support. The problem is complicated by the fact that patients with sickle cell anemia are subject to the ordinary abdominal complaints as are other persons, and the question of differential diagnosis is important.

Another group of symptoms include intense pains in the joints and muscles, fever, and leukocytosis, which, together with a functional murmur of anemic origin, closely imitates acute rheumatic fever. These pains in the joints may be related very closely to the rather definite changes in the bones detected by x-ray frequently in sickle cell anemia.

The x-ray findings in the bone[76] are not specific for sickle cell anemia but appear to be similar to those found also in congenital hemolytic icterus and in erythroblastic anemia. There is a thickening of the frontal, parietal, occipital, and temporal bones, with thinning of the internal tables and very thin or absent outer tables. The diploë are very prominent and seem to extend beyond the outer table. In the long bones there are seen a thinning of the cortex, an expansion of the shaft, and medullary trabeculations. Striations are also seen in the pelvis and scapulae. It appears that the explanation of the x-ray findings

[76] Moore, J. Missouri M. A., 26:561, 1929; Vogt and Diamond, Am. J. Roentgenol., 23:625, 1930; Brandau, Am. J. M. Sc., 180:813, 1930; Lewald, Radiology, 18:792, 1932; Grinnon, Am. J. Roentgenol., 34:297, 1925.

in the bone is the hyperactivity of the bone marrow and the subsequent hyperplasia which begins in early life when the cortices of the bone marrow are not firm enough to stop the overgrowth of the marrow. The joint pains may well result from the internal pressure of the expanding bone marrow.

Certain thrombogenic phenomena in visceral vessels[77] have been described in sickle cell anemia that give rise to definite clinical conditions and may be the basis of the acute abdominal pains. Particularly striking are the involvements of the central nervous system that have been attributed to this cause. Cook[78] published the first account of neurologic symptoms in the presence of sickle cell anemia. It involved a seven-year-old Negro boy who suffered loss of consciousness and in whom evidence was found of a subarachnoid hemorrhage with cerebral softening. Cook apparently considered the condition coincidental. The second report is that of Arena,[79] who reported the symptoms of cramping abdominal pains, headache, vertigo, stupor, and right hemiplegia in a colored boy aged six years. Bloody spinal fluid was present. Arena appends a second case with similar findings that he had seen and cited personal communications from Sydenstricker and from Cooley covering three more cases. Baird[80] describes a patient forty-six years old with sickle cell anemia who also developed a cerebral accident, and Kampmeier[81] cites the case of a colored boy, ten years old, who suffered repeated attacks of disturbance referable to the central nervous system, during the last of which there was hemiplegia.

Anderson and Ware[82] charted the most frequent signs and symptoms summarized from forty-nine reported cases of sickle cell anemia in such a way as to show their comparative incidence. Several of those shown are based on the anemia. Others are either coincidental or have a relation not yet understood.

Patients with active sickle cell anemia have pronounced remissions and relapses. During the remissions, in which the dis-

[77] Yater and Mallori, *loc. cit.;* see n. 63.   [79] *Am. J. Dis. Child.,* 49:722, 1935.

[78] *J. Med.,* 11:541, 1930.   [80] *M. Bull. Vet. Admin.,* 11:169,,1934.

[81] *Arch. Neurol. & Psychiat.,* 36:1323, 1935.

[82] *Loc. cit.;* see n. 47.

ease assumes the latent form, the symptoms of the active phase may all be present, except in a milder degree, or there may be only a few indefinite complaints.

The close resemblance of sickle cell anemia to familial hemolytic jaundice is often brought out. The similarities and differences have been summarized by Wollstein and Kreidel[83] and Sydenstricker.[84] The similarities are as follows: Both of them are familial, with the same type of anemia, jaundice, erythropoietic activity, bone changes, hemolytic crises associated with increase of jaundice, excretion of pigment, diminution of red cell count and hemoglobin, and abdominal pain referable to the spleen. Phagocytosis of red blood cells and deposition of iron pigment occur in the liver in both conditions. The differences are: Sickled erythrocytes characterize sickle cell anemia and microcytes are regularly found in congenital hemolytic icterus. Fragility of the red cells is usually but not invariably increased in hemolytic icterus and is usually normal in sickle cell anemia. The spleen is always large in hemolytic icterus. In infants and young children with sickle cell anemia the spleen may be large or normal, while in older children and adults it may be small. The icterus is much deeper in hemolytic jaundice, and the icteric index is higher. The absolute differentiation of the two conditions depends upon the demonstration of the sickling trait and sickle cells in the circulation, which is specific for sickle cell anemia. Another point in the differentiation is that there seems to be no racial preference for congenital hemolytic icterus, while with sickle cell anemia there is a great predominance, if not exclusive occurrence, in Negroes.

The significant pathological changes are found mainly in the spleen, bone marrow, liver, and blood vessels. These changes have been succinctly described by Diggs with Ching[85] and other colleagues, from whose reports the following summary is made.

There is a great variation in the size of the spleen—the smallest recorded weighing 0.87 grams(?)[86] and the largest 960

[83] Loc. cit.; see n. 54.   [84] South. M. J., 25:620, 1932.   [85] Loc. cit.; see n. 60.

[86] Diggs, J. A. M. A., 104:538, 1935 (see discussion, Corrigan); Diggs, Pullman, and King, South. M. J., 30:249, 1937.

grams.[87] The pathological condition found in the spleen in sickle cell anemia is characterized by a series of progressive changes from congestive enlargement to fibrotic atrophy. The earliest demonstrable lesion is congestion of the reticular spaces with sickled erythrocytes and dilatation of the capillaries in the Malpighian corpuscles. At this stage the spleen is enlarged, dark purple, and soft. Then in the areas of intense congestion in the region of the terminal arterioles hemorrhages occur. Later these hemorrhages organize, the vessel walls become greatly thickened, and there are pigmentary changes and a deposition of mineral salts. The lumens of the vessels become narrowed and a stasis is produced. Around the vessels is an inflammatory reaction, and thrombi with infarction are common. The whole spleen is not affected with the same lesion simultaneously, and several different processes may be seen at the same time, but ultimately the pulp becomes completely replaced with fibrous tissue in which incrustations of iron and calcium are entrapped. In the last stages the spleen is reduced to a small wrinkled mass, often buried in adhesions. Diggs says that these changes, such as congestion of the pulp, hemorrhages, infarcts, vascular changes, siderotic deposits, fibrosis, and atrophy, occur in other diseases. The peculiar deformity of the erythrocytes is the one feature that is specific for sickle cell anemia in all stages of the process and is not found in these other conditions. It is the combination of sickle cells with the lesions that makes the spleen in sickle cell anemia unique. Rich[88] claims to have found a lesion which distinguishes the spleen from that which is found in any other disease. This specific lesion is "a pronounced Malformation of the sinuses immediately about the Malpighian bodies leading to the formation of pools of blood partially or completely surrounding the Malpighian bodies." He examined the sections of spleens from five thousand consecutive autopsies and identified this lesion in sixty-two cases, although he admits the sickled cells were also found along with the spleen lesions.

There is general agreement among those who have made ex-

[87] Lash, *Am. J. Obst. & Gynec.*, 27:79, 1934.

[88] *Bull. Johns Hopkins Hosp.*, 43:398, 1928.

aminations of the bone marrow in sickle cell anemia that the marrow is hyperplastic and that the flat and cancellous bones of the trunk and the shafts of the tibia and femur are filled with red marrow. This same change may also be found at times in the bones of the calvarium, scapula, clavicles, sternum, ribs, ilium, humerus, radius, ulna, tibia, and fibula but not usually in the smaller, more distal bones of the foot or in the bones of the wrist or in the long bones of the hand. The color of the marrow may vary, depending on the degree of congestion, the amount of fat, and the pathological changes that are present, but the usual color is a uniform dark red to purplish-black. The marrow from · the shafts of most of the long bones has a consistency of soft jelly and is readily scooped out of the medullary cavity. Microscopically the bone marrow presents a picture of great cellularity and congestion. The capillaries and the tissue spaces are filled with greatly elongated, pointed, and curved sickle cells. The stasis shares with the excessive erythrogenesis in accounting for the color of the marrow. The predominating nucleated cells are of a primary undifferentiated type. Neutrophilic and eosinophilic granulocytes in various stages of maturation are conspicuous. Islands of megaloblasts and nucleated red blood cells are scattered throughout. Most of the nucleated erythrocytes are round, but sickled nucleated erythrocytes are demonstrable. Megakaryocytes are present in increased numbers. There are occasional lymphocytes and cells of large mononuclear type, the latter sometimes containing within their cytoplasm ingested red blood cells, nuclear fragments, and brown and black pigment granules giving a variable iron reaction. In addition to this abnormal hematopoiesis and blood stasis there is evidence of degenerative and reparative processes in the marrow. The lesions found include thrombosis, infarction, necrosis, hemorrhage, granular and crystalline pigment deposits, hyalinization, fibrosis, abnormal calcification, and new bone formation.

In the long bones the red marrow is not confined to the medullary cavity but fills the widened Haversian canals of the cortex, which is, in general, thicker than normal. New bone formation is observed in the shafts, usually taking the form of delicate linear trabeculae but in some instances taking the form of concentric layers of lamellated bone adjacent to the cortex and parallel to it or of thin sheets of bone perpendicular to the cortex. Occasionally there is a complete replacement of the marrow cavity with new bone. The surfaces of the bones as a rule appear normal, but gross roughening and irregular periosteal new bone formation is observed in some of the bones, being most marked in the tibia and fibula of the older patients with leg ulcers. Other bones of the body show less marked changes. Diggs, after describing these lesions, says that it is his opinion that the bone changes in sickle cell anemia are, even in their most marked form, nonspecific. He also states that the appearance of the bone in this disease indicates that the bone marrow is primarily involved. Two factors appear to be working in opposite directions—one the hyperplastic marrow tending to increase its volume at the expense of bone and the other the sclerosing factors tending to replace marrow and to substitute in its place osteoid-tissue or new bone.

The liver is consistently moderately enlarged. The lesions met with are congestion, degenerative changes and pigmentation, marked enlargement of the Kupffer cells, which are actively phagocytic toward sickle cells, granular and fatty degeneration of the parenchymal cells, usually most marked around the center of the lobule, and fibrosis. These changes are most often not of a marked degree, and they do not form a conspicuous feature of sickle cell anemia.

The tendency to capillary stasis, thrombosis, and infarction has been often noticed and is probably related to the shape of the sickled cells. The organs most often involved are the spleen, liver, kidneys, and lungs, and several instances of involvement of the central nervous system have been described. Bauer[89] emphasizes the mechanical obstruction of the blood vessels by the disfigured, elongated erythrocytes. Anemia is only one sequel of sickle cell anemia. Other features of the disease, such as thrombosis, ischemia, necrosis, and fibrosis, are due to the intravascular effect of the abnormal cells. Additional con-

[89] *Arch. Surg.*, 41:1344, 1940.

ditions that may be found in sickle cell anemia are massive bilateral cortical necrosis of the kidney, reticulo-endotheliosis, and polycythemia vera.

Sickle cell anemia has been treated both surgically and medically. The former type of treatment, consisting entirely of splenectomy, is based on the activity of the spleen in this disease, which is believed to be a factor in the production of anemia. Medical treatment is mainly supportive and anti-anemic.

Sydenstricker[90] first suggested splenectomy in sickle cell anemia because (1) of the similarity of the disease to congenital hemolytic icterus, which condition is improved by removal of the spleen, (2) of the compensatory activities of the hematopoietic tissues as evidenced by the excessive output of reticulated and nucleated erythrocytes and high white cell counts and splenomegaly, and (3) of evidences of splenic involvement in crises of abdominal pain. The first splenectomy actually performed was by Hahn and Gillespie,[91] and since then until the present time about a dozen such operations have been performed, although it is believed that many more than this have been done but have remained unreported. Hahn and Gillespie claimed that during the month of postoperative observation their patient was greatly improved by the operation. The results obtained by subsequent authors have varied greatly, and there is no unanimous opinion as to the value of the operation. Ching and Diggs[92] say that at the time of their publication the cases had been too few, the age groups too limited, and the preoperative data too meager to allow a fair appraisal of the procedure. They advise that if splenectomy be given further trial it should be frankly on an experimental basis and attempted only in cases in which the spleen is enlarged, since the removal of small spleens may not only be valueless but it may be, as was in their case, impossible and may impose on the patient an unnecessary operative risk. Later Landon and Patterson[93] reported two cases of splenectomy in sickle cell anemia which were ob-

[90] South. M. J., 17:177, 1924.

[91] Loc. cit.; see n. 11.

[92] Loc. cit.; see n. 74.

[93] J. Pediat., 7:472, 1935.

served postoperatively over a period of seven and five years, re-spectively. They felt that both patients were benefited. In each case the spleen was very large (630 and 655 g., respec-tively). As has always been observed, the sickling tendency per-sisted. Their cases also continued to show moderate, variable anemia. They concluded that splenectomy as a therapeutic measure in sickle cell anemia, while not as definitely indicated as in certain other anemias associated with splenomegaly, is of benefit if the spleen is very large and offers more hope than any other form of treatment. The immediate striking postoperative improvement is not sustained, but the patients continue to be generally more comfortable, more normal, and less susceptible to the usual complications that characterize the disease.

Most of the usual antianemic medications have been tried in sickle cell anemia, but most authors concede that this form of treatment is unsatisfactory. Iron, arsenic, calcium, iodides, alkalies, and general supportive measures have been used with-out apparent benefit. Liver or liver extracts have been given by Sydenstricker,[94] Levy and Schnabel,[95] Cardoza,[96] and Anderson and Ware,[97] who failed to observe any benefit. Levy[98] reported marked improvement in three patients, but the diagnosis is questionable in one of these cases, and in the others the anemia was mild. Brandau[99] added fresh spleen to his patient's diet for twenty-five days, with slight and temporary improvement. Transfusion has proved to be of aid in relieving the acute symp-toms of anemia and to serve in tiding over a critical period, but its effect has been only temporary. Impressed by theories of Bancroft[100] concerning coagulation and peptization of colloids of the nervous system in pathological states, Torrence and Schnabel[101] believed that the acute pains in sickle cell anemia were due to changes in the aggregation or dispersion of the body colloids in some way and reasoned that physicochemical proper-ties of potassium thiocyanate would relieve the pains. In a sin-

[94] M. Clin. North America, 12:1451, 1929.

[95] Am. J. M. Sc., 183:381, 1932.

[96] Loc. cit.; see n. 22.

[97] Loc. cit.; see n. 47.

[98] Ann. Int. Med., 3:47, 1929.

[99] Arch. Int. Med., 50:635, 1932.

[100] J. Phys. Chem., 35:1185, 1931.

[101] Ann. Int. Med., 6:782, 1932.

gle case in which this substance was used they reported prompt relief of pain, but there was no alteration in the underlying conditions. Diggs,[102] using seven cases of sickle cell anemia, made a careful appraisal of the antianemic effect of whole liver, liver extract by mouth, liver extract subcutaneously, desiccated hog's stomach, bone marrow extract, iron, and transfusion. In six cases in which treatment with one or more of these medications was used there was no alteration in the clinical condition. In one three-year-old child there was improvement in the clinical condition and of the anemia following transfusion and the administration of liver.

Summary.—Sickle cell anemia appears to be one disease in which there is a more or less complete racial segregation. If those people in whom there is a probability of an immediate or remote infusion of Negro blood are excluded, it is doubtful if there is a single genuine instance of sickle cell anemia in a white person. There is no satisfactory explanation for this well-established susceptibility of Negroes and immunity of white people to the condition.

Sickle cell anemia is apparently secondary to a congenital anomaly known as sicklemia in which there is a defect of the hematopoietic system manifested by the production of erythrocytes that show under certain conditions a specific form of poikilocytosis. The defect is inherited as a Mendelian dominant. It is probable that the erythrocytes, being abnormal, are rapidly removed from the circulation, and, when the rate of this process exceeds the rate of formation of new cells, anemia develops. Until anemia does develop, persons with sicklemia may enjoy good health. Surveys of groups of the Negro population show that from 4 to 15 per cent, depending on the technic used for demonstrating it, have sicklemia.

The poikilocytotic changes of the erythrocytes, known as "sickling," may occur in the circulation, but it is best demonstrated *in vitro*, for which suitable technics have been developed. Under the conditions of these methods a much larger part of the erythrocytes may undergo sickling than usually occurs *in vivo*.

[102] *Am. J. M. Sc.*, 187: 521, 1934.

When typical, the sickled cells may be easily differentiated from other forms of poikilocytosis. The erythrocytes become elongated and assume a crescentic shape with filamentous processes at the ends. Many studies have been made to determine the factors which lead to sickling. The chief condition for the change in shed blood is the exclusion of air and is obtained by sealing a drop of blood beneath a cover slip or under paraffin oil. There is some reason to believe that anoxemia might lead to sickling of cells in the circulation.

Most of the symptoms in sickle cell anemia, oftentimes very vague in nature, appear to be due to the anemia, which may be very marked, and to certain vascular phenomena which are believed to be the result of the mechanical effect of the distorted erythrocytes, leading to agglutination thrombi and capillary stasis. These same changes may also account for the pathological findings in the disease, consisting chiefly of hypertrophy and finally fibrosis of the spleen, hypertrophy of the bone marrow, thinning of bone, and ulceration of the skin of the lower extremities.

No therapeutic procedure has any effect on the sickling trait, and there seems to be no effective treatment for sickle cell anemia. Patients with the disease have remissions and relapses, with a continual progression in severity, until they succumb to secondary infection or develop an anemia severe enough to cause death.

HEMOPHILIA

It appears that hemophilia is an extremely rare disease in Negroes. Bullock and Fildes,[103] in 1911, collected all but six of the known papers on hemophilia in the world. They found but three papers reporting four cases of the disease in Negroes among a total of over nine hundred cases. Since then only one additional case has been reported, making altogether five instances. All were found in the United States, the first by Had-

---

[103] *Eugenics Laboratory memoirs XII; treasury of human inheritance*, Parts V and VI, Sec. XIV*a*, "Hemophilia" (London: Cambridge University Press, 1911).

lock,[104] the second by Steiner,[105] the third and fourth by Buck,[106] and the fifth by Crandall.[107] There have probably been more than these five cases, because at least two others in the family of the patient reported by Hadlock, an uncle and the father, died of hemorrhages following insignificant injuries. Crandall does not accept the case of Steiner or one of those reported by Buck because they occurred in females, and it is known that, while females transmit the disease, they do not suffer from it. The second case of Buck also comes in for criticism because the bleeding in this patient, as well as in the first one, was not as severe as it usually is in hemophilia. And there was only one attack in each, and both were comparatively easily controlled. Crandall believes that some type of purpura would explain the condition in at least one of these cases. The two patients of Buck attained the ages of twenty-four and thirty years, respectively, and hemophiliacs rarely reach the third decade of life without some serious hemorrhagic manifestations.

The only acceptable cases, then, are the one by Hadlock, in a seven-year-old boy, and the one by Crandall, in a ten-year-old boy. Since the former is reported as being in a mulatto, Crandall claims his as being the only one in a full-blooded Negro, although the only support for this claim is the statement by the mother of the child that all known members of the direct family were very dark.

The clinical, physical, and laboratory findings in Crandall's case were typical of those identified with hemophilia.

Pachman[108] has, since, described three additional cases in colored children. There were for two of them a definite family history and genealogy which were fairly typical. The diagnosis was questionable in the third case, but the history and x-ray findings were characteristic of hemophilia. Campbell[109] adds another. Of the thirty-four descendants of the grandmother of his patient, there were, in all, five bleeders.

[104] *Tr. Acad. Med.*, 7:241, 1874.

[105] *Bull. Johns Hopkins Hosp.*, 11:44, 1900.   [107] *Am. J. M. Sc.*, 192:745, 1936.

[106] *M. Rec.*, 58:149, 1900.   [108] *J. Pediat.*, 10:809, 1937.

[109] *M. Ann. District of Columbia*, 8:294, 1939.

OTHER BLOOD DYSCRASIAS

Agranulocytosis is believed to be unusual in Negroes. The first case was described by Tally and Griffith,[110] the second by Newman,[111] and the third by Norris.[112] Norris is of the opinion that the disease is infrequent in colored people because they usually bear their pains without resource to the drugs with which agranulocytosis is often associated. In the case he described, the patient was in the habit of taking large quantities of quinine, and it is believed this was the provoker of the neutropenia. If so, it is the second one described to be due to quinine, the first one having been reported by Groen.[113] No cases of agranulocytosis developed among many African natives with pneumonia and treated with sulfopyridin and sulfanilamide compounds.[114]

The literature contains very little reference to leukemia in Negroes. That it does occur among them is certain. The author has seen several cases in a small hospital, and among them were included chronic myelogenous leukemia and acute and chronic lymphatic leukemia. In Senegal, Rivoalen, Montagne, and Goez[115] observed five cases of leukemia associated with malaria.

The first two cases in Negroes of the blood disease variously known as erythroblastosis, embryonal hematopoietic persistence, and erythroleukoblastosis, have been described by Andrews and Miller.[116] The condition is characterized by persistent jaundice, edema, petechiae and ecchymoses, and anemia. The blood shows abnormal red cells, varying from early erythroblasts to normoblasts. These cells may amount to as much as 83 per cent of the total red cell count.

The hemolytic anemia that often develops after the administration of sulfanilamide is said to occur oftener in Negroes than

[110] M. Clin. North America, 13:1079, 1930.

[111] Texas State J. Med., 30:452, 1934.

[112] J. Lab. &. Clin. Med., 22:124, 1936–37.

[113] Nederl. tijdschr. v. geneesk., 78:3444, 1934.

[114] Hutton, East African M. J., 16:74, 1939.

[115] Bull. Soc. path. exot., 30:152, 1937.   [116] Am. J. Dis. Child., 50:673, 1935.

in whites. Among the 3 cases of this type of anemia reported by Harvey and Janeway[117] from Johns Hopkins Hospital, 2 were colored. From the same institution Wood[118] later reported that of 522 patients taking sulfanilamide, 21 developed acute anemia. Sixteen of the 21 were colored, but the proportion of the 522 patients which belonged to this race is not given. Schnitzer[119] describes 3 cases in colored persons and states that in a personal communication Myers[120] claims to have seen 12 cases of acute hemolytic anemia, 10 of whom were colored. Willis[121] reports the disease in a Negro infant four days old.

Blood parasitic diseases are so prevalent among Africans that it is difficult to determine the normal blood picture of the natives. Beaudisnet[122] believes that, in addition, defective nutrition is a factor in the peculiar blood picture of African Negroes. He finds that the average red blood cell count of male natives is 4,555,000 and of females, 4,087,000. The hemoglobin values (Tallquist) average 77.5 per cent for both sexes—80 per cent for the males and 77.5 per cent for the females. The color index is 0.87 for males and 0.89 for females. It was impossible to give a formula representing the white cell picture because of the prevalence of malaria and filariasis. There is often a leukopenia with white cell counts averaging 6,000 per cmm. but with counts as low as 4,000 per cmm. The outstanding feature of the differential count was a marked eosinophilia. Most cases examined showed 40–50 per cent eosinophils, but in some the counts reached 70 per cent and never below 30 per cent. The eosinophils increased at the expense of the neutrophils. Trowell[123] complains of the difficulty of diagnosing anemias in natives because of the lack of blood standards for them. He found the mean diameter of the native red cells to be 7.88 μ as compared to 7.17 μ for Europeans. Hennessey[124] found hemoglobin to vary

[117] *J. A. M. A.*, 109:12, 1937.

[118] *J. A. M. A.*, 111:1916, 1938. [119] *Ohio State M. J.*, 35:1204, 1939.

[120] Price and Myers, *J. A. M. A.*, 112:1021, 1939.

[121] *Yale J. Biol. Med.*, 10:275, 1938. [123] *East African M. J.*, 15:402, 1938.

[122] *Bull. Soc. path. exot.*, 30:147, 1937. [124] *East African M. J.*, 13:210, 1936.

from 9.0 g. to 15.77 g. per 100 cc. of blood, the average being 13.1 g., 20 per cent less than the figure for Europeans.

The lower hemoglobin values of American Negro infants have often been pointed out. Munday *et al.*[125] have confirmed this by finding the average values for white infants during the first year of life to be 0.5–1.0 g. per 100 cc. of blood higher than those for Negro infants. The colored babies showed a greater variation in their hemoglobin values than did the whites. Despite these differences in hemoglobin, there were no racial differences in the red blood cell counts.

In two reports from Africa[126] it is shown that the blood sedimentation rate of apparently healthy natives is much lower than that of Europeans. This is attributed to the large amount of parasitic disease.

A case reported by Futcher[127] and another by Lowe[128] appear to be the only instances reported of polycythemia vera (erythremia) in Negroes.

[125] *Am. J. Dis. Child.*, **55**:776, 1938.

[126] Zschucke, *Arch. f. Schiffs- u. Tropen-Hyg.*, **44**:363, 1940; Lassman, *Ann. Soc. belge de méd. trop.*, **19**:557, 1939.

[127] *Boston M. & S. J.*, **191**:304, 1924.   [128] *Tri-State M. J.*, **13**:2679, 1941.

HOOKWORM

There seems to be a marked relative resistance of the Negro to hookworm, expressed as a resistance both to invasion by the parasite and to the injurious effects after invasion. Chandler[1] says this is proved in the South, where Negroes and whites live under identical conditions and have practically the same sanitary habits. Here Negroes have markedly lighter infestations and also suffer less ill effects from a given degree of infestation than do the whites. According to Smillie and Augustine,[2] in one of the most heavily infested counties in Alabama less than 9 per cent of the rural colored children of school age harbored over 100 worms and less than 1 per cent over 500, whereas of the white rural school children in the same county over 50 per cent harbored over 100 worms and 14 per cent over 500. In six different counties in different parts of the state less than 4 per cent of the colored children harbored over 100 worms and only 0.4 per cent over 500, whereas of the white children 33.3 per cent harbored over 100 worms and 7.4 per cent harbored over 500. Knowlton,[3] examining soldiers from Florida and the Carolinas, obtained an average of 155.3 worms per individual in whites and only 38.3 in Negroes. Clinical cases in Negroes in southern United States are said to be extremely rare, while the prevalence of the anemic, emaciated, mentally retarded white hookworm victim in certain parts of the South is well known. Concerning hookworm infestation in Jones County, Mississippi, Howard[4] says the infestation rate of 22.6 per cent among Negro children (75.8 per cent among white children) is low. It has been noted often before that the Negroes of the southern states seem to possess a relative immunity, or at least when living under apparently the same environment as the whites they have generally shown a markedly lower rate of infestation. Among the colored school children there was practically no clinical evidence of infestations, and in those specimens of stools from them found to

[1] *Hookworm disease* (New York: Macmillan Co., 1929).

[2] *J. A. M. A.*, 85:1958, 1925.

[3] *J. A. M. A.*, 70:701, 1919.   [4] *South. M. J.*, 18:668, 1925.

be positive for hookworm ova only a few ova could be demonstrated. Howard notes that a similar resistance is found in the West Indian Negro as compared with the coolies (East Indians) imported to the West Indies as laborers.

Gordon,[5] in West Africa, studied a series of 137 Negroes, 14 of whom had an average of over 10,000 eggs per g. of feces, and failed to find any noticeable effects on the hemoglobin percentage, the physique and general fitness, or the mentality of the cases examined, or any association between hookworm infestations with nephritic disturbances. The possibility of some association between hookworm infestations of more than 15,000 eggs per g. of feces and a low standard of energy was suggested, but the number of cases was not large enough to be conclusive.

Cort et al.[6] found that in several groups of people in Panama who were Indian-Negro mixture with little white blood the resistance to the effects of hookworm infestation was astonishingly great, even in places where the people were very poor and appeared undernourished and had malaria to contend with as well. In contrast to this, in two localities where the population had a marked infusion of white blood, the people looked distinctly anemic, and there were numbers of individuals evidently suffering from severe clinical hookworm diseases, although the intensity of hookworm infestation was no greater than the Indian-Negro groups and distinctly lighter in some. In the Indian-Negro groups there was no significant correlation between intensity of infestation and hemoglobin percentage, while in the Indian-white groups a definite correlation was observable.

Smillie and Augustine[7] expressed the opinion that the lighter infestations observed in Negroes might be due to the greater thickness of the skin in the Negro than in the white race, a suggestion further borne out by the rarity in Negro children as compared with white children of "creeping eruption," a condition caused by the penetration of certain types of hookworm larvae.

[5] Ann. Trop. Med. & Parasitol., 19:429, 1925.

[6] Am. J. Hyg. ("Monographic series"), 9:215, 1929.   [7] Loc. cit.; see n. 2.

Africa can be divided into two sharply defined hookworm areas—north and south of the Sahara Desert. The former is a smaller but very heavily infested region. It includes Egypt, which is especially heavily ridden with hookworm. The southern area, which makes up the habitat of the Negro, is extensive, but the infestation, even in the most heavily infested part, is comparatively small. The northern boundary of this southern area where hookworm exists extends in an almost straight line across the whole of Africa at about 10° north. The southern boundary begins at about 5° south on the west coast and extends southeastward to about 25° south on the east coast. The northern hookworm area of Africa is infested with *Ankylostoma duodenale*, while the southern area (Negroes) is infested with *Necator americanus*. The latter species is also the type that is almost exclusively found in North, Central, and South America. Since these countries have been in close contact with equatorial Africa through the importation of slaves, it is believed that the parasites were brought into them by native Africans and slavers. While information is meager concerning the type of hookworm infestation among American Indians, there is slight evidence that it is with *A. duodenale*.

It has been suggested that the relative immunity of the Negro to hookworm is due to his long contact with the parasite in Africa, a theory that must assume, first, that there is an acquired immunity associated with hookworm disease and, second, that Negroes have been exposed to this immunizing effect longer than most other races, since their resistance is greater.

THE DIET OF THE NEGRO: DEFICIENCY DISEASES

Reference is often made to the diet of the Negro in discussions of his diseases. If the diseases are those which occur with a relatively low frequency, such as dental caries and peptic ulcer, the diet is spoken of as plain but wholesome and as a considerable contributory factor in preventing the diseases. If, on the other hand, the conditions discussed are of high frequency, such as rickets and tuberculosis, the diet is often considered as being of much influence, since it is deemed highly inadequate both in quality and in quantity. The divergence of these views about the Negro's diet indicate that it is not a fixed one but varies greatly with groups and individuals as it does among other people. Despite the myth of pork chops and chicken, there is nothing racially specific about what colored people eat. If there is anything common to their food, it is that it is a diet of a community—the South. Its characteristics are those of the food of the majority of the people of that part of the county, both white and colored. In both races this southern diet may be embellished, as the result of better economic circumstances and a greater sophistication in the matter of taste, but its basic attributes remain for the most part unchanged.

The attributes of the southern diet are accounted for by the fact that the South is an agricultural country devoted for the most part to the cultivation of a single product, cotton. The greatest part of the energy of man, beast, and land is expended in the production of this staple. On the small farms of the sharecropper and the tenant farmer as well as on the large plantations the minimum amount of ground is used for growing food, and that which is produced is of such nature as to require minimum attention. Cabbage, greens of various sorts, beans, and other vegetables which grow quickly and easily are the vegetables of choice for kitchen gardens. Fowl and swine are preferred to cattle because they require less care and space.

During the summer months the food of the southerner, even under the humblest circumstances, is adequate and highly desirable. Its virtues, especially those of the provincial "pot-liq-

uor," have in recent years been extolled in the Senate by en-
thusiastic representatives of the South. But, owing to the lack
of time and of space for the cultivation of food products for
more than current needs and to the lack of proper means
of preservation when excess quantities are available, together
with a complete cessation of income between crops, the food
during the winter months is of very poor quality, consisting
mostly of corn meal, molasses, salt pork, dried beans, and grits.
It is during this period, which may be considerably extended
under certain circumstances, that deficiency diseases occur. It
is a reflection of the agricultural habits of the South that during
"fat" years, when the high price of cotton stimulates its most in-
tensive cultivation, the occurrence of deficiency diseases is higher than in "lean" years, when there is presumably more time and
land for the production of food.[1] Wheeler[2] suggests that the
boll weevil might be a blessing in disguise in that it diverts the
farmer of the South from cotton to food production.

The likes and dislikes of people for certain foods are determined
by habits created for the most part during childhood and retained with tenacity through adult life. Foreign people bring
their food habits to this continent. Native-born migrants within
the borders of this country cling to the local dishes to which
they have been accustomed. The newly rich surreptitiously obtain the homely dishes of earlier days. In the same way Negroes
in the North maintain the taste for the foods, both good and
bad, to which they were accustomed in the South. The northern
markets learn to cater to their wants, and wise northern whites
have learned that colored neighborhoods are the sources of the
largest varieties of green foods. There is a large demand for
viscera of food animals, known locally as "chitterlings" (intestines), "smelts" (spleen), "lights" (lungs), and "tripe" (stomach). (Viscera, which have certain desirable qualities as food,
form a staple diet also for certain Central European and Balkan
people, as well as for Eskimos.) Southern colored people in the
North retain also their taste for the less desirable parts of the
southern diet, such as salt pork, corn meal, molasses, and so

[1] Tucker, *South. M. J.*, 28:603, 1935.   [2] *South. M. J.*, 23:299, 1930.

forth, but when their use is excessive it is not likely to be confined to any one season, as in the South.[3]

Hess and Unger[4] described the diet of the colored inhabitants of Columbus Hill in New York City, a community made up of West Indian Negroes and where at that time practically every child had rickets. In the West Indies their diet was largely made up of fresh vegetables and fruits, but in New York City, owing to low incomes and the lesser availability of fresh foods, the diet consisted of meat, fish, rice, potatoes, and only a small quantity of fruit. The observation was made that these people over-cooked their vegetables, a fact that also applies to most southern people.

Whipple and Baynham[5] found in St. Louis, Missouri, that the colored children in the elementary schools showed a smaller percentage of malnutrition than the white children. However, the preschool Negro children were not in so good physical condition as the white preschool children. Bad food habits, they claim, were more noticeable in the Negro children than in white children.

In Africa the nature of the diet of the natives depends on the cultural pattern of the various tribes—on whether they are nomadic, agricultural, or pastoral. It is, for the most part, uncontrolled, and both its quantity and its quality are subject to the vagaries of nature.[6] Much attention has been given recently in the African medical literature to the inadequacy of the native diet and to the nutritional diseases resulting therefrom. While food deficiencies occur in the natives living in their natural conditions, they have been augmented a great deal through the influence of European colonists, especially in labor camps, schools, asylums, and prisons. In South Africa among the Bantus one of the chief articles of diet was at one time millet seed,

[3] For a description of the southern white diet showing its similarity to the Negro diet see Vedder, *Arch. Int. Med.*, 18:137, 1916; Siler, Garrison, and McNeal, *Arch. Int. Med.*, 14:293, 1914.

[4] *J. A. M. A.*, 70:900, 1918.   [5] *J. Missouri M. A.*, 22:305, 1925.

[6] See Hintze for a description of the edible foods in various parts of the country (*Geographie und Geschichte der Ernährung* [Leipzig: Georg Thieme, 1934]).

but this was supplanted by maize, which was introduced by the Dutch.[7] The latter cereal lacks certain essentials that millet has, and deficiency diseases have appeared if they were absent previously or increased if they were already present.

A rather thorough   of the African diets has been made in recent years,[8] and it was shown that the natives were, on the whole, an undernourished population. Many of the local diseases, including deficiency diseases, have malnutrition as their basis. The deficiency of the diet is not only in vitamins but also in calcium, phosphorus, iron, iodine, and in complete proteins.[9]

Two important deficiency diseases of Negroes are pellagra and rickets, the former being found in Negroes of Africa and southern United States and the latter chiefly in those of northern United States.

PELLAGRA

Although known for centuries in Europe, pellagra has been recognized as an important disease in this country only since the beginning of this century. It was first found in large amounts in prisons and other institutions where hygienic conditions were very poor, but it was soon found to be prevalent in the general population, especially among the poor whites and Negroes of the South, although it is agreed both in America and in Europe that it is not necessarily a disease of poverty. Following its establishment as an endemic disease in this country, a series of surveys of its prevalence was made which were handicapped because its recognition was not at all times certain and because it was not a reportable disease—a condition which still prevails in many communities. Clinicians are now recognizing that there is a large amount of subpellagra that must be added to estimates of the extent of the disease.[10]

[7] Corkhill, Lancet, 1:1387, 1934.

[8] Africa, 9:145, 1936; see also subsequent pages by a series of authors writing from various localities.

[9] Hall, The improvement of native agriculture in relation to population and public health (London: Oxford University Press, 1936); Dumont, Ann. Soc. belge de méd. trop., 13:261, 1933; Rev. de méd. et d'hyg. trop., 27:36, 1935.

[10] Evans, Illinois M. J., 76:458, 1939.

In studies of the prevalence of pellagra where comparisons could be made, it was found that the disease was from two to five times more frequent in white people than in Negroes. On the other hand, the case fatality was just as many times higher in Negroes than in whites.[11] Reece, in showing that pellagra is a major problem in the South, pointed out that in 1933 there were approximately 70,000 cases, with an average mortality of 5 per cent. In Texas alone there were 12,000 cases, the white mortality being 13.9 per cent and the Negro mortality 51.8 per cent. The highest mortality of both white and colored was in South Carolina, the colored being 69.5 per cent and the white 24.8 per cent. The lowest mortality was in Maryland, where it was 2.2 per cent for the colored and 0.5 per cent for the whites. Before the discovery of the cause of pellagra, the difference in the morbidity of Negroes and whites was attributed to the segregation of the races with the idea that the disease was infectious in nature and transference from the whites to Negroes was minimal.

Pellagra in both white and Negroes is closely associated with the southern diet, whose vitamin B complex deficiency is determined to a great extent by the conditions incident to the extensive cultivation of cotton in the South, as have been discussed above.

Grimm believed that pellagrous insanity was found oftener in Negroes, but no other clinical difference between the two races has been established except in the color characteristics of the skin lesions, which are modified in the Negro because of his basic pigmentation.

The first recognition of pellagra in Africa outside of Egypt was in 1912 by Stannus,[12] who found it in Sierra Leone among Negroes. Since then it has been disclosed that the disease is endemic in various degrees among Negro natives throughout the

---

[11] Lavinder, *Pub. Health Rept.*, 27:2076, 1912; 28:2035, 1913; Grimm, *Pub. Health Rept.*, 28:427, 1913; Siler, Garrison, and McNeal, *Arch. Int. Med.*, 15:98, 1915; 18:173, 1916; Sydenstricker and Armstrong, *Arch. Int. Med.*, 59:883, 1937; Sydenstricker and Armstrong, *South. M. J.*, 30:14, 1937; Jobling and Petersen, *J. Infect. Dis.*, 21:109, 1917; Reece, *South. M. J.*, 28:472, 1935.

[12] *Tr. Roy. Soc. Trop. Med. & Hyg.*, 5:112, 1911–12.

country. Stannus[13] reviewed the various reports of its occurrence and pointed out that certain conditions considered as
separate entities were, in fact, manifestations of pellagra. This
was especially true of various edema diseases among children.[14]

Contrary to the American writers, Corkhill[15] says pellagra is
not a disease that proclaims itself in classical textbook form in
dark-skinned races and that very often it must be distinguished
from malaria and syphilis.

Scott[16] says the so-called "central neuritis" of Jamaicans is a
form of pellagra. It is also probable that the different forms of
edematous diseases reported in Haiti are analogous to those in
Africa and form a part of the picture of pellagra.

RICKETS

The Negro has figured prominently in the history of rickets
and was an important factor in the establishment of the facts
that led to the final discovery of the cause and cure of the disease. It had been long known that colored people in large cities
suffered severely with rickets. Hess[17] frankly stated that of all
races the Negro was most subject to rickets and that this tendency was so marked that it might be safely said that over 90 per
cent of the colored babies had the disease and that even a majority of those that were breast fed showed some signs of this
disorder. This statement could be confirmed by observation in
colored communities of many bow-legged, pot-bellied, "double-
jointed," pigeon-breasted babies, the cause of which was unknown but suspected to be associated with poverty, slums, im-
pure air, confinement, and the want of sunlight. On the other
hand, in Africa rickets among the natives was unknown, and
even in the deep South among the Negroes of the plantations it
was uncommon. These facts, together with the fact that rickets

---

[13] *Trop. Dis. Bull.*, 33:729, 1936.

[14] Williams, *Arch. Dis. Childhood*, 8:423, 1933; Trowell, *Arch. Dis. Childhood*, 12:193,
1937; Gillan, *East African M. J.*, 11:88, 1934; Stones, *East African M. J.*, 12:113, 1935;
Carman, *Tr. Roy. Soc. Trop. Med. & Hyg.*, 9:22, 1928–29; Sharp, *Tr. Roy. Soc. Trop.
Med. & Hyg.*, 28:411, 1935.

[15] *J. Trop. Med.*, 37:177, 196, 214, 245, 265, 314, 1934.

[16] *Ann. Trop. Med.*, 12:109, 1909. [17] *J. A. M. A.*, 69:1583, 1917.

was also prevalent among Italians, East Indians, and Chinese, that it occurred with a high rate among the poor of London, and that it was unusual anywhere in the zone 40°–60° north and south of the equator were important clues in the establishment of the cause of rickets.

Hess,[18] in order to test the efficacy of cod-liver oil in preventing and curing rickets, gave this substance to a large number of Negro babies in the notorious San Juan Hill district of New York City, where the disease exacted a dreadful yearly toll of death. His experiments clearly demonstrated the efficacy of cod-liver oil. The next step was to show, also with Negro babies, that exposure of the body to sunlight and the carbon arc favorably affected the disease as did cod-liver oil. Then it was found that irradiation of certain foodstuffs had the same effect. Following this, the nature of vitamin D was determined and found as a constituent of the organs of the body and of rickets-preventing foods. In this way the problem of rickets in Negroes was solved. Pigmentation that is a protection where sunlight is intense is a hazard where sunshine is less available. The effects of race, geography, and climate in the distribution of the disease are resolved into questions of antirachitic substance in food, in the amount of available sunshine, the amount of pigmentation of the skin, the amount of clothing worn, and the amount of time spent out of doors.

It is to the credit of public health officials that, owing to the energetic education of mothers concerning the means of preventing rickets and to the free distribution of cod-liver oil in poor communities, rickets among Negroes is now as unusual as it was formerly common.

OTHER DEFICIENCY DISEASES

Very few references in the American literature can be found to racial comparisons of other deficiency diseases, from which it can be concluded that probably little or no outstanding differences have been recognized. Scott and Hermann[19] described one Negro case among several white cases of beriberi among the rice

---

[18] *Ibid.* [19] *J. A. M. A.*, 90:2083, 1938.

farmers of Louisiana but give no estimate of the relative occurrence of the condition in the two races. Youmans[20] made a
review of the various vitamin-deficiency diseases in this country
and refers to no others than those described above. Youmans
worked in a clinic situated in an area densely populated with
Negroes, and his attention would probably have been called to
marked deficiency diseases among these people.

The high frequency of scurvy in African natives has been
pointed out.[21] Bernstein and Weiner showed that the Bantu
mine recruit retained vitamin C, while the European excreted it,
showing that the former had a high degree of vitamin unsatura-
tion. Zschucke[22] says that, as long as the nutrition of the natives
of West Africa is based on local products, there is little likelihood of vitamin deficiency except in some chronic diseases
where there is a greater demand for vitamin C. The diet in
Tanganyika is short of proteins and green stuff but is rich in
carbohydrates.[23]

[20] *J. A. M. A.*, 108:15, 1937.

[21] Turner, *The diet of the South African natives in their kraals* (Pretoria: Government
Printer, 1909); also in *Transvaal M. J.*, 4:183, 1909; Maynard, *South African M. J.*,
14:271, 1918; Dyke, *Lancet*, 2:513, 1913; Walker, *South African M. Rec.*, 19:128,
1921; Fox and Stone, *South African J. M. Sc.*, 3:7, 1938; Bernstein and Weiner, *South
African J. M. Sc.*, 2:37, 1937; Spencer, *South African M. Rec.*, 24:386, 1926; Ross,
J. M. A. South Africa, 5:596, 1931.

[22] *Arch. f. Schiffs- u. Tropen-Hyg.*, 44:281, 1940.

[23] Culivick and Culivick, *East African M. J.*, 16:43, 1939.

MENTAL DISEASES

The psychoses are among those diseases which the advocates of the benefits of slavery cite in proof of their claims.[1] These authors point out that before emancipation Negroes, except for a few epileptics and aments, were practically free of insanity but that since the Civil War mental diseases have increased, until now they are equal to and in some cases exceed those in white people. It is stated that this increase is due to the stress of existence under independence as opposed to the ease of life during slavery. As with other diseases about which similar claims are made, it is difficult to prove their validity, because no records were kept of disease conditions among slaves, and all the information we have consists of impressions or what has been passed along by word of mouth. Since the value of a slave depended entirely on the amount of work he could perform, it is not likely that anyone short of a violent maniac or a completely deteriorated individual would be considered mentally ill and unsuitable to be retained as a laborer. Even at the present time the comparative statistics on insanity in whites and Negroes are grossly inaccurate, owing to differences between and within localities in the indications for commitment and in the facilities for the care of white and colored insane patients. In many places in the South it is the practice not to confine white or colored patients with mental disease unless they are destructive to life or property. There is a great difference in the institutional facilities for colored and white. When colored patients are hospitalized, it is always in public institutions, while white patients have access to both public and private hospitals. Since most statistics concerning mental disease deal with patients in public institutions, it is evident that they do not give accurate data on the prevalence of insanity.

Powell[2] says that in 1860 there was 1 insane Negro in Georgia to every 10,584 Negro inhabitants; in 1870 there was 1 to 4,225

[1] Mays, Boston M. & S. J., 136:537, 1897; Powell, J. A. M. A., 27:1185, 1896; McKie, J. A. M. A., 28:537, 1897; O'Malley, Am. J. Insan., 71:309, 1914; Green, J. Nerv. & Ment. Dis., 41:697, 1914.

[2] Loc. cit.; see n. 1.

inhabitants; in 1880, 1 to 1,764; and in 1890, 1 to 943. Green[3] claims that in the Georgia State Sanitorium in 1870 there was 1 colored patient to 5.6 whites, in 1880 there was 1 colored to 4 whites, and in 1900 it was 1 colored to 2.2 whites. These figures may not actually represent the relative occurrence of mental disease in whites and in Negroes but the relative facility with which Negroes were admitted as patients.

In 1910 the United States census of the insane in hospitals showed that for the whole country the rate of first admission for whites was 68.7 per 100,000 population and for Negroes 44.6 per 100,000. The admission rate for native-born whites was 57.9 and for foreign-born whites 116.3 per 100,000. In 1923 the census showed the white admission rate for native-born whites to be 69.5 per 100,000 and the Negro rate 56.4. The native-born white admission rate was 56.8, and the foreign-born rate was 113.2 per 100,000. Ten years later, in 1933, the last statistics available which separated races, the white admission rate was 56.2 and the colored rate 61.8 per 100,000. The native-born and foreign-born white rates were, respectively, 51.2 and 92.6 per 100,000. Concerning the 1933 data, the report says that they do not necessarily indicate that mental disease is more prevalent in Negroes, as they may be influenced by the fact that many white patients are in private institutions and homes and are therefore unavailable for enumeration. It is seen that the relative increase of Negro patients in institutions for mental disease in the United States is greater than it is for whites, although it is impossible to say if this increase is bona fide or due to an increase in the facilities for caring for Negro patients.

The relative number of insane Negro patients fluctuates greatly between states. As a rule, the rate is higher and exceeds that of whites in the northern states and is lower and less than the whites in the southern states. This, however, is not true in all instances, since in some of the southern states the rate is high and, in some cases, exceeds the white rate. The higher rates in the North are probably due to the concentration of Negroes in cities, where the rates are generally higher. In New York State,

[3] *Loc. cit.;* see n. 1.

where nearly all colored people are urban, Malzberg[4] found that the admission rate to insane hospitals during 1929–31, inclusive, was 150.6 per 100,000 for Negroes and 73.7 per 100,000 for whites. In Cincinnati, from July 1, 1936, to July 1, 1937, according to Wagner,[5] the Negro admission rate was 189.2 per 100,000, while the white rate was 95.1 per 100,000. Both the Negro and the white rates in Cincinnati exceeded those in New York, and in both places the colored rate was about twice that of the white.

Jacobs[6] made a comparative study of the incidence of insanity among Negroes and whites in Georgia, Alabama, and Illinois for the decade 1923–32. Georgia has 8.8 per cent of the total Negro population of the United States, but Negroes in Georgia furnish only 5.5 per cent of the total Negro first admissions to insane hospitals. Alabama has 8.2 of the total Negro population but supplies 5.5 per cent of all Negro first admissions in the entire country. On the other hand, Illinois, with only 2.3 per cent of the Negro general population, has 6.1 per cent of Negro first admissions to state hospitals. In all three states the Negro first admissions were higher than those of whites, but there is less racial difference in Georgia and Alabama than in Illinois, the Illinois Negroes having over twice the incidence of the Illinois whites. The excess of Negro first admissions in Illinois is attributed to the more complex environment of this state, to the selective influence of migration, to a relatively greater number of Negro males, and to less racial discrimination. It is suggested that it is further explained by the practice on the part of southern institutions of accepting only the more severe cases among Negro applicants, thus predisposing a smaller percentage of discharges, and subsequent readmissions, among Negroes. Jacobs also found that Negroes have a higher percentage of first admissions under age twenty than do whites, and the whites have a higher percentage of first admissions in the group sixty and above than do Negroes. White readmissions in the three states

[4] *Human Biol.*, **7**:471, 1935.

[5] *Am. J. Psychiat.*, **95**:167, 1938.

[6] *Bull. Univ. Georgia School Med.*, **38**:No. 2a, 1938.

constitute a much higher percentage of the total white admissions than do Negro readmissions of the total Negro admissions. In both races during 1923, and in the whole country, the admission rate for dementia praecox was higher than for any other mental disease. Among the whites 41,7 per cent of all mental diseases was of this type, while it formed 36.5 per cent of all Negro mental diseases. Manic-depressive psychoses made up 21.3 per cent of Negro admissions and 15.3 per cent of white admissions. Alcoholic psychoses were less in Negroes, being 1.2 per cent of the admissions as compared to 2.1 per cent for the whites. Epilepsy made up 4.8 per cent, and psychoneuroses and neuroses made up 0.3 per cent in colored people as compared with 4.0 per cent and 1.1 per cent of white admissions for the same diseases. Syphilis, including general paresis and cerebral syphilis, accounted for 6.7 per cent of Negro admissions and 4.2 per cent of the white. There was very little difference between the two races in the percentage of admissions for all other mental diseases.

In Georgia, Green[7] found that brain tumor, traumatic psychoses, infective-exhaustive type of psychoses, psychoses accompanying pellagra, and epileptic psychoses occurred about equally in the white and in the colored populations. The psychoses accompanying nerve or brain disease (chorea, tabes, paralysis agitans), alcoholic and drug psychoses, involutional melancholia, paranoiac conditions, constitutional inferiority, imbecility and idiocy, were more frequent in the white than in the colored. Senile psychoses, general paresis, dementia praecox, and manic-depressive psychoses were more prevalent in colored than in white.

In New York, according to Malzberg, dementia praecox was the leading psychosis among Negroes, accounting for 29.5 per cent of all the first admissions and providing a rate of 44.4 per 100,000. This disease was also first among the whites, but the first admission rate was 19.2 per 100,000, and it formed 26 per cent of all first admissions. General paresis ranked second among Negroes and fourth among the white population, including 16.6

[7] *Loc. cit.;* see n. 1.

and 9.4 per cent, respectively, of the total of the first admissions. The rates of admission were 25.0 for Negroes and 7.0 for the white population. The manic-depressive psychoses ranked third in frequency among both racial groups, but the Negroes had a rate of first admission of 17.4 and the whites 10.0. The alcoholic psychoses ranked fourth among the Negroes but sixth among the whites. The corresponding rates were 15.1 and 4.3, respectively, a ratio of 3.5 to 1. Psychoses with cerebral syphilis have low rates of first admission, but the Negro rate exceeded the white. The lowest rates among Negroes were found in the psychoneuroses and neuroses, paranoiac conditions, involutional melancholia, psychoses due to drugs and to pellagra. For all the major psychoses, except senile psychoses, the Negro population had higher rates than the white population. The lower rate of the senile psychoses is probably due to the fewer persons of the older ages among the colored. The sex differences in the psychoses were about the same in both races.

Karlan[8] investigated all first admissions from the New York State prisons to the Dannemora State Hospital over a period of ten years. During this period the rates of mental disease per 1,000 commitments to the state institutions of correction were 26.9 for the whites and 36.4 for the colored. Calculated on the basis of the annual population of prisons, the rates of functional psychoses per 10,000 inmates were the same for white and colored—93.3. Prison psychoses, schizophrenia, manic-depressive psychoses, and the group called "other psychoses" were each at a lower rate in Negroes, while psychoses due to syphilis were at a higher rate than in whites. Karlan estimates that the incidence of psychoses in the general population is higher in Negroes than in whites but that the excess is due to cultural, social, and economic causes rather than to a racial predisposition.

O'Malley[9] found no significant difference in the occurrence of dementia praecox in white and in colored. Manic-depressive psychoses, toxic psychoses, senile and presenile psychoses, paranoia and paranoid states, involutional melancholia, depression, and hysteria formed higher proportions of the mental diseases in

[8] *Psychiatric Quart.*, 13:160, 1939.   [9] *Loc. cit.*; see n. 1.

white than in colored patients. On the other hand, infective-exhaustive psychoses, organic brain disease, undifferentiated psychoses, general paresis, defective states, and epilepsy were higher in the Negro.

Wagner[10] found in Cincinnati that the incidence of all forms of psychoses, with the exception of involutional melancholia and hysteria, was greater in the Negro than in the Caucasian. Particularly outstanding was the occurrence of alcoholic psychoses and psychoses associated with syphilis of the nervous system, each of which was about 2.5 times more frequent in the colored and which together equaled almost all other psychoses combined. This high rate of alcoholic psychoses is in disparity with the reports of some other writers who have observed a comparative immunity of Negroes to the toxic effects of alcohol as well as of other drugs (see chap. iii, p. 98). On comparing the incidence of the various mental diseases in Cincinnati and in New York, it is found that in Cincinnati, for white and colored combined, the alcoholic psychoses are over 3.5 times and the psychoses associated with syphilis 2.5 times more frequent than in New York. In New York both the alcoholic psychoses and the psychoses associated with syphilis are about 3.5 times more frequent in Negroes than in whites, while in Cincinnati both are 2.5 times more frequent in Negroes. On the other hand, the total schizophrenia and the total manic-depressive psychoses are both more frequent in New York, the former about 5 times and the latter about 2 times. Schizophrenia is about twice as frequent in New York Negroes as in New York whites and about 1.5 times as frequent in Cincinnati Negroes as in the whites of this city. Manic-depressive psychoses occur about 2 times oftener in the colored of both places than in the whites.

Bailey[11] found among recruits during World War I that the Negro had a high rate of mental deficiency and an extremely low rate of alcoholism. In several southern states, however, the white mental deficiency exceeded that of the colored in the same state. While habits in regard to the use of alcohol were about the same in white and in colored, the rate of alcoholic psychosis

[10] Loc. cit.; see n. 5.   [11] Arch. Neurol. & Psychiat., 7:183, 1922.

among the recruits was about one-tenth as much as the average
for the United States. With the exception of epilepsy, all other
neuropsychiatric conditions in the Negro were less than the
average for the United States. Epilepsy was about 1.5 times
more frequent than the average rate.

Davenport[12] summarized the reported rates of epilepsy in
various races and groups represented among draftees during
World War I and found that the rate per 1,000 for Negroes was
5.13 and the rate for drafted white men was 5.15 per 1,000.

Da Lacerda[13] pointed out that neuroses in the Negro are rare.
The most prevalent form of insanity is mania of persecution.
Hysteria is also rare, and the mental effects of drugs are less.

It is often claimed that suicide is an infrequent occurrence
among Negroes and that it is usually associated with the so-
called superior races. An analysis of suicides in Cincinnati by
Piker[14] shows that over a period of ten years the colored suicide
rate was about 2.3 times that of whites. While there was little
difference between the rates of Negro males and white males,
the colored female rate was nearly four times greater than the
white female rate. Both male and female colored suicides were
younger than the whites. Alcoholism was involved in suicides
among white people more often than among colored. Poison
was the favorite method of suicide by all but was particularly
the choice of Negro females, 93.5 per cent of whom used some
sort of toxic substance as compared with 88.2 per cent of white
females. Poison was the instrument of suicide chosen by 60.5
per cent of Negro males and 49.5 per cent of white males. There
was very little difference between the racial groups in the use of
other methods of suicide. Fewer of the Negro suicides (2.3 per
cent) were psychotic than the white suicides (8.1 per cent). No
studies have been made to corroborate these unexpected findings
of Piker. In a study of suicide among Negroes in Washington,
D.C., Prudhomme[14a] divided suicides into those that were
successful and those that were unsuccessful. The Negro as a
group furnished a smaller proportion of successful suicides,
while the number of attempted but unsuccessful suicides, ap-

[12] *Arch. Neurol. & Psychiat.*, 9:555, 1923.   [14] *Am. J. Psychiat.*, 95:97, 1938.

[13] *Pan-Am. M. Congress*, No. 26, 1893.   [14a] *Psychoanalyt. Rev.* 25:187, 372, 1938.

pears to be as large if not larger than in the white population. The explanation of these facts is largely found in the psychosocial setting of the Negro in America and not in any biologic trait. Zilboorg[15] declares that suicide is not necessarily a phenomenon of advanced races but is probably as old as natural death. He cites its occurrence among primitive races and describes the method used by the Sudan natives, which consists of holding the breath until death occurs. Zilboorg believes that suicide, whether in civilized or in primitive people, is basically an identification with the dead.

Certain qualitative differences in the psychoses of Negroes and whites have been pointed out. Bevis[16] finds catatonia in dementia praecox occurs twice as frequently in colored patients in southern hospitals for mental diseases as it does in white patients. Psychoses with dissociation were most numerous in the Negro, compensatory psychoses came next, while repression psychoses were the least. Bannister[17] in a small series of cases found a high rate of maniacal or exalted types of insanity. Green[18] says that manic-depressive psychosis is oftener of the manic type (elated, active, boisterous) in Negroes than in whites. O'Malley[19] also remarks about the frequency of catatonia in schizophrenia and exaltation in manic-depressive psychoses. Lind[20] describes what he calls the phylogenetic elements of the Negro's psychoses. He attempts to correlate cited hallucinations and dreams of psychotic Negroes with what he believes are the characteristics of the native African's beliefs and customs. Barnes[21] says that 39.6 per cent of Negro paretics had hallucinations, while only 17.3 per cent of the whites had them.

Wagner[22] could not find any indications of trends or "coloring" in the psychoses of colored people, in spite of the fact that claims have been made that the Negro psychotic reaction is more likely to be bizarre, on a religious basis, and transitory. While Negro psychoses were appreciably greater in incidence, according to Wagner, they otherwise fail to differ from those in

[15] *Am. J. Psychiat.*, 92:1347, 1935-36.

[16] *Am. J. Psychiat.*, 1:69, 1921.

[17] *Am. J. Insan.*, 44:455, 1887.

[18] *Am. J. Insan.*, 73:618, 1917.

[19] *Loc. cit.;* see n. 1.

[20] *Psychoanalyt. Rev.*, 4:303, 1917.

[21] *New York State J. Med.*, 98:767, 1913.

[22] *Loc. cit.;* see n. 5.

white people and certainly lack any quality that could be considered Negroid. ,

Malzberg is of the opinion that the excess of alcoholic psychoses and general paralysis in the Negro can be attributed to deleterious social surroundings, but that the excess of dementia praecox and manic-depressive psychoses cannot be explained in terms of purely environmental factors. He suggests that a less stable, more emotional makeup of colored people than of whites is a factor. Such emotional instability, he says, is more likely to be a fruitful ground for functional mental disease. Later Malzberg[23] partly retracted these statements .and substituted the theory that migration is responsible for the high Negro insanity rates. He claims that 90.7 per cent of the Negroes admitted to all institutions for mental disease in New York State were born elsewhere in the United States, while only 34.3 per cent of the native whites were born outside of New York. The average annual rate of admissions for colored people born in New York was 40.0 per 100,000, a rate corresponding to that of the general population. On the other hand, the rate of those born elsewhere was 186.2. From this data it is believed to be a justifiable conclusion that migration is in itself and through attendant circumstances, particularly a less-secure economic existence, an important contributory factor in the causation of mental disease. Wagner does not agree that colored people are less stable emotionally than white people or that New Yorkers, both white and colored, have a greater emotional lability than the population of Cincinnati, and the greater incidence of functional psychoses in Negroes and New Yorkers cannot be explained in this way. Nor is there any reason, he states, to believe that a change in climate associated with migration is any more than a minor and incidental factor in the development of psychotic symptoms.

The more exacting, completely integrated society such as exists in a large metropolitan city, has a more telling effect on both whites and Negroes as manifested by the relative greater incidence of the functional psychoses. Further, all migrant groups appear to be more liable to "functional" reactions during the period through which they are learning to adjust themselves to new standards and strange customs.[24]

---

[23] *Am. J. Phys. Anthropol.*, 21:107, 1936.

[24] Odegaard, *Ment. Hyg.*, 20:546, 1936; Pollock, *Ment. Hyg.*, 10:596, 1926.

Wagner attributes much of the excessive insanity rates of colored people to the facts that one-fourth of the total unemployed in Cincinnati are colored, that 85 per cent of the Negroes live on incomes considered inadequate to maintain a minimum standard of living, and that the mortality rate for all causes is twice as great as for whites.

There have been very few recorded observations on mental disease among natives of Africa. A number of writers have mentioned that there is very little insanity among them, and most of the discussions on mental disease in American Negroes are introduced with this statement, but there is doubtful authority for the opinion. Shelley and Watson[25] say they cannot offer an accurate opinion concerning the incidence of insanity in the general population of Nyasaland, which numbers about one and one-half million natives, because a mentally disordered native does not come under observation until he is uncontrollable and dangerous to his fellows. However, from the figures available to them, it would appear that there is one mental patient to every 15,537 people. This is conceded to be a gross underestimate of the true state of affairs. The largest part of a group of 84 insane patients was made up of schizophrenics (35.7 per cent). Other conditions, in order of their frequency, were affective psychoses (21.4 per cent), epileptic psychoses (13.09 per cent), psychopathic constitution (8.3 per cent), dementia (7.16 per cent), general paresis (4.7 per cent), psychoses associated with organic brain disease (3.57 per cent), confusional states (toxic-infective, neurospirochetosis) (2.3 per cent), oligophrenia (2.3 per cent), and undetermined (1.1 per cent). Hallucinations occurred in 31 per cent of the patients, but illusions were very uncommon. Delusions associated with things or conditions introduced by Europeans occurred in 100 per cent of the general paretics and 80 per cent of the schizophrenics, but for all disorders the average for this type of delusion was 47.6 per cent. Shelley and Watson believe that the confusion arising from the introduction by Europeans of new ideas regarding government, commerce, and morals is a large factor in the mental disorders of the native.

[25] *J. Ment. Sc.*, 82:701, 1936.

In Kenya, Gordon[26] finds that the largest group of mental disorder among the natives is neurospirochetal in origin (21.6 per cent). This type of disease made up 10–15 per cent of the mental diseases of Europeans. Schizophrenia accounted for 19.2 per cent of the native and 20–25 per cent of the European insanity. Senile, alcoholic, manic-depressive, and paranoid psychoses were less in percentage in the natives than in Europeans, while epilepsy, drugs other than alcohol, and physical disease caused more mental disease in the native than the European. He found that all the schizophrenics were among the educated natives.

Marchand[27] says epilepsy is often met with among the natives of the French Lower Congo and believes trypanosomiasis, alcoholism, syphilis, and intoxications from parasites are important factors.

In South Africa[28] schizophrenia and psychopathic constitutions make up 39.4 per cent of mental disease among the natives. Epilepsy, manic-depressive psychoses, and neurospirochetosis account for, respectively, 13.8 per cent, 7.35 per cent, and 5.6 per cent of the mental diseases.

Bosselman and Kraines[29] describe a thirteen-year-old colored boy with sickle cell anemia who developed mental changes, including aphasia. The occurrence of multiple, small cerebral hemorrhages is suggested as the most likely cause.

Mettler et al.[30] say there is a racial variation in the blood-cerebrospinal fluid barrier of normal children. The normal quotient of the blood bromide content divided by the cerebrospinal fluid bromide content ranges from 2.9 to 3.5. In 11 per cent of white children and 75 per cent of colored children the quotient was less than 2.9, and in 89 per cent of white children and 25 per cent of colored children it was above 2.9.

Because it is claimed that the level of intelligence among Negroes and the specific psychological traits of colored people are

[26] East African M. J., 12:327, 1936.

[27] Rev. de méd. et d'hyg. trop., 29:165, 1937.

[28] Annual report of the Commissioner for Mental Hygiene, Union of South Africa (1934).

[29] Am. J. Psychiat., 94:709, 1937–38.   [30] Psychiatric Quart., 11:620, 1937.

of importance in explaining mental diseases in them, psychiatrists very often refer to the large literature on these subjects. As to intelligence, opinion varies from that of Boas, who says there is no difference between white and colored people, to that of Davenport, who says that it is on a considerably lower level in Negroes. The psychological traits ascribed to colored people are not at all flattering to them and are in keeping with the conventional vaudeville stage conception of the Negro character. Most of the literature on the intelligence of Negroes and their psychological traits has the attributes that it is strongly biased and is based on faulty technics of observation. For this reason it is not possible or desirable to review or to appraise what has been written.

MONGOLOID IMBECILITY

The interest in the racial aspect of mongolism arises from the writings of Langdon-Down,[31] who is responsible for the recognition of the disease as a clinical entity, and of Crookshank,[32] who developed a theory of racial atavism to account for the condition. Langdon-Down, in 1866, noted the departure from the normal of the facial features of a certain type of feeblemindedness and attempted a classification of the cases by arranging them around various ethnic standards. He believed that a considerable portion of them could be referred to one of the great divisions of the human family other than the class from which they have sprung. On the assumption that certain types of imbecility were patterned on the physical traits of certain races, he introduced the terms Mongolian imbecility, Negroid imbecility, Malayan imbecility, American imbecility, and Tartar imbecility. The propriety of this idea is, however, no longer in favor, and all these terms have been discarded, with the exception of Mongolian imbecility. But the resemblance of the facial features in this disease to those of the Mongol are superficial and perhaps only accidental, since the condition can be readily recognized in pure Chinese[33] by the departure from

[31] *London Hosp. Rept.*, 3:259, 1866.

[32] *The Mongol in our midst* (3d ed.; New York: E. P. Dutton & Co., Inc., 1931).

[33] Trumpeer, *J. A. M. A.*, 79:14, 1922; Demuth, *Ztschr. f. Kinderh.*, 33:110, 1922; Brousseau, *Mongolism* (Baltimore: Williams & Wilkins, 1928); Sweet, *J. Pediat.*, 5:352, 1934.

278 THE BIOLOGY OF THE NEGRO

the usual Chinese features. For this reason Bleyer[34] prefers the term Mongoloid imbecility rather than Mongolian imbecility.

Crookshank advanced the theory that Mongoloid imbecility is a form of atavism referable to an anthropoid progenitor of the Mongol race. Since the Negro and certain other races were believed by him to have different origins, he assumed that it was impossible for Mongoloid imbecility to occur in the Negro and these other races. In addition to his theory being based on unsound anthropological knowledge, there were, in reality, reports in the literature, at the time of his writing, of five cases of the disease in colored people which he refused to accept as bona fide. Since then other cases have been described in Negroes as well as in a total of thirty-one races and countries, including several races which Crookshank believed were immune to the condition.

While the actual occurrence of Mongoloid imbecility in the Negro is now unquestioned, there is a difference of opinion as to its frequency. Bradley[35] and Dunlap,[36] who reported, respectively, one and three cases, consider it rare in the Negro. Rambar[37] concludes from his experience that it is comparatively less common than in the white race. Mitchell and Cook[38] reported four cases and state their belief that "mongolism in the Negro is probably not as uncommon as it is generally believed. Instances of it are not always recorded." Bleyer,[39] who described a series of eight cases of Negro mongolism, concludes after a comparative racial study that the proportion of mongoloidism in the colored race is about the same as it is among the mentally defective of any race. Gesell[40] published results of a canvass of 56 institutions for the feeble-minded in various parts of the country, which yielded a total of 115 Negro Mongoloid imbeciles, including 31 cases assembled from the literature and 1 case reported by him. As a result of this study, Gessel is of the opinion that clinical mongoloidism in colored people is much

[34] *Am. J. Dis. Child.*, 44:503, 1932.

[35] *Arch. Pediat.*, 44:724, 1927.

[36] *J. Pediat.*, 2:615, 1933.

[37] *Arch. Pediat.*, 52:58, 1935.

[38] *J. A. M. A.*, 99:2105, 1932.

[39] *Loc. cit.*; see n. 34.

[40] *J. A. M. A.*, 106:1146, 1936.

more frequent than is commonly supposed and that carefully analyzed statistics suggest that the condition occurs with almost equal frequency in black and white populations. The latest report is that of Scott,[41] who was able to discover within three years 9 cases of Negro mongoloidism among the patients of the out-patient clinic of Provident Hospital in Chicago. His cases together with 1 other found in the literature, besides the 32 found by Gesell, make a total of 42 cases reported. Thompson[42] canvassed schools, hospitals, and institutions and discovered 21 additional cases of the disease among Negro children. Although about 9 per cent of the population of the United States is Negro, only 1 per cent of the total Mongoloids is to be found in this race.

As far as can be ascertained from the clinical reports of the cases of Negro Mongoloid imbecility found in the literature, there are no peculiarities of the disease referable to this race.

[41] *Arch. Pediat.*, 54:410, 1937; 56:4, 1939.

[42] *Proc. Am. Ment. Deficiency*, 63:91-94, 1939.

MUSCULAR DYSTROPHY

The first and only authentic report, until recently, of a case of muscular dystrophy in a Negro was apparently made by Austrégesilo,[1] who described in 1913 the condition in a Brazilian Negro boy, age twelve years, seen in the author's clinic at Rio de Janeiro in 1908. No family history was obtainable, and from the physical findings the condition was diagnosed as pseudo-hypertrophic muscular atrophy of Duchenne. Photographs of the patient reproduced by Pearson[2] show: (a) contractures of the forearms and atrophy of the arms and of the shoulder girdle with winged scapulae; (b) the method of "climbing up his legs" from the prone position; (c) the great enlargement of the calves; (d) lumbar lordosis; (e) myopathic facies. Prior to the publication of this case Eschner is cited by Cardoza[3] as saying that in statistical studies of the progressive myopathies no case had been encountered or observed in Negroes. But Hurwitz[4] claims that "pseudo-hypertrophic muscular dystrophy can no longer be accepted as occurring in the white alone since authentic cases have been described in Negro children," although no reference is given to such cases, other than the one by Austrégesilo. Cardoza[5] found in the clinics of Provident Hospital in Chicago a second case of progressive muscular atrophy in a nine-year-old Negro boy for whom clinic records are available over a period of seven years. The greatest amount of dystrophy in this patient involved the upper part of the body, so that at first glance it might be classified as of the facioscapulohumeral type of Lan-douzy-Déjérine. He showed the myopathic facies, the transverse smile, and the muscular wasting of the facial, scapular, and humeral group muscles. However, the boy also showed wasting of the muscles of the lower extremities and of the pelvic girdle, for which reason Cardoza believes that "mixed muscular dystrophy" is the more accurate diagnosis.

[1] *Nouv. iconog. de la Salpêtrière*, 26:430, 1913.

[2] *Ann. Eugenics*, 5:179, 1933. [4] *Arch. Neurol. & Psychiat.*, 36:1294, 1936.

[3] Personal communication. [5] Personal communication.

Recently Lowe[6] reported muscular dystrophy of the same type in two colored girls who were sisters. Biopsy of the calf muscles of both cases revealed focal atrophy, fragmentation of striated muscle fibers, hyaline changes, and adipose-tissue infiltration between the muscle bundles. Glycin therapy produced some subjective results in each case, but vitamin E therapy had no effect.

[6] *Tri-State M. J.*, 13:2679, 1941.

DIABETES MELLITUS

The unequal distribution of diabetes among certain races, such as the high rate among Jews and the low rate among Chinese, suggests the possibility that there may also be a rate for Negroes that is different from the average. At one time this was believed to be the case, in that these people were given credit for a relative immunity to the disease. Most authors refer to this former opinion, but no data can be found to account for its origin. The earlier editions of Osler's *Principles and practice of medicine* state that "diabetes is comparatively rare in the colored race," but in the later editions this statement is amended with, "but not so uncommon as it was formerly supposed." It is not known whether this change in opinion is due to an actual change in the incidence of the disease or to a more accurate investigation of the real conditions. Whatever the previous rates have been it is now true that there is not a very significant difference between Negroes and Caucasians in the occurrence of diabetes.

Lemann[1] is accredited with the first publication giving actual statistics showing comparisons between whites and Negroes as to diabetes. He reported the incidence of the disease among 61,298 white patients and 40,265 colored patients in the Charity Hospital at New Orleans over a period of eleven years, from 1898 to 1908, inclusive. Later[2] he added further observations on 92,042 white and 68,004 colored patients observed over another eleven years extending from 1909 to 1919. A third group[3] was also added which included 91,948 whites and 66,673 colored, who were admitted from 1921 to 1926. In the first group the incidence of diabetes among the whites was 0.73 per 1,000 patients, and among the colored it was 0.47 per 1,000 patients. In the second group the white rate was 1.4 per 1,000 and the Negro rate 0.86 per 1,000; and in the third group the white and colored rates were, respectively, 2.3 and 3.4 per 1,000. From the first period to the second the white diabetics increased 100 per cent,

---

[1] *New Orleans M. & S. J.*, 63:461, 1911.

[2] *Am. J. M. Sc.*, 162:226, 1921.   [3] *J. A. M. A.*, 89:659, 1927.

and from the first to the third period they increased 215 per cent. The increases of the colored at the same times were, first, 82 per cent and then 623 per cent. These increases may not at all mean an increase in the incidence of the disease. Greater awareness of the disease and the facilities for treatment are probably the most important factors in bringing about the apparent increase.

At Atlanta Bowcock[4] found from 1921 to 1928, among 26,858 colored hospital and clinic admissions, 113 admissions for diabetes, giving an incidence of 4.2 diabetic admissions per 1,000 general admissions. No comparable figures are given for whites.

Leopold[5] shows that for the three-year period 1929-31 in the Johns Hopkins Hospital Out-Patient Department, 457 of the 31,519 white admissions were diabetic, and 189 of the 14,954 Negro admissions had the disease. These give rates for white and colored as 14.5 and 12.7 per 1,000, respectively. These figures illustrate the inaccuracy of quoting admission rates as being identical with morbidity rates. It is difficult to believe that the colored rate of 3.4 per 1,000 in New Orleans and 4.2 per 1,000 in Atlanta[6] is increased in Baltimore 3-4 times. At Johns Hopkins Hospital is a well-known clinic for diabetes which attracts a larger proportion of diabetics than do less well-known medical centers. The statistics from this clinic exaggerate the proportion of the disease, and unless the clinic is equally well known to both white and colored and unless the inducement to seek treatment at the clinic is the same for both groups, the statistics may not be used as a basis of racial comparisons.

Bowcock says 70 per cent of his cases were in women as compared with the very slight excess of women shown by Joslin among white diabetics. He believes that probably the cause of this excess is the high rate of obesity among colored women. Of 26 Negro females whose weights he obtained, 23, or 92 per cent, were more than 10 per cent overweight. No reason is given as to why the remainder of the group, consisting of more

---

[4] *South. M. J.*, 21:994, 1928.　　　　[5] *Ann. Int. Med.*, 5:285, 1931-32.

[6] Leopold erroneously quotes these figures as 3.4 per cent and 4.2 per cent.

than 100, were not weighed, a routine procedure in nutritional diseases. One wonders if those cited were weighed only because of their large size. Leopold found 67 per cent of his colored patients to be overweight, to which he compares the 77 per cent overweight found by Joslin among 1,000 white diabetics. The colored between ages forty and sixty years were found to be 86.4 per cent overweight.

Support of the theory of Warthin and Wilson[7] that syphilis is a factor in diabetes is denied by the facts concerning the disease in Negroes according to Lemann.. He states that, although his colored patients have a high rate of syphilis, their incidence of diabetes is less than that of whites with less syphilis. Likewise, the percentage of syphilis in colored diabetics is no higher than in nondiabetics.

Bowcock says that diabetes begins about ten years earlier in the Negro. The maximum incidence occurred in the sixth decade of Leopold's cases and in the fifth decade of Lemann's series. In whites, as reported by Joslin, the maximum was in the sixth decade.

Diabetes in the Negro seems to be a comparatively mild disease according to Bowcock. Over 44 per cent of his patients were known to last over two years. One case was known to last at least seventeen years. Leopold reports 19 per cent of his cases as having a duration of over five years.

Gangrene was observed as a complication in 14 per cent of the white diabetics and in 21 per cent of the colored diabetics in Lemann's series. It occurred in 15 per cent of the colored cases studied by Bowcock and in only 4 per cent of Leopold's group. The proneness of the Negro to vascular degeneration and his bad hygiene are claimed by Lemann to account for a higher incidence of gangrene.

Leopold refers to the mortality records for Baltimore during the years 1928, 1929, and 1930, where the average diabetic death rate was 28.7 per 100,000 whites and 18.3 per 100,000

[7] *Am. J. M. Sc.*, 153:157, 1916.

colored. Diabetic deaths were 2.21 per cent of the total white deaths and 0.89 per cent of the total colored deaths.

For 1936 the mortality from diabetes among the general white population in the United States is estimated from the returns of the Bureau of the Census to be 23.4 per 100,000, and for the entire Negro population it is estimated to be 14.4 per 100,000. Of the total white deaths those from diabetes were 1.4 per cent, and of the total colored deaths those from diabetes were 0.95 per cent. The white female diabetic death rate was 1.6 times that of the white male, while the colored female rate was 1.7 times that of the colored male.

An analysis of the mortality experience of the Metropolitan Life Insurance Company by Dublin and Lotka[8] shows that, during the five years from 1931 to 1935, the standardized death rate from diabetes for colored men is 10 per cent less than that for white men, while that of Negro women is practically identical with that of white women. When the races are divided into age groups it is found that there is a relatively high mortality rate among Negroes in early adult and middle life, especially in the females. Between ages twenty-five and forty-four the Negro male exceeds the white male rate, being 1.5 times as great.

Over a period of twenty-five years there was a steady increase in the death rates from diabetes for all groups except the white males, which have been remarkably stable. The increase of the colored female rates, however, has been most marked. At the beginning of the period (1911) diabetic deaths among colored women were less than among any other group. But they have increased more rapidly than the other groups, so that by 1933 the rate was the highest of all.

Among the factors listed by the authors which have served to increase the diabetic death rate in general, those which operate particularly among the colored people are, first, the rapidly growing proportions of older persons and, second, the shift of large groups from rural to urban life with greater probability of recognition of the disease.

[8] *Twenty-five years of health progress* (New York, 1937).

ALCAPTONURIA

Of the twenty-one cases of alcaptonuria reported in this country, the only instances of the disease in Negroes were described by Abbott.[9] Of five siblings in a colored family, two, a male and a female aged thirteen and eight years, respectively, excreted homogenistic acid. The available histories of the parents, grandparents, aunts, and uncles did not disclose evidence of the condition among them:

[9] *Science*, 94:365, 1941.

DISEASES OF THE HEART AND BLOOD VESSELS

Since 1928 heart disease has killed more colored people than any other disease. This has been true for white people since 1912. Before heart disease became the leading cause of death, tuberculosis ranked first place for both races. The exchange in rank of the two diseases has been due both to an increase in deaths from heart disease and to a decrease in deaths from tuberculosis.

In dealing with the published comparative racial statistics of heart disease the obvious untrustworthiness of clinical and mortality data must be kept in mind. The unreliability of such information has often been expressed, especially by Dublin, who said: "We shall always be troubled with our figures for heart disease until there are a larger number of autopsies and the standards of medical practice are generally raised."[1] Also in this connection White and Jones stated that "no single series of patients—private, hospital or clinic—gives a correct incidence of heart disease."[2]

With heart diseases, as with most other diseases, the question arises, in comparing the white and colored races, whether the differences shown are due to actual racial differences or due to other and unspecific differences. The Negro race is predominantly one of hard physical laborers and one characterized by strong emotions, both of which factors may have a telling effect on the cardiovascular system. There are few primary heart diseases. Certainly the four major causes of heart disease—hypertension, arteriosclerosis, syphilis, and rheumatism—affect the heart only secondarily as a part of processes that have much wider distributions. The incidence of heart disease in a race, then, depends both on the incidence of these diseases and on the susceptibility of the heart and blood vessels to their effects. Also the various forms of heart disease have varying distributions among the age groups, and races having different age-group compositions will have different rates of heart disease.

It has been claimed that diseases of the heart have a higher

---

[1] *Am. Heart J.*, 1:359, 1925–26. [2] *Am. Heart J.*, 3:302, 1928.

mortality rate among Negroes than among whites. Thus Gover shows that in ten southern states[3] for the years 1921-23 the Negro rate, excluding coronary disease, was 58.5 per cent higher than the white rate and that ten years later, 1931-33, it was 61 per cent higher. For the five years 1931-35 the average mortality rate per 100,000 for the same ten states, calculated from the United States *Mortality statistics* and the estimated populations for each year, was 170.4 for the whites and 200.5 for the colored. However, over the same period, the average rate for the remainder of the Registration Area, which included the entire United States since and including 1933, was 236.4 per 100,000 whites and 170.4 per 100,000 colored, which is just the reverse for the southern states. For the entire Registration Area for the years 1931-35, inclusive, the rates are shown in Table 13. The average white rate was 227.5 per 100,000 and the average colored rate 184.7.

It thus appears that, while heart disease in the South is more prevalent in colored people than in white, in the northern states and in the country as a whole it is more prevalent in white people. In this connection it must be recalled that the above statistics apply to all "colored" people, a term used for races not considered white and including—besides Negroes—Mexicans, Japanese, Chinese, Indians, and others. In the United States at the last census year, 1930, the non-Negro part of the colored people amounted to 17 per cent. In the above ten southern states it amounted to 5.8 per cent.

In the industrial experience of the Metropolitan Life Insurance Company,[4] involving 3,198,737 deaths from all causes over twenty-five years, 2,575,443 of which were white and 623,294 colored, the death rate from heart disease in Negroes exceeded, on an average, that in whites by 39 per cent among males and no less than 64 per cent among females. Among males the differ-

---

[3] Florida, Kentucky, Louisiana, Maryland, Mississippi, North Carolina, South Carolina, Tennessee, Virginia, and the District of Columbia (*J. Negro Educ.*, 6:276, 1937).

[4] *Twenty-five years of health progress* (New York: Metropolitan Life Insurance Co., 1938).

ences between the rates of the white and colored are relatively small between the ages ten and twenty-five years, but from then on the picture changes abruptly. For the next twenty years of life there is a large and growing difference between men of the two races, which reaches its maximum of 112 per cent at ages thirty-five to forty-four years. The relative excess then falls off, until at sixty-five to seventy-four years it is only 15 per cent. Among females the situation is very different. The smallest excess of the colored rate over that for white females is 27 per cent, recorded at ages ten to fourteen years, and again at the oldest

TABLE 13

RELATIVE MORTALITY OF WHITE AND COL-
ORED FROM HEART DISEASE, 1931–35

Year	White	Colored
1935............	244.5*	186.6
1934............	239.3	196.3
1933............	229.0	184.7
1932............	217.9	174.5
1931............	207.0	181.3

* All figures per 100,000 population.

ages sixty-five to seventy-four years. At ages fifteen to nineteen years the colored rate is more than 1.5 times that of the white, falls off slightly during the next five years, but then mounts sharply, reaching a maximum at ages thirty-five to forty-four, when it is no less than 2.75 times the white rate. The excess is somewhat smaller in the next ten years and declines thereafter very sharply.

Dublin,[5] of the Metropolitan Life Insurance Company, is of the opinion that to a certain extent these large differences may be discounted as being due to relatively poor certification of the causes of death among Negroes, for these differences between the two races in cardiac mortality at ages past thirty-five years are much larger relatively than are those found in the death rates from all causes combined. It is likely, he states, that in a

[5] Ibid.

large proportion òf cases in which the deceased had no regular medical attendant, the diagnosis of heart disease was frequently put down even without good evidence of its presence. On the other hand, he believes that the differences are too large to be dismissed altogether in this manner. Part of them certainly can be explained by the incidence of syphilitic heart disease in Negroes. Part also may be due to the effect of arduous manual work and of exposure, particularly if there existed any damage to the heart from other causes. By and large, the proportion of persons doing this type of work is greater among Negroes than among whites, even for industrial policyholders.

These facts about the higher incidence of cardiac disease among Negroes are supported by the observations of Allen,[6] who states that, of a group of one thousand Negro male factory workers in the Cincinnati metropolitan area, 55.6 per cent were found to have significant cardiovascular abnormalities. This rate is notably higher than that of 33.5 per cent found among two thousand white workers in that locality. This difference in rates closely approximates the difference in the local mortality rates over a period of years. A striking number of men under forty years of age were found to have significant cardiovascular lesions. The rates were definitely higher among those overweight and with albuminuria and glycosuria. A high percentage of the Negro workers were unaware of any unsound condition of their circulatory system. Laws[7] found that 3.3 per cent of the white and 4.9 per cent of the colored patients admitted to Grady Hospital in Atlanta had heart disease. Judging from admissions to the clinic in Galveston, Stone and Vanzant[8] and Schwab and Schulze[9] are of the opinion that heart disease is 1.7–1.8 times more prevalent in colored than in white. Likewise, Wood, Jones, and Kimbrough[10] state that in Virginia the rate of heart disease in Negroes is almost twice that in Caucasians.

Attempts have been made to discover racial differences in the

---

[6] *Am. J. Pub. Health*, 22:579, 1932.

[7] *Am. Heart J.*, 8:608, 1935.   [9] *Am. Heart J.*, 7:223, 1931.

[8] *J. A. M. A.*, 89:1473, 1927.   [10] *Am. J. M. Sc.*, 172:185, 1926.

distribution of heart disease among the various etiologic types.[11] In several of these studies the cases were not divided into clear-cut etiologic types but into groups of combinations of disease processes, any one of which could alone produce heart disease, and it was impossible to discover which was the primary cause.

ARTERIOSCLEROTIC AND HYPERTENSIVE HEART DISEASE

In most instances these two forms were grouped together. By far and large they form the largest group among the various causes of heart disease in both races, and the rates are about the same in white and in colored. In the whites the average is about 66.6 per cent of all heart disease, and in the colored these diseases make up about 64.9 per cent of all heart cases. However, in the statistics that separate arteriosclerosis and hypertension it is shown that arteriosclerosis causes relatively more heart disease and hypertension causes relatively less heart disease in white people than in colored people. Stone and Vanzant found that 50.5 per cent of the colored heart cases were caused by hypertension as compared to 45.3 per cent of the white cases. Arteriosclerosis produced 19.8 per cent of the white cases and 6.3 per cent of the colored. In the same clinic a few years later Schwab and Schulze found 42.4 per cent of the white cases and 63.2 per cent of the colored cases were due to hypertension, and 35.9 per cent of the white and 13.7 per cent of the colored were produced by arteriosclerosis. Arteriosclerosis is a disease primarily of advanced age, and the lower rate of this condition in Negroes might mean a lower proportion of the upper-age-groups in this race.

Hedley points out that Negroes dying in the arteriosclerotic-hypertensive group of heart disease do so at an earlier age than whites. In this series the average colored age at death was 54.6 years, and the average white age was 66.6 years. The peak of colored deaths was at forty to forty-nine years, and of the white deaths it was sixty to sixty-nine years. In the whites 40.4 per

[11] Stone and Vanzant, *loc. cit.*; see n. 8; Schwab and Schulze, *loc. cit.*; see n. 9; Davison and Thoroughman, *South. M. J.*, **21**:465, 1928; Wood, Jones, and Kimbrough, *loc. cit.*; see n. 10; Laws, *loc. cit.*; see n. 7; Hedley, *Pub. Health Rept.*, **50**:1127, 1935; Geiger *et al.*, *Am. Heart J.*, **12**:137, 1936.

cent of these deaths occurred at age seventy years or more, but only 16.7 per cent occurred at this time among the colored. Death occurred before forty years in 0.6 per cent of the whites ´ and 12.9 per cent of the colored.

HYPERTENSION

The proneness of Negroes to hypertension and its resultant or concomitant cardiac and renal changes has been noted and studied by several investigators. Adams[12] made several blood pressure readings on each of 5,074 male employees and one reading on each of 9,000 applicants for employment. About one-third of these were colored and the remainder white. The average white systolic pressure was 121 mm. and the diastolic 81 mm.; for the colored—systolic 128 mm., diastolic 85 mm. In each age group·the Negro systolic pressures were 4–13 mm. higher than those of the whites, and the diastolic pressures were 2–6 mm. higher. Beyond forty years of age the pressures of the colored men advanced more rapidly than the whites. The maximum differences of the average systolic pressures in the age groups occurred at ages forty-six to fifty years and at fifty-six to sixty years, where the colored systolic pressures were, respectively, 11 mm. and 13 mm. higher. In other age groups they were 4–9 mm. higher. The maximum difference in diastolic pressure was in the forty-one-to-forty-five-year and fifty-six-to-sixty-year groups, which in both instances amounted to 6 mm. over the white. The average of the maximum systolic pressures of all five-year age groups from eighteen to sixty-five years was 205 mm. for the whites and 222 mm. for the colored. The average of the minimum systolic pressures was 79 mm. for both races. Damage to the aortic valve in hypertension, as evidenced by an increased pulse pressure, occurs earlier and more frequently in Negroes. Jaffé[13] found, in his autopsy experience at the Cook County Hospital in Chicago, that hypertension and malignant nephrosclerosis were much more prevalent in Negroes and

[12] *Am. J. M. Sc.*, 184:342, 1932.

[13] *Centralbl. f. allg. Path. u. path. Anat.*, 55:209, 1922.

also that the average age at death was lower. Moritz and Oldt[14] made a detailed study of arteriolar sclerosis in an autopsy population of 1,177 individuals. Negroes made up 20 per cent of this population but furnished 30 per cent of the cases of chronic hypertension, indicating again that the disease has a higher incidence among them than among the whites. Analysis of the ages of the hypertensive cases showed that the mean age of the colored cases was eight years lower than that of the white cases. These patients with hypertension died either of uremia, cardiac failure, or cerebral hemorrhage, but about the same percentage of colored and white died of each of these causes. Histological studies of each type, distribution and severity of arteriolar changes in white and colored nonhypertensives and hypertensives showed no racial differences.

Schulze and Schwab[15] applied the various theories that have been applied to explain hypertension to account for the difference between white and colored people. They deny the role of inheritance, since hypertension is supposed to be absent in native Africans, and there is not enough intermixture with whites to account for the departure from this African characteristic. Moreover, they say, the Mendelian law of inheritance is not in accord with the excess of hypertension in Negroes over whites, which amounts to 2.5 times. The effect of the change from African to American climate is considered, but, although Europeans and Americans show a lowering of blood pressure in the tropics, there is no evidence that the contrary circumstances produce opposite results. Although syphilis is present in Negroes, its role in hypertension is questionable.[16] Likewise diet and obesity are unsuitable as explanations of hypertension. Schulze and Schwab resort to the theory of nervous factors to account for the high rate of hypertension in colored people. They believe that the true explanation is the stress and strain incident to adjustment to a new civilization. Jaffé[17] was of the

[14] Am. J. Path., 13:679, 1937.　　　　　[15] Op. cit., 11:66, 1936.

[16] For a discussion of the relation of syphilis to hypertension see Horine and Weiss, Am. Heart J., 6:121, 1936.

[17] Loc. cit.; see n. 13.

opinion that the large amount of hypertension in Chicago Negroes was due to their recent migration from the South.
Polak[18] says fibroids, which are very prevalent in colored women, have no effect on blood pressure, although a relation between these two conditions has been suggested.

Schwab[19] determined the results of the vasomotor test of Hines and Brown[20] on 172 whites and 153 Negroes between the ages of fifteen and thirty-five years. In this test the hand and wrist were put in cold water at $4°-5°$ C., and while in the bath blood pressure readings were taken 30, 90, and 150 seconds after immersion. He found that the elevation of blood pressure is more marked in Negroes and concluded that there is a quantitative racial difference in reaction to a standard vasomotor stimulus, indicating a more sensitive vasomotor mechanism in the Negro. This evidence is used in support of the neurogenic theory of hypertension.

SYPHILIS

This disease is the second largest cause of heart disease in Negroes and is reported to be three to six times more frequent in them than in white people, among whom syphilis is the third largest cause of heart disease. Syphilis of the cardiovascular system is discussed in more detail in the section on syphilis (pp. 178-80).

DISEASES OF THE CORONARY ARTERIES: ANGINA PECTORIS

Most investigators who have studied the question agree that coronary disease and the closely associated condition, angina pectoris, have a much lower incidence in Negroes than in white people. White[21] states that the "full-blooded Negro rarely or never" has angina pectoris. The United States *Mortality statistics* for 1932 show that 0.94 per 100,000 white people and 0.13 per 100,000 colored people died of this disease. Mills[22] studied

[18] *Am. J. Obst. & Gynec.*, 4:227, 1922.

[19] *Proc. Soc. Exper. Biol. & Med.*, 32:583, 1935.

[20] *Ann. Int. Med.*, 7:209, 1933.

[21] *Heart diseases* (2d ed.; New York: Macmillan Co., 1937).

[22] *Arch. Int. Med.*, 46:741, 1930.

the geographic distribution of angina pectoris in this country, using the mortality statistics of the Registration Area for 1927 as the source of his data. The death rate in the southern states, like in most warm countries, was low, being one half of what it was in the northern states. In the South the Negro death rate was much lower than the low rate of the whites in the same states. Among the cases of heart disease reported by Wood, Jones, and Kimbrough,[23] 5.3 per cent of the colored patients gave a history of paroxysmal heart pain as against 10.2 per cent of the whites. Davidson and Thoroughman[24] found no angina among their 257 Negro heart cases, nor did Schwab and Schulze[25] find any among 5,936 Negro dispensary patients, although they did find 11 cases among 4,252 white patients in the same clinics. Stone and Vanzant[26] reported that 3 per cent of 501 white persons with heart disease had angina pectoris, while only 1.5 per cent of 201 Negroes with heart disease had angina. Laws[27] gave 4.4 per cent and 1.1 per cent as the incidence among 365 white and 280 Negroes, respectively, with heart ailment.

In the experience of the Metropolitan Life Insurance Company,[28] the mortality rate for angina pectoris among white and colored policyholders is about the same, 7.0 and 7.3 per 100,000, respectively. While the white male death rate, 11.1 per 100,000, exceeds the Negro male rate, 6.7 per 100,000, that of Negro females, 6.0 per 100,000, exceeds that of white females, 4.9 per 100,000.'

Levy[29] states that there is no significant difference in the incidence of angina pectoris among the colored and white races, although in his own experience the more advanced degrees of sclerosis are less common in the Negro. In a detailed examination of 476 autopsies in which there were lesions of the coronary arteries or aorta, Bruenn, Turner, and Levy[30] found that ad-

[23] Loc. cit.; see n. 10.

[24] Loc. cit.; see n. 11.

[25] Op. cit., 7:710, 1931.

[26] Loc. cit.; see n. 8.

[27] Loc. cit.; see n. 7.

[28] Loc. cit.; see n. 4.

[29] Diseases of the coronary arteries and cardiac pain (New York: Macmillan Co., 1936).

[30] Am. Heart J., 11:34, 1936.

vanced arteriosclerosis of the coronary arteries had a relative racial occurrence of 34 whites to 1 Negro, although the relative representation of two races in the autopsy series was 12 whites to 1 Negro. The incidence of anginal pain in Negroes with arteriosclerotic coronary arteries was about the same as in whites with the same lesions. They express the belief that the impression established in the literature that anginal pain is infrequent in Negroes is due to the fact that advanced sclerosis of the coronary arteries is relatively rare among them. It is pointed out that the presence or absence of hypertension has no effect on the incidence of anginal pain. Hedley[31] showed that fatal disease of the coronaries was much less frequent among colored people in Washington, D.C., and in Philadelphia. Between 1933 and 1937, deaths from coronary occlusion increased 78 per cent among the whites in Philadelphia but showed no increase in Negroes.

Gager and Dunn[32] found that the incidence of coronary thrombosis for 600 white patients was 3.8 per cent, and for an equal number of Negro patients it was 0.8 per cent. Burch and Voorhies,[33] in a review of medical case histories at Charity Hospital, New Orleans, assembled from 1928 through 1937, revealed a relatively low incidence of coronary occlusion and angina pectoris in the Negro. After correcting their data for differences in admissions, the ratios of white to Negro in the incidence of these diseases were 7:2 for coronary occlusion and 4:1 for angina pectoris. Flaxman[34] showed that 7.2 per cent of 432 whites and 2.5 per cent of 93 Negroes with hypertension died as a result of coronary thrombosis. Peery and Langsam[35] found that coronary arteriosclerosis occurs about 4 times as frequently in whites as in Negroes. Coronary thrombosis was the cause of death in 4.4 per cent of the whites and 3.4 per cent of the Negroes with hypertension. In fatal arteriosclerosis without hypertension, coronary thrombosis occurred in 36.4 per cent of the whites and

[31] *Public Health Rept.*, 50:1127, 1935; 54:927, 1939.

[32] *Med. Ann. District of Columbia*, 2:112, 1933.

[33] *Am. J. Med. Sc.*, 198:685, 1939.   [34] *Ann. Int. Med.*, 10:748, 1936.

[35] *Arch. Int. Med.*, 64:971, 1939; *Am. Heart J.*, 17:424, 1940.

2.5 per cent of the Negroes. In the whole series of fatal cardio-vascular disease, hypertensive and nonhypertensive, coronary thrombosis occurred in 2.9 per cent of the Negroes and 13.2 per cent of the whites.

The incidence of marked coronary sclerosis found at autopsy by Johnston[36] was 24 per cent for white males, 9 per cent for Negro males, 10 per cent for white females, and 4 per cent for Negro females. Coronary occlusion with myocardial infarction, either recent or old, was found in 9 per cent of the white males, 4 per cent of the Negro males, 4 per cent of the white females, and 2 per cent of the Negro females. Ashman,[37] using electro-cardiography, found nine times as much myocardial infarction in white patients as in colored.

Weiss[38] does not agree with most of the opinions that coronary occlusion and angina pectoris are less in colored people. He claims that the data supporting these opinions are inaccurate. It is pointed out that hypertension, considered a potent factor in causing coronary sclerosis, is not always taken into account in comparison of the races. He presented data indicating that in his experience there was little difference in the incidence of coronary sclerosis in white and Negro hypertensives. These findings are supported somewhat by Peery and Langsam[39] but are contrary to those of Flaxman,[40] who found coronary thrombosis three times as often in white hypertensives as in Negro hypertensives. If high blood pressure is the essential factor in producing coronary disease, there should be a very high incidence among Negroes because of the large amount of essential hypertension among these people; yet those people who see many Negro patients are not impressed with an unusual frequency of coronary thrombosis but are impressed by the frequency of essential hypertension and those conditions that are manifestly associated with it.

·Weiss also says that the true incidence of angina pectoris cannot be obtained from hospitalized heart cases, because the his-

[36] *Am. Heart J.*, 12:162, 1936.　　[37] *Tri-State M. J.*, 13:2686, 1941.

[38] *Am. Heart J.*, 17:711, 1939; *Internat. Clin.*, 4:201 (3d. ser.), 1940.

[39] *Loc. cit.*; see n. 35.　　[40] *Loc. cit.*; see n. 36.

tory of cardiac pain is usually obscured by myocardial, cerebral, and renal failure. In making racial comparisons of the incidence of angina he insists that the Negroes and whites should be of the same economic, social, and intellectual class, since it has been shown that the disease is more prevalent in the well-to-do educated than it is in more humble people. He gives statistics concerning the occurrence of angina among white and colored patients of an outpatient clinic, presumably of the same indigent class. Angina has a low rate in both races but a lower rate in the Negroes. He infers that the lower rate in the latter is due to their inability to describe pain. Schwabe and Schulze[41] made it clear that their white and colored dispensary patients were of "practically the same social stratum and worked and lived under similar conditions," yet they did not find a single case of angina pectoris among 5,936 Negroes but did find 11 cases among 4,252 whites.

Several discussions have appeared in the literature on the cause of the difference in the occurrence of angina pectoris in Negroes and white people. These have been based on the assumption that the nervous system plays an important role in the disease, manifested either by spastic contractions of the coronary vessels or by an undue sensitivity to pain produced by pathological processes in the heart. It has been pointed out that individuals suffering with angina pectoris are of the highstrung, nervous type, sensitive to the stresses and strains of modern life. Roberts says: "It occurs usually in the sensitive, nervous type as the Jew or in the tense efficient American, rather than the dull, happy Negro or the calm accepting Chinaman."[42] In this respect, angina pectoris and pyloric spasm are similar, and both are unusual in colored people. He says further that the Negro is insensitive to pain and has not the stresses and strains on his nervous system that the whites have. Houston[43] speaks of the spasmogenic aptitude in whites as the basis of their angina pectoris as contrasted to the placidity of the Chinese, in

[41] *Op. cit.*, 7:710, 1931.

[42] *Am. Heart J.*, 7:21, 1931.   [43] *M. Clin. North America*, 12:1285, 1929.

whom angina pectoris is infrequent. Libman[44] separated people according to sensitivity to pain and devised a test for this purpose, which consists of pressing on the mastoid. While he does not apply this test to colored people, he suggests a lack of sensitivity to pain in these people as the explanation of a low incidence of angina pectoris.

These theories might be given more credence were it not for the contradictory facts of hypertension in Negroes. Exactly the same qualities of the nervous system have been offered to explain both hypertension and angina pectoris in whites. In Negroes emotional factors are used to explain their high rate of hypertension, a lack of them is used to explain their low rate of angina pectoris. A theory cannot "blow hot and cold."

RHEUMATIC HEART DISEASE

In most instances rheumatic heart disease is reported to be much less in colored people than in whites. The low rate of rheumatic fever in these people was noted years ago by Osler and by Weir Mitchell. In the various studies of heart disease reported above, the rheumatic form is given as occurring two to three times more frequently in white people. To these can be added the statement of Davis and Weiss[45] that rheumatic heart disease in New England occurs twice as frequently in the white as in colored people.

OTHER FORMS OF HEART DISEASE

Congenital heart disease, thyrotoxic heart disease, subacute bacterial endocarditis, miscellaneous and unclassified forms of heart disease, are of nearly the same rate in the two races, with a tendency to be slightly higher, if anything, in the white race.

THROMBOANGIITIS OBLITERANS

This disease, first thought to be confined to Jews, and later found often in white Gentiles, is being discovered with increasing frequency in Negroes. Although apparently only eight Negro cases have been reported in the literature,[46] there are undoubtedly many other cases that have not been reported. Several such unreported cases in Negroes in Chicago have come to the attention of the writer in recent years. The report of Yater differed from the others in that the cases were studied histologically and found to be pathologically typical of the disease. In three cases the veins as well as the arteries were affected. Smoking was not uniformly heavily indulged in by the patients.

As reported above, Moritz and Oldt[47] found that cerebral hemorrhage as the terminal event in hypertension occurred no more often in Negroes than in hypertensive whites. Because of ' the higher incidence of hypertension, cerebral hemorrhage kills more Negroes per 100,000 population annually than it does whites, the rates being for 1935, 92.7 for colored and 73.8 for whites.

Systematic studies of heart and blood vessel diseases of Negroes in other countries than the United States seem not to have been made. Heimann, Strachan, and Heyman[48] seem to believe that heart disease among the Kaffir, Hottentot, and Eurafrican city dwellers in Johannesburg is rather common, and, although syphilis is very prevalent among these natives, the commonest form of heart disease is the rheumatic type. Of 152 cases of heart disease, 64 were due to rheumatism, and 39 were due to syphilis. Bacterial endocarditis was found in 14 and pericarditis in 8. There were 25 patients with degenerative lesions. While hypertension was not particularly studied, several cases of extremely high blood pressure are mentioned. Donnison[49] confirms the fact that rheumatism is the chief cause of heart disease in Africa (Kenya) but denies the frequency of any form of heart disease. He examined over 14,000 natives and found only 10 cases of valvular disease, all of which were most probably rheumatic in origin. Donnison[50] also made many blood pressure

[46] Parson, *Texas State J. Med.*, 32:546, 1936 (1 case); Smith, *Texas State J. Med.*, 32:462, 1936 (1 case); Gemmil, *Atlantic M. J.*, 24:244, 1925–26 (1 case); Yater, *Am. Heart J.*, 13:511, 1937 (5 cases).

[47] *Loc. cit.*; see n. 14.   [49] *Brit. M. J.*, 1:478, 1929.

[48] *Brit. M. J.*, 1:344, 1929.   [50] *Lancet*, 1:6, 1929.

readings of Kenyan natives from fifteen to seventy or eighty
years of age and compared them with white blood pressures.
Up to the fourth decade the figures for the two races approximately agree, but after that the blood pressure in the native
tends to come down, while in the whites it continues its tendency to rise until the eighth decade. It was very uncommon to
meet with a systolic blood pressure in a native above 144 mm.
Hypertrophy of the heart, angina pectoris, and coronary thrombosis are extremely rare. Jex-Blake[51] also says that essential hypertension is rare in Kenya. In 1,100 autopsies none showed
calcified arteries or arteriosclerosis. Atheroma of the aorta was
common. According to Dubois,[52] hypertension is uncommon in
the Congo. A case of bradycardia is described by Stones,[53] who
says heart block is unusual in Africans. Blackaby[54] says bacterial endocarditis is unusual in African natives.

A frequency of aneurysms of the heart in Africans has been
reported by Hall[55] and McFie,[56] who think that malaria is the
basis of these lesions, and they suggest that it acts in one of two
ways: either the circulation in the heart muscle is blocked by
the presence of large numbers of parasites in the capillaries and
arterioles,[57] or it is blocked by a massive obstructive endarteritis
which they say is characteristic of the disease.[58]

Thonnard-Neumann[59] examined 500 West Indian Negro laborers and their wives in Panama. Included were 255 active
workers, 102 ambulatory patients, and 142 bed patients. The
average age was forty years. Considering above 140 mm. as abnormal blood pressure, he found that 33.5 per cent had hyper-

[51] East African M. J., 11:286, 1934.
[52] Ann. Soc. belge de méd. trop., 12:133, 1932.
[53] East African M. J., 12:89, 1935.
[54] East African M. J., 12:394, 1935.
[55] Edinburgh M. J., 13:322, 1903.
[56] Report of the Accra Laboratory (new ser.), (1916).
[57] Dudgeon and Clarke, Lancet, 2:153, 1917.
[58] McFie and Ingram, Ann. Trop. Med., 14:147, 1920.
[59] Arch. f. Schiffs- u. Tropen-Hyg., 34:183, 1930.

tension. Because 54.5 per cent of these had a positive serologic reaction for syphilis, and the configuration of the heart and aorta was typical of syphilitic aortitis and endocarditis, he was of the opinion that the hypertension was caused by lues. He recognized only 4 cases of true essential hypertension, the criteria for which he considered to be elevated blood pressure, normal blood vessels, negative urinary findings, and a negative reaction for syphilis. He also writes of the unusualness of angina pectoris and apoplexy and the frequency of arteriosclerosis and chronic kidney disease.

DISEASES OF THE KIDNEY

The literature on kidney diseases discriminates very little between those occurring in Negroes and in whites. The chief source of information is the various mortality statistics. These data are likely to be inaccurate, because in death returns attention is more likely to be concentrated on the primary cause and this reported as the cause of death rather than nephritis, which may be only the terminal or secondary condition. Most of the mortality statistics fail to distinguish between the various forms of nephritis. This, however, is to be expected, since the accurate differentiation between the anatomical and clinical varieties of kidney disease is beyond the facilities of most of the physicians whose death reports make up the bulk of the data represented in mortality statistics. The United States *Mortality statistics* lists nephritis under the headings, "acute nephritis," "chronic nephritis," and "nephritis unspecified." The Metropolitan Life Insurance Company[1] gives their data as "acute nephritis" and "chronic nephritis." From their discussions it appears that chronic nephritis refers only to the kidney of essential hypertension.

For 1930 the United States *Mortality statistics* gives the mortality rates per 100,000 population from nephritis in general for each race in thirteen southern states (Table 14).

The large variations between states for each race is probably due to differences in accuracy of registration. But it is clear that in each state the mortality of Negroes is much higher than that of whites. The average mortality per 100,000 population for all registration states in 1930 was, for acute nephritis, 2.44 for whites and 12.4 for Negroes; for chronic nephritis 75.6 for whites and 98.3 for Negroes; and for nephritis, unspecified, 7.0 for whites and 20.4 for Negroes.

The Metropolitan Life Insurance Company shows the average annual death rate among its policyholders (1911–35) for acute nephritis to be for white males 4.8, colored males 14.7,

[1] *Twenty years of health progress* (New York: Metropolitan Life Insurance Co., 1937).

white females 4.1, and colored females 14.5. For chronic nephritis the rates were white males 61.6, colored males 124.5,
white females 65.7, and colored females 122.5.

In Africa, according to Hennessey,[2] the commonest fatal nephritis was what he called proliferative hyalizing glomerulitis.
Since cardiovascular diseases are relatively uncommon, so is the
nephritis associated with them also uncommon.

TABLE 14

RELATIVE MORTALITY OF WHITE AND NEGRO
FROM NEPHRITIS, 1930

State	White	Negro
Alabama...............	80.3*	126.5
Arkansas.............	63.0	106.7
Florida...............	106.5	138.9
Georgia...............	100.7	145.5
Kentucky.............	77.8	219.0
Louisiana.............	110.6	89.2
Maryland.............	135.6	182.4
Mississippi............	88.6	137.3
North Carolina.........	90.4	133.7
Oklahoma.............	47.6	71.5
South Carolina.........	116.3	155.7
Tennessee:.............	63.9	128.7
Virginia...............	98.5	171.7

* All figures as per 100,000 population.

With many of the acute infectious diseases, even with those in
which the attack rate is lower in Negroes, the case fatality is
higher for the colored people. Part of this higher death rate is to
be accounted for by a greater susceptibility to penumonia,
which is often a complication and the terminal event. But it is
also probable that part of it can be explained by a greater
effect on the kidneys. The higher rates for essential hypertension and the extension of acute nephritis, with a high morbidity
rate, into chronic nephritis can explain the excess of chronic
nephritis mortality.

[2] *East African M. J.*, 15:329, 1938.

CHAPTER V

SURGICAL DISEASES

SURGEONS who have had considerable clinical experience with Negroes commend them as excellent surgical risks.[1] They are stoic in their reaction to pain and discomfiture, do not easily go into shock, take anesthesia well, resist infection, and show remarkable powers of recovery. Most colored people live strenuously, both in their work and in their pleasures, a reflection of which is in the many severe injuries they receive either as accidental industrial injuries or as the result of altercations. Some of these injuries are so extensive and serious as to merit an almost hopeless prognosis. Yet many times they recover with ease and with remarkably little disablement. The first person to undergo a successful cardiac suture was a Negro, which was as much a tribute to the hardihood of the patient as it was to the skill of the surgeon, who, incidentally, was himself a Negro—the late Dr. Daniel H. Williams.

Probably the most outstanding feature of Negroes as surgical patients is their resistance to infection. Resistance to bacterial invasion, as the account of their medical diseases shows, is not a general one. To some organisms, on the contrary, they are highly susceptible. But for those organisms that are concerned with surgical sepsis, particularly the suppurative cocci, they seem to have a high degree of immunity. This relative immunity is probably also a part of their resistance to scarlet fever, erysipelas, measles, and certain suppurative skin affections. It may, in addition, be related to the ability of Negroes to readily form granulation tissue, and this in turn be related to the tendency to

---

[1] Reichenbach, *J. Anthrop. Soc.*, 11:64, 1864; Plehn, *Deutsche med. Wchnschr.*, 22: 544, 1896; Fernandez, *South African M. J.*, 4:34, 1896–97; Matas, *Tr. Am. S. A.*, 14: 483, 610, 1896; Fletcher, *Tr. M. A. Alabama*, 49:22, 1898; Lofton, *New Orleans M. & S. J.*, 54:530, 1901–2; Greely, *M. Rec.*, 8:10, 1912.

form hyperplastic scar tissue, the so-called "fibroplastic diathe-sis" of Rosser.[2] When surgical infection does occur, it often can be adequately described by the name used by the older sur-geons, "laudable pus," indicating a low-grade infection with thick yellow pus and much granulation tissue. This resistance of colored people to surgical infection is included in the concep-tion of Holmes[3] of the "resistant ectoderm" of the Negro.

All too often the stamina of Negro surgical patients is offset by diseases that seriously increase the risk of surgery. Those diseases which are particularly active in this respect—syphilis, hypertension, heart disease, renal disease, and tuberculosis—are at the same time those that have a relative high incidence in the Negro.

[2] *Am. J. Surg.*, 37:265, 1923.　　　[3] *Am. J. Phys. Anthropol.*, 12:139, 1928.

PEPTIC ULCER

The racial and geographical distribution of peptic ulcer is mostly studied for its possible contribution to the solution of problems concerned with the etiology of the disease. This has been the chief interest in peptic ulcer as it occurs in Negroes. Since it appears to have been shown that the disease attacks these people differently than it does white people, it is believed that an explanation of the difference will yield important information on the causes of peptic ulcer. However, the facts obtained have been used to support first one theory and then another, without convincingly establishing any one of them.

Most writers believe that gastric and duodenal ulcers occur less frequently in colored people. The amount of difference between them and white people that has been claimed ranges from a very slight degree to an almost complete immunity. Robinson, on one hand, says "the Negro and lesser pigmented races are immune (to peptic ulcer); the white race alone is susceptible."[1] Steigman,[2] on the other hand, believes that the Negro, as such, is neither more nor less reactive to the causes of peptic ulcer than the white race.

Frank[3] and the discussants of his paper were among the earlier ones who wrote of the low rate of peptic ulcer in colored people. Frank described two cases of duodenal ulcer and one of gastric ulcer with the opinion that they were of unusual occurrence. Rodman[4] says he never saw a case in a Negro with symptoms definite enough to warrant a diagnosis of gastric ulcer. He quotes from a study made by Storck of the New Orleans Board of Health statistics between 1893 and 1903. Among 48,500 white deaths there were 60 deaths due to gastric ulcer, and among 30,012 colored deaths there were 13 deaths due to the disease. There were 58 gastric ulcers found among 6,800 white medical cases, while among 4,900 Negro medical cases only 2

[1] *Am. J. Digest. Dis.*, 2:353, 1935.

[2] *Am. J. Digest. Dis.*, 3:310, 1936–37.   [3] *Kentucky M. J.*, 20:74, 1922.

[4] *Surgery, its principles and practice*, eds., Keen and DaCosta, 4:1142 (Philadelphia: W. B. Saunders, 1921).

gastric ulcers were discovered. Adams,[5] also in New Orleans, listed the diseases encountered over a period of seven years among 5,047 industrial employees, one-third of whom were colored. There were only 6 instances of peptic ulcer among the colored, while there were 80 cases among the white.

Sturtevant and Shapiro[6] cite 7,700 autopsies performed at Bellevue Hospital, New York, between 1904 and 1922, among which were disclosed 120 gastric ulcers, 118 being in white patients and 2 in colored patients. There was no record of duodenal ulcers being found in the colored, although there were 44 in the whites. The proportion of the 7,700 autopsies which was colored is not given, but it is probable that it was greater than 1 in 60, which is the proportion of colored gastric ulcers to the total number.

Rivers[7] took careful histories of 200 Negroes in Texas and could find but 1 person who gave a history of symptoms indicating peptic ulcer. Steigman,[8] at Cook County Hospital, Chicago, shows that 12.7 per cent of the peptic ulcers occurred among the colored admissions, which amounted to 27.7 per cent of the total admissions. Boland[9] found at the Grady Hospital, Atlanta, Georgia, over a period of ten years, that 1 in every 254 white patients admitted had a peptic ulcer, while 1 in every 504 colored admissions had the condition, giving a white-colored ratio of 2:1. Boland showed, however, that perforation occurred equally often—in 31 per cent—in both races.

Quite different from any of these reports is that of Jaffé,[10] who, on the basis of autopsy evidence at the Cook County Hospital, claimed that he found no real difference in the occurrence of peptic ulcer in the colored and white races. In 5.23 per cent of 4,128 white autopsies and 3.5 per cent of 2,850 colored autopsies, he found either peptic ulcers or scars of peptic ulcers. The ulcer incidence increases with age, and when the statistics are corrected for this factor, Jaffé says the difference between

[5] *Am. J. M. Sc.*, 184:342, 1932.

[6] *Arch. Int. Med.*, 20:74, 1922.   [8] *Loc. cit.;* see n. 2.

[7] *Arch. Int. Med.*, 53:97, 1934.   [9] *Ann. Surg.*, 102:724, 1935.

[10] *Centralbl. f. allg. Path. u. path. Anat.*, 63:379, 1935.

the two races is even less. The relation of gastric ulcer to duo-denal ulcer in the whites was 1.3:1, while in the colored it was 1.2:1. Peptic ulcer was the chief lesion and cause of death in 38.4 per cent of the whites and 27.8 per cent of the colored with ulcer. According to these statistics there is less difference be-tween male and female in the occurrence of peptic ulcer in the Negro than in the white.

Clark's[11] autopsy experience in the Canal Zone is at variance with those in the United States. He found that 5.3 per cent of the West Indian Negro laborers had gastric ulcers, while 2.5 per cent of the South American mestizoes and 2.3 per cent of the North American whites in Panama had gastric ulcers.

In Africa the evidence for the low occurrence of peptic ulcer in the natives appears to be conclusive. Beyers[12] was able to collect only 4 cases among 18,000 hospital inmates of the Jo-hannesburg Non-European Hospital during the years 1921–26. Autopsies at Johannesburg[13] show a rate of 0.9 per cent among 4,773 European autopsies and a rate of 0.14 per cent among 9,472 Bantu autopsies. The rate for Eurafricans was between these extremes, being 0.48 per cent. In the European, peptic ulcer occurred seven times more frequently in the males than in the females, but in the Bantu males it was only two times as frequent as in the females.

A series of reports on peptic ulcer in East Africa shows that Roberts[14] in Uganda discovered in the records of the hospital at Mulago evidence of 30 patients in whom the diagnosis of peptic ulcer had been confirmed in the course of 7,019 major opera-tions. In a series of 947 post-mortems performed at the same hospital, 3 deaths were found to be due to peptic ulcer, giving an incidence of 0.317 per cent. From Tanganyika Connell[15] re-ports that in thirteen years he found 5 cases of peptic ulcer that were verified at operation, about 1,200 operations being per-

[11] *Proc. M. A. Isthmian Canal Zone* (1914).

[12] *J. M. A. South Africa*, 1:606, 1927.

[13] Eagle and Gillman, *South African J. M. Sc.*, 3:1, 1938.

[14] *East African M. J.*, 14:88, 1937.   [15] *East African M. J.*, 14:89, 1937.

formed annually. Bainbridge,[16] in Nairobi, refers to 18 peptic ulcers in natives, 10 of whom were operated upon and 2 who died while undergoing medical treatment. Enzer[17] records 1 case in a Swahili, while Vint[18] discovered only 1 healed gastric ulcer in 1,800 autopsies. Vassalo,[19] in Zanzibar, reports a relatively large number of duodenal ulcers among the Swahilis. There were 108 cases in 8,317 operations. Some of the operations, however, included Arabs, Indians, and Goans. Vassalo thinks the great prevalence of hookworm might be related to the high incidence of duodenal ulcer in the Swahilis.

Bergsma[20] calls attention to the high rate of peptic ulcer in the natives of Ethiopia. Within two years he had seen over 200 cases, some of which were operated on. Europeans in this country seldom had peptic ulcer. Bergsma believes that the large amount of ulcer in the natives is due to a favorite and widely used article of diet, namely, a thin cake of bread which is rolled into the form of a cornucopia and filled with a sauce containing 50 per cent cayenne pepper. This sauce was irritating to the degree that it caused blistering on the lips of Bergsma when he attempted to eat it.

Various interpretations have been suggested of the findings concerning peptic ulcer in the Negro, and different uses have been made of them in explaining the etiology of the disease. Boland[21] stresses dietary factors and claims that the diet of the southern Negro is a preventive for him of peptic ulcer. He points out that it includes fresh green vegetables, peas and beans of various sorts, and cereal. Bread made from corn meal, much fish, and little meat are other characteristics. Artificially fabricated foods are not used. Boland supports his theory with the observations of McCarrison,[22] who located in a remote part of the Himalayas several tribes of primitive East Indian people whose food consists of milk, eggs, fruit, vegetables, and very

[16] *East African M. J.*, 14:90, 1937.

[17] *East African M. J.*, 14:91, 1937.

[18] *East African M. J.*, 14:91, 1937.

[19] *East African M. J.*, 14:83, 1937.

[20] *Arch. Int. Med.*, 47:144, 1931.

[21] *Loc. cit.;* see n. 9.

[22] *J. A. M. A.*, 78:1, 1922.

little meat and sugar. These people are remarkably free of peptic ulcer but acquire it on moving to areas where the disease is indigenous.

Rivers,[23] on the other hand, believes that the Negro's diet is very deficient and inadequate but that, in spite of this, colored people have little peptic ulcer because they are habitually a slow-moving, easy-going, carefree people, while white people are beset with worry, fear, anxiety, and other emotional tensions. Robinson[24] says that the colored race is "skipped by the disease" because it is genetically insusceptible. Steigman[25] summarizes these views and points out the interesting fact that for his colored patients in the Cook County Hospital the average duration of symptoms of peptic ulcer was about five years, while the average time they had been in Chicago was about eleven years. He was of the opinion that during the six-year interval various psychoneurogenic stimuli, in addition to disturbed gastrointestinal physiological processes, were developed that precipitated the disease, these stimuli being the effect of a new environment. They were not peculiar to colored people but applied also to white people who go from areas principally agricultural, as is the South, to areas principally industrial, as is the North. Steigman expressed the opinion that the theory of racial selectivity as a unique feature of the peptic ulcer syndrome could not be substantiated.

In seeking an anatomical basis for the low incidence of peptic ulcer and of certain biochemical findings in the stomach of African natives, Gillman[26] made morphological studies of the cardioesophageal junction on material obtained from Bantus a few minutes after death from violent trauma. He found that the epithelium in the lower end of the esophagus is a half to four times as thick as that described for the European. The deep esophageal glands are constantly found in the lower end of the esophagus, where they may be very highly developed. The lower superficial or cardiac glands of the esophagus and the

[23] *Loc. cit.;* see n. 7.   [25] *Loc. cit.;* see n. 2.

[24] *Loc. cit.;* see n. 1.   [26] *South African J. M. Sc.,* 2:18, 1937.

cardiac glands of the stomach of the Bantu are not considered to be separate entities, while they are regarded as separate in the European. The zone of the cardiac glands in the stomach is much smaller in the Bantu than in the European. The glands are simple, branched tubules. The deep esophageal glands are definitely mucus-secreting glands, while the cardiac glands and superficial cells of the gastric glands do not secrete a true mucin. The constantly found and well-developed lymph nodules and lymphoid tissue at the extremities of the cardiac zone are other features of the Bantu. This highly developed adenoid tissue constitutes a large perijunctional ring extending around the lower part of the esophagus and upper end of the stomach. The interglandular connective tissue varies in degree of development but contains particularly oxyphil leukocytes, many of which contain very coarse eosinophilic granules. Mast cells are absent.

Fractional gastric analyses after test meals were made of northern Nigerians by Rose,[27] of southern Nigerians by Ellis,[28] and of South African Bantus by Barnes and Gordon.[29] The results show that the acid response is, on the average, lower than that by Europeans. There were more hypochlorhydric and less hyperchlorhydric curves among the Bantus than among the Nigerians. Lower hydrochloric acid secretion might indicate that there is a higher incidence of pernicious anemia (*q.v.*), but this does not seem to be borne out by the evidence available.

[27] *West African M. J.*, 8:10, 1935.

[28] *West African M. J.*, 8:16, 1935.   [29] *South African J. M. Sc.*, 2:75, 1937.

CHOLELITHIASIS

The statistics regarding the frequency of gall-stones in the Negro vary exceedingly. This, according to Jaffé,[1] is to be expected, because of the lack of uniformity of the material on which the figures are based. Some of the data are based on clinical diagnoses and some on autopsy findings, and in both cases there may be wide variations in sex and age factors. It is obvious that the occurrence of gall-stones in a group as determined by clinical findings will be considerably less than that determined by necropsy, since in the former instance the discovery of the calculi depends on the production of symptoms or on an accidental finding during a laparotomy, while with autopsies the presence or absence of gall-stones is definite in each member of the autopsy population. Since the occurrence of cholelithiasis is unusual below the age of twenty years and is usually at its maximum at about the seventh decade, and since it is two to three times more frequent in females than males, it is evident that the age and sex composition of either clinical or autopsy groups will markedly affect the amount of gall-stones found.

Rodman,[2] without giving any other statistics, says that of 106 cases of gall-stones operated on in Louisville, only 1 was in a Negro. No autopsy performed on a Negro in the Louisville City Hospital showed gall-stones. From these facts he concluded that gall-stones are unusual in colored people and offered the opinion that their more active life, better teeth, stronger digestion, abstinence from highly seasoned foods, and less malaria were responsible. Keen[3] and Graham, Cole, Copher, and Moore[4] say that gall-stones in colored people are very infrequent, without giving statistics to support their opinion.

Mosher[5] found in the autopsy records of Johns Hopkins Hos-

[1] *J. Lab. & Clin. Med.*, 18:1220, 1933.

[2] Gould and Warren, *International textbook of surgery*, 2:739 (1905).

[3] *Surgery, its principles and practice*, eds. Keen and DaCosta, 4:1142 (Philadelphia: W. B. Saunders, 1921).

[4] *Diseases of the gallbladder and bile ducts* (Philadelphia: Lea & Febiger, 1928).

[5] *Bull. Johns Hopkins Hosp.*, 12:253, 1901.

pital that among 1,018 whites there were gall-stones in 7.85 per cent, and among 634 Negroes there were gall-stones in 5.51 per cent. The largest percentage (14.86) in the white group occurred in the age group sixty-one years and over, this group making up 14.2 per cent of all whites. The largest percentage (15.05) in the colored group occurred in the age group fifty-one to sixty years, which made up 14.5 per cent of all Negroes.

Clark[6] cites 1,088 autopsies of West Indian Negroes (Jamaicans) employed as laborers in the Canal Zone, in which 24, or 2.21 per cent, showed gall-stones. He was of the opinion that the West Indian in the Canal Zone showed more cholelithiasis than the same race in temperate zones and that this was probably due to a high rate of intestinal infection and of malaria in the former.

Ludlow[7] analyzed the autopsy records of Lakeside Hospital, Cleveland, for data relative to the racial incidence of gall-stones. Among 1,488 white autopsies there were calculi in the gall-bladder of 6.97 per cent, while among 1,734 colored autopsies there were gall-stones in 4.32 per cent. He refers to Scheult, who found 11 clinical cases of cholelithiasis among 64,126 West Indian Negroes in Trinidad, a rate of 0.017 per cent. In 7,557 autopsies of the same people there were 5 with gall-stones, a rate of 0.07 per cent.

No gall-bladder calculi were disclosed by Mitchell[8] in 85 coroner's autopsies of male Negroes in Chicago, while only 2 were found in 37 autopsied female Negroes. In 1,225 white male autopsies, 28 instances of gall-stones were found, and in 248 white female autopsies, 20 instances were found.

In 2,621 autopsies of people over twenty years of age performed by Jaffé[9] in Cook County Hospital over the period January 1, 1929, to June 30, 1932, gall-stones were found in 9.03 per cent. Among the white males there were 6.76 per cent gall-stones, in colored males 1.04 per cent, in white females 17.57 per cent, and in colored females 10.23 per cent. White

[6] *Ann. Surg.*, 59:107, 1914.

[7] *Surg., Gynec. & Obst.*, 50:51, 1930.

[8] *Ann. Surg.*, 68:289, 1918.

[9] *Loc. cit.*; see n. 1.

males, therefore, had gall-stones 6 times more often than colored
males, and white females have calculi 1.7 times as frequently as
colored females. The ratio of males to females in the white
group with gall-stones was 1:2.6, and the ratio in the colored
group was 1:9.8. It was pointed out that the mixed cholesterol-
bile, pigment-calcium stone was by far the predominating type
in both races, but it made up a larger proportion in the white
group than in the colored. On the other hand, the bile-pigment
stone made up a larger proportion in the colored group than in
the white group. There was no racial difference in the number
of stones found. Deaths due indirectly or directly to gall-stones
were more frequent in the whites than in the Negroes. The
mortality rate was 18.2 per cent of the whites with biliary calculi and 6.2 per cent of the colored with calculi. Jaffé is of the
opinion that differences among charity hospital patients in
diets, occupation, mode of living, or in disposition to infections
of the gall-bladder were insufficient to account for the greater
disposition of white people to biliary calculi. He suggests that
differences in nervous and endocrine influences upon the tonus
and emptying of the gall-bladder may be important and should
be the subject of comparative studies.

There is little or no information about gall-stones among
African natives. Garnier and Prieur[10] assumed there were no
differences from other people. De Lange[11] refers to the rarity of
gall-stones and speaks of this fact being noticed by the early
English physicians.

[10] *Pathologie du foie et des voies biliaires: nouveau traité de médicine* (Paris: Masson,
1928).

[11] *Presse méd.*, 42:352, 1916.

UROLITHIASIS

The relative immunity of Negroes to urinary calculi has been vaguely known for a long while, but the subject has only relatively recently received any amount of actual study upon which conclusions may be based. This recent interest has come about because of the bearing that the geographical and racial distribution of urolithiasis has on theories concerning the causes of urinary calculi.

Hoffman[1] pointed out that the mortality in the United States from urinary calculosis per 100,000 was 9 for white males, 7 for colored males, 4.1 for white females, and 2.7 for colored females. Joly[2] says that urinary stone is almost unknown in Africa outside of Egypt and that in the United States the Negro is less liable to stone than the whites. Hinman[3] writes that the "most notable stone districts (India, Mesopotamia, South China) lack proper sanitation and suitable food, but the African Negro, similarly deficient, is almost immune to stone." Holmes and Coplan[4] describe the very interesting situation in Florida, where there is an unusually high incidence of urolithiasis among the white natives but an almost complete absence among the Negroes of that state. In one hospital in Miami, 29.4 per cent of 489 white urological cases, over a period of three years, showed urinary calculi. But during a period of five years only 1 Negro, a mulatto, was admitted to the hospital with urolithiasis. The amount of Negro admissions for other conditions is not given. Inquiry by them of 5 other physicians in the state with practice among Negroes disclosed 3 other cases.

Among 5,900 autopsies in West Virginia, Reason[5] found 64 white cases of urinary calculi and 14 colored cases. The percentage of the autopsies which was colored is not known, yet the authors state definitely from these figures that urolithiasis is uncommon in the colored race.

[1] *M. Rec.*, 101:532, 1922.

[2] *Stone and calculous diseases of the urinary organs* (St. Louis: C. V. Mosby, 1929).

[3] *Principles and practice of urology* (Philadelphia: Saunders, 1935).

[4] *J. Urol.*, 23:477, 1930.   [5] *J. Urol.*, 34:148, 1935.

Cary[6] obtained the statistics from several hospitals in and near Richmond, Virginia. Among 126,543 white patients and 48,032 colored patients were found 990 white and 111 colored cases of urolithiasis. For all cases the ratio of colored to white was 1:3.39. For ureteral and renal stones alone, the ratio was 1:3.56. For the individual institutions the ratios varied from 1:2.10 to 1:3.61 for all urinary stones and from 1:2.14 to 1:3.81 for ureteral and renal stones alone. If the ratio of cases of stones in the city of Richmond is calculated on the basis of the populations of the city, the Negro-white ratio would be 1:5.06. In the instances where the comparison could be made, it would seem that the economic level of the two races has little effect on the ratio of urinary stones.

Vermooten[7] reports that an analysis made for him of the records of 1,000,000 admissions of natives to the various hospitals in South Africa showed that in only 1 case was the diagnosis made of renal calculus. He also examined the records of the Johannesburg General Hospital covering a period of fourteen years. During this time 126,000 white and 91,000 colored patients were admitted to the wards. Of the white patients, 273 were proved to have had renal or ureteral calculi, while only 1 native African possibly may have had a renal or ureteral calculus.

Recent work[8] indicates that diet is the important factor in the causation of urinary calculi. Foods with an acid ash and adequate vitamin A content protect against calculi, while those with an alkaline ash and deficient vitamin A predispose to calculi. Holmes and Coplan[9] suggest that the large consumption of citrus fruits with their high alkaline ash is responsible for the high incidence of calculosis in southern Florida (and southern California) among the whites. The climate is not conducive to the consumption of foods that have an acid ash, these foods being also the ones that contain vitamin A. They indicate that,

[6] *J. Urol.*, 37:651, 1937.

[7] *J. A. M. A.*, 109:857, 1937.

[8] Higgins, *New England J. Med.*, 213:1007, 1935.

[9] *Loc. cit.;* see n. 4.

while the low incidence of urinary calculi in the Negro remains unexplained, it is true he is less likely to go to extremes in the use of alkaline ash foods and is more likely to adhere to a meat and bread diet. In Africa, Vermooten refers to the work of Fox,[10] who finds that the native diet in South Africa has an extremely low calcium diet, an acid ash, and a high vitamin A content, a diet that ideally complies with Higgins' experimental work.

[10] *South African M. J.*, 10:25, 1936.

HYPERTROPHY OF THE PROSTATE

The opinion has been prevalent that the Negro enjoys a relative immunity to hypertrophy of the prostate gland. Rodman[1] accepted this view and was supported by a similar belief, ascertained by inquiry, on the part of several outstanding southern surgeons. Clark[2] likewise was under the same impression. McIntosh[3] described as a medical curiosity a case of enlarged prostate in a Negro. Matas,[4] on the other hand, found in his experience that hypertrophy of the prostate was more frequent in the Negro and that operative removal was more fatal. Day[5] cited 5 cases in Negroes and 30 cases in whites observed over the five-year period 1916–20, but does not state the proportion of patients of the two races from whom the cases came. He came to the opposite conclusion of Matas, namely, that enlarged prostates were less frequent and less often fatally operated on in Negroes.

Randall[6] in his book refutes the statement that the Negro is to a degree racially immune to enlarged prostate. He points out that in 314 autopsies of Negroes there were found 41 instances of the condition, representing 13 per cent. In the white race 833 autopsies produced 179 cases, a rate of 20.2 per cent. The average age at death in the whites was 54.6 years, while in the Negro it was 42.3 years. Only 34 per cent of the colored died past fifty years, while 62.8 per cent of the whites lived beyond this recognized threshold of the onset of prostate trouble.

Smith and Jaffé[7] examined the prostate in 1,093 autopsied males above thirty years of age. They established the measurements of a normal gland and determined hypertrophy by a 10 per cent increase in size, by a nodular instead of a uniform

---

[1] *Surgery, its principles and practice*, eds., Keen and DeCosta, 4:1150 (Philadelphia: W. B. Saunders, 1921).

[2] *Maryland M. J.*, 38:222, 1897–98.

[3] *M. Rec.*, 54:350, 1898.

[4] *Tr. Am. S. A.*, 14:483, 1896.   [5] *J. Urol.*, 5:19, 1921.

[6] *Surgical pathology of prostate obstruction* (Baltimore: Williams & Wilkins, 1931).

[7] *Urol. & Cutan. Rev.*, 36:661, 1932.

structure, and by trabeculation of the bladder mucosa. In 757 white bodies there were 111, or 14.6 per cent, instances of prostatic hypertrophy, and in 336 colored bodies there were 42, or 12.5 per cent, instances of the condition. They found, however, that in the sixty-one-to-seventy-year age group the percentage of Negroes with hypertrophied prostate was twice that of the whites.

Hirsch[8] says prostate size, prostate nodulation, and bladder trabeculation discovered at autopsy are not enough to establish the presence of enlarged prostate. He claims that there must be clinical evidence of urinary obstruction. There are many instances, he states, of apparent prostatic enlargement in the Negro as judged by the anatomical findings but in which there are no clinical symptoms referable to the findings. He still insists that hypertrophy is not nearly as frequent in Negroes as in whites.

Kahle and Beacham[9] report 223 operations for prostatic obstruction in Charity Hospital, New Orleans, during two and one-half years. Of these, 120 were in whites and 113 in Negroes. Seventeen of the colored patients and 3 of the white were under fifty years of age.

Derbes, Leche, and Hooker[10] find that 0.78 per cent of the white patients admitted to the State of Louisiana Charity Hospital over the ten-year period 1927–36 were treated for enlarged prostates, while 1.024 per cent of the colored admitted during the same period were treated for the same condition. The colored patients entering the hospital with prostatic hypertrophy were, on an average, five years younger than the whites.

Burns[11] gathered reports of 2,281 cases of prostatic obstruction from medical centers in five southern states. Of this number 1,136, or 49.8 per cent, were colored and 1,145, or 50.2 per cent, were white. From these figures he infers the disease occurs with equal frequency in the two races.

[8] *Urol. & Cutan. Rev.*, 36:821, 1932.   [10] *J. Urol.*, 38:383, 1937.

[9] *Urol. & Cutan. Rev.*, 37:99, 1933.   [11] *J. Urol.*, 44:177, 1940.

D'Aunoy, Schenken, and Burns[12] studied microscopically prostate glands, removed at operation, for evidences of hypertrophy. No clinical evidence is given. The white patients from whom hypertrophied glands were removed represent, over the period from January 1, 1933, to June 30, 1937, 0.25 per cent of 58,093 white general admissions. The colored patients operated on for prostatic hypertrophy represent, over the same period, 0.48 per cent of 37,717 colored admissions. These percentages are given as the relative occurrence of enlarged prostate in the colored and white patients. They represent the relative number of operations and not necessarily the comparative incidence of the disease. The figures given are the averages for the whole period, but, when the annual figures are plotted, it is seen that beginning with the middle of 1935 the colored operation rate far exceeded the white, when previously the reverse was true. Hypertrophied prostate occurred at an earlier age in the colored. The mean colored age was 62.9 years and the mean white age was 66.5 years. The greatest incidence in both races was in the seventh decade, when the white rate was higher. The white rate was also higher in the eighth decade, but in the fifth and sixth decades the colored rates were higher.

Walker[13] made inquiries as to the occurrence of hypertrophied prostate in the natives of Africa. The opinion was unanimous that the condition was rare. It is believed that the explanation is that the natives usually do not live longer than fifty years.

[12] *South. M. J.*, 32:47, 1939.   [13] *Brit. M. J.*, 1:297, 1922.

GOITER

SIMPLE COLLOID GOITER

The various surveys made in all parts of the world to determine the geographic distribution of endemic goiter have included most of the areas where Negroes live. The incidence of simple colloid goiter among these people, as among other races, is controlled by the local content of iodine in the soil, water, and food. There does not seem to be any racial immunities or predispositions as such, although racial habits concerning the use of foods containing iodine may determine whether or not the intake of iodine is insufficient to prevent hyperplasia of the thyroid. Hygienic conditions as determined by the social and economic levels may likewise be of importance in explaining variations within a goitrous or nongoitrous district of the amounts of goiter in colored people. The relative amount of goiter in white and colored people varies usually within small limits from district to district. In some places the percentage of people affected is higher in the whites, and in others the reverse is true.

In the United States the amount of goiter in Negroes varies with that in white people within the same area, being high in the endemic districts and low in the nonendemic ones. Goldberger and Aldinger[1] found that 20.3 per cent of 9,978 white school girls and 13.6 per cent of 1,106 colored school girls in New York City had enlarged thyroids. Likewise Cohen[2] found in Manhattan that 15.9 per cent of 5,119 white girls and 13.5 per cent of 1,106 colored girls had goiters. Oleson[3] reported that in Denver, Colorado, 27.3 per cent of the white girls examined had goiters, as well as did 26.3 per cent of the colored girls. In Cincinnati he[4] found the condition among 26.4 per cent of the white boys, 28.2 per cent of the colored boys, 39.0 per cent of the white girls, and 45.1 per cent of the colored girls. On the other hand, Oleson found a much larger comparative incidence among the colored in Tennessee.[5] There were 9.5 per cent cases

[1] *Am. J. Dis. Child.*, 29:780, 1935.

[2] *Am. J. Dis. Child.*, 31:676, 1926. [4] *Ibid.*, 39:1777, 1924.

[3] *Pub. Health Rept.*, 40:1, 1925. [5] *Ibid.*, 44:865, 1929.

in white boys as against 15.4 per cent in colored boys, and 23.5 per cent in white girls as compared to 35.5 per cent in colored girls. This excess in Tennessee is likewise shown by Mustard and Waring,[6] who found in Murfreesboro 9.1 per cent in the white and 27.0 per cent in the colored school children. In Rutherfords County, 3.6 per cent of the white boys, 8.9 per cent of the colored boys, 11.7 per cent of the white girls, and 17.0 per cent of the colored girls were affected. On comparing urban and rural districts he found for the latter that 7.5 per cent of the whites and 7.7 per cent of the colored were affected. The above figures for Murfreesboro represent the urban findings. Still another study from Tennessee is presented by Youmans,[7] who found in patients of Nashville, ranging in age from fifteen to eighty-two years, an incidence of 19 per cent in 273 colored patients and 15 per cent in 227 white patients.

Jones,[8] with not very convincing figures, states that goiter is less in the Negroes than in the whites of Atlanta, Georgia, and the Southeast.

Oleson was of the opinion that unfavorable social and economic conditions among the colored were responsible for the higher rate in Tennessee but that local conditions may be responsible for local variations. Youmans states that the diet and hygienic situation of the colored in his group was superior to that of the whites in his group. It has been suggested that the high rate of goiter in some districts of otherwise nonendemic areas of the South might be related to the fact that cabbage makes up a large part of the diet of both white and colored. This plant contains organic cyanides which have been shown to produce thyroid hyperplasia in experimental animals.[9]

While the whole of Africa has by no means been surveyed for the presence of goiter in the natives, it has been discovered that there are areas where goiter is endemic. Among these are certain parts of the basin of the Congo.[10] Another is described by

[6] *J. A. M. A.*, 88:714, 1927.

[7] *South. M. J.*, 22:966, 1929.   [8] *J. A. M. A.*, 71:712, 1918.

[9] Webster, Marine, and Cipra, *J. Exper. Med.*, 57:121, 1933.

[10] Means, *The thyroid and its diseases* (Philadelphia: Lippincott, 1937).

Blacklock[11] at Mopra, along the Zambesi River in East Africa. Means states that the goiters in old endemic areas, like those of Africa, are likely to be very large. Very large fibrous and cystic goiters are described by Cloistre[12] among Africans in Madagascar.

TOXIC GOITER

Most of the recent literature on the subject seeks to prove that Negroes are not immune to the various forms of toxic goiter as was formerly believed and expressed by such authors as Bram,[13] Harris,[14] and Rodman.[15]

Herrmann[16] saw in Lakeside Hospital, Cleveland, Ohio, over a period of five years, forty colored patients with thyrotoxicosis. The total number of patients from which these were drawn is not given, nor is the comparative number of white patients. But he concludes that toxic goiter is not uncommon among colored people and that all varieties of the symptom complex may be observed in them. Harris[17] stated that iodine therapy in the Negro with toxic adenomas is harmful. Herrmann, however, finds no contraindication for iodine administration in any form of goiter. The reaction to iodine therapy and subtotal thyroidectomy is essentially the same in the Negro as in the white. It is pointed out that psychic shock, financial worries, and domestic difficulties play a part in precipitating the symptom complex and that removal of these irritating factors should be an essential part of the postoperative treatment.

Cohn[18] believes that a few years ago thyroid disease was rare among Negroes in the South, particularly in Louisiana, but that now comparatively large numbers of cases of goiter are seen that include almost every type: acute suppurative thyroiditis, adolescent goiter, nodular toxic and nodular nontoxic goiters, dif-

[11] *Tr. Roy. Soc. Trop. Med. & Hyg.*, 18:395, 1924–25.

[12] *Bull. Soc. path. exot.*, 23:342, 1930.

[13] *Goiter: non-surgical types and treatment* (New York: Macmillan, 1924).

[14] *Tri-State M. J.*, 1:80, 1929.

[15] *International textbook of surgery*, 2:739 (Philadelphia: W. B. Saunders, 1905).

[16] *Surg., Gynec. & Obst.*, 55:221, 1932.

[17] *Loc. cit.*; see n. 14. [18] *South. Surg.*, 4:417, 1935.

fuse nontoxic and diffuse toxic goiters, as well as malignant disease.

Porter and Walker[19] found records of thirty-seven cases of hyperthyroidism in Negroes in Richmond, Virginia, a nonendemic area. They say that the disease is proportionately as common as in the white race of the same district but that there is a difference in the reaction of the Negroes and the whites, which is more quantitative than qualitative. While the vascular system is more severely affected in the colored patients, the nervous system is less affected. Even when the basal metabolism is elevated and there is restlessness, tremor, and the usual evidences of stimulation in a degree of great severity, these disappear with remarkable promptness after subtotal thyroidectomy.

Maes, Boyce, and McFetridge, in a series of papers,[20] admit that thyrotoxicosis in New Orleans has about the same incidence in Negroes and whites but that it is a much more fatal disease in the former and that it arises on a different basis and runs a different course. They state that the disease in the white patient arises as "virgin pathology," in a gland which is not the seat of previous disease. But in the Negro it arises on the basis of a previous nontoxic diffuse goiter. They point out further that operation is more likely to be fatal in the colored patients than in the whites.

Leahman and Shearburn[21] confirmed the higher mortality of toxic thyroid in Negroes. Although the incidence of the disease was about the same as in whites, the operative mortality in Negroes was 9.43 per cent as compared to 0.84 per cent in whites. The preoperative and postoperative treatments were the same in both cases. They express the belief that thyrotoxicosis presents a separate problem in the Negro.

Walsh and Pool,[22] on the other hand, deny the seriousness of thyroidectomy in Negroes. They found that convalescence

[19] *Ann. Int. Med.*, 11:618, 1937–38.

[20] *Am. J. Surg.*, 24:232, 1934; *West. J. Surg.*, 42:456, 1934; *Ann. Surg.*, 105:700, 1937.

[21] *Ann. Surg.*, 109:712, 1939.

[22] *Am. J. M. Sc.*, 199:255, 1940.

after operation was easier and more rapid. Little medication, such as narcotics and sedatives, was necessary.

Walsh and Pool doubt the role of psychogenic factors in thyroid disease among colored people, since the Negro is not the high-strung, nervous, self-centered personality in which these factors are important. They insist that mimicry of the thyroid-disease complex is a means of escape from what they consider to be other and more pressing dangers and discomforts. Thyroid disease commends itself for mimicry because of its obviousness. If this be true it strengthens the argument for the psychogenic origin of thyroid disease rather than contradicts it, as claimed by Walsh and Pool.

NEOPLASMS

There is probably no type of neoplasm that occurs in one race to the exclusion of others, although there is a considerable variation among races as to the incidence of tumors as a whole and as to the distribution of the various types of tumors and of the organs affected. Some of these variations are due to differences in the nature of the causal stimuli to which races are exposed and which are incident to the habitat and habits of the races, while other variations are without an obvious explanation and are attributed to inherent racial characteristics. The Negro, both in America and in Africa, shows a definite type of tumor distribution that is more or less peculiar to him.

BENIGN TUMORS

Every type of benign tumor that is generally met with has been found in Negroes, and there are none found in this race that are not found in other races. With the exception of fibromyomata and keloids (if the latter can be called a true neoplasm), there seems to be little reference in the literature to an unusual prevalence or rarity in Negroes of any type of benign tumor. From this it probably can be gathered that there is little variation from the general population in the occurrence of nonmalignant neoplasms. Statements have been made in the literature that ovarian cysts are very unusual in colored women,[1] but within recent years no such claims have appeared, and inquiry among surgeons who have had extensive experience with colored patients discloses no lack of the occurrence of these tumors. Occasionally the finding of an unusual tumor in a colored patient is reported with the unwarranted inference that if the tumor is rare in white people it is much more rare to find it in a Negro.

In Africa many types of nonmalignant tumors have been reported, but more to show that the natives do have these tumors rather than to point out any peculiarities of the people in this respect or to give accurate statistics. Owing to the lack of medical supervision of the large majority of native Africans, it is not

[1] Stone, *Washington M. Ann.*, 17:253, 1913.

possible to make definite statements about the incidence of tumors among them. The difficulty has been pointed out of differentiating in natives between true neoplasms and inflammatory tumors associated with certain parasitic diseases. Indeed the chronic inflammation incident to such diseases is often the basis of neoplasms, both benign and malignant.

Kegel,[2] in presenting 35 cases of adamantinomata of the jaw, says that, while the proportion of Negro patients to whites in the surgical wards of Johns Hopkins Hospital is 1:6, the proportion of adamantinomas is 11 colored to 1 white, indicating an unusually high incidence among colored patients. He refers to Miller,[3] who says, "slowly growing unilateral jaw tumors are not infrequent in colored people and often attain a huge size," and to Westmoreland,[4] who operated on 43 "follicular odontomas," all save one in Negroes. Graves[5] described a case in a colored boy, and Ivy and Curtis[6] described 11 white cases and 5 colored.

Of a total of 45 cases of rhabdomyoma of the heart appearing in the literature, only 1 case has been reported in a Negro.[7] There is no way of determining from these facts whether the condition is more or less rare in colored people than white, although the author accepts them as indicating a greater rarity. Harper and Feder[8] report a rhabdomyoma of the sternocleidomastoid muscle in an elderly Negro man. The tumor lay dormant for fifty years, then became malignant. It was operated upon, but metastases appeared later in the lungs. This is believed to be the first report of a rhabdomyoma of the sternocleidomastoid muscle and the first instance of the tumor in the skeletal muscle of a Negro.

Cushing and Eisenhardt[9] emphasized the rarity in Negroes of

[2] *Arch. Surg.*, 25:498, 1932.

[3] *Philadelphia Acad. Surg.*, 16:35, 1914.   [6] *Ann. Surg.*, 105:125, 1937.

[4] *Surg., Gynec. & Obst.*, 12:188, 1911.   [7] Hueper, *Arch. Path.*, 19:372, 1935.

[5] *Am. J. M. Sc.*, 154:313, 1917.   [8] *Surgery*, 6:76, 1939.

[9] *Meningiomas: their classification, regional behavior, life history, and surgical end-results* (Springfield and Baltimore: Charles C. Thomas, 1936).

intracranial meningiomas. Bradford[10] says that if Cushing and Eisenhardt inferred this statement to also apply to intraspinal meningiomas it may not be accurate, since he found 3 of 4 intraspinal meningiomas in Negro women.

FIBROMYOMATA OF THE UTERUS

Fibroids of the uterus occur much more frequently in colored women than in white, but the exact relative incidence of the tumor among colored and white is unknown, although several estimates have been made. Matas,[11] in New Orleans, says that fibroids are five times more frequent in colored women than in white, a ratio which Anspach[12] also accepts. Kelly[13] cites the autopsy figures of Johns Hopkins Hospital, in which 33.7 per cent of colored women over twenty years of age showed fibroids, while 10 per cent of white women over twenty years of age showed the tumor. Miller[14] says the ratio is 9:1. Of 150 cases of fibroids admitted to Charity Hospital, New Orleans, during the first few months of 1921 and analyzed by him, over 91 per cent were in colored patients. For the ten-year period from 1913 through 1922, there were 2,352 colored cases in this hospital as against 263 white cases, or 90 per cent colored and 10 per cent white. The youngest colored patient among the 150 with tumors was twenty years of age and the oldest seventy-six; 51 per cent were between thirty and forty years of age; and the average age was just over thirty-six years. The youngest white patient was twenty-one and the oldest fifty-seven; 38.5 per cent were between thirty and forty years of age; and the average age was 38.5 years. Rosser[15] places the ratio of colored to white as 4:1 and Alsobrook[16] as 5:1. Cohen[17] found among 1,000 consecutive cases of fibroids, also at Charity Hospital, 103 in white women and 897 in colored. Still another study from Charity

[01] South. Surg., 3:721, 1940.   [11] Tr. Am. S. A., 14:483, 1896.

[21] Gynecology (Philadelphia and London: Lippincott, 1921).

[13] Myomata of the uterus (Philadelphia and London: Saunders, 1909).

[14] New Orleans M. & S. J., 76:461, 1923–24.

[15] Am. J. Surg., 37:265, 1923.

[16] New Orleans M. & S. J., 84:317, 1931–32.   [17] South. M. J., 23:875, 1930.

Hospital by Levy and Meyer[18] showed that there were operated in ten years (1926–35) 712 white patients with fibroids and 5,109 colored patients, or 12.2 per cent and 87.7 per cent, respectively. Of total whites admitted to the hospital 2.5 per cent showed fibroids, and of total colored admitted 16.5 per cent showed the tumor. They also refer to the experience of Greene at the Grady Hospital, Atlanta, Georgia, who found that 80 per cent of 500 laparotomies performed on colored women disclosed fibroids. Miller[19] says that one-third to one-half of colored women over fifty years of age have fibroids. Incidentally, exactly the same statement is made concerning women in Germany.[20] Peaslee[21] states that "very few women die above the age of forty at the Home for Colored Women in New York City who are free of fibroids."

Balloch[22] refers to Jackson, who says fibroids are prevalent among the Negroes of Barbados. There have been few trustworthy observations as to the occurrence of fibroids in native African women. Miller[23] states that, according to reports, the tumor is rare in Africa.

Fibroids are noted for the extreme size that they may attain, and a number of surgeons have pointed out how large these tumors may be in colored women without the patients suffering any discomfort or even being aware of the presence of the growth. However, among the nine largest solid noncystic fibroids collected from the literature by Owing,[24] ranging in weight from sixty-five pounds to ninety-five pounds, only one was found in a colored patient. This one weighed eighty-seven pounds and was described by Penrose.[25]

No adequate explanation has ever been given for the excessive occurrence of fibroids in colored women. It is usually at-

[18] *New Orleans M. & S. J.*, 89:418, 1937.   [19] *Loc. cit.*; see n. 14.

[20] Klob, *Pathologische Anatomie der weibliche Sexual-Organe* (1864).

[21] *Ovarian tumors* (New York: D. Appleton, 1872).

[22] *M. News*, 64:29, 1894.

[23] *Am. J. Obst. & Gynec.*, 16:662, 1928.

[24] *Arch. Surg.*, 27:897, 1933.   [25] *Am. J. Obst. & Gynec.*, 35:106, 1897.

tributed to an inherent racial characteristic. Balloch[26] says it is a part of a fibroid diathesis of Negroes which is expressed not only by a tendency to fibromyomata formation but also by a predisposition to keloids, elephantiasis, lymphogranulomatosis, and other conditions. A number of theories have been suggested to account for fibroids in general, but none of them, except that proposed by Witherspoon, also explains why the tumor occurs in colored people more often than in whites. Witherspoon points out that a relation of ovarian activity and fibroids has for a long while been suspected because of several facts: namely, the tumor occurs after puberty, it is frequently associated with metrorrhagia and sterility, it may grow rapidly during pregnancy, and it regresses in growth during the puerperium and menopause. He[27] brings fibroid formation and ovarian function in closer relation by his contention that the fundamental cause of the tumor is an excessive stimulation by the ovarian follicular hormone of the endometrium and myometrium. Hyperestrinism, according to him, causes not only hyperplasia of the endometrium but also a cellular metaplasia and proliferation of the uterine muscle cells, bringing about a subsequent development of uterine fibroids. In general, he contends that multiple follicular cysts of the ovary may be the source of an excessive amount of the estrogenic principle whose action results in the formation of fibromyomata. Witherspoon and Butler[28] have attempted to apply this hypothesis in explanation of the greater frequency of fibroids in colored women. They believe that the ovarian and myometrial findings in one hundred and twenty-five cases of fibroids in the Negro furnish evidence which confirms their ideas. Their contention is that uterine-fibroid development in the white and in the colored woman has the same source, namely, prolonged estrin stimulation resulting from ovarian follicle-cyst formation, but that Negroes have a greater frequency of fibroid occurrence because chronic pelvic infection, resulting in ovarian damage and dysfunction, is more common in them than

[26] *Loc. cit.*; see n. 18.

[27] *Surg., Gynec. & Obst.*, 61:743, 1935.   [28] *Surg., Gynec. & Obst.*, 58:57, 1934.

in white women. The pelvic infection found frequently in colored women is of the type that produces a thickened capsule and a disturbed blood supply of the ovaries, resulting in mechanical block to rupture of the follicle and subsequent cyst' formation. This damage is permanent, and once the hyperestrin secretion is initiated, it persists as long as ovarian tissue remains active.

This theory of Witherspoon is susceptible to a number of criticisms. In the first place, estrin stimulates other organs than the uterus, particularly the breasts and the Fallopian tubes, but there is no evidence of tumor-like proliferations or even hyperplasia in these organs in patients with fibroids. Again it is doubtful that the epithelium in follicle cysts remains active for any length of time after the failure of the Graafian follicle to erupt. It is probable that it soon undergoes pressure atrophy. Further, no effort has been made to find if patients with fibroids or with follicle cysts or even with chronic pelvic infections secrete more estrin than normal women, although quantitative methods are available for this purpose.

KELOID

The predisposition of Negroes to keloid formation is well known, although it is a condition, like albinism, that is more conspicuous on dark skins than on white, and it is possible that much of the excess in colored people is more apparent than real. It is, nevertheless, very common among these people. Casual observation in a colored community discloses numerous examples of the disfiguring growth. Illustrations of keloids in textbooks are almost invariably taken from Negro subjects, and in the American literature, when certain features of the tumor are reported, the cases in illustration are likely to be in colored people. Nevertheless, keloids are by no means uncommon among white people, as the numerous case reports and extensive discussions of cause, prevention, and treatment in the European literature will attest. The predisposition of the Negro seems to be not solely a characteristic of a race but a concomitant of pigmentation, since other dark but non-Negro races, such as

Hindus,[29] Malayans,[30] Australians,[31] and Tahitians,[32] also have keloids more commonly than white people. Exactly how much more common the condition is among Negroes is difficult to say, for milder forms and those which occur in unexposed sites are not often presented for examination and treatment. On the other hand, it is inaccurate to regard the patients of a physician or a clinic as an adequate sampling of the population in estimations of keloid frequency.

Fox[33] found 3 cases in 8,382 white patients and 76 in 11,486 Negroes, a ratio of Negroes to white persons of about 19:1. Hazen[34] saw 1 keloid in 2,000 white patients with cutaneous diseases and 14 in an equal number of Negro patients.

Patients with keloids seem to have some special predisposition to connective-tissue overgrowth. Normal people react to injuries of tissue with contracted atrophic scars, while those with the keloid tendency produce large hypertrophic scars that are out of all proportion to the degree of injury. Insignificant pinpricks may lead to extremely large tumors. When it was fashionable to pierce the ears for earrings, it was common to see large lobulated tumors on ears of people predisposed to keloids. Often keloids are held to be spontaneous in origin, in that no injury at the site involved is recalled. Surgical incisions of susceptible people are considered a problem, although an early prophylactic exposure of the incision to x-rays is thought to prevent the development of keloids.

On the basis of chemical and experimental observation, Justus[35] has the opinion that hyperthyroidism is a predisposing

[29] Spitzer, *Handb. der Haut- und Geschlechtskr.*, 14: Part II, 285, 1928; Powell, *Indian M. Gaz.*, 34:280, 1899.

[30] Wooley, *Am. J. Dermat. & Genito-Urin. Dis.*, 11:481, 1907; Steiner, *Arch. f. Schiffs- u. Tropen-Hyg.*, 15:13, 1911; Linton, *Ethnology of Polynesia and Micronesia* (Chicago: Field Museum of Natural History, 1926), p. 59.

[31] Bohrod, *Arch. Dermat. & Syph.*, 36:19, 1937.

[32] Briffault, *The mothers* (New York: Macmillan Co., 1927), Vol. 1.

[33] *J. Cutan. Dis.*, 26:67, 109, 1908.

[34] *J. Cutan. Dis.*, 32:705, 1914.   [35] *Arch. f. Dermat. u. Syph.*, 127:274, 1919.

factor in the genesis of keloids, and Krzysztalowicy[36] has impli-
cated chronic infections about the hair follicles and sebaceous
glands. It has been pointed out that the tendency to keloids
may be inherited and familial in nature.[37]

The susceptibility of Negroes to keloids may be seen in Africa
in an even more striking manner. The natives utilize this tendency to hypertrophic cicatrization for purposes of ornamenta-
tion.[38] While tattooing is a method of decoration of the body of
fair-skinned people, scarification is regarded as the analogous
procedure in dark-skinned primitive races because of the sharp
relief of the white scars. Herskovits and Herskovits[39] give an
excellent description of scarification and its results among an
African colony in South America. The site of these decorative
incisions often show marked keloids. White says: "In South
America we have the keloid which is almost impossible to escape
in the healing process."[40]

Bohrod[41] calls attention to the fact that scarification, like
tattooing, has an underlying sexual basis[42] and that among
Africans those persons with the best designs on their bodies—
those designs which stand out boldly from the surrounding
skin, as would those in which keloids developed—mated early
and left the largest number of progeny. Since there is in this
way a selective breeding of people susceptible to keloids, and
since the tendency to keloids is believed to be inherited, the result has been, according to Bohrod, the production of a race
that has a widespread inborn trait of susceptibility to the keloid
process.

Keloid is a condition that is manifested in the skin. The question arises whether there is an analogous process that takes

[36] *Monatschr. f. prakt. Dermat.*, 49:38, 1909.

[37] Wolf, *Wien. med. Wchnschr.*, 86:722, 1936.

[38] Matas, *Tr. Am. S.A.*, 14:483, 1896; Pautrier, Woringer, and Esquier, *Bull. Soc. franç. de dermat. et syph.*, 39:310, 1932.

[39] *Rebel destiny* (New York: McGraw-Hill, 1934).

[40] *Internat. J. Med. & Surg.*, 47:313, 1934.   [41] *Loc. cit.*; see n. 31.

[42] Grosse, *The beginning of art* (New York: D. Appleton, 1900), p. 78.

place in the internal organs of people who are susceptible to the disease. If the keloid dyscrasia indicates a tendency of the connective tissue to develop far in excess of its needs, it would be expected that keloid-like tumors would appear also in internal organs during the course of repair of tissue injuries. But, since no such condition is evident, it is probable that keloidosis is a process due to some peculiarity of the skin about which nothing is known other than that this peculiarity appears to be associated in some way with the presence of pigment. · Connective-tissue formation is not only a reparative process but is also a mechanism of defense, operating to wall off and localize injurious processes. There seems to be no better utilization of this function of connective tissue in colored people as a result of a fibrous diathesis. To the contrary, the lack of a connective-tissue reaction in tuberculosis is a noteworthy feature of the disease in colored people.

CANCER

In the United States.—A review of the literature on cancer in the Negro as compared to other peoples reveals that there are considerable racial differences in regard not only to the incidence of cancer in general but also in the age and sex incidence and in the organs most frequently affected. It likewise shows that the debate concerning the increase of cancer involves Negroes as deeply, if not more so, than other people.

There have been three important sources of statistics on the comparative distribution of cancer in white and colored people in America. First are the mortality statistics of the United States Bureau of the Census for the Registration Area. Since 1933 this has included all Negroes living in the United States. Several writers have dealt with this information, but Holmes[43] has been the most recent and probably the most thorough. Second is the mortality experience among the industrial policy-holders of the Metropolitan Life Insurance Company, which has been analyzed by Dublin, using first the experience from 1911 to 1916, dealing with 37,666 white and colored cancer

[43] *Am. J. Cancer,* 25:358, 1935.

deaths,[44] then with that from 1911 to 1922, dealing with 90,175 white and colored cancer deaths,[45] and finally that from 1911 to 1935, dealing with 262,046 colored and white cancer deaths.[46] The third source is the necropsy material at Johns Hopkins Hospital consisting of 6,670 records which were studied by Pearl and Bacon.[47] In addition to these statistics there are a number of clinical and pathological reports in the literature dealing with various features of cancer in colored people.

Statistics are in agreement that cancer in general affects colored people much less than it does the white races.[48] In ten southern states in 1921–23 it ranked sixth place as a cause of death, while it was in third place in 1931–33. For colored people in 1921–23 it ranked seventh, and in 1931–33 it was sixth. In 1934 cancer in the entire Registration Area had attained second place for white people but remained in sixth place for colored. For white people cancer as a cause of death was exceeded only by heart disease, while for colored people it was exceeded, in order, by heart disease, tuberculosis, pneumonia, kidney diseases, and cerebral hemorrhage. At all times the white rate exceeded the colored, but in later years the amount of the excess had decreased.

Holmes calculated the death rates from cancer in the several age groups over twenty for the colored and white populations for 1930. He pointed out that the total cancer rate for white males is higher in every age group than for the colored males, except in the age groups twenty-five to twenty-nine years, thirty to thirty-four years, and forty to forty-four years. On a whole, the differences in the mortality of white and colored males are not great in the earlier age groups, but these differences increase rather rapidly in the more advanced ages, becoming twice as

[44] *Mortality statistics of insured wage-earners* (New York: Metropolitan Life Insurance Co., 1919).

[45] *Cancer mortality among insured wage-earners and their families* (New York: Metropolitan Life Insurance Co., 1925).

[46] *Twenty-five years of health and progress* (New York: Metropolitan Life Insurance Co., 1937).

[47] *Arch. Path.*, 3:963, 1927.   [48] Gover, *J. Negro Educ.*, 6:276, 1937.

high for white males in ages over sixty-five. Colored females show higher rates than white females in the age groups up to the sixtieth year, after which the rates for the white females become the higher. While with whites the rates for females are much higher than those for males in the earlier age groups, and lower after age seventy, except in extreme old age, the mortality in the colored female is higher than for males in all age groups. One of the causes of these sex differences in total cancer is cancer of the female genitalia. Cancers of this type occur with relatively greater frequency in the earlier years in colored than in white females. Cancer of the female genitalia is the only form of cancer in which the mortality is higher in the colored population than in the white and is also the only one in which race differences decrease with age.

Holmes finds that cancer of the breast in both white and colored is more prevalent than any other form of cancer except cancer of the female genitalia. The noteworthy features of cancer of the breast are that its excess above other forms of cancer (other than of the genitalia) is greater in colored women than in white women and that there is less racial difference in cancer of the breast than in other forms. Holmes suggests three possible causes for the relative frequency in colored women, namely, the ease of diagnosis, the frequent early removal in white women, and the greater frequency of trauma in colored women.

Cancer of the peritoneum, intestines, and rectum is found by Holmes to be higher in colored females below ages forty-five than in white females, which is accounted for by him by the prevalence in colored women of rectal stricture and other rectal trouble.

In all other forms of cancer than that of the reproductive system, breast, peritoneum, intestines, and rectum, the male death rate is higher. In buccal cancer the excess of male mortality is very great in the whites but much less in the colored. Cancer of the skin shows enormous racial differences in older age groups, the rates being much higher in whites, especially in white males. Notwithstanding this fact, the skin-cancer rates in the younger age groups are actually higher in the colored than in the white, and in Negro females they continue to be higher until after fifty years of age. In cancer of the stomach and liver the rates for the colored exceed those for whites for both sexes up to age group fifty- to fifty-four years, after which there is an excess mortality of the whites which increases greatly with age.

Holmes is at a loss to explain the racial differences in the incidence of cancer. Diagnosis is not the sole factor, because skin cancer, which is relatively easier to detect than internal cancers, shows even greater racial differences in incidence than do cancers less likely to be detected. Then also racial differences are most marked as age increases, and there is no reason that any form of cancer is better diagnosed in youth than in old age. Evidence seems to contradict some other writers who believe the effect of civilization has been to increase cancer in Negroes. Those diseases of civilization, the so-called degenerative diseases of later life which impair vitality, affect the Negro at an earlier age than they do the whites, but cancer at old age, when these degenerative diseases are most active, is less prevalent in colored people than in whites. Holmes thinks that the most probable interpretation of racial differences in cancer incidence is that it is a result of inherent differences in race, the nature of which he does not venture to say.[49]

The analysis by Dublin and his associates of the cancer mortality statistics of the Metropolitan Life Insurance Company[50] discloses race-sex-age distribution of total cancer and of the standard organ-group cancers to be similar to those pointed out by Holmes. Over the twenty-five-year period, the death rate among white males was consistently higher than that for colored males. The excess white mortality at ages one to seventy-four years, however, decreased from 101 per cent in 1911-15 to 47 per cent in 1931-35, but even in the earlier period of 1911-15 the rate among white females was only 9 per cent in excess of that of colored females, and in recent years colored females showed by a small margin the higher mortality. The more recent data show that the death rate from cancers of the stomach

[49] See also Gover, *U.S. Pub. Health Bull.*, Nos. 248 and 252, 1940.

[50] *Twenty-five years of health and progress.*

and liver among white persons exceeded that among colored by 30 per cent for males and 16 per cent for females at ages one to seventy-four years. For cancer of the stomach alone the death rate for white males averaged about 20 per cent higher than that of colored males. Among females, on the other hand, the death rates were practically identical for colored and white females. Malignant tumors of the liver and gall-bladder showed a defi-nitely higher rate for the whites in each sex. The mortality for cancer of the peritoneum, intestines, and rectum grouped to-gether is higher for white persons than for the colored, amount-ing to 74 per cent among males and 28 per cent among females during 1931–35. Cancer of the intestines alone shows a higher death rate for white persons than for the colored in each sex and at every age-group period. For cancer of the rectum and anus, however, the rates for white females are considerably lower than for colored females at ages under sixty-five years. Over the en-tire twenty-five year period the mortality from cancer of the genital organs among colored females, aged one to seventy-four years, was 43 per cent higher than that among white females, and over the last five years of this period it amounted to 57 per cent. In the age range twenty to forty-four years the colored female death rates were about twice those for white females in the more recent years. During the five-year period 1931–35 there was virtually no difference in the mortality from breast cancer between white and colored females at ages one to seventy-four years. In ages under fifty-five years the colored mortality is slightly higher, and past fifty-five years slightly lower. The mortality from cancer of the buccal cavity among white males was twice that of colored males, but that of colored females slightly exceeded that of white females. The data on cancer of the skin indicate that colored persons are relatively immune to this form of cancer. The rate for white males was about three times that of colored males. This excess increases steadily with advancing age, until at age group sixty-five to seventy-four years there were nine deaths of white men for every one among colored men. Similarly, white females showed higher rates than colored females at the older ages, but the differences were much less than those for males. The rate for cancer of "other organs" or unspecified cancer was higher among the whites than among the colored, amounting to 44 per cent for males and 22 per cent for females. The deaths in the various subdivisions of this group were too small among the colored for accurate comparison, but cancer of the prostate did show a 20 per cent excess of colored males over white males.

Because of the higher degree of accuracy which is permitted, Pearl and Bacon[51] utilized the necropsy material of Johns Hopkins Hospital to show the comparative racial incidence of cancer. This material consisted of 6,670 autopsies, 3,911 of which were white and 2,759 colored. The authors point out that in this necropsied population malignant tumors of all sorts taken together occur two to three times more frequently among white persons than they do among colored persons. This racial difference is much more marked relatively for malignant tumors which are not carcinomatous (i.e., for sarcoma or other types). A careful critical examination of the most trustworthy available statistical data for general populations (Baltimore, New York City, Chicago, New York State, Maryland, Pennsylvania) leads to the similar conclusion that, in general, malignant new growths occur with considerably greater frequency in the white race than in the colored. All lines of evidence concur in support of this conclusion—necropsy records, age-corrected rates for general populations, and death rates for age and sex. The only apparently significant exception to this general conclusion is found in the fact that, during the childbearing ages, colored females exhibit a higher incidence of malignancy than do white females. The generally less frequent occurrence of neoplasms in the male Negro may indicate a lower susceptibility of truly genetic racial origin, reflecting a real biologic differentiation of colored from white in this respect.

It is pointed out that the colored persons in the necropsied population who die with malignant tumors tend to do so at an earlier age, on the average, than do whites. The only exception is in the case of the female sarcomatous group.

[51] *Loc. cit.;* see n. 47.

Clinical experience bears out the mortality statistics as to the relative immunty of colored people to cancer of the skin. Fox,[52] in an extensive experience with colored patients in clinics in Washington, Baltimore, and New York City, found epitheliomas to be 13.3 times more frequent in white than in colored people but also states that sarcoma, both cutaneous and surgical, is slightly more prevalent in colored patients. He claims that he had never seen an epithelioma of the face in a full-blooded Negro but had seen it on the prepuce and occasionally in the mouth. Of 374 consecutive cases of epithelioma at New York University, he saw only 1 case of squamous cell carcinoma of the skin in a colored person, and this was in a mulatto. At Harlem Hospital there had been only 1 instance of a basal cell carcinoma of the nose, also in a mulatto. He did see in Brazil 1 case of epithelioma of the face in a full-blooded Negro. A United States naval officer stationed in Haiti reported to him the finding of 3 cases of epithelioma of the skin in full-blooded natives of that country. Fox refers also to earlier observations on this question, especially to those of Tiffany,[53] who found no epitheliomas in the Negroes, constituting 36 per cent of a total of 4,930 patients. These observations as to the rarity of epithelioma in Negroes were corroborated in discussions by Johnston and Yandell.

Of 2,000 dermatological cases in colored people, Hazen[54] saw not a single case of basal cell or squamous cell carcinoma, although 8 cases of the latter were referred to his clinic from the surgical services. On the other hand, among 2,000 white dermatological cases were 30 instances of skin cancer. Hazen also points out the rarity in colored people of precancerous skin lesions, especially the seborrhoeic warts or patches.

Hopkins and Studdiford[55] described an unusual case of multiple epitheliomas of the face in a five-year-old Negro boy. Associated with these tumors was a generalized dermatosis characterized by hyperpigmentation and depigmentation. Although

[52] *J. Cutan. Dis.*, 26:109, 1908; *Arch. Dermat. & Syph.*, 29:408, 1934 (discussion).

[53] *Tr. Am. S. A.*, 5:260, 1887.

[54] *J. Cutan. Dis.*, 31:705, 1913.   [55] *Arch. Dermat. & Syph.*, 29:408, 1934.

no arsenic was known to have been taken therapeutically or accidentally, these epitheliomas were assumed to be the sequel of arsenical poisoning because of the histological but not chemical recognition of arsenic trisulphide crystals in sections. This assumption was criticized in the discussion of the paper. Further discussion also brought out additional views on the occurrence of epitheliomas in colored people. Finnerud in Chicago, Shelmire in Dallas, and Tauber in Cincinnati declared these tumors, according to their experience, to be either absent or rare in Negroes.

In New Orleans, Howles[56] also came to the conclusion that skin cancer is very definitely less common than in whites. Among 2,200 cases of this condition in Charity Hospital, 71 per cent were in white males, 20.4 per cent in white females, 2.4 per cent in colored males, and 1.6 per cent in colored females. In Negroes the cheeks and lips were most frequently involved. Howles stated that in a survey of 11,587 cancer deaths (source unstated), 3 per cent were due to cutaneous cancer in white males, 2 per cent in white females, 0.2 per cent in colored males, and 1.1 per cent in colored females.

Hyde[57] believes that much of the Negro's immunity to skin cancer is due to the protection against the cancer-producing actinic rays of light afforded by his pigmentation. He also suggests, without saying how, that the skin in some way protects the internal organs against cancer.

In 1899 Gilchrist[58] called attention to the rarity of melanomas in colored people. He reported one such case and says that previously only two others had been reported. Later literature indicates that they are probably not so rare as believed by Gilchrist but that they are far less numerous than in white people, although not so common as they appear to be in the natives of Africa. There can be found reported a total of thirty-seven cases,[59] including one by Gilchrist and two before him.

---

[56] *New Orleans M. & S. J.*, **89**:143, 1936.   [57] *Am. J. M. Sc.*, **81**:11, 1906.

[58] *J. Cutan. & Gen.-Urin. Dis.*, **17**:117, 1899.

[59] Hazen, *South. M. J.*, **13**:345, 1920 (1 case); Sutton and Mallia, *Arch. Dermat. & Syph.*, **8**:325, 1923 (1 case); Lee, *Proc. Path. Soc. Philadelphia*, **27**:83 (new ser.), 1925

The belief is expressed that melanomas in colored people might be more prevalent than the literature suggests. Ewing[60] mentions the occurrence of these tumors in the Negro and suggests the possibility that they and the pigmented nevi are often overlooked because of the difficulty in observing them, on account of the deep pigmentation of the surrounding skin. The clinical behavior of melanoma in colored people, at least in those of America, seems to be the same as in white people. It has the same histological and gross appearance and the same deadly outcome. Bauer[61] believes the histological diagnosis is more difficult in the Negro.

Most of the melanomas in Negroes arise in the soles of the feet or in the nail-beds, and trauma seems to play a prominent role. Matas,[62] who also called attention to the rarity of melanoma in colored people, believes that pigment production is a normal function of the Negro's skin and that it is under a well-developed physiological control, while in the white race pigment is limited to a few scattered areas, and its physiological control is poorly developed. This may be suggested by the fact that the very dark Negro shows an even distribution of pigment in the skin of the entire body, only the palms of the hands and the soles of the feet showing a lesser degree of pigmentation. There is also less pigment about the nails. The predilection of melanomas for the soles of the feet and the nails may be related to this lesser pigmentation. Sutton and Mallia[63] point out the fact that while melanomas occur in horses, they are more frequent in gray and light-colored animals than in dark ones; the analogy,

---

(1 case); Weidmann, *Arch. Dermat. & Syph.*, 16:667, 1927 (1 case); Bauer, *Arch. Path.*, 3:151, 1927 (1 case); Adair, Pack, and Nicholson, *Bull. Assoc. franç. p. l'étude du cancer*, 19:549, 1930 (1 case); Knighton, *South. M. J.*, 24:354, 1931 (1 case); Rosenthal, *Am. J. Cancer*, 15:2290, 1931 (1 case); Dickson and Jarman, *Ann. Surg.*, 95:470, 1932 (1 case); Herold, *New York State M. J.*, 36:1418, 1936 (1 case); Menage, *South. M. J.*, 23:875, 1930 (5 cases); Bishop, *Am. J. Cancer*, 16:523, 1932 (9 cases); Butterworth and Klauder, *J. A. M. A.*, 102:739, 1934 (6 cases); Quinland, *J. Nat. M. A.*, 28:49, 1936 (3 cases); Affleck, *Am. J. Cancer*, 27:120, 1936 (2 cases).

[60] *Neoplastic diseases* (Philadelphia: W. B. Saunders Co., 1928).

[61] *Ayer Clin. Lab. Bull.*, 10:5, 1926.

[62] *Loc. cit.*; see n. 38.   [63] *Loc. cit.*; see n. 59.

however, is not a good one, since the color of these horses is not due to a lack of melanin but to melanin in various states of oxidation. The 158 cases of carcinoma of the stomach disclosed at autopsy in the Los Angeles County Hospital by Harding and Hanking[64] had a racial distribution as shown in Table 15. Fitts[65] studied fifty cases of gastric cancer in the Negro, which represents the incidence of the disease among 40,000 general hospital admissions in Atlanta over a period of eight years. He also compared the findings to those in 50 cases in white people.

TABLE 15

RACIAL DISTRIBUTION OF GASTRIC CARCINOMA

Races	Number of Autopsies	Number of Malignant Tumors	Per Cent	Number of Carcinomas of Stomach	Per Cent
Caucasian.............	5,142	805	15.7	123	2.4
Mexican..............	2,295	117	5.1	20	0.9
Negro................	460	37	8.0	8	1.5
Yellow...............	103	11	10.7	3	2.9

Among the colored patients there were 39 males and 11 females, and in the whites there were 35 males and 15 females. Pain was present in 76 per cent of the colored patients and 44 per cent of the white. Vomiting occurred in 58 per cent of the colored and 16 per cent of the white. The tumor could be palpated in 34 per cent of the white patients and in 54 per cent of the colored, in whom the disease was usually more advanced at the time of examination. Achlorhydria seemed to be more frequent in the colored. Gastric syphilis often simulated gastric carcinoma and occurred often in colored subjects. Leather-bottle stomach was reported in a colored woman by Haines,[66] who says this condition is comparatively rare in white men, is rarer in white women, and extremely rare in colored women. Although gastric cancer is unusual in the first two decades of life, a case in a colored male aged twenty years is reported by King.[67]

[64] *Am. J. Cancer*, 16:561, 1932.

[65] *South. M. J.*, 24:110, 1931.

[66] *M. Rec.*, 142:183, 1933.

[67] *J. A. M. A.*, 101:520, 1933.

Hoffman,[68] Deaver and McFarland,[69] and Maes and McFetridge[70] state that carcinoma of the breast is quite common among American Negro women. Cohn[71] showed from statistics of the Charity Hospital, New Orleans, that the incidence in colored women was even higher than in white women—1.6 breast carcinomas per 1,000 Negro admissions as compared to 0.9 such tumors per 1,000 white admissions. There were more nulliparous Negro women with the cancer than there were white nullipari, and the age of the colored averaged 4.7 years younger than that of the white.

Quinland[72] found carcinoma of the breast to occur second in frequency in Negro women, carcinoma of the cervix uteri being first. Among males, the prostate, not the digestive tract, was the organ most often affected. Gover[73] also calls attention to the relatively high incidence of cancer of the genitalia in colored women.

Carcinoma of the thyroid is believed by Losli[74] to be rare in the American Negro, as it is also in the African Negro. He reports a single case in an American Negro but refers to five additional ones reported to him by personal communication.

Contrary to Rodman[75] and Barney,[76] who say they never saw carcinoma of the penis in the Negro and therefore imply its rarity, Thomas[77] and McCoy[78] each report a case in a colored patient. Of 5 patients treated by Shivers,[79] 4 were colored. Howze[80] reports 6 of 17 cases in Negroes. Leighton[81] cites 5 colored cases and states there is no racial exemption of penile cancer unless it be in Jews.

[68] *Some cancer facts and fallacies* (Newark, N.J.: Prudential Life Insurance Co., 1925).

[69] *The breast: its anomalies, its diseases and their treatment* (Philadelphia: P. Blakiston Sons & Co., 1917).

[70] *Am. J. Surg.*, 33:5, 1936.

[71] *Ann. Surg.*, 107:716, 1938.

[72] *Arch. Path.*, 30:393, 1940.

[73] *U.S. Pub. Health Bull.*, No. 252, 1940.

[74] *South. Med. & Surg.*, 101:592, 1939.

[75] *Ann. Surg.*, 35:655, 1902.

[76] *Ann. Surg.*, 46:890, 1907.

[77] *Ann. Surg.*, 63:755, 1916.

[78] *Urol. & Cutan. Rev.*, 20:481, 1916.

[79] *J. A. M. A.*, 89:446, 1927.

[80] *Virginia M. Monthly*, 51:550, 1924.

[81] *Am. J. Cancer*, 16:251, 1932.

Since the time Rokitansky[82] made the famous statement that there is an antagonism between tuberculosis and cancer, a voluminous literature has developed which is about equally divided in denying and affirming its truth. Probably some light on this question can be shed by a study of cancer statistics in colored people in relation to the fact that they are so prone to tuberculosis. Since tuberculosis is more prevalent in Negroes and cancer is less prevalent, it may be taken to mean that cancer is suppressed in colored people because of tuberculosis, but it is significant that the tuberculosis rate in white people is 0.8 times that of cancer, and the tuberculosis rate in colored people is 2.5 times the cancer rate. If tuberculosis suppresses cancer it does so less effectively in white people than it does in colored. There are places in Africa where the natives have not yet come in contact with white people, and therefore tuberculosis is practically absent. It would be interesting in this connection to compare the incidence of cancer among such people with those among whom tuberculosis is prevalent.

Petersen,[83] on mapping the distribution of cancer in the United States, finds that cancer of the mouth increases as the Negro goes north, although the mortality rate is high in Louisiana. In Kentucky and Maryland cancer of the breast is higher than elsewhere, and in Kentucky and Louisiana cancer of the skin is higher than in other states. Petersen suggests that these geographical variations in cancer mortality among Negroes are related in some way to meteorologic conditions (!), although factors such as the reliability of the statistics or facilities for diag-' nosis might be responsible.

In Africa.—Information concerning cancer among the natives of Africa is not obtained in the same manner or with the same degree of completeness as it is for the Negroes of the United States. The large majority of the natives have no medical supervision whatsoever, and that which is available is in most cases characterized by the lack of facilities, interest, or ability. The published data consist of reports of individual observers

[82] *Handbook of pathological anatomy* (Philadelphia: Blanchard & Lea, 1855).

[83] *Arch. Dermat. & Syph.*, 30:425, 1934.

concerning material that has come within the field of their observation from which nothing more than a superficial estimate
can be made of the conditions that exist at large.

The facts that are now available give a much different idea
from that formerly held. It was at one time almost universally
believed that cancer was quite rare among Africans. This opinion was formed as a result of the information of travelers or
medical people with limited contacts with the natives. But,
with a larger exploitation of the country and with the wider establishment of hospitals and laboratories, and with the use of
modern means for the diagnosis of cancer, this opinion has been
reversed, and it is now conceded by authorities that cancer is
common in Africa. The occurrence of many types of malignant
growths has been established, but there are some peculiarities
of cancer among the natives which, if not characteristic of
Africa, are at least different from cancer as found in the Negroes
of America. Some of the outstanding features of African cancer
are the prevalence of primary carcinoma of the liver, the prevalence of melanoma, the unusualness of carcinoma of the stomach, and the prevalance of skin cancer.

No pretense is made of covering all the literature on cancer in
the natives of Africa, but the following review of that which has
been available gives a fairly accurate picture of the present
status of the question. It must be remembered that the figures
cited below represent an uncertain number of people and in
most cases cannot be used as the basis for calculating the rates
of tumor occurrence. It is certain that they represent an underestimate rather than an overestimate.

Adler and Cummings[84] are convinced that the reports of the
rarity of cancer in African aborigines and its increase on contact with Europeans are untrue and that the increase is only apparent and due to the better facilities for diagnosis that such a
contact brings. Des Ligneris[85] found in northern Transvaal 81
malignant tumors, nearly all advanced. They consisted of 6
carcinomas, 58 sarcomas, and 17 melanomas. All but 1 of the
melanomas had origin in the leg or foot. The author remarks

[84] *Ann. Trop. Med.*, **17**:535, 1923.   [85] *J. M. A. South Africa*, **1**:102, 1927.

about the lower degree of virulence of these melanomas, which is like those in gray horses, and not of the malignancy of those in Europeans. The sarcomas arose in various sites, the majority, however, involving the extremities. With one exception the carcinomas were skin epitheliomas.

In central Africa Mouchet and Gerad[86] found, in addition to 3 benign connective-tissue tumors, 9 malignant ones, which included myxofibrosarcoma, small cell sarcoma, lymphoblastic sarcoma, and fusiform cell sarcoma; 18 carcinomas, among which were 9 primary in the liver and 4 in the breast; 3 melanomas; and 1 mixed tumor of the parotid.

Besides numerous lipomas, fibromas, angiomas, myxomas, sebaceous cysts, and adenomas, Surmont and Sava[87] found 10 sarcomas, an epithelioma of the eyelid, 1 of the vulva, 9 carcinomas of the digestive tract, including 6 primary in the liver, 1 of the esophagus, 1 of the parotid, and 1 of the pancreas, 5 carcinomas of the breast, 1 glioma of the brain, and 2 mixed tumors. They noted the absence of carcinoma of the stomach. All the subjects of this communication lived in savagery.

During three years' surgical work in a hospital in the Belgian Congo, Guillot[88] found in the natives the following neoplasms: a basal cell carcinoma of the temporal region, an adenocarcinoma of the stomach, an adenocarcinoma of the head of the pancreas with metastases in the liver, metastatic carcinoma of the liver (primary not found), and spindle cell sarcoma of the popliteal space. Guillot expresses the belief that, as medical service for the natives becomes better organized, it will be discovered that malignant growths are even more common. In another communication[89] he reported a dermoid cyst of the ovary, a fibroid of the uterus, and a cyst of the broad ligament.

Arnsmont[90] describes 2 cases of primary carcinoma of the liver, 2 melanomas (1 of the foot and 1 of the orbit), 1 osteosarcoma, and 2 cancers whose nature was undiagnosed.

[86] Bull. Soc. path. exot., 19:564, 1926.

[87] Bull. Assoc. franç. p. l'étude du cancer, 16:136, 1927.

[88] Bruxelles méd., 10:1224, 1930.

[89] Bull. Soc. path. exot., 23:205, 1930.   [90] Bull. Soc. path. exot., 23:109, 1930.

Among 1,963 autopsies of native mineworkers, Fischer[91] disclosed 16 primary carcinomas of the liver, 2 of the bladder, 1 of the pancreas, 2 lymphosarcomas, and 1 round cell sarcoma.

Plazy[92] points out that malignant tumors, originally considered rare in natives, are found more and more as the pathology of the race is understood. There is no special racial immunity, and all varieties of benign and malignant tumors have been met with. He describes a case of primary carcinoma of the liver and points out the prevalence of this tumor according to other reports in the literature. This predilection for the liver may probably be explained, according to him, by the overwork of the liver in the tropics but more likely by the frequency of hepatic parasites.

Ram[93] reports an instance of carcinoma of the esophagus and says it is uncommon as compared with other tumors.

Of 2,551 deaths in a hospital in Cameroon, Ledentu[94] found 13, or about 0.5 per cent, due to cancer, partly confirmed by autopsy. Among the patients in the hospital there were cancers at the rate of only 7 per 100,000, although among the population at large, as determined by frequent visits, there were 16 cancers per 100,000, and there would be more if the visits were increased in frequency. Of 63 cases of cancer, 25 per cent were of the digestive tract, 11 per cent being primary in the liver. Most of the cancers occurred between the ages thirty to forty years. Cancer of the skin made up 20.6 per cent and cancer of the breast 17.4 per cent (4.7 per cent in males). Carcinomas formed 60 per cent and sarcomas 40 per cent of the whole.

Thibaut,[95] in Matadi, Congo, autopsied 3 cases of cancer—a carcinoma of the colon, a carcinoma of the breast, and a round cell sarcoma of the deltoid region.

Sequira and Vint[96] examined histological preparations of

[91] *South African M. J.*, 6:359, 1932.

[92] *Bull. Soc. path. exot.*, 26:1015, 1933.

[93] *East African M. J.*, 11:368, 1934.   [94] *Bull. Soc. path. exot.*, 27:282, 1934.

[95] *Ann. Soc. belge de méd. trop.*, 14:519, 1934.

[96] *Brit. J. Dermat.*, 46:361, 1934.

2,228 lesions in natives which were submitted to them for diagnosis and found 482 malignant tumors. These specimens came from the natives of Kenya, of which there are about 3,000,000, the majority being of Bantu origin. Of the 482 cancers, 182 were located in the skin and adjacent mucous membranes, including 130 cases of squamous cell carcinoma, 2 basal cell carcinoma, and 52 melanomas. It was believed that the high proportion of squamous cell carcinomas is largely attributable to chronic tropical ulcers, on the basis of which cancer develops. In addition, there were reported from another laboratory 57 malignant skin tumors, including 30 squamous cell carcinomas and 15 melanomas. This shows that in the two territories where the laboratories were located, malignant melanoma is much commoner than in European countries. Among these natives both sexes seemed to be equally affected by malignant tumors. In the combined melanomas of the two groups, by far the commonest site of the tumors is the foot (39 out of 67). There was no evidence of the occurrence of pigmented nevi in these natives. Although the histologic picture was that of malignant melanoma, the disease was usually only locally malignant. Metastases occurred but were much rarer than in Europeans. Provided that there was no lymph node involvement, excision of the tumor seemed to be all that was required for a complete cure.

Smith and Elmes[97] classified 500 tumor specimens collected over a period of eight years from the natives at Lagos, Nigeria. These are regarded as a fair representation of the type of tumor occurring in Nigeria, since they came from all parts of the country. The series included 225 carcinomas, or 45 per cent, of which 155 were of the glandular type, 63 squamous, and 7 basal cell; 180 sarcomas, including 10 Kaposi tumors, 40 melanomas, 18 mixed parotid tumors, 17 endotheliomas, 13 adamantinomas, 2 cylindromas, 2 peritheliomas, 2 teratomas, and 1 chorionepithelioma. The chief locations of these tumors, in order of frequeney, were the skin, lymph glands, liver, bones, female genitalia, orbit, parotid region, breast, and limbs. Twenty-nine,

[97] *Ann. Trop. Med.*, 28:461, 1934.

or 5.8 per cent, of the tumors occurred in children under ten years of age. Ten of them were round cell sarcoma of the orbit.

Strachan[98] found the only striking difference between cancer in whites and Negroes of South Africa to be the high incidence of primary carcinoma of the liver among Negroes (Bantu) and its occurrence at an early age. In 2 of the 37 cases of this tumor definite bilharzial lesions were present—ova with fibrosis and bilharzial pigmentation. In others there was some evidence of bilharzial pigmentation but no bilharzial cirrhosis. In 30 of the 37 cases there was a definite degree of cirrhosis, which, it is suggested, may be of etiologic significance.

Appelmans and Ducuroir[99] report a case of bilateral glioma of the retina; van den Branden[100] reports a glioma of the cord; another of the retina is described by Dubois.[101] These 3 gliomas were in natives of the Belgian Congo. The patient of Appelmans and Ducuroir was two years of age, that of Branden was forty years of age, and that of Dubois two to three years of age.

Smith[102] gives 8 examples of Hodgkin's disease and another possible one in the natives of Nigeria. In 6 cases the diagnosis was based on histological findings alone; in 3 Gordon's test was carried out in addition. The test was definitely positive in 2 cases. The third case was not typical histologically and must be regarded as doubtful. Material from 4 cases was cultured for diphtheroid bacilli, and this organism was isolated in all. Cultures of one strain of the isolated organisms inoculated into animals gave negative results.

Berman[103] points out the inaccuracy of Hoffman's data, showing the rarity of malignant tumors in native Africans. He estimates that the average death rate from cancer is 18.8 per 100,000 for the Bantu people of South Africa. He had available 735 cases of malignancy in South African Bantus as reported

[98] *J. Path. & Bact.*, 39:209, 1934.

[99] *Ann. Soc. belge de méd. trop.*, 15:155, 1935.

[100] *Bull. Soc. path. exot.*, 13:34, 1920.

[101] See discussion in Appelmans and Ducuroir, *loc. cit.*

[102] *Lancet*, 2:874, 1935.   [103] *South African M. J.*, 1:12, 1935; 5:54, 1940.

in the literature, together with those of his own.[104] The 735 malignant growths were composed of 455, or 61.9 per cent, carcinomas, 266, or 36.2 per cent, sarcomas, and 14, or 1.9 per cent, other malignant tumors.

Of the 235 carcinomas that he himself gathered among the male Bantu mineworkers, 90.5 per cent were of the liver. Among them carcinomas of the skin and the stomach were absent. Carcinoma of the lung was comparatively rare, while carcinoma of the bladder was frequent. Among the Bantus of the cities carcinoma was relatively common among males after middle age, but primary hepatic carcinoma occurred much less frequently than among the mineworkers. The average incidence for the two groups was 37.4 per cent. Among the Eurafricans liver cancer had a low frequency, not differing materially from that in Europeans. Berman showed that the high frequency of liver cancer is a characteristic of most pigmented races (Javanese, Chinese, Philippine Islanders, Japanese), but, of all, the rate is highest among the Bantus, being about forty times the rate among Europeans.

Prates[105] confirms the high frequency of carcinoma of the liver among the Bantus. This tumor occupies first place in the list of the whole of the neoplasms found in the natives of the Portuguese colony of Mozambique. This is not true of the whole of Portuguese East Africa, the excessive rates being sharply circumscribed in one area. It is an interesting fact that among the mineworkers that Berman reported as having frequent liver carcinomas, those that were recruited from the Portuguese colonies developed the tumor three times more often than those from other parts of South Africa.

Gillman[106] points out the relation of the high frequency of primary carcinoma of the liver to the number of multinucleated cells in the liver of normal Bantus. While about 5 per cent of

[104] Hawes, *St. Barth. Hosp. Rept.*, 41:161, 1905; Pirie, *M. J. South Africa*, 17:87, 1921; Leipoldt, *M. J. South Africa*, 20:257, 1925; Watkins, *M. J. South Africa*, 20:257, 1925; Des Ligneris, *loc. cit.*; see n. 85; Bayers, *J. M. A. South Africa*, 1:606, 1927; Fischer, *J. M. A. South Africa*, 3:511, 1929; *South African M. J.*, 6:359, 1932; Strachan, *J. Path & Bact.*, 39:209, 1934; McVicar, *South African M. Rec.*, 23:315, 1925.

[105] *South African M. J.*, 14:95, 1940. [106] *South African M. J.*, 5:46, 1940.

the liver cells are binucleated in the European, from 10 to 34 per cent of the liver cells show this condition in the Bantu. In the latter people the liver cells are often tetranucleated, although sextinucleation is rare. Most of the other Bantu organs also show this finding, leading Gillman to say that multinucleation is a distinctive feature of normal Bantu organs. He believes that the multiple nuclei arise by a mitosis. In view of the fact that primary carcinoma of the liver is the only malignant neoplasm that is markedly excessive in the Bantu, it is doubtful that multinucleation is an important factor, since other organs without high cancer involvement also show multiple nuclei.

Des Ligneris[107] reports having found a carcinogenic substance in the normal liver of noncancerous Bantus as well as in the uninvolved part of the liver from people with cancer. Although carcinogenic substances have been found in the liver (cancerous or uninvolved) of white cancerous patients,[108] they are not found in the liver of normal white subjects.[109] Hieger suggests that the liver of the Bantu acts as a depot for the carcinogenic substances and that the high incidence of liver cancer among these people is a consequence of some dietary factor.

Berman gives data that indicate that diet is an important factor in the causation of carcinoma of the stomach. The food of the Bantu mineworker, while modified to some extent from the strictly native diet, is much more primitive than that of the urbanized Bantu, whose food is practically the same as that of the European. Among the mineworkers there was no cancer of the stomach and intestines, while among the urbanized Bantus cancer of the alimentary tract made up 25.8 per cent of the cancers in the male and 10.1 per cent of the cancers in the female. While carcinoma of the alimentary tract increases on urbanization, carcinoma of the liver decreases.

Vint[110] examined 2,378 tissues from natives of Kenya, on the east coast of Africa, and in 546, or 23 per cent, discovered malignant changes. The types of tumor were as follows: car-

[107] *Am. J. Cancer*, 39:489, 1940.

[108] Shabad, *Bull. biol. et méd. expér.*, 3:252, 1937.

[109] Hieger, *Am. J. Cancer*, 39:496, 1940. [110] *Lancet*, 2:628, 1935.

cinoma, 277 cases (50.7 per cent); sarcoma, 178 (34.4 per cent); melanoma, 59 (10.8 per cent); endothelioma, 15 (2.7 per cent); teratoblastoma, 14 (2.5 per cent); chorioepithelioma, 2 (0.3 per cent); hypernephroma, 1 (0.1 per cent). Malignant growths of the skin are of the utmost importance in the East African native, accounting for 36.4 per cent of the total. Only 2 basal cell cancers were seen. The large number of squamous cell carcinomas is due to the prevalence of malignant change in tropical ulcers of the leg. Of a series of 282 such ulcers, 2 per cent were found to be malignant. There were 25 carcinomatous and 4 sarcomatous growths of the breast, 5.3 per cent of the entire series. Five of these carcinomas and 2 of the sarcomas were in males. There were found 15 cancers of the male genital organs, including 9 epitheliomas of the penis, all from uncircumcised natives (in most of the tribes circumcision is practiced), and 13 cancers of the female genital tract. Only 1 carcinoma of the body of the uterus and 1 uterine sarcoma were observed, epitheliomas accounting for the majority of the growths of the female genitalia. The incidence of liver tumors was high, as in most African statistics; of the 38 cases in this series, 31 were liver-cell growths and 7 of bile-duct origin. Cirrhosis was usually present in these cases. Gastrointestinal cancer was not common. The author points out that, while this series may be considered representative of the native population of Kenya, it accounts for only a small proportion of the tumors found throughout the colony. Figures obtainable for the age incidence are unreliable, but the maximum would seem to fall in the decade thirty to forty years.

Ellis[111] believed that he obtained evidence of the relation of chronic mastitis to carcinoma of the breast from the relative occurrence of these two conditions in African native women. Of the women that he examined, 51 per cent had the nodules of chronic mastitis, and 14 per cent had cysts of the breasts. Nodularity is twice as common among these people as among English women, while, on the other hand, carcinoma of the breast is

[111] Brit. J. Surg., 25:39, 1937.

unusual in African women[112] and common in the English.[113] Ellis thinks, therefore, that chronic mastitis is not a precancerous lesion.

In a letter from Khartoum, Horgan[114] cites interesting figures on the incidence of melanomas in the Sudanese. Of 438 malignant tumors examined in the years 1930–35, 31, or approximately 7 per cent, were melanomas. Eighteen of these were from the foot. A similar incidence is recorded among the Nigerians—10 melanomas, all of the foot, occurring among 90 malignant neoplasms seen in 1930–33. Hewer[115] also calls attention to the prevalence of melanomas in the Sudanese. A total of 47, or 1.9 per cent, of these tumors were found among 2,500 specimens sent to the Wellcome Tropical Research Laboratory for diagnosis. About 95 per cent of 200 Sudanese, ranging in color from light brown to coal black, were found to have easily detectable nevi. Of the 47 melanomas, 28, or 59.5 per cent, were from the foot, and 35, or 74.5 per cent, were on the lower extremity. Hewer calls attention to the differences between the American and the African Negro in the incidence of melanoma. Part of the differences may probably be explained by the fact that the bare feet of the Sudanese are constantly exposed to puncture wounds from thorns, while such trauma is usually absent in the American Negro. In the Sudan these tumors are at least as common in coal-black natives as in light-skinned Arabs, so that trauma appears to be a more important predisposing factor than skin color.

[112] D'Abreu, *Brit. J. Surg.*, 22:456, 1935.

[113] Ferguson, *South African M. J.*, 6:802, 1932.

[114] *Lancet*, 2:156, 1935. [115] *J. Path. & Bact.*, 41:473, 1933.

MISCELLANEOUS SURGICAL DISEASES

VON RECKLINGHAUSEN'S DISEASE

Fibroma molluscum, or Von Recklinghausen's disease, is, according to Weiss,[1] undoubtedly extremely rare in Negroes. The literature and personal communications confirmed this. He reports, however, two typical and extensive cases in Negroes—one a female aged twenty-two years and the other a male aged forty-six years. One other case in a Negro has since been described by Heuer and Bell.[2]

CHONDRODYSPLASIA: HEREDITARY MULTIPLE CARTILAGINOUS EXOSTOSES

Hale[3] says this disease affects few Negroes in America; Anglo-Americans predominate in case reports. Lewin[4] states that the condition is rare in the colored race. Ehrenfried,[5] on reviewing the literature, was able to find only 1 case in a Negro among a total of 99 collected cases.[6] Ray[7] found 58 additional white cases and another colored case. Mahorner[8] added a third Negro case. Scott[9] discovered 5 more cases, all members of a single Negro family. These cases of Scott illustrate the usual familial character of the disease, which shows a tendency to conform to the Mendelian law of inheritance, occurring predominantly in males, in the ratio of 3 to 1 in females.

PYLOROSPASM

Roberts[10] says pylorospasm is strikingly infrequent in Negroes, a fact which seems to him to support the etiologic theory based on the assumption of a "spasmogenic aptitude." He thinks the psychologic attitude of whites is one of struggle, while that of the Negro, like that of the Chinese, is one of calm. The former race has a psychology which results in an irritability of the sympathetic nervous system, which tends to respond in the

[1] *Arch. Dermat.*, 3:144, 1921.

[2] *Ann. Surg.*, 94:15, 1931.

[3] *Ann. Surg.*, 92:92, 1930.

[4] *Surg., Gynec. & Obst.*, 45:48, 1927.

[5] *J. A. M. A.*, 63:502, 1917.

[6] Ashhurst, *Ann. Surg.*, 63:167, 1916.

[7] *Arch. Pediat.*, 47:152, 1930.

[8] *J. Pediat.*, 10:1, 1937.

[9] *Am. J. Dis. Child.*, 57:1075, 1939.

[10] *J. A. M. A.*, 97:459, 1931.

form of spasm to the slightest stimulus. Bokus[11] eliminates pylorospasm as the cause of pyloric obstruction in Negroes and looks for organic lesions, even though they are obscure.

Boland[12] confirms the general impression that acute intestinal obstruction occurs more often in Negroes. His experiences in Atlanta show it to be twice as prevalent as in whites. Of the total known causes, appendectomy was the operation which led to the largest number of obstructions. The mortality in the obstructions was high. There is no explanation, according to Boland, of this higher tendency among Negroes.

Deaths from appendicitis, according to most American statistics, appear to be higher in Negroes than in whites. This might not be an indication of the comparative frequency of appendicitis but of the availability of diagnosis and surgical treatment or of willingness to undergo operation. Among native Africans appendicitis is often believed not to occur. Assali and Cusset[13] do not agree with this and state that it is their opinion that it occurs oftener than it is reported, as the natives do not recognize the disease and accept it as an ordinary gastrointestinal disturbance. They report a case among French Senegalese troops in Marseilles. Pales[14] says the relative proportion of appendicitis in native Africans and in whites is about 3:10. He thinks the factors involved that account for the difference are physiological, pathological, and anatomical, the last one being most important. Among the anatomical characteristics of the Negro appendix are: It is more often placed internal and retrocecal, the point of implantation on the cecum is more terminal, it is more vascular and has more lymphoid tissue, and the mesoappendix is more developed.

With American material Bayon[15] finds the musculature of the

[11] M. Clin. North America, 12:1061, 1929.

[12] Ann. Surg., 98:698, 1933.

[13] Bull. Soc. path. exot., 23:996, 1930.

[14] Ann. d'anat. path., 11:563, 1934.

[15] Anat. Rec., 19:239, 1920.

white appendix probably stronger than that of the Negro, the vascularity of the Negro appendix richer and its lymphocytes poorer than in whites, and the white appendix shorter and wider. Bayon thinks that, although statistics concerning appendicitis are uncertain, the anatomy indicates that Negroes might be less prone to the disease. Quinland[16] calls attention to the large number of stercoral appendices removed from colored patients with symptoms simulating acute or chronic appendicitis.

In South Africa Erasmus[17] says that appendicitis is eight times more frequent in Europeans than in the Bantus, although complications occur much more often in the latter. This he attributes to a low initial resistance, to the inefficiency of early localization of peritonitis, and to a low resistance to protracted sepsis. The disease in the Bantu is rare below the age of fourteen and occurs more in those on a European diet.

HERNIA

Connell[18] says there is no dearth of hernias among native Africans. He operated on 208 cases within a period of about two years, with a mortality of 2.4 per cent. There was a striking immunity of the females to hernia, there being only 2 women among the 208 cases.

Boland[19] speaks about the large number of hernias in American Negroes, with a high rate of strangulation.

ACUTE EMPYEMA

In an analysis of 124 cases of acute empyema thoracis admitted to the Charity Hospital in New Orleans made by Ochsner and Gage,[20] it was found that a higher percentage occurred in the white race (64.4 per cent) than in the colored (35.4 per cent). Tuberculosis was the underlying lesion in 19.7 per cent of the colored patients and in 8.7 per cent of the white patients. There were only slight racial differences in the occurrence of the

[16] *J. Nat. M. J.*, 32:55, 1940.

[17] *South African M. J.*, 13:601, 1939.   [19] *Loc. cit.;* see n. 12.

[18] *Brit. J. Surg.*, 18:16, 1930.   [20] *Ann. Surg.*, 94:25, 1931.

other causes, which included lobar pneumonia, influenza, and lung abscess. The mortality of the white patients was 10 per cent and of the colored 25 per cent.

Burpee[21] made similar observations in Augusta, Georgia. Of 85 cases of acute empyema, 57, or 65 per cent, were in whites and 28, or 33 per cent, in Negroes, although the community from which the patients came contained only 43 per cent Negroes. Complications were twice as frequent in the colored patients. The mortality was 10.5 per cent for the whites and 39.2 per cent for the colored.

BILIARY DISEASE

Boland[22] found among 65,000 Negro patients in Atlanta (1925–35) 88 cases of disease of the biliary tract, while among 75,000 white patients there were 755 instances of the same disease. Boland believes the simple diet and manual labor of Negroes to be responsible for these racial differences. The symptoms and course of the disease were the same in both groups.

GAS BACILLUS INFECTIONS

Veal[23] found in New Orleans that Negro admissions were less than half of the whites but that they furnished 60 per cent of the cases of gas bacillus infections. The mortality from this infection was four times as high in the colored as in the white patients.

MALFORMATIONS

Johnston[24] says that polydactylism (six fingers or six toes) is perhaps commoner among Negroes, at least in Africa and the West Indies. Among the Bahama Negroes it seems to be particularly frequent. Davenport,[25] likewise, says polydactylism is apparently common in Negroes. He cites a case of twins, both

---

[21] *Arch. Pediat.*, 53:449, 1936.

[22] *J. M. A. Georgia*, 26:185, 1937.

[23] *New Orleans M. & S. J.*, 89:432, 1937.

[24] *The Negro in the New World* (New York: Macmillan Co., 1910).

[25] *Am. J. Phys. Anthropol.*, 2:147, 1919.

with the condition. Cummins and Sicomo[26] described the dissection of the feet of an adult Negro with polydactylism.

Magalpaes[27] reported an instance of dolichopododactylism in a Negro.

In a single Negro family Grand[28] found 3 cases of cleft foot. The family consisted of 3 affected members (father and 2 of 4 children) and 12 normal people.

Pilonidal sinus is a condition rarely found in Negroes, according to Saleeby and McCarthy.[29] They could discover only 4 cases of it in Negroes previous to the one they found in a colored boy, aged eighteen years. They could offer no reason for its lesser occurrence in Negroes other than pigmentation, which in some way might prevent it.

Davis[30] showed that in 15,520 deliveries of Negro women 7 congenital clefts of the lip and palate in the infants were found, giving a ratio of 1 in about 1,788. In 11,638 white deliveries there were 13 congenital clefts, giving a ratio of about 1 in 895.

Duperron and Ruelle[31] give an illustration presenting a case of hermaphroditism in an African native in Lobi.

Schurmeier[32] examined 15,000 white and 5,000 Negro drafted soldiers and found 1 deformity in each 277 whites and 1 in each 395 Negroes. The predominating deformity in Negroes was polydactylisms, occurring equally in the feet and hands. The predominating deformity in the whites was syndactylism.

FRACTURES

Matas[33] reported that both the frequency of and the fatality from fractures was higher in whites than in Negroes. He uses this to prove that Negroes, at least in Louisiana, do not have more rickets than do whites and that the recuperative powers of Negroes exceed those of whites.

[26] Anat. Rec., 23:211, 1922.

[27] Brazil Med., 33:116, 1919.

[28] Am. J. Dis. Child., 51:338, 1936.

[29] Ann. Surg., 105:634, 1937.

[30] Ann. Surg., 84:363, 1924.

[31] Ann. d'hyg., 8:453, 1905.

[32] Am. J. Phys. Anthropol., 5:51, 1922.

[33] Tr. Louisiana State M. Soc., 1901.

Weaver[34] found that head injuries, including skull fractures, when of comparable severity are less fatal in Negroes. In his series the Negro mortality was 16.0 per cent and the white mortality 27.6 per cent.

POSTOPERATIVE EVISCERATION

Surgical wounds break open much oftener in white patients than they do in Negroes. Boland[35] suggests that this fact may be related to the greater tendency of colored people to form scar tissue.

[34] *Surg., Gynec. & Obst.*, 50:499, 1930.   [35] *South. M. J.*, 29:1228, 1936.

CHAPTER VI

OBSTETRICS AND GYNECOLOGY

THE survival of a race depends on a positive balance of reproduction over mortality. Since Negroes have not only been able to survive but to also show moderate increases in population wherever they may be, it is evident that their fertility and fecundity are adequate. These functions must be all the more efficient because they must compensate for an excessive death rate as well as for the inefficiency of reproduction that must maintain under primitive conditions where there is little or no medical supervision.

It is generally believed that women living under primitive conditions, as do most native Africans, go through pregnancy and delivery with comparative ease and with little inconvenience. Most of the writings that express this opinion are of an old date, however, and are chiefly by nonmedical people, mainly anthropologists. Marchand, more recently,[1] marveled at the natives' vitality and power of recovery after delivery. He doubted whether serious puerperal sepsis ever took place. He recounted pathological conditions ending in recovery under which European women would have died. On the other hand, Mitchell[2] states that it is a mistake to believe that native women deliver with less difficulty than do European women. Severe labors are frequent, and the maternal and fetal death rates are high. Mitchell finds that most difficult labors are due to (1) flat pelvis, (2) general contraction, (3) funnel pelvis, and (4) native toxic remedies. Among the Uganda women, flat pelves are frequent. The true conjugate averages 102 mm. in comparison to 110 mm. for Europeans, and the transverse diameter is 109 mm. as compared to the European 132 mm. These flat pelves, as well as the general contracted and funnel pelves, are of the same type found in white women. Rickets, which may also produce

---

[1] *South African M. J.*, 6:329, 1932.   [2] *East African M. J.*, 15:177, 206, 1938.

them, does not occur in Africans. Preston[3] likewise says that childbirth among native women varies very little from that in European women. They have the same difficulties and complications. He gives the external pelvic measurements of three groups of native women and compares them with those of white women. On an average, the native women have smaller measurements. They possess a miniature rather than a distorted pelvis. From an analysis of his experiences in a maternity hospital, he found that in regard to presentation among 217 deliveries there were 132 left occipito-anterior, 58 right occipito-anterior, 15 right occipito-posterior, 3 left occipito-posterior, 3 left sacro-anterior, 2 right sacro-anterior, 2 transverse, and 2 face. Of 215 of these cases, 176 delivered themselves normally, 22 were forceps deliveries, and 3 were delivered by cesarean section; there were 2 craniotomies, 2 bipolar versions, 5 internal rotations, and 5 manual deliveries. There were 18 tears of the perineum and 2 of the vaginal wall. Antepartum hemorrhage, not very severe, occurred 4 times. Only 1 case of retained placenta was observed. There were 1 set of triplets, 3 sets of twins, and 1 case of hydramnios. Two cases of marginal placenta praevia occurred. There was not a single case of eclampsia and only 3 or 4 cases of slight albuminuria. One patient delivered a cyclocephalian type of monster. No instance of ruptured uterus was seen. During the course of two years there were 5 maternal deaths—1 from sepsis and shock following craniotomy, 2 from surgical shock after cesarean section, 1 from sepsis of unstated cause, and another from hypostatic pneumonia following puerperal sepsis. There were, in all, 14 cases of puerperal sepsis.[4]

In the United States the pioneer work of Williams[5] and his pupil, Riggs,[6] at Johns Hopkins Hospital remains to the present

[3] *East African M. J.*, 13:215, 1936.

[4] For other discussions of obstetrics among African natives see Johnson, *South. M. J.*, 7:76, 1902; Wells, *South African M. Rec.*, 23:398, 1925; Anderson, *Kenya & East African M. J.*, 6:62, 1929; Abbatucci, *Rev. d'hyg.*, 54:95, 1932.

[5] *Obstetrics* (New York: D. Appleton & Co., 1915); *Obstetrics*, 1:241, 1899; *Tr. Am. Gynec. Soc.*, 26:260, 1901.

[6] *Johns Hopkins Hosp. Rept.*, 12:241, 1904.

as the best observations of the comparative features of pregnancy and delivery in colored and white women. They were largely instrumental in calling attention to the importance of rickets among Negroes in producing contracted pelves and obstructed labor.

Riggs classified the pelves he encountered into 4 types, occurring among Negro and white pregnant women in the following frequency: among whites—normal, 90.75 per cent; generally contracted, 4.62 per cent; simple flat, 3.33 per cent; and rachitic, 1.28 per cent; among Negroes—normal, 65.18 per cent; generally contracted, 23.16 per cent; rachitic, 9.7 per cent; and simple flat, 1.94 per cent. The abnormal pelvis, therefore, was found in colored women 3.76 times more often than in white women. The generally contracted pelvis occurred approximately 5 times more frequently, the simple flat pelvis about 1.7 times less frequently, and the rachitic pelvis about 8 times more frequently in colored women than in white.

Previous to the report of Riggs, Williams had found in Johns Hopkins Hospital a larger percentage of normal pelves among two series of colored women—80.17 per cent and 81.17 per cent, respectively. Riggs explains this by the fact that his own figures were taken from the records of the hospital, while those of Williams were taken from both the hospital and the outpatient service. The abnormal pelves tended to be more concentrated in the hospital because of the necessity of greater care.

Williams made a final report in 1911 on observations of 4,750 white and colored obstetrical patients. The proportion of important abnormal pelves occurring among the two racial groups is presented in Table 16. The distribution of abnormal pelves within each race is shown in Table 17.

Riggs also showed that the duration of labor in Negroes with normal pelves was about two hours and twelve minutes shorter than that in white women with normal pelves; in Negro women with generally contracted pelves the duration of labor was shorter by about three hours and fourteen minutes than that in white women with contracted pelves. But with the simple flat and rachitic pelves, the duration of labor in Negroes was five hours and seven hours and fifty minutes, respectively, longer than in white women with the same types of pelves. Spontaneous delivery occurred less frequently, and operative delivery was required more frequently in white women, in spite of less contracted pelves. This was due to the fact that the colored infants were smaller and the heads more easily molded, thus compensating for the usually smaller size of the pelves.

TABLE 16

THE INCIDENCE OF ABNORMAL TYPES OF PELVIS
IN WHITE AND NEGRO OBSTETRICAL PATIENTS

Types of Pelvis	Whites (Per Cent)	Negroes (Per Cent)
Rachitic	0.80	10.80
Generally contracted	4.70	21.40
Simple flat	2.57	0.66
Funnel	5.87	6.43

TABLE 17

THE DISTRIBUTION OF ABNORMAL TYPES OF
PELVIS IN WHITE AND NEGRO WOMEN

Types of Pelvis	Whites (Per Cent)	Negroes (Per Cent)
Funnel	44.00	15.43
Generally contracted	34.29	53.73
Simple flat	14.86	1.06
Generally contracted, rachitic	4.00	26.60
Atypical	2.28	0.53
Flat rachitic	0.57	2.66

With the use of a modification of Thom's roentgenological method, Torpin and Holmes[7] studied the pelvic inlet of four hundred Negro women and compared the results with a similar study made by Caldwell[8] and others. The types of pelves are divided into four groups: (1) the gynecoid—the normal pelvis, occurring in 58.5 per cent whites and 60.25 per cent Negroes; (2) the anthropoid—occurring in 18.1 per cent whites and 31.0 per

[7] *Am. J. Obst.*, 38:594, 1939.   [8] *Am. J. Obst.*, 26:479, 1933.

cent Negroes; (3) the android—the male type of pelvis, with an incidence of 22.2 per cent in whites and 6.75 per cent in Negroes; and (4) the platypelloid—simple flat, nonrachitic pelvis, occurring in 0.9 per cent whites and 2.0 per cent colored. The pelves in Negro women, as in the white, tended to be round. Operative interference was less in Negroes, probably because of a lower incidence of the android type of pelvis.

An analysis of 13,658 consecutive deliveries at or near term at Johns Hopkins Hospital made by Peckham[9] showed that colored women, both primiparae and multiparae and regardless of age (types of pelvis were not taken into account), had consistently longer labors than white women. In both races there was an increased duration of labor in the older age groups which was more marked among colored than among white women. He also found[10] that fetal mortality is higher in the Negro than in the white race, regardless of the duration of labor, and that the colored infant tolerates prolonged labor correspondingly less well. In both colored and white a precipitate labor (under three hours) is associated with an increased risk to the child. After three hours very little change is noted in fetal mortality in the whites, until the twenty-four-hour duration is reached, after which it rises proportionately to the increase in length of labor. A similar rise occurs among the colored except that it begins when the duration exceeds twelve hours. He likewise found[11] a higher fetal mortality in the toxemias of pregnancy among Negroes than among whites.

Levy,[12] in a study of five hundred women of each race, stated that pelvic contractions were not more frequent in the colored women of New Orleans. Except for the interspinous and intercristal diameters, which were shorter, all other measurements—intertrochanteric, Baudelocque, diagonal conjugate, and true conjugate—in Negroes were identical with those in white women. Eclampsia and nephritic toxemia were about equal in frequency in colored and in white women. Nausea and vomiting

[9] *Am. J. Obst. & Gynec.*, 24:751, 1932.

[10] *Ibid.*, p. 372.

[11] Peckham, *J. A. M. A.*, 101:1608, 1933.   [12] *South. M. J.*, 19:886, 1926.

were less in Negroes. He did not see a single case of true toxic vomiting in a colored patient. Negroes showed less postpartum injury and less puerperal sepsis.

Pride[13] compared the pelves of Negro and white women in the South (Memphis) and in the North (Chicago). With both races the diameters of northern women were larger than those of southern women. But in both places the diameters of the white women were slightly larger than those of the colored women. The external conjugate of the latter averaged about 0.25 cm. less than in the white and the other diameters about 0.5 cm. less. He states that labor in the Negro women was more difficult than in the white, although his figures show that spontaneous delivery occurred in 95.45 per cent of the colored and 92.2 per cent of the white, while operative interference was necessary in 4.55 per cent of the colored and 7.8 per cent of the white. Abnormal conditions of the child and stillbirths were much higher in the Negro.

Miller[14] found eclampsia of about the same incidence in both races. Placenta praevia was less frequent, but the mortality was higher in the colored. Puerperal sepsis was less in the colored, presumably because abnormal labor occurred less often. Obstetrical injury, except for fistula, was less. The larger number of fistulas resulted from neglect more than from anything else.

McCord,[15] among others, points out the prevalence of syphilis as the cause of complications in obstetrics among Negroes. Of six hundred colored women with positive Wassermanns, 35 per cent had premature births, 33 per cent of the cases ended disastrously, and 25 per cent had hypertension.

The distinctive features of gynecology among Negroes are the high incidence of fibroids (see under "Neoplasms," chap. v, pp. 329-32), and of suppurative infections of the generative tract. The description of these conditions as usually seen has been given by Miller.[16] He states that chronic pelvic inflammatory disease

---

[13] *Am. J. Obst. & Gynec.*, 31:495, 1936.

[14] *South. M. J.*, 25:733, 1932.

[15] *Am. J. Obst. & Gynec.*, 11:850, 1926; 13:389, 1927.   [16] *Loc. cit.;* see n. 14.

was the most frequent condition for which the colored woman seeks hospitalization at the Charity Hospital in New Orleans. The statistics there show that it is roughly twice as frequent in the colored race as in the white. The disease begins as an acute salpingitis which is usually neglected and becomes chronic. The pathological changes that may develop are incredible. Large and widely disseminated suppurative lesions are found, consisting of multiple pus pockets sometimes containing a quart or more of thick suppurative exudate. The organs of the pelvis are displaced or destroyed and replaced with sacs of pus. The infection is of a low grade, and the mortality in colored women is small, amounting to about 3.1 per cent, which is only 1 per cent higher than in white women with a lesser degree of tubal disease. Sterility occurs early in the process. Radical surgical treatment is most often necessary, although Murray[17] presented a series of cases showing that in many instances conservative treatment may be used.

Miller says fibroids originate considerably earlier in colored women than in white. Like tubal disease, these tumors frequently exhibit a degree of pathological change that is astounding. In well over half the cases, Miller found that the growths could be palpated abdominally, and in about a third of the cases they were visible as projections on the abdominal wall. Multiple fibroids are the rule, and the tumor mass may reach the umbilicus, the costal margin, or even higher. In these enormous growths large veins course over the top and often can be palpated through the peritoneum before the actual cavity is opened. Rupture of these veins occurs, but only rarely. Various degrees and types of degeneration usually can be found, and sometimes the necrotic tissue becomes infected. Tubal disease and fibroids often occur together. A tumor impacted in a deep pelvis and complicated by suppurative disease of the adnexa offers a difficult problem to the surgeon. The hazards involved are shock, loss of blood, generalized peritonitis, injury to the bowel or bladder, and ligation or severance of the ureters.

[17] M. Rec., 140:145, 1934.

CHAPTER VII

DISEASES OF THE SKIN

THE differences in the anatomy and physiology of the skin of the Negro suggest that there might also be differences in the diseases that affect the skin. Whether or not these are the factors that are responsible; it is true that many reports and studies establish the fact that there are certain peculiarities of skin disorders in colored people when compared with white people. The differences established are not only in the incidence of many diseases but also in the clinical and pathological manifestations. The same factors that are common in determining the racial differences of many other diseases, such as occupation, economic status, living conditions, hygienic habits, and so forth, undoubtedly play a role in determining the peculiarities of skin diseases in Negroes. Again, the majority of Negroes live in tropical and near-tropical countries, and the skin diseases inherent to these climates will tend to be segregated in these people. But some of the outstanding differences between Negroes and whites cannot be accounted for by any of the known factors that influence disease and are usually assigned to inherent racial attributes.

The appearance of cutaneous lesions in Negroes is greatly modified by the presence of the characteristic dark pigmentation. The brilliant display of color changes upon which the diagnosis of many conditions in white skins depends is absent, obscured, or modified in dark skins. For instance, the description of lesions in erythema multiforme that says they are "bright red in color, gradually fading to a violaceous hue" or in pityriasis rosea that says they are "yellowish, pinkish or reddish, scaly patches" has no meaning as such for the Negro's black skin. Nevertheless, erythema multiforme and pityriasis rosea are readily diagnosed in the Negro because experienced dermatologists have learned to recognize equivalents of these color changes in dark skins as well as to depend upon concomitant nonchromatic changes. Loewenthal[1] has pointed out that there are but two color changes in black skin—pallor and increased pigmentation. The former is seen where there is stretching of the skin, as in edema; in interference with the blood supply, where there is masking of the pigment, as occurs in keratoses, acanthosis, and fungus growths, in some postinflammatory conditions; and in certain atrophies. Further darkening of the skin is seen in chloasma and where there is a folding of the epidermis, which brings more pigment-bearing cells into a given area of skin surface. And even in the very darkest there is some increase of pigmentation on prolonged exposure to intense sunlight. Most dermatologists will agree that even in very black skins a certain degree of hyperemia can be detected in inflammatory conditions as areas of dark purplish color.

It is believed that as a whole the Negro is more resistant to skin diseases than is the white. This fact is probably what Holmes[2] had in mind when he spoke of the resistant "ectoderm" of the Negro, although his evidence is not convincing, since he obtained it from the United States *Mortality statistics* under the heading of deaths from "diseases of the skin and cellular tissues" and from the general mortality of the exanthematous diseases, which are not primarily diseases of the skin. It is also believed that the Negro loses this resistance on intermixture with whites, and statistics are cited that show that certain conditions which are unusual in the pure Negro and common in the whites occur at rates in hybrids that are between these.

Of the primary lesions of the skin the macule is the most easily overlooked, especially when erythematous in nature. Thiroux[3] maintains that an erythematous macule manifests itself on black skin by a lighter patch, while Fishbein[4] says it shows as an increasingly bluish-black tinted area. Loewenthal[5] says the discrepancy may be accounted for by assuming that a pure ery-

---

[1] *J. Trop. Med.*, 39:209, 250, 260, 276, 295, 1936; 40:266, 277, 324, 1937; 41:21, 41, 58, 187, 1938.

[2] *Am. J. Phys. Anthropol.*, 12:139, 1928.   [4] *J. A. M. A.*, 95:1689, 1930.

[3] *Bull. Soc. path. exot.*, 2:532, 1909.   [5] *Loc. cit.*; see n. 1.

thema darkens the skin, while the presence of edema, so often the concomitant of erythema, causes pallor by stretching. Purpuric spots are extremely difficult to detect except in the lighter portions of the skin, and then only in the lighter-colored Negro. Unless there are lesions on the mucous membranes, purpura may not be diagnosed. Sometimes the macule is an area of depigmentation, in which instance it may readily be seen.

Loewenthal states that the papule does not differ noticeably from that seen in the white skin. In general it tends to be lighter in color than the surrounding skin, although there is no fixed rule which determines whether it be lighter or darker than other parts of the skin.

The wheal is always of a lighter tint, as the pigment layer is stretched by the acute subepidermal edema. Otherwise it has no peculiarity in the Negro. Vesicles and pustules are pale from the masking of the pigment layer and are readily recognizable. Ulcers, fissures, and crusts are in no way different from similar lesions on the white skins. Scales are light in color, however dark the skin from which they are shed.

The principal students of skin diseases in Negroes in this country have been Fox and Hazen. The former[6] compared the incidence of various lesions in 2,200 Negroes and 2,200 whites with skin diseases in Washington and Baltimore. Hazen[7] reported the comparative occurrence of various diseases among 2,000 Negro and 2,000 white dermatological cases seen in Washington and New York City. Later he[8] extended his observations to 11,729 Negroes with skin diseases other than syphilitic. Loewenthal has been concerned with the skin diseases of African natives and has published a series of articles[9] dealing with this subject. There have also been published many noteworthy papers by various authors dealing with the characteristics of certain skin diseases in Negroes in addition to numerous case reports of unusual dermatological conditions in colored people.

Fox, in his article, lists 65 different diagnoses, of which 36 occurred less frequently in the Negro, 22 occurred more frequent-

[6] Fox, *J. Cutan. Dis.*, 26:67, 1908.   [8] *Arch. Dermat. & Syph.*, 31:316, 1935.

[7] *J. Cutan. Dis.*, 32:705, 1914.   [9] *Loc. cit.*; see n. 1.

ly, and 7 occurred in about the same frequency in Negroes and in whites. In only a few, however, were the differences significant, and in many instances the number of cases of a given disorder were too small to make comparisons accurate. Erythema multiforme was found to be twice as common in whites. Lichen planus occurred one-third less in the colored. There were 25 cases of rosacea in the whites as compared to 1 in Negroes. Sycosis was diagnosed 16 times in the white patients and 9 times in the colored ones. Urticaria appeared twice as often in Negroes as in whites. There were half as many instances of lupus vulgaris in the colored as in the white. Psoriasis occurred much more often in whites.

Hazen found that the diseases which occur more frequently in the Negro are:

Chloasma	Keloid
Cicatrix	Miliary lupoid (tuberculosis)
Dermatitis papillaris capitis	Pellagra
Dermatitis papulosa nigra	Pityriasis corporis
Dermatitis vegetans	Pityriasis facei
Erythema ab igne	Pyoderma
Fibroma	Scabies
Granuloma inguinale	Tinea tonsurans
	Vitiligo

Those that occur more frequently among white people than among Negroes are:

Acrocyanosis	Pediculosis capitis
Carcinoma basocellulare	Pediculosis pubis
Carcinoma spinocellulare	Pruritis (various)
Clanus	Psoriasis
Dermatitis factitia	Recklinghausen's disease
Dermatitis herpetiformis	Rosacea
Dermatomycosis	Tinea cruris
Herpes simplex	Tinea sycosis
Lichen planus	Tinea ungulum
Lymphoblastoma	Verruca filiformis
Melanoma	Verruca plana
Molluscum contagiosum	Verruca plantaris
Nevus pigmentosus	Verruca senilis
Nevus vascularis	Verruca vulgaris
Neuroses	Xanthelasma
Paronychia	Xanthoma

Loewenthal[10] says that the dermatoses which are particularly common in Negroes are: (1) the fibroplastic diseases, (2) lichenoid diseases, (3) lichenification, and (4) dermatosis papulosa nigra. Those that are comparatively rare in Negroes are: (1) conditions due to trauma from light, (2) those due to external irritants, and (3) those to which there appears to be a natural resistance, including psoriasis, rosacea, eczema, seborrheic dermatitis, alopecia senilis, alopecia areata, lichen tropicus, pruritis, and cancer. Ziemann[11] gives as unusual among African Negroes the following diseases: lichen tropicus, seborrhea capitis, acne rosacea, seborrhea, ichthyosis, psoriasis, papillae filiforme hypertrophicum, epidermolysis bullosa hereditaria, Quincke's edema, dermatitis solaris, furunculosis, and carbuncle.

Some of the diseases which have been prominently discussed in relation to their occurrence and behavior in Negroes are reviewed below.

PSORIASIS

In the white race psoriasis is so common that it attracts little attention, constituting about 2.7 per cent of all skin diseases. In colored people, however, the disease is believed to be so unusual that at one time some dermatologists doubted its existence. But so many cases have now been reported, each as a rarity, that the sum total of them amounts to a considerable number, and, while the disease is still uncommon among these people, it is not so unusual as formerly believed. Rufz,[12] with a large experience among the Negroes of Martinique, had never seen psoriasis among them. Morison[13] reported 26 cases of psoriasis in 500 white patients, against 2 cases in black males and 4 in female mulattoes in a total of 500 Negro patients. Corlett[14] stated that he had never seen psoriasis in a Negro. Fox[15] found 49 cases among 2,200 whites (2.22 per cent) and 10 cases among an equal number of Negroes (0.45 per cent). In 2,000 consecutive

[10] *Loc. cit.;* see n. 1.

[11] *Arch. f. Schiffs- u. Tropen-Hyg.*, 33:68, 1929.

[12] *Bull. Acad. imper. de méd.*, 24:1051, 1859.

[13] *M. News*, 53:439, 1888.

[14] *Brit. M. J.*, 2:839, 1906.

[15] *Loc. cit.;* see n. 6.

cases of skin disease in whites Hazen[16] found 82 cases of psoriasis, and in 2,000 cases of skin disease among Negroes he found 10 cases. Later he[17] reported the finding of 89 instances of psoriasis among 11,729 Negro dermatological patients, there being 12 cases in the last 1,000 patients. He states, with this experience, that the disease is not nearly so rare as alleged but that it is still rare in the full-blooded Negro. Dade[18] reported 3 cases in Negroes. Wright[19] reported 1 case, as did also Parounagian.[20] Knowles, in the discussion of Wright's presentation, claimed to have seen "a few cases" in lighter-colored Negroes. Morison says that the spots of psoriasis in the Negro are covered with a more yellowish, less shining crust than in the white. When punctate, the crust is thicker than usual and is easily rubbed off, leaving a deep red, bleeding surface, the blood oozing freely from the minute vessels. He says the disease is easily cured in Negroes and that he had seen no relapses and had not obtained histories of previous attacks. No other writer has reported such differences in the behavior of psoriasis in Negroes and in whites. Parounagian definitely states that the scales in his case were perfectly white and that the disease was not easily cured, the patient having had a relapse within two months.

Loewenthal,[21] Ziemann,[22] and Heim[23] reported the infrequency of psoriasis also in the natives of Africa.

DERMATOSIS PAPULOSA NIGRA

Castellani[24] described and named as dermatosis papulosa nigra a disease which he had observed to be extremely common among the Negroes of Jamaica and Central America. Later, and with Duval,[25] he described the condition more completely and showed that it may occur in Negroes of this country who have never been abroad. In a well-marked case the lesions

[16] *J. Cutan. Dis.*, 32:705, 1914.

[17] *Arch. Dermat. & Syph.*, 31:316, 1935.

[18] *J. Cutan. Dis.*, 27:207, 1909.

[19] *Arch. Dermat. & Syph.*, 9:398, 1924.

[20] *Arch. Dermat. & Syph.*, 13:106, 1926.

[21] *Loc. cit.;* see n. 1.

[22] *Loc. cit.;* see n. 11.

[23] *Dermat. Ztschr.*, 23:357, 1916.

[24] *J. Trop. Med.*, 28:1, 1925.

[25] *Arch. Dermat. & Syph.*, 18:393, 1928.

consist of black or dark-brown papules, somewhat cupoliform or at times flattened, situated on the face, principally on both malar regions, being rare or absent on the lower parts of the face and chin. A few papules may be present on the forehead, the maximum diameter of each papule varying between 1 mm. and 4 or 5 mm. They are not pruriginous or painful. In early cases the surface of the papule is smooth, but later it may become slightly rough and verrucoid. The disease usually begins during youth, often at the age of puberty or soon after with the appearance of two or three papules. The condition gradually becomes more marked, the papules increasing in number and in size the older the patient becomes. It is common to see middle-aged men and women with their faces studded with these black papules. Diasio[26] shows that the lesions may be more widespread than believed by Castellani.

Histologically the pars papillaris of the derma is greatly increased in density, presenting a keloid appearance and forming a protuberant and branching projection which assumes a papillomatous arrangement, although the layers of the surface epithelium have not proliferated.

The etiology is unknown. The condition does not affect the general health. Treatment is unsatisfactory, and there is no tendency to spontaneous cure.

Michael and Seale[27] made further histological studies and showed the most prominent features to be irregular acanthosis, hyperpigmentation, rudimentary hair follicles, and immature sebaceous elements. Added to these were a moderate catarrhal inflammation of the cutis and degeneration of the collagenous tissue. From their obervations they believe this dermatosis to be a nevus. They examined 2,230 colored school children in Houston, Texas, and found the incidence of the disease to be 6 or 12 per cent and more prevalent in the female than in the male. The many reports made in the literature confirm the fact that it is a very common disease among Negroes. Hazen[28]

[26] *Arch. Dermat. & Syph.*, 27:751, 1933.

[27] *Arch. Dermat. & Syph.*, 20:629, 1929.

[28] *Arch. Dermat. & Syph.*, 31:316, 1935.

speaks of it as one of the dermatologic peculiarities of the race. Dermatologists admit that before the descriptions of Castellani the disease had been diagnosed as flat warts, tiny nevi, and a host of other conditions.

LUPUS ERYTHEMATOSUS

There have been varying opinions concerning the frequency of lupus erythematosus in Negroes. The interest in this question arises because, among other reasons, of a suggested relation of this disease to tuberculosis.

In 1918 Wise[29] stated that lupus erythematosus in the Negro was relatively uncommon in his experience. In the discussion Ochs said that he had observed a number of cases in Negro patients and that the disease was more extensive in them than in white patients ("extensive" apparently referring to the area involved). Bechet, on the same occasion, stated that he had observed instances in Negro patients occasionally, agreeing that the condition was more extensive in these than in white patients. On the other hand, Gilchrist[30] held that lupus erythematosus is rare in the Negro race, while lupus vulgaris is common. Further discussions brought out opinions by Hasse that the reverse was true and by Strauss that lupus erythematosus is rare in Negroes and the result of treatment poor. Klauder[31] presented a case of the disease in a Negro, feeling that the rarity of the condition warranted the presentation. For the same reason Kirby-Smith[32] describes two additional cases. Andrews[33] made the comment that the disease is uncommon in the Negro. Fox[34] found practically the same incidence of lupus erythematosus in white and in colored. Hazen found about three times more cases in the whites. In his larger series of Negro patients the incidence was about 4.7 per 1,000. Noel[35] believes that lupus erythematosus is exceptional in African Negroes and reports what

[29] *J. Cutan. Dis.*, 37:354, 1919.   [31] *Arch. Dermat. & Syph.*, 7:121, 1923.

[30] *Arch. Dermat. & Syph.*, 1:597, 1920.   [32] *J. Florida M. A.*, 26:141, 1939.

[33] *Diseases of the skin* (Philadelphia: Saunders, 1930).

[34] *Loc. cit.*; see n. 6.   [35] *Ann. de dermat. et syph.*, 9:372, 1928.

he believes to be the first case in a Sudanese woman. Rufz[36] did not observe a single case in Martinique during the course of twenty years of practice. Cummer[37] has collected from the literature altogether thirty case reports of lupus erythematosus in Negroes, most of which were presented as rarities. He found in New Orleans the incidence of the condition among white patients with skin disorders to be 3.5 per 1,000 and among the Negroes with skin diseases 0.6 per 1,000. The age incidence and results of treatment were about the same in the two races. The deeper pigmentation of the lesions of lupus erythematosus in Negroes seems to be the result of the normal pigment *plus* erythema rather than hyperpigmentation.

ACNE VULGARIS

Fox[38] claimed that acne is relatively infrequent in the Negro and in support of this statement offered his own statistics as well as those of Rufz,[39] Dyer,[40] and Morison.[41] He believes that not only is acne less frequent in Negroes but that it is milder and that well-marked cases of acne indurata are rarities. This difference between white and colored is even more marked if mulattoes are excluded. Hazen,[42] on the other hand, found that acne vulgaris is about as common among Negroes as among whites and that the disorder does not respond any more readily to treatment than it does in white people. According to Ziemann,[43] acne rosacea is seldom seen in the Negro, while acne vulgaris occurs frequently. Hinrichsen and Ivy[44] found that acne vulgaris occurred slightly more often in Negro high-school boys in Chicago than in white high-school boys. The incidence in the white and colored girl students was about the same.

[36] *Loc. cit.;* see n. 12.

[37] *Arch. Dermat. & Syph.,* 33:434, 1936.

[40] *Tr. Louisiana State M. Soc.,* p. 257, 1895.

[41] *Loc. cit.;* see n. 13.

[43] *Jadassohn's Handb. d. Haut- u. Geschlechtskr.,* 12:Part 1, 1910–16.

[44] *Arch. Dermat. & Syph.,* 37:975, 1938.

[38] *Loc. cit.;* see n. 6.

[39] *Loc. cit.;* see n. 12.

[42] *J. Cutan. Dis.,* 32:705, 1914.

AINHUM

Ainhum, a disease almost completely confined to Negroes, consists of the formation of a narrow strip of hardened skin, the so-called "constricting ring," which gradually involves the whole circumference of the little toe at the level of the digito-plantar fold. This constriction forms a deep circular furrow, which slowly increases in depth and length and follows the absorption of the tissues, including the bone, underneath the ring. As a result of either injury or gangrene, the process terminates in spontaneous amputation of the toe distal to the ring. The distal part of the toe is usually enlarged to two or three times its normal size and before falling off assumes the form of a tumor attached by a pedicle to the rest of the toe. The amputation takes place at the second or third joint or through the phalanx. The ring is located near the proximal joint of the toe. Such is the description of ainhum as given by Bloom and Newman,[45] who review the literature and present a case.

The disease was first described clinically by Clarke[46] in 1860 as occurring among the natives of the African Gold Coast and was referred to as "dry gangrene of the little toe." The name "ainhum" was given by Da Silva Lima and is a word used by the Nagos, an African tribe, to describe the malady. While the majority of the cases have been reported in African Negroes, it also has been found infrequently among Hindus, Arabs, and Chinese. It is of rare occurrence in white people. Until 1911 only thirty cases had been reported in the literature from the United States, all in Negroes from the Gulf states and from North and South Carolina. More recently Friedman,[47] Bloom and Newman,[48] and Irgang and Alexander[49] each reported one case of ainhum occurring in Negroes residing in New York who had migrated from southern states. Horwitz and Tunick[50] cite six cases in New York City, one of whom came from the British

---

[45] *Arch. Dermat. & Syph.*, 27:783, 1933.

[46] *Tr. Epidermol. Soc., London*, 1:76, 1860.

[47] *Am. J. Roentgenol.*, 31:349, 1934. [49] *Arch. Dermat. & Syph.*, 30:508, 1934.

[48] *Loc. cit.*; see n. 45. [50] *Arch. Dermat. & Syph.*, 36:1058, 1937.

West Indies and the remainder from the southern states. These authors also give excellent descriptions of the clinical picture and pathology, from which the following is abstracted.

The disease usually affects men from twenty to forty years of age, but occasionally women and children suffer from it. Patients with it are often in otherwise good health. The Wassermann may or may not be positive, but, if positive, and antisyphilitic treatment is given, the course of the disease is not affected, although iodides given intravenously (Irgang and Alexander) will often relieve the pain, which may be severe when there is ulceration. Ainhum is frequently familial in occurrence.[51]

The histopathology of the disease indicates that the tissue beneath the constricting ring atrophies, and the bone undergoes rarefaction, fragmentation, and absorption. Endarteritis and periarteritis of the vessels are seen distal to the band, with atrophy of the part proximal to the ring and fatty degeneration and edema of the distal bulbous portion.

The etiology of ainhum is entirely unknown. Wellman[52] collected the following theories, which had been proposed in explanation up to the time of his writing: (1) that ainhum is a lesion of leprosy; (2) that it is caused by injuries to toes incident to barefootedness; (3) that it is due to a trophoneurosis; (4) that it is a circumscribed scleroderma; (5) that it is a congenital spontaneous amputation; (6) that it is the result of self-mutilation by ligatures, the wearing of toe rings, and so on. Wellman shows how none of these theories can hold. Horwitz and Tunick state that the disease is probably a mechanical process produced by a fibrotic constriction which is induced by mechanical or infectious injury.

KERATOSES

According to Hazen, the rarity of keratotic and precancerous lesions of the skin in colored people is in keeping with and prob-

---

[51] Maas, *Arch. f. Schiffs- u. Tropen-Hyg.*, 30:32, 1926; Da Silva Lima, *Arch. Dermat & Syph.*, 6:637, 1880.

[52] *J. A. M. A.*, 46:636, 1906.

ably related to their lesser tendency toward malignant growths of the skin. Callosities and corns were rarely seen by him in the dispensary, although there is no lack of these lesions among the general Negro population. Verruca vulgaris was only rarely a cause of complaint, and large and multiple warts were practically never seen. Likewise plantar warts, seborrheic warts, juvenile flat warts, and small pedunculated warts were excessively rare in Hazen's experience.

Ambler and Stout[53] discuss the occurrence of porokeratosis, or Mibelli's disease, in Negroes. This is a condition in which there is a marked hyperkeratosis at the sweat-duct openings. Almost ninety cases have been reported, but these authors did not disclose a single instance in Negroes by a careful search of the literature. Hutchins,[54] the first American author to describe a case, stated he had seen lesions resembling those of Mibelli's disease on the scrotum of a young Negro boy but had no opportunity to study the case. Ambler and Stout claim to be the first to record a detailed report of an instance of the disease occurring in the Negro race. It concerned a laborer aged thirty-five years, living in San Francisco, but who was born in Arkansas. The lesions were located on the hands, arms, shoulders, scalp, scrotum, and right thigh. There were no characteristics that distinguished this case from those found in white patients.

XERODERMA PIGMENTOSUM

Xeroderma pigmentosum is another disease considered rare in colored people. Loewenthal[55] cited three cases in African native children, all in one family. A case of multiple epitheliomas and pigmentosis in an American Negro described by Hopkins and Studdiford[56] is believed to be a form of xeroderma pigmentosum. King and Hamilton[57] report a colored girl who had lesions with histological and other features of the disease. These three cases apparently form the extent of the known occurrence of xeroderma pigmentosum in Negroes.

[53] Arch. Dermat. & Syph., 29:21, 1934.

[54] J. Cutan. Dis., 14:373, 1896.   [56] Arch. Dermat. & Syph., 29:408, 1934.

[55] Brit. J. Dermat., 50:66, 1938.   [57] Arch. Dermat. & Syph., 42:570, 1940.

MULTIPLE HEMORRHAGIC SARCOMA OF KAPOSI

In 1922 Jojot and Laigret[58] described a case of multiple tumors in a Bantu Negro of Cameroon. Ziemann and Sklarek[59] expressed the belief that it was one of Kaposi's sarcoma. In 1934 Ellis[60] reported another case in an American Negro, supposedly full-blooded, and quoted Pardo-Castello[61] as having described one previously. Andrews[62] reported a fourth case, and Loewenthal[63] presented a fifth one in a Negro native of British East Africa, giving histological evidence that the tumor was derived from vascular endothelium. These five cases are said by Loewenthal to be the only ones recorded in Negroes, although he admits that the lack of trained dermatologists in Africa might be responsible for others not having been found there. Since then others have been described in Africa[64] and additional ones located that were missed by Loewenthal.[65] McLean states that about 10 per cent of all sarcomas in native Africans are of the Kaposi type. There is no additional reliable information on the occurrence of these tumors in American Negroes.

These tumors, while called sarcomas, appear to occupy a position, as far as malignancy goes, midway between generalized nonpigmented benign growths and those of the malignant melanotic type. They often terminate fatally, but in some instances spontaneous involution with complete recovery has been noted. Arsenic has apparently proved to be curative in a considerable number of cases, although the doubt has been expressed whether these were actually specimens of Kaposi's sarcoma.

TUBERCULOSIS

Most dermatologists who have discussed the question have expressed surprise at the lack of an excessive frequency of tuber-

[58] *Bull. Soc. path. exot.*, 15:956, 1922.

[59] *Loc. cit.*; see n. 43. [60] *Arch. Dermat. & Syph.*, 30:706, 1934.

[61] *Bol. Soc. cubana de dermat.*, 2:100, 1931.

[62] *Arch. Dermat. & Syph.*, 26:549, 1932. [63] *Arch. Dermat. & Syph.*, 37:972, 1938.

[64] McLean, *East African M. J.*, 16:308, 1939.

[65] Smith and Elmes, *Ann. Trop. Med.*, 28:468, 1934.

culosis of the skin in Negroes in view of their susceptibility to other forms of tuberculosis. All agree that the various forms that tuberculosis of the skin may take, including lupus vulgaris, Boeck's sarcoid (see chap. iv, section on "Tuberculosis" p. 144), scrofuloderma, tuberculosa verrucosa cutis, and the tuberculids, are no more frequent in colored people than in Caucasians. There has been much discussion of the reason for this without definite conclusions other than that it is an expression of specific resistance of the skin to tuberculosis in Negroes.

KELOIDS

The remarkable tendency of the Negro's skin to keloid formation is discussed in chapter iv, section on "Neoplasms" (pp. 332–35). It has further dermatologic interest in that this tendency may influence in many instances the appearance and behavior of various skin diseases. The characteristic lesions of a given disease may have superimposed keloidal growths, especially those in which there is inflammation and destruction of tissue.

CANCER OF THE SKIN

(See chap. iv, pp. 335–55)

EXTERNAL IRRITANTS

One of the most unique characteristics of the Negro's skin is its resistance to external irritants.

It is well known in industry that the Negro is less sensitive to the action of skin irritants than the white man. In such occupations as work on grinders and driers in dye factories, where there is exposure to irritating dust and dyes, many industrial concerns will employ Negroes because they have found by actual experience that Negroes are less sensitive to skin irritation. The same is true of dry cleaning establishments where cutaneous irritation from solvents is a major hazard.[66]

During the World War, when large forces were employed in the manufacture of munitions, this resistance of the Negro's skin was in striking evidence. Among the whites so employed the

[66] Schwartz and Tulipan, *Occupational diseases of the skin* (Philadelphia: Lea & Febiger, 1939).

toxic action on the skin of chemicals used in the production of explosives was a serious problem, but among the Negro employees under the same conditions this was a negligible factor.

The statistics of Fox show that dermatitis venenata occurred twice as often in the whites as in the colored. Ivy poisoning was found in twenty-two of the white patients and in only eight of the Negroes. Fox made inquiries about the experience of other dermatologists with ivy poisoning in colored people and received replies that indicated either that there was complete immunity or that the condition was exceptional. Hazen says in one place[67] that dermatitis venenata due to ivy is almost as common in the two races and, in another place,[68] that ivy poisoning is less frequent in Negroes.

The pigment of the skin of the Negro, and probably also an excessive sebum secretion, protects him against trauma from light. In the series of Fox, miliaria and heat rash occurred six times more frequently in the whites, and Hazen's figures also confirm this. The latter, in addition, points out the resistance of dark skin to x-ray burns. Loewenthal[69] extends the conditions to which colored skins are comparatively immune to include senile keratosis, sailor's skin, and xeroderma pigmentosum. There seems, however, to be a higher frequency of dermatitis due to cold, according to Fox.

DISEASES AND ANOMALIES OF PIGMENTATION

The skin of Negroes as well as of whites may show either a decrease or an increase of pigment, but in Negroes the more conspicuous process is that in which the pigmentation is less than normal, while in whites the reverse is true. For this reason each of the conditions is emphasized in the literature according to the race affected.

Pigmentary changes may be partial or complete, congenital or acquired. The congenital forms are various degrees of albinism, and the acquired forms are vitiligo or acquired leukoderma.

---

[67] *J. Cutan. Dis.*, 32:705, 1914.

[68] *Arch. Dermat. & Syph.*, 31:316, 1935.   [69] *Loc. cit.*; see n. 1.

In albinism there is a congenital deficiency of pigmentation, the degree and extent of which is variable. The various degrees have been classed differently by writers. Pearson, Nettleship, and Usher,[70] and Stannus[71] have presented classifications, each of which has six, but not comparable, divisions, embracing forms of the anomaly ranging from complete albinism to the form in which there is one or more small pigmented spots. Stannus doubts if there are ever states of complete albinism, since microscopic examination invariably discloses some pigment in the eye. But for practical purposes complete albinism designates the condition where no melanin is found either grossly or microscopically in the skin. Most authors avoid extended classifications and are content with describing all forms as either complete or partial.

It has been believed that albinism occurs more frequently in Negroes than in other races, but most writers point out the lack of accurate statistics to prove this and attribute the opinion to the fact that albinism is much more conspicuous in Negroes than in whites and is therefore observed and described more often. Excellent descriptions have been made by, among others, Pearson, Nettleship, and Usher,[72] Stannus,[73] and Loewenthal[74] of the disease in African Negroes and by Musser[75] of American Negroes. Complete albinism, indeed, makes a very striking appearance in the Negro, who may have all the anatomic features of his race, including kinky or even "peppercorn" hair, but with white skin and hair and pink or blue eyes. The color of the skin is not that of normal white people but is of a milky color, or of a pinkish color when the blood capillaries are visible beneath the translucent epidermis. The skin may otherwise be normal, although it often shows changes due to irritation from the solar rays as a result of the lack of protective pigment. Thickening,

[70] *Research memoirs: a monograph on albinism in man* ("Biometric series, IX," [Draper's Co., 1908]).

[71] *Biometrika*, 9:333, 1913.

[72] *Loc. cit.*; see n. 70.

[73] *Loc. cit.*; see n. 71.

[74] *J. Trop. Med.*, 40:4, 1937.

[75] *M. Clin. North America*, 7:781, 1924.

inflammation, excoriation, ulceration, and severe abscess formation have been described. Roberts[76] reported an instance of
malignant epithelioma arising from irritation of the skin in an
African Negro albino. The eyes may be pink in the Negro when
the condition, which is unusual, approaches absolute albinism.
Small amounts of pigment in the eye color the iris so that it appears blue, hazel, gray, or sometimes orange. Errors of refraction are constantly present in albinos and may take the form of
hypermetropia or myopia, usually associated with a high degree
of astigmatism. Keratoma has also been noted. A frequent abnormality is absence of the fovea centralis, with accompanying
nystagmus. There is a constant photophobia, owing to the absence or diminution of uveal pigmentation. Albinos are said to
be usually of low mental ability and to have a short span of life.

Albinism is inherited as a recessive in true Mendelian fashion,
as is shown by the family histories of Negro albinos both in
Africa and in this country. In Africa albinos are looked upon
with superstition by the natives and are treated as outcasts.
This results in interbreeding of albinos and is probably the
source of the reports of tribes of white Negroes in the interior of
the continent. Consanguinity among albinos emphasizes the
inheritable quality of the condition and leads Penrose[77] to believe that there is a strong indication that the main pathogenic
factor is a single recessive gene. In a discussion of the genetics
of albinism, Cockayne[78] concluded from data on interbreeding
of albinic Negroes with albinos of other races that the anomaly
in all races represents the same defect carried by the same gene.

Negroes with partial albinism, often called piebald Negroes,
like complete albinos, are particularly noticeable, and for this
reason the frequency within the race of the condition has probably been overemphasized. The disease may present itself as
basically albinism upon which are superimposed normally pigmented areas of skin of various sizes, or the affected individual

[76] *East African M. J.*, 15:148, 1938.

[77] *The influence of heredity on disease* (London: Lewis, 1934).

[78] *Inherited abnormalities of the skin and its appendages* (London: Oxford University Press, 1933).

may be fundamentally of a normal black color with one or more variously sized areas of typical albinic skin. Stannus says that when the area is very small and single, and for some reason or other this is frequently located at the corona of the penis, the lesion is referred to as a spotting. The curiosity attached to piebald Negroes has occasionally lead to the exhibition of some of these people in circuses, where they are exploited as so-called "leopard men."

As with complete albinism, partial albinism is inherited as predictable by the Mendelian law. Both types are permanent, and no kind of treatment, including various forms of irradiation, causes the formation of pigment in the white areas, although instances have been described in which complete albinos have spontaneously developed small areas of pigmentation.

XANTHISM

Pearson and Stannus describe a condition in Negroes of uniform hypopigmentation of the skin which is designated as xanthism. It is characterized by a skin color of reddish brown, red, or warm brown, with eyes of a light-brown or hazel color. Loewenthal states that xanthism is a fairly common phenomenon in Africa and is often observed in more than one member of a family. He also believes the condition tends to disappear with advancing years, as by far the greatest number of cases seen were in children. In America it is probably unsafe to diagnose xanthism in Negroes on the basis of skin color alone, since various shades of brown skin and light hair may be due to intermixture with other races.

VITILIGO

The acquired loss or diminution of pigment in the skin is known as vitiligo. It occurs spontaneously and from unknown causes. One or more areas of depigmented skin appear which grow in size and coalesce to form bizarre shapes. The degree of depigmentation may be complete, and the affected skin has the appearance of that of complete albinos. The process has been known to proceed to the extent that the entire body becomes white. The structure or function of the skin does not change, except when due to the absence of melanin. It is said that the deprived skin is more susceptible to inflammation, and it is certainly more easily injured by intense sunlight.

The disease is intractable to treatment, but some cases are known in which spontaneous improvement has occurred and partial restoration of pigment has followed exposure to actinic rays. Much publicity is often attached to these unfortunate people, and in the newspapers they are referred to as "Negroes who turn white."

CONSECUTIVE DEPIGMENTATION

Loss of pigmentation often occurs in the skin of the Negro as the sequel of various diseases, and the process is known as consecutive depigmentation or secondary leukoderma. The diseases known to have this result are syphilis, yaws, certain fungous diseases, pyrogenic and toxic dermatoses, virus diseases (herpes zoster and varicella), leprosy, and pinta. The loss of pigment varies in amount and extent, but in most cases it is a temporary condition.

A curious industrial depigmentation occurring in Negroes was observed by Oliver, Schwartz, and Warren.[79] Colored workers who used rubber gloves continually in their work were observed to gradually lose the pigment of the skin covered by the gloves, although parts of the body that could have come in contact with the rubber were in some cases affected. McNally[80] made the same observation but did not refer to the above previous publication. The writers agree in incriminating, as the active agent, an antioxidant containing monobenzyl ether of hydroquinone and free hydroquinone. Since hydroquinone decomposes into formaldehyde, McNally tested the ability of the latter to depigment the skin, but negative results were obtained. Oliver, Schwartz, and Warren did obtain depigmentation by applying the monobenzyl ether to the skin in patch tests. A later and more thorough investigation[81] confirmed this and eliminated hydroquinone as the active element in causing the

---

[79] *J. A. M. A.*, 113:927, 1937.　　[80] *Indust. Med.*, 8:405, 1939.

[81] Schwartz, Oliver, and Warren, *Pub. Health Rept.*, 55:1111, 1940.

skin changes. The loss of skin color is temporary, since on discarding the rubber gloves the pigmentation returns.

Increasing evidence of the relation of certain vitamins, especially vitamin C, to pigmentation is beginning to stimulate interest in the bearing vitamins have on the color of Negroes. Certain European people are known to consume large quantities of lemon juice in order to maintain a desirable degree of pallor. Vitamin C will also inhibit, under certain conditions, the *in vitro* formation of melanin from dopa oxidase and the proper substrate. Attempts to change the color of Negroes by feeding large quantities of ascorbic acid have failed.

CONGENITAL INCREASE OF PIGMENT

The pigment in the skin of many Negroes is just about at the saturation point, and increases in amount are inconceivable. Nevertheless, Stannus,[82] Levin,[83] and Weidman[84] have described such cases in localized areas which Loewenthal believes to be examples of nevi.

ACQUIRED HYPERPIGMENTATION

Hazen[85] points out that chloasma occurred more frequently in his colored group of patients than in the whites and that it was found more often in the mulattoes than in either the dark Negroes or the whites. Fox,[86] on the other hand, noted that it was found much oftener in whites. Hyperpigmentation of parts of the skin following either local or systemic disease is so frequently seen that it may be regarded as a normal concomitant of any inflammatory disease of the skin in Negro subjects.[87] Loewenthal gives a long list of conditions described in the literature as having left pigmented areas in Negroes. If careful comparisons are made of black skin exposed to intense sunlight with that adequately protected, some increase in pigmentation may be observed.

[82] *Loc. cit.;* see n. 71.

[83] *Arch. Dermat. & Syph.*, 27:141, 1933.

[84] *J. Cutan. Dis.*, 37:517, 1919.

[85] *J. Cutan. Dis.*, 32:705, 1914.

[86] *Loc. cit.;* see n. 6.

[87] Garzon, *Arch. Dermat. & Syph.*, 9:821, 1929.

GRANULOMA INGUINALE

Granuloma inguinale, also known as granuloma venereum and ulcerating granuloma of the pudenda, is a specific, chronic, progressive, superficial ulceration involving the skin and subcutaneous tissues, usually of the genitocrural and genitoanal regions. It is spread by direct contact, most often sexual. Although distinctly different diseases etiologically, granuloma inguinale (venereum) and lymphogranuloma inguinale (venereum) are often confused in the literature and in the clinics because of the similarity in names and in the areas involved and because both processes are fundamentally granulomas, although each has distinctive features which can be demonstrated, if not always grossly, usually histologically. The technics used in making the differential diagnosis between the two conditions are discussed by Butts.[88]

In 1926 Fox[89] gathered reports of 150 cases of granuloma inguinale in the United States, including 15 cases of his own. Ten years later D'Aunoy and von Haam[90] collected 101 more cases from the literature and added 294 additional ones which were observed in a single hospital in New Orleans over a period of only five years (1931–35). Very few cases have been reported as such since this publication, probably because the disease is no longer a curiosity and because more attention is now being paid to the etiology and to the nature of the pathological process.

The overwhelming majority of the cases in this country has been in Negroes, some authors even saying it is found exclusively in them. In the D'Aunoy and von Haam series the ratio in the two races was 9 colored to 1 white. This same proportion was found by Fox, but Harris,[91] in his study of 195 cases, observed the ratio to be only 4:1. Some authors[92] insist that race plays no part in the susceptibility to this infection and that the apparent predilection of colored people for granuloma inguinale

---

[88] *Am. J. Syph.*, 21:544, 1937.

[89] *J. A. M. A.*, 87:1785, 1926.

[90] *J. Trop. Med.*, 17:747, 1937.

[91] *Laryngoscope*, 40:707, 1930.

[92] Scott, *Northwest Med.*, 25:40, 1926; Cole, Miskjian, and Rauschkolb, *Dermat. Ztschr.*, 53:127, 1928; De Metta, quoted by D'Aunoy and von Haam, *loc. cit.*

is due to differences in sexual hygiene and moral standards. Bahr-Manson,[93] Sutton,[94] Grindon,[95] and Galloway[96] say that the disease is found predominantly in young Negro women, but D'Aunoy and von Haam, Fox, and Harris show that the number of males infected exceed the females.

Most clinicians see or recognize the disease only when it is an extensive, destructive, angry-looking, foul-smelling ulceration involving the whole pudendal region and highly infected with secondary invaders. But when identified in its early stages, it is seen as a small, clean area of red granulation tissue which begins as an inguinal subcutaneous granuloma. About 6 per cent of the cases are extragenital.[97] Pund and Gotcher[98] describe an instance of granuloma inguinale involving the body of the uterus, the tubes, and the ovaries. Another case, simulating carcinoma, affected the cervix uteri.[99]

The characteristic and constant feature of granuloma inguinale is the presence of the so-called Donovan bodies, which are round or rodlike structures found lying within cysts in the cytoplasm of large mononuclear cells scattered in various numbers throughout the granulation tissue. The absolute clinical diagnosis of the disease must be made by the demonstration in smears or tissue sections of the Donovan bodies which have distinct tinctorial characteristics. The significance of these structures is not positively known, but the evidence is increasing that they are the etiologic agent. They cannot be cultured on artificial mediums or in chicken embryos, nor can they infect lower animals, according to Dienst, Greenblatt, and Sanderson[100] and Carter, Jones, and Thomas.[101] The former authors aspirated the fluid from an early lesion of the disease and, finding the fluid

[93] Manson's tropical diseases (Baltimore: William Wood & Co., 1936).

[94] Diseases of the skin (St. Louis: C. V. Mosby, 1935).

[95] J. Cutan. Dis., 31:236, 1913.   [96] Brit. J. Dermat., 9:133, 1897.

[97] Greenblatt, Turpin, and Pund, Arch. Dermat. & Syph., 38:358, 1938.

[98] Surgery, 3:34, 1938.

[99] Pund and Greenblatt, J. A. M. A., 108:1401, 1937.

[100] J. Infect. Dis., 62:112, 1938.   [101] J. Infect. Dis., 64:314, 1939.

free of bacteria but rich in Donovan bodies, inoculated it into a Negro subject. A bubo was thereby produced from which could be aspirated a fluid showing a marked increase of Donovan bodies.

The disease is subject to many spontaneous remissions and relapses, and in the late stages a permanent cure is difficult to accomplish. In the early stages tarter emetic given intravenously, as shown by Hazen, Howard, Freeman, and Scull,[102] has a very beneficial effect. In fact the response to this drug constitutes a means of therapeutic diagnosis.

PEDICULOSIS

Both Fox and Hazen were impressed with the differences in the occurrence of pediculosis capitis and pediculosis corporis which they observed in white and in colored patients with skin diseases. Fox found the former condition ten times more frequent in whites, and, while the latter condition was actually slightly more frequent in Negroes, he was of the opinion that the amount of pediculosis corporis was really small for the colored people he studied in view of their unclean habits. Hazen states that lice in the hair of Negroes is very rare, his statistics showing three cases in the colored as against sixty-six in the whites, both figures being obtained from the same number of skin cases. He says that the explanation suggested by Fox that the Negro mother takes especial care of the heads of her children does not seem to explain this racial immunity, for one would expect to find pediculosis in those at least who people the slums, and this is apparently not the case. Fox found that pediculosis pubis was 2.5 times more frequent in whites, while Hazen found the ratio 4 of white to 1 of the Negro. Murray[103] says that the the pediculi pubis become the same color of the host. They are black on the black African and light colored on the European. This statement seems not to have been confirmed.

Fox says scabies is found more frequently in whites, while Hazen says the reverse is true.

[102] *J. A. M. A.*, 99:1410, 1932.

[103] *Tr. Roy. Soc. Edinburgh*, 22:567, 1861.

DISEASES PRODUCED BY FUNGI

Loewenthal[104] gives a detailed description of the diseases caused by vegetable parasites in African Negroes and of the organism involved but gives little information about their relative frequency in Negroes and other races. Fox found seventeen cases of tinea capitis in two thousand whites with skin diseases and fifty-six cases in an equal number of Negroes. He refers to a similar proportion in the statistics of Morison.[105] Fox says both favus and chromophytosis appear to be more common in the Negro than in the white. Hazen shows tinea cruris to be very rare in the colored, but tinea tonsurans was exceptionally common. He states he was not successful in curing a single case with local applications. Tinea versicolor, according to him, is almost never diagnosed in the Negro, probably because the spots, instead of being darker than the normal skin, are often considerably lighter. Hazen says dermatomycosis is relatively infrequent in the Negro race. It is found in students who use a common gymnasium, but in the laboring class it is excessively rare. This is not due to an indifference to mild symptoms of the disease, because examination of the feet of patients admitted to the dispensary and hospital discloses the true paucity of dermatomycoses. Likewise tinea sycosis and tinea unguium are met with great infrequency.

[104] *J. Trop. Med.*, 40:324, 1937; 41:21, 41, 58, 187, 1938; 42:20, 36, 53, 99, 159, 1939.

[105] *M. News*, 53:439, 1888.

CHAPTER VIII

DISEASES OF THE EYE, EAR, NOSE
AND THROAT

PEOPLE who live under primitive conditions are often credited with a higher development of the senses than scientific investigation justifies. To some extent this is true of the eyesight and hearing of native Africans. It appears that, as the result of a greater dependence for existence on the senses, the sense organs are used with more directness and concentration. A greater acuity of vision, hearing, and smell may be more psychological, more the result of a lesser sensory inhibition and, to some extent, of habituation and concentration than of some organic or anatomical development. It is more likely that the apparent better development of the senses among primitive people depends chiefly on the fullest use of the same quality of organs that other people possess.

Schwarzbach[1] found that of 1,853 natives in South Africa, 1,509 possessed the same power of sight as Europeans, while 259 had better vision and 87 weaker vision. An instance of 20/60 vision was noted in a Kaffir girl fourteen years of age. There was not a single case of color-blindness. Roy[2] examined 5,000 African Negroes from 100 tribes in 22 colonies. He was impressed with the general excellence of vision among these people but noticed that the eyesight was, as a rule, better in those living south of 5° latitude than in those living north of this line, where they came in more intimate contact with other races and where their eyes showed lesions from purulent ophthalmia, variola, and irritation from sand. The average vision of the natives was found to be 12/5, and in one instance it was 20/5. With some individuals a correction of two or three diopters of either hypermetropia or myopia could improve vision up to 9/5 and even 11/5. He noted the ability of natives to see to a great depth in

---

[1] *Brit. M. J.*, 2:1731, 1898.   [2] *Arch. Ophth.*, 48:73, 1919.

water. There was also a remarkable degree of night vision.· Although there is evidence that the rods of the retina determine the relative amount of diurnal and nocturnal vision, Roy could himself detect no difference in the histology of the Negro's retina, nor could he learn of any investigation showing a difference. Refraction showed that almost all the eyes of the natives were emmetropic, provided there was no alteration of the cornea from previous disease. Simple hypermetropia and hyperopic astigmatism each occur in about 2.5 per cent, while myopic astigmatism and simple myopia are found in 1.5 per cent. None of these refractive errors in vision required more than a small amount of correction. The power of accommodation was better than the accepted standards of white accommodation. The belief is expressed that the good eyesight of African Negroes is due, in addition to the simple life they lead, to the large amount of protective pigment that is found in all parts of the eye, especially in the conjunctiva and retina.

The chief lesions of the eye came from purulent ophthalmia, variola, syphilis, filariasis, trypanosomiasis, and sand irritation. Roy[3] describes the high susceptibility of the native eye to syphilis in contrast to its small sensitivity to the effect of trypanosomiasis.[4]

Although comparatively few studies of the eyesight of Negroes in the United States have been made, it seems that, on the whole, their eyes are somewhat better than those of white people, although by comparison with Negroes in Africa, there is evidence of a deteriorating influence of 'Western civilization. Kollock[5] was certain that the eyesight of colored people had decreased in quality since slavery. He pointed out that cataract had become just as common as in white people, but myopia was still rare. Xerosis conjunctiva was believed to be peculiar to Negroes, especially to their children. Burnett,[6] Ray,[7] and

---

[3] *Ibid.*, 50:28, 1921.

[4] For further discussion of vision and diseases of the eye in African Negroes see Wieser, *Arch. d. Julius Klaus Stiftung f. Vererbsforsch.*, 3:85, 1927.

[5] *Ann. Ophth. & Otol.*, 2:121, 1893.

[6] *Arch. Ophth.*, 13:187, 1884.   [7] *New York M. J.*, 64:86, 1896.

Bruns[8] have listed the relative occurrence of the various eye diseases in white and in colored patients. Their results are not in agreement, and the racial differences noted are in most cases not significant. Diseases of the lids, conjunctivae, muscles, optic nerve and retina, eyeball, and orbit are found more often in white people, while diseases of the cornea, iris, ciliary body, and choroid are more prevalent among colored, owing to the higher rate of syphilis. They agree that there is little difference in the occurrence of cataract. Belt[9] found fewer abnormal eyes among colored students in the public schools of Washington, D.C., than among white students. Among the whites 25 per cent were astigmatic, and among the colored 10 per cent were astigmatic.

The most outstanding difference in diseases of the eyes between Negroes and whites is the almost complete immunity of the former to trachoma. This is true of Negroes both in Africa and in America, although in both countries the disease is very prevalent among other races with whom Negroes often come in contact. Jones[10] reviewed the literature and ascertained by questionnaire the experience of outstanding ophthalmologists with trachoma among Negroes. There was an agreement that the disease was either entirely absent or rare. Not accepting the immunity of Negroes to trachoma was Van Millingen,[11] who studied the disease in Constantinople. In this city there are about four thousand Negroes, and Van Millingen found trachoma to be as prevalent among them as among the many other races there. Bordley[12] describes an accute inflammatory disease in the eyes of Negroes that simulates trachoma and may often be mistaken for it. The onset is sudden, with swelling of the lids, seromucous discharge, edema of the bulbar conjunctiva, apparent follicular enlargements in the palpebral papillary overgrowth of the tarsal conjunctivae, pain, and photophobia. The disease is obstinate, in spite of active treatment. It is distinguished from trachoma in that it ultimately

[8] *Tr. Am. Ophth. Soc.*, **39**:87, 1905.

[9] *Handbook Pan-American medical congress, no. 520* (1893).

[10] Thesis, University of Chicago, 1931

[11] *Ann. d'ocul.*, **114**:179, 1895.   [12] *Bull. Johns Hopkins Hosp.*, **18**:37, 1907.

gets well, leaving no scar tissue. No pannus is formed and there is no evidence of contagion. Testa[13] attempted without success to treat trachoma with the blood of Negroes.

Crooks[14] states that there are distinct racial differences in the occurrence of color-blindness. He tested 2,279 colored students at Hampton Institute and found 3.75 per cent of 1,628 males to be color-blind and none of 651 females. Among another group of 2,019 males he found the incidence of the condition to be 3.91 per cent. Color-blindness to red was found in 1.04 per cent and to green in 2.87 per cent, the ratio of the two conditions being 1:3. He formerly said color-blindness did not occur in Negro females, but he later found one instance. The findings concerning color-blindness among Negroes made by other writers[15] were grouped with his to yield an average incidence of 3.75 per cent. This figure may be compared with 8.22 per cent, the incidence for American whites averaged from the findings of Miles,[16] Haupt,[17] and Garth,[18] 7.95 per cent the average incidence among European whites,[19] 2.3–2.5 per cent for Mexicans,[20] 6.6 per cent for Chinese,[21] 2.3 per cent for Indians,[22] and 4.0 per cent for Jews.[23]

Arcus senilis is believed to occur at an earlier age and more rapidly in Negroes than in whites.[24]

Schilder and Parker[25] say that the pupillary changes described by Westphal[26] as occurring in psychiatric conditions are

[13] Gior. de med. mil., 79:172, 1931.

[14] Science, 80:269, 1934; Am. J. Phys. Anthropol., 19:453, 1934; Human Biol., 8: 451, 1936.

[15] Garth, Science, 77:333, 1933; Clements, Science, 72:203, 1930.

[16] Gen. Psychol., 2:535, 1929.

[17] J. Comp. Psychol., 6:291, 1926.   [18] Loc. cit.; see n. 15.

[19] Von Planta, Arch. f. Ophth., 120:253, 1928.

[20] Garth, loc. cit.

[21] Kilborn and Beh, Science, 79:34, 1934; Chang, Nat. M. J. China, 18:806, 1932.

[22] Garth, loc. cit.; Clements, loc. cit.

[23] Garth, loc. cit.   [24] See under "Queries," J. A. M. A., 103:939, 1934.

[25] Arch. Neurol. & Psychiat., 25:838, 1931.

[26] Deutsche med. Wchnschr., 33:1080, 1907.

found more often in Negroes than in whites. These changes consist of irregular reaction to light, ranging from a prompt reaction to absolute rigidity, frequently with sluggishness but always with changes in form. These phenomena are said to be due to a coincidence of constitutional, psychic, and anatomicotoxic factors.

Michel[27] says that an anatomical congenital feature of the Negro eye is a symmetrical overlapping fold of equal width around the cornea of both eyes. Routil[28] says that the direction of the palpebral fissure in Negroes is downward from the inner canthus to the outer canthus, while that of the Mongol is downward from the outer canthus to the inner, and that of the European is straight. Rollin[29] denies this and says each of the three types of palpebral fissure can be found in Europeans and Negroes and at about the same rate.

Beiglemann[30] describes a case in a Negro of transient myopia in chronic anterior uveitis.

Walraven[31] removed a fibroadenochondroma and a fibrosarcoma from the eyes of native Africans.

Not many comparisons of Negroes and whites relative to diseases of the ear, nose, and throat have been made, and most of those available were published many years ago. Schepegrell[32] found that "post-nasal catarrh," which is dubbed "American catarrh" by Europeans, occurs about nine times more frequently in whites than in Negroes. Chronic aural diseases, both suppurative and nonsuppurative, are from four to six times more frequent in white patients. Congestive and hypertrophic conditions of the nose as well as abnormalities of the septum are likewise of less frequency in Negroes. A tabulation of all diseases which Schepegrell could compare in the two races shows each one of them to be excessive in varying degrees among white

[27] M. News, 61:461, 1892.

[28] Ztschr. f. morphol. Anthropol., 32:69, 1933.

[29] Ztschr. f. Augenh., 89:95, 1936.

[30] J. A. M. A., 95:1660, 1930.

[31] Ann. d'ocult., 164:955, 1927.

[32] Ann. Ophth. & Otol., 4:589, 1895.

people. Dunbar[33] presents data to show practically the same conclusions.

Roy[34] found the natives of Africa to have good hearing, both bony and aerial. There was little otitis and no labyrinth disease. He believed the Eustachian tube of Negroes to be larger, which might account for some of their immunity to ear disease. Perforations of the septum and palate, owing to syphilis, were frequently found.

Goldmann and Kully[35] reported on a series of twenty-one patients in Cincinnati during 1929–32 with fusospirochetal angina. Of these 52 per cent were Negroes. There were seven deaths, all colored patients. Six of the ones who died had untreated chronic dental infections.

[33] *Virginia M. Semi-Monthly*, 21:176, 1894.

[34] *Ann. Otol., Rhin. & Laryng.*, 29:79, 1920.   [35] *J. A. M. A.*, 101:358, 1933.

CHAPTER IX
DENTAL DISEASES

RACIAL comparisons of teeth have been made by anthropologists because they are a part of the anthropologically important skull and because in their own right they have importance by reason of useful phylogenetic characteristics exhibited in development and in their modeling. The teeth have likewise been of extreme interest to the physician, not only for reasons of oral hygiene and general health, but also because of the highly instructive information that comparisons of tooth anatomy and disease among races have contributed concerning the relation of food and food accessories to odontology. In both respects the study of the Negro's teeth has yielded extremely useful data.

The evolution of the teeth may be traced from lower species of animals to man. Even though human teeth may show wide variations, their pattern conforms to a fundamental primitive type which is anthropoid in nature. The phylogenetic as well as the ontogenetic development of human dentition, with frequent references to the Negro, has been discussed by Gregory[1] and Schultz.[2] It appears that races show evolutionary changes in the teeth that are alike in nature but different in degree. Hellman[3] says the teeth of whites show the most changes and those of Negroes least. The especial instability in form of the third upper and the second lower molars is well known to odontologists. The trend is toward a reduction in the number of cusps from five, a more primitive form, to a lesser number. Sullivan[4] quotes Schwertz[5] as having shown that five cusps are found in

[1] *J. Dent. Research*, 2:89, 215, 357, 607, 1920; 3:87, 1921.

[2] *Dental Cosmos*, 67:935, 1053, 1925.

[3] *Proc. Am. Philosoph. Soc.*, 67:157, 1928.

[4] *Am. J. Phys. Anthropol.*, 3:255, 1920.

[5] *Studien und Förschungen zur Menschen- und Völkerkunde*, Vol. 13:(Stuttgart, 1915).

73 per cent of Australians, 34 per cent of Negroes, 3 per cent of Alamans, and 2 per cent of Hungarians. Hrdlička,[6] who has attempted to stimulate renewed interest in the anthropological aspects of tooth morphology, called attention to a peculiar type of incisors prevalent among certain races. These teeth, usually the upper incisors, are called "shovel-shaped" teeth because of a marked hollowing-out of the lingual surface. Among the Japanese shovel-shaped teeth are found at the rate of 69 per cent. They occur in 1.0 per cent and 0.6 per cent, respectively, of white males and females, 4.0 per cent and 3.2 per cent of Negro males and females, 33.0 per cent and 26.0 per cent of Hawaiian males and females, and 53.0 per cent and 62.5 per cent of Chinese males and females. From his discussions Hrdlička does not regard these teeth as pathological, although they may conceivably be so. Attempts to apply an index representing the relation of the breadth to the width of teeth failed to indicate any usefulness of the index in classifying races because of wide variations within and between the races.

Suk,[7] among others, describes the precociousness of tooth eruption among Negroes. Among a group of native Africans the teeth began to erupt very early, and dentition was completed in a relatively short time; at the age of eighteen several individuals had all four of the third molars erupted; one boy about thirteen or fourteen years of age already had thirty-two teeth. Eruption takes place gradually, but an acceleration occurs in Negroes at the ninth and tenth years and in whites at the eleventh and twelfth years.

It is, however, in the field of dental pathology, especially that concerned with caries, anomalies, and dental malformations, that the greatest differences between Negroes and whites are found. Colored people are well known for the excellent quality of their teeth, a fact that has been depicted in song and caricature but also well substantiated by scientific observation both in this country and in Africa. Suk, one of the earlier of the modern writers, examined 1,008 Zulus of Natal and Zululand (492 males

[6] *Am. J. Phys. Anthropol.*, 3:429, 1920; 6:195, 1923.

[7] *Am. J. Phys. Anthropol.*, 2:351, 1919.

and 516 females), ranging in age from six to nineteen years. The results were compared with those obtained among 694 boys in Prague whose ages ranged from less than four years to twenty years. He stated that the Zulus in general had a fine set of teeth. The individual teeth were well developed, well differentiated, very seldom discolored, and the cusps well formed. Additional cusps (the cusps of Carabelli) were not rare. Crowding of teeth and displacements were met with in a few cases only. Fairly frequent was the trema (central diastema) in the upper jaw. There were not many anomalies. A supernumerary conical tooth behind the upper-right permanent median incisor was found in 4 individuals. There were 10 individuals ranging in age from nine to nineteen years with tooth deficiencies, having 1 to 4 teeth missing. There were 6 instances of permanent and temporary teeth existing together. Among the white boys examined, 10.0 per cent of the upper-jaw teeth and 11.2 per cent of the lower-jaw teeth were decayed. Among the Zulus, 0.48 per cent of the upper and 0.86 per cent of the lower-jaw teeth in males were carious, and 0.98 per cent of the upper and 1.39 per cent of the lower teeth in females were carious. Of the whites, 74.3 per cent of the individuals had decayed teeth, while 6.3 per cent of males and 14.6 per cent of the females among the Zulus had decayed teeth. Little difference in the type of teeth affected in the two races was found. While he had no detailed data for the so-called "civilized" natives living in the towns (teachers, preachers, and servants), he did notice that these had poorer teeth than those living under primitive conditions.

Staz[8] examined in South Africa 300 each of primitive Bantus, urban Bantus, and Europeans with ages ranging from fifteen to thirty years. Altogether 28,000 teeth were observed. The percentage of mouths affected with caries, the number of affected teeth, and the number of cavities per carious mouth were all higher in the Europeans. The figures were much reduced in the urban Bantu and least in the primitive Bantu, who was markedly immune to caries. The lower first molar and then the upper first molar were the most susceptible to caries in the Europeans,

[8] *South African J. M. Sc.*, 3:1, 1928.

while in both classes of Bantus the lower second molar develops the most cavities, then the lower first molar. The first molar of the natives was somewhat protected because it was usually markedly worn. Pits and potential cavities were ground down, leaving a highly polished surface, which was resistant to caries. The primitive Bantu tooth had as many potential cavities as that of the urban Bantu, but as long as the primitive mode of life is maintained, these cavities do not develop. Attrition of the molars was relatively marked in the primitive Bantu, present to a lesser extent in the urban Bantu, and comparatively rare in the European. Attrition appeared to be associated with diet, shape of the jaw, and development of the masticating apparatus. Staz says the average primitive Bantu arch is superior to that of the urban, which in turn is better than that of the European. In each group, to a limited extent, development of caries is in inverse ratio to the degree of attrition of the molars. According to pH determination of saliva, the oral environment in the primitive Bantu seems to be neutral or slightly acid, while in the European there is a greater acid concentration and a reaction at an intermediate position in the urban Bantu.

In contrast to their reaction to caries, the Bantu is highly susceptible to degeneration of the gingival and adjacent tissues. Gingivitis and deposits of calculus were common in both groups of the natives, while the gums of the Europeans were the healthiest. Staz suggests that this susceptibility may be related to pigmentation of the gums, which occurs frequently in the primitive Bantu.

It is pointed out that the immunity of the natives to caries exists in spite of a diet poor and deficient in essential food factors and just above starvation level. The intake of calcium and phosphorus is barely sufficient for their needs. There is often a vitamin C deficiency, and latent scurvy is common. The marked attrition found in the primitive Bantu is thought probably to be due to the prominence of maize in his diet. On the other hand, the large consumption of this food and of sour milk is considered as an important factor in his resistance to dental caries.

Osborn and Noriskin[9] investigated another group of Bantus, apparently with a different background than those studied by Staz. Their subjects were between nine hundred and one thousand new labor recruits for the South African mines, who were examined shortly after arrival at the compounds. While no examinations were made in the native kraals, the authors estimated that about 20–30 per cent of the subjects there had caries which is a low figure according to European standards but high in comparison with some other native groups. On European food the laborers developed caries to the extent that 58 per cent of them were affected. The examination of the natives disclosed a number of dental irregularities which included many supernumerary teeth, accidental fractures of the teeth, pigmented enamel, marked diastema between the first upper and lower incisors, and cramping of the anterior portions of the jaws, with cramping of the second incisors. There were few unerupted or missing teeth. It was noticed that the natives still practiced filing of the teeth. Contrary to the findings of Staz, marginal gingivitis and periodontal disease were rare in the kraals but not in the Johannesburg compounds.

Osborn and Noriskin attempted to correlate various items of the diet with the development of caries in the natives. None of the items in the traditional native diet, with the possible exception of sweet potatoes, showed either a positive or a negative correlation with an increased percentage of carious cases. A greater incidence of the disease was associated with the assumption of a European diet. They suggested that those items of the new food which, when eaten regularly, caused the increased incidence of caries were machine-ground mealie meal, white bread, and refined sugar or foods containing it. It is believed that the carbohydrates of sugar cane and wheat are accompanied, in the natural or crude state, by a "protective agent" which when removed in the process of refining causes decay.[10]

Friel and Shaw[11] stated that the Zulus, in their native state,

[9] *J. Dent. Research*, 16:431, 1937.

[10] Oranje, Noriskin, and Osborn, *South African J. M. Sc.*, 1:57, 1935.

[11] *Brit. Dent. J.*, 52:309, 1931.

have exceptionally sound teeth; but when they emigrate to towns where Europeans live they immediately develop caries. Colyer[12] cites studies of natives of central and southeastern Africa. In the former the inhabitants of three districts had an incidence of caries of 1 per cent or less. Their diet is said to consist mainly of millet porridge, to which is added in the rainy season corn, pumpkins, beans, and potatoes. In southeastern Africa caries was found to be rampant among groups of natives of Bantu descent. Here the staple foods were mealies and Kaffir corn, but sugar also was consumed in large quantities in cereals, tea, and coffee, and also eaten alone. One family of 6 members was said to consume 6 pounds of sugar each week. Price,[13] who has made extensive studies of the racial distribution of caries, reported on the disease in Africa. In Kenya, where the natives live largely on milk, blood, and meat, he found among 88 persons (2,516 teeth) only 4 with caries (10 teeth); and among 19 boys (546 teeth) only 1 with caries (2 teeth). An additional group of 10 persons revealed no caries. In Uganda, another group of natives with similar food habits had no caries among 37 persons. In the Belgian Congo, on the other hand, Price found that 53 per cent of 77 persons in the Bozora Mission had caries, affecting 7.2 per cent of their teeth. Here corn, beans, sweet potatoes, and bananas were used as food. Le Bourbis[14] also gives evidence that caries may occur at a high rate among African Negroes. He reported on a branch of the Bantu family in Cameroon, in western Africa, among which caries was very active. Their diet consisted largely of carbohydrates, including bananas, sweet potatoes, taro, corn, and sugar cane; meat was rare; fish was more available, eaten raw or obtained dry from traders. Among 2,196 individuals, 64 per cent showed no attrition; of these about two-thirds had caries; 36 per cent had varying degrees of attrition, but five-sixths of these had caries.

[12] *Dental surgery and pathology* (5th ed.; London: Longmans, Green & Co., 1923).

[13] *J. Am. Dent. A.*, 20:1648, 1933; 23:417, 876, 1936; *Dental Cosmos*, 77:841, 1935.

[14] *Rev. de stomatol.*, 30:581, 1928.

These findings suggest that attrition is not always associated with freedom from caries.

The statistics that are available in the United States likewise show on an average a much lower incidence of dental caries in colored people. The largest group of statistics bearing out this statement was that produced by a dental survey of school children aged six to fourteen years, made in 1933–34 in 26 states, under the supervision of the United States Public Health Service. The survey included 1,356,433 white children and 81,883 colored children. The incidence of gingivitis, caries, malocclusion, and the amount of indicated or already performed dental treatment were determined. The voluminous data is not presented so that a comparison of the entire number of each race can be made, but in counties where there are both white and colored the percentage incidence of each condition in each race can be compared. On a whole it can be said that, while there are large variations from place to place in the rates of each condition for each race, the incidence of caries in the colored children is remarkably uniformly lower than in the white children. On the other hand, gingivitis appears to be in excess among colored children. It seems that malocclusion occurs with only slight differences between the two races.

Blackerby[15] finds that dental health conditions among Negro children in rural and semirural communities of Tennessee are generally better than those of white children of the same or similar communities. His examination of 1,117 colored and 11,674 white children showed that 80.2 per cent of the latter and 67.5 per cent of the former needed dental care. The average number of dental defects for each examined child was found to be 4.16 among the white children and only 2.29 among the Negroes. If the comparison is limited to defective children only, the racial difference in average number of defects per defective child is still marked, the average being 5.18 for the whites and 3.39 for the colored. The differences in the races are most pronounced

15 J. Am. Dent. A., 26:1574, 1939.

in the ages six to fourteen years and tend to become less marked with increasing age.

Banting[16] found 6.2 per cent of Negro children and 9.2 per cent of white children in Detroit to have decayed teeth. In Ann Arbor 2.3 per cent of Negro boys and 1.4 per cent of Negro girls had decayed teeth in comparison to 7.7–8.1 per cent of white boys and 6.6–11.7 per cent of white girls. Steggerda and Hill[17] found the incidence of Jamaicans having carious teeth and the percentage of carious teeth in the mouths of these people to be much higher than the same figures for Navajo and Maya Indians but less than those for a community of Dutch people in Holland, Michigan. Mills[18] finds that, while Negro children in all areas show less caries than do the whites, the incidence of the disease among them varies in the same way as it does among the whites. These variations are associated with the distance from the tropics, the distance from the mouth of rivers, the degree of hardness of the drinking water, and the amount of salt used in seasoning food.

An attempt to explain the difference between Negroes and whites in the occurrence among them of caries and related conditions would elicit a discussion of the voluminous literature and multitudinous opinions on the causes of dental disease. Such a review would only show that there is no single theory thus far suggested that will adequately explain all features of tooth decay. The data concerning Negroes are often cited to show the importance of diet, because the fact stands out clearly that those Africans who are free of caries on their native diet will promptly develop it when they either partly or entirely discard their customary food and adopt that of white people. But what element native food contains or does not contain that makes it effective in preventing decay is not known. Vitamins of various kinds, carbohydrates, bacteria of different sorts, minerals, and an as yet unknown substance have figured in the speculations made.

[16] *Dental Cosmos*, 51:310, 1909.

[17] *J. Dent. Research*, 15:233, 1935–36.   [18] *J. Dent. Research*, 16:417, 1937.

Part of the difference between Negroes and whites may be inborn and inheritable, because the food habits of Negroes and whites in the United States are not markedly divergent. These racial differences for dental disease are most pronounced in childhood, when inherited influences are probably most effective. It appears that by the time adult life is attained, the racial differences in the incidence of dental disease have disappeared, probably because both races have by then been subjected to the pernicious influences of modern diets and the inherited protection of Negroes has been overcome.

AUTHOR INDEX

Abbatucci, 107, 363
Abbott, 286
Abel, 39
Abramavich, 88
Abreu, d', 355
Adachi, 40, 49, 54, 93
Adair, 343
Adams (C. C.), 91
Adams (J. M.), 292, 308
Adler, 347
Affleck, 343
Ahmann, 231, 234, 235, 236, 239, 240
Aitken, 95
Alarcón, 147
Alden, 237
Aldinger, 322
Alexander, 378, 379
Aley, 190
Allen (E. H.), 128
Allen (F. J.), 105
Allen (F. P.), 290
Almeida, de, 96
Alsobrook, 329
Alves, 224
Ambler, 380
Amdur, 276
Anderson (D. D.), 150
Anderson (E.), 62
Anderson (G. V.), 363
Anderson (W. W.), 236, 237, 238, 239, 242, 248
Andes (J. E.), 91
André, 177
Andree, 93
Andrews (G. C.), 376
Andrews (G. R.), 381
Andrews (H. S.), 252
Annecke, 193
Anspach, 329

Appelmans, 351
Archibald, 230, 232
Arena, 242
Aristotle, 47
Armstrong, 262
Arnsmont, 348
Aron, 57
Aronson, 125, 126
Ashford, 193
Ashhurst, 356
Ashman, 297
Ashmead, 49
Assali, 357
Asserson, 124
Atkinson, 162, 164
Auerbach, 144
Augustin, 211, 213
Augustine, 255, 256
Aunoy, d', 189, 190, 321, 389, 390
Austregesilo, 280

Bacon, 336, 340
Baelz, 49
Baetz, 163
Bahrawy, 49, 50
Bailey, 271
Bainbridge, 310
Baird, 242
Balfour, 194
Ballard, 138
Balloch, 330, 331
Bancroft, 248
Bannister, 273
Banting, 406
Barlow, 74
Barnard, 127
Barnes (F. M.), 273
Barnes (H. D.), 312
Barnes (I.), 45, 46, 47, 48

409

Barney, 345
Bauer (J.), 246
Bauer (J. H.), 212, 213
Bauer (J. T.), 343
Baurvens, 95
Baynham, 260
Bayon, 357, 358
Beacham, 320
Bean, 24, 25, 75, 76, 78, 79, 80
Beatty, 139
Beaudisnet, 89, 253
Bechet, 376
Beck, 235
Becker, 40, 54
Beeuwkes, 213
Beh, 396
Beiglemann, 397
Belding, 157
Bell, 356
Belt (E. O.), 395
Belt (T. H.), 213
Benedict, 96
Bercovitz, 176
Bergsma, 310
Berman (C.), 351, 352, 353
Berman (L.), 25
Bernstein (F.), 83, 84
Bernstein (M.), 66
Bernstein (R. E.), 265
Bevis, 273
Beyers, 309
Bianchi, 177
Bibb, 231, 234, 235, 236, 239, 240
Binford, 74
Bishop, 343
Blache, 189, 190
Black, 201
Blackaby, 301
Blackerby, 405
Blacklock, 324
Blake, 217
Bleyer, 278
Bloch (B.), 39
Bloch (R. G.), 128, 138

Bloom, 168, 378
Boas, 277
Bötticher, 209
Bogen, 138
Bohrod, 333, 334
Bokus, 357
Boland, 308, 310, 357, 358, 359, 361
Bolk, 25
Bonnet-Lyon, 54
Bordley, 395
Borman, 209
Borrel, 106, 107, 113, 115
Bosselman, 276
Bowcock, 283, 284
Boyce, 325
Bradford, 329
Bradley, 278
Brailey, 127
Bram, 324
Branche, 181
Brandau, 235, 241, 248
Branden, van den, 104, 351
Brandt, 189
Brault, 54
Brennemann, 49, 50
Briffault, 333
Broca, 30, 36
Brock (B. G.), 168
Brock (B. L.), 134, 138, 139
Brodnax, 36
Brousseau, 27
Brown, 294
Browne, 65
Browning, 2
Bruck, 86
Bruen, 209
Bruenn, 295
Brumfield, 157, 158
Bruns, 395
Brunstig, 35
Bryant, 128
Bryce, 74
Buck, 251
Bullock, 250

Bullowa, 203
Bunting, 239
Burch, 296
Burhans, 92
Buri, 172
Burke, 213
Burnett, 394
Burns, 320, 321
Burpee, 276, 359
Burr, 172
Burrows, 105, 115
Bushnell, 100, 108, 146
Butler (C. S.), 184, 185
Butler (V. W.), 331
Butterworth, 343
Butts, 389

Cain, 108
Caldwell, 365
Calmette, 104
Cameron, 69, 227
Campbell, 117, 238, 240, 251
Cardoza, 231, 232, 235, 237, 238, 248, 280
Carley, 194
Carman, 263
Carr, 227, 228
Carter (B.), 390
Carter (H. G.), 138
Carter (H. R.), 163, 166, 210, 212, 213
Cary, 317
Cason, 179
Casper, 136, 141, 142, 144, 146, 148
Castana, 230, 231
Castay, 108
Castellani, 374, 375, 376
Castor, 54, 75
Cauchi, 200, 209
Chadwick, 139
Chandler, 255
Chang, 396
Chason, 201
Chatard, 206, 207
Chen, 97
Chesney, 160

Chesterman, 191
Ching, 237, 238, 240, 243, 247
Chudzinski, 74, 75, 76
Cippes, 139
Cipra, 323
Clark (E.), 58
Clark (G. C.), 319
Clark (H. C.), 194, 309, 314
Clark (T.), 149, 158, 163, 167, 168, 170, 171, 173, 181
Clarke (C.), 301
Clarke (F.), 231
Clarke (R.), 378
Clements, 396
Clemow, 199
Clevers, 104
Cloistre, 324
Cluver (E. H.), 225
Cochrane, 101, 105
Cockayne, 385
Cohen (F.), 322
Cohen (J.), 329
Cohn (I.), 324, 345
Cole, 163, 168, 170, 171, 181, 189, 313, 389
Colyer, 404
Combes, 54
Connell (W. J.), 309, 358
Connolly, 70
Cook, 209
Cook (W. C.), 242, 278
Cooke (J. V.), 174, 175, 180, 231, 233
Cooley, 229, 230, 232, 234, 235, 236, 237, 239, 242
Copher, 313
Coplan, 316, 317
Corkhill, 261, 263
Corlett, 373
Cornell (B. S.), 228
Cornely, 128, 207, 208
Cornia, 190
Corrigan, 238
Cort, 256
Costa, da, 313, 319, 397
Cozenanette, 198

Crabtree, 126
Crafts, 96
Crandall, 251
Crichton, 209
Crocker, 225
Crombie, 224
Crooks, 396
Crookshank, 277, 278
Crouch, 221
Crouzon, 54
Crum, 201, 216
Culivick, 265
Cummer, 377
Cummings, 347
Cummins (H.), 360
Cummins (S. L.), 100, 106, 109, 114
Cunningham, 71
Curtis, 328
Cushing, 328, 329
Cusset, 357
Cutler, 139

Dade, 374
Däubler, 58
Danforth, 74
Davenport, 31, 33, 34, 36, 37, 38, 42, 43,
    44, 45, 46, 47, 48, 62, 73, 272, 277, 359
Davidson, 167
Davis (D.), 299
Davis (J. S.), 360
Davis (W. S.), 39
Davison, 179, 208, 291, 295
Day, 319
Deadman, 174
Deaver, 345
Demuth, 277
Deniker, 23
Denney, 197
Dennison, 180
Derbes, 320
Des Ligneris, 347, 352, 353
De Wolf, 189
Deycke, 147
Diamond, 241

Diasio, 375
Dickson, 343
Dienst, 390
Diggs, 231, 234, 235, 236, 237, 238, 239,
    240, 243, 244, 246, 247, 249
Dill, 92
Dixon, 25
Dolgopol, 139, 235, 237
Donadio, 104
Donnelly, 122, 139
Donnison, 300
Dorno, 35
Doull, 202
Dowdeswell, 224
Dowling, 195
Dresbach, 232
Drolet, 124
Dublin, 4, 7, 12, 206, 219, 285, 287, 289,
    335, 338
Dubois (A.), 301, 351
Dubois (W. E. B.), 3, 80
Duckworth, 77
Ducuroir, 351
Dudgeon, 301
Duff, 209
Duke, 223, 224, 225
Dumas, 107
Dumont, 261
Dunbar, 398
Dunlap, 278
Dunn, 296
Duntley, 36, 40
Duperron, 360
Durieux, 104
Duval, 374
Dyer (I.), 377
Dyer (R. E.), 208
Dyke, 265

Eagle, 309
Eastland, 237
Eckstein, 74
Economo, von, 81
Edwards (E. A.), 36, 40

Edwards (H. R.), 127, 128
Eggeling, 74
Ehrenfried, 356
Eisenhardt, 328, 329
Ellis (F. A.), 381
Ellis (H.), 93
Ellis (M.), 312, 354, 355
Elmes, 350, 381
Emerson, 254
Enzer, 310
Epstein, 136
Erasmus, 358
Eschner, 280
Esquier, 334
Evans (F. A.), 227, 228
Evans (F. D.), 231, 233
Evans (L. S.), 145
Evans (V. L.), 261
Evans (W.), 54
Everett, 142, 143
Ewing, 343
Eykmann, 57

Fabyan, 207
Fales, 202
Feder, 328
Fenner, 210
Ferguson, 355
Fernandez, 305
Ferris, 145
Fildes, 250
Finger, 166
Finnerud, 342
Fischer (O.), 209
Fischer (W.), 87, 199
Fischer (W. O.), 349, 352
Fishbein, 370
Fishberg, 112
Fisher, 139, 144
Fitts, 344
Fitzgerald, 87
Flahiff, 132
Flaxman, 296, 297
Fletcher, 305

Fleure, 63
Flippin, 145
Fong, 181
Fornara, 104
Fort, 77
Foster, 96, 174
Fox (F. W.), 265, 318
Fox (H.), 164, 166, 184, 185, 186, 333, 341,
    371, 373, 376, 377, 383, 388, 389, 390,
    391, 392
Francine, 172
Francis, 221
Frank, 307
Franklin, 238
Frazier, 162
Freeman, 217, 391
Freer, 58
Frei, 188, 190
Freilich, 145
Friedlander, 227
Friedman, 378
Friel, 403
Frobisher, 213
Frost, 219
Futcher (P. H.), 37
Futcher (T. B.), 254

Gage, 358
Gager, 296
Gaines, 139
Galloway, 390
Galton, 60
Garnier, 315
Garrison, 260, 262
Garth, 396
Garzon, 388
Gass, 127
Gauld, 127
Geiger, 291
Gemmil, 300
Gerad, 348
Gesell, 278, 279
Giacomini, 74
Giglioli, 224
Gilchrist, 164, 342, 376

Gillan, 263
Gillespie (A. M.), 209
Gillespie (E. B.), 230, 237, 247
Gillman, 309, 311, 352, 353 ·
Glaser, 179
Gleick, 223
Godfrey, 50
Goez, 252
Goldberger, 322
Goldblatt, 189
Goldmann; 398
Goldsmith, 94
Gordon (A.), 145
Gordon (F. B.), 222
Gordon (H. L.), 81, 160, 161, 275
Gordon (M. S.), 312
Gordon (R. M.), 256
Gorgas, 110, 204
Gortner, 39
Gotcher, 390
Gougerot, 178
Gould, 313
Gover, 15, 208, 288, 336, 338, 345
Graham, 230, 235, 313
Grand, 360
Grasset, 199
Gravellat, 108
Graves (G. O.), 145
Graves (S.), 328
Gray, 189, 190, 191
Greely, 305
Green, 266, 267, 269, 273
Greenblatt, 390
Greene, 330
Gregory, 399
Griffith, 252
Grigorjewa, 88
Grimm, 262
Grindon, 390
Grinnon, 241
Groen, 252
Grosse, 334
Grove, 86
Grun, 74

Günther, 93
Guild, 139
Guillot, 348
Guthrie, 237

Haam, von, 189, 389, 390
Hadlock, 250, 251
Hahn, 229, 237, 240, 247
Haines, 344
Hale, 356
Hall (A. D.), 261
Hall (D. G.), 301
Hall (F. G.), 92
Hamil, 254 ·
Hamilton, 380
Hamman, 238
Hammarsten, 93
Hanking, 344
Hansmann, 237
Harding, 344
Hargan, 224
Hargrove, 237
Harley, 187
Harmon, 220, 222
Harper, 328
Harrell, 91, 140
Harris (E. W.), 324
Harris (J. A.), 96
Harris (R.), 389, 390
Harrison (E. F.), 127
Harrison (T. R.), 223
Harvey (A. M.), 253
Harvey (D.), 90
Hassee, 376
Haupt, 396
Hausen-Pruss, 235, 237
Hausman, 67
Hawes, 352
Hawk, 65
Hayden, 231, 233
Hazen, 157, 162, 163, 164, 166, 167, 168,
    179, 181, 333, 341, 342, 371, 372, 374,
    375, 376, 377, 379, 380, 383, 388, 391,
    392
Hecht, 172

Hedley, 179, 291, 296
Hedrick, 214
Heim, 161, 164, 165, 169, 180, 181, 374
Heimann, 179, 180, 300
Heller, 167, 173
Hellman, 399
Henderson (D. L.), 84, 85
Henderson (J. M.), 90
Hennessey, 253, 304
Hepburn, 60
Hermann (A. G. R.), 264
Hermann (C.), 49
Herold, 343
Herrick, 228, 239
Herrmann, 324
Herskovits (F. S.), 334
Herskovits (M. J.), 11, 24, 28, 31, 37, 45, 46, 334
Hertz, 235, 237
Hess, 260, 263, 264
Hetherington (H. W.), 125, 126, 133
Hetherington (J.), 74
Heuer, 356
Hewer, 160, 165, 355, 356
Heyman, 179, 180, 300
Hickerson (V. P.), 126
Hickerson (W. D.), 126
Hieger, 353
Higgins (C. C.), 317, 318
Higgins (J. B.), 237
Hill (L. C.), 95
Hill (T. J.), 406
Hillemand, 108
Hindman, 172, 208
Hines, 294
Hinman, 316
Hinrichsen, 377
Hintze (A.), 30, 34
Hintze (K.), 260
Hirsch, 159, 160, 197, 199, 214, 320
Hirschfeld (H.), 82, 83, 84, 85
Hirschfeld (L.), 82, 83, 84, 85
Hoffman, 6, 199, 316, 345, 351
Hoffmann, 213

Holmes (L. P.), 365, 370
Holmes (R. J.), 316, 317
Holmes (S. J.), 1, 7, 13, 206, 215, 306, 335, 336, 337, 338
Homma, 59
Hoof, van, 104
Hooker, 320
Hopkins (H. H.), 179
Hopkins (R.), 197, 341, 380
Horan, 75
Horgan, 225, 355
Horine, 293
Horwitz, 378, 379
Houseal, 235
Houston, 298
Howard (D. C.), 218
Howard (H. H.), 255, 256
Howard (W. J.), 391
Howard (W. T.), 225
Howells, 209
Howles, 342
Howze, 345
Hrdlička, 38, 69, 72, 73, 400
Hruby, 139
Hubbard, 172
Huck, 236, 237, 240
Hudson, 212, 213, 222
Hueper, 328
Hunter, 157
Huntingdon, 25
Huntoon, 22, 23
Hurt, 189, 190
Hurwitz, 280
Huschke, 78, 79
Hutchins, 380
Hutchinson, 54
Hutton, 252
Hyath, 77
Hyde, 342

Ingalls, 73
Ingram, 301
Irgang, 378, 379
Isaacs, 132

Israel, 134, 138
Ivey, 173
Ivy (A. C.), 377
Ivy (H. I.), 328

Jackson, 330
Jacobi, 145
Jacobs, 268
Jaeger, 93
Jaffe, 145, 238, 292, 293, 308, 313, 314, 315, 319
Jamison, 228
Janeway (C. A.), 253
Janeway (T. C.), 179
Jarman, 343
Jason, 157
Jeans, 174, 175, 180
Jennings, 209
Jessner, 54
Jex-Blake, 301
Jobling, 262
Johnson (C. S.), 1
Johnson (S. F.), 363
Johnston, 341
Johnston (C.), 297
Johnston (H. H.), 1, 359
Jojot, 381
Joly, 316
Jones (C. A.), 188
Jones (C. P.), 390, 395
Jones (E. G.), 167, 323
Jones (T. D.), 179, 287, 290, 291, 295
Jones (W. H. S.), 196
Jordan, 40
Josephs, 235
Joslin, 283, 284
Junge, 209
Justus, 333

Kahle, 320
Kahn, 85, 86, 116
Kampmeier, 91, 227, 242
Kanner, 156
Karg, 40
Karlan, 270

Kartschagin, 36
Keegan, 78, 81
Keen, 307, 313, 319
Kegel, 328
Keith, 25, 61
Kellar, 139
Kelly (F. B.), 206
Kelly (F. C.), 90
Kelly (H. A.), 329
Kerim, 177
Kersten, 104
Kettlekamp, 139
Kilborn, 396
Killingsworth, 231, 232, 235
Kimbrough, 179, 290, 291, 295
King (H.), 380
King (J. C.), 243
King (M. K.), 344
King (R. L.), 145
Kirby-Smith, 376
Kirschner, 177.
Kitchen, 213
Klatz (H. G.), 189
Klatz (O.), 213
Klauder, 238, 343, 376
Kleine, 199
Klob, 330
Kneberg, 66, 67
Knighton, 343
Knowles, 374
Knowlton, 255
Kollman, 60
Kollock, 394
Koppel, 190
Korb, 231, 235, 239
Kraines, 276
Kreidel, 235, 237, 238, 243
Kroo, 199
Krzysztalowicy, 334
Kully, 398
Kuppisch, 143

Lacerda, da, 272
Laigret, 381

Lamb (A. R.), 179
Lamb (D. S.), 73
Lambert, 74
Lambin, 232
Lambkin, 161, 165, 168
Landis, 125, 126, 133
Landon, 247
Landouzy-Déjérine, 280
Landsteiner, 85, 86, 87, 88, 166, 237
Langdon-Down, 277
Lange, de, 315
Langsam, 296, 297
Lanier, 71
Larsen, 50
Lash, 244
Lasnet, 107
Lassman, 254
Laurens, 95
Lavinder, 262
Lawrence, 230, 232
Laws, 179, 290, 295
Leahman, 325
Le Bourbis, 404
Leche, 320
Ledentu, 349
Le Double, 74
Lee (H.), 190
Lee (P.), 229, 230, 232, 234, 235, 236, 237, 239
Leighton, 345
Leipoldt, 352
Lemann, 145, 157, 158, 173, 282, 284
Lennette, 222
Leopold, 283, 284
Leto, 232
Levaditi, 176
Levin, 388
Levine (M. I.), 140
Levine (P.), 85, 86
Levine (S. A.), 223
Levine (W.), 171
Levy, 235, 248, 295, 330, 366
Lewald, 241
Lewin (P.), 356

Lewin (W.), 225
Lewis, 84, 85
Lewisohn, 145
Leyden, von, 172
Lhamon, 58
Libman, 299
Lillie, 179
Lind, 273
Lindberg, 129
Ling, 179
Linton, 333
Livingstone, 159
Lloyd (J. H.), 172
Lloyd (W.), 213
Locchi, 74
Loewenthal, 95, 370, 371, 373, 374, 380, 381, 383, 384, 386, 388, 392
Lofton, 162, 305
Logie, 126
Long, 105, 144, 146, 147, 148, 151
Longcope, 144, 228
Loon, van, 177
Lortat-Jacob, 54
Losli, 345
Loth, 74
Lotka, 7, 206, 219, 285
Love, 218
Lowe, 254, 281
Lucke, 172
Ludlow, 314
Lumsden, 121
Lutrario, 177
Lya, 88
Lyon, 70

Maas, 379
McArthur, 160, 161, 162, 168, 169
McBatts, 74
McCaffrey, 129, 130
McCain, 129
McCarrison, 310
McCarthy, 360
McCarty, 230, 235
McConnell, 172

McCord (J. R.), 367
McCord (W. M.) 92
McCoy, 345
McCrae, 179, 207
McFarland, 345
McFetridge, 325, 345
McFie, 301
McIntosh, 319
Mack, 231, 233
McKenzie, 220
McKie, 266
McKinley, 215, 222
McLean, 381
McLeod, 96
McNally, 387
McNeal, 260, 262
McNeill, 167
McPhedran, 125, 126, 131, 133, 134
McVicar, 352
Macy, 254
Maes, 325, 345
Magalpaes, 360
Mahaffey, 213
Mahorner, 356
Mall, 74, 79, 80
Mallia, 342, 343
Mallori, 238, 242
Maloney, 172
Maly, 62
Malzberg, 268, 269, 273, 274
Mandl, 178
Manoiloff, 88
Manson-Bahr, 213, 224, 390
Manteufel, 104
Marchand (A.), 276
Marchand (L.), 362
Marchoux, 211
Marine, 323
Markoe, 139
Marshall, 87
Marten, 34
Martin (C. F.), 189, 190
Martin (C. J.), 95
Martland, 179

Mason, 237
Matas, 305, 319, 329, 334, 343, 360
Mathis, 104
Matiegka, 62
Matthews (H. O.), 227
Matthews (R. J.), 105, 115
Matthews (W. R.), 237
Matthewson, 190
Maxcy, 157, 158
Mayer, 208
Maynard, 265
Mays, 266
Means, 323, 324
Meillon, de, 193
Memmesheimer, 34
Menage, 343
Merzbacher, 177
Metta, de, 389
Mettler, 276
Meyer, 330
Michael, 375
Michel, 74, 397
Miescher, 95
Miles, 396
Milian, 54
Miller (A. J.), 252
Miller (C. J.), 329, 330, 367, 368
Miller (C. P.), 87
Miller (G. S.), 23
Miller (K.), 5
Miller (M. B.), 328
Mills, 294, 306
Miskjian, 389
Mitchell (A. G.), 278
Mitchell (J. P.), 362
Mitchell (W.), 299, 314
Miyamoto, 231, 235, 239
Mohr, 62
Monash, 51, 53, 54, 55, 57
Monglond, 89
Montagne, 252
Montpelier, 54
Moon, 75
Moore (A. T.), 74

Moore (J. E.), 139, 163, 168, 170, 171, 176, 181
Moore (S.), 241, 313
Moreau, 107
Morgan, 174
Moriarty, 70
Morison, 161, 373, 374, 377, 392
Moritz, 293, 300
Mosher, 313
Mouchet, 104, 348
Moulin, 209
Müller, 104
Mulherin, 235
Mulholland, 145
Munday, 254
Murphy, 139
Murray (A.), 391
Murray (P. M.), 368
Musser, 206, 207, 384
Mustard, 323
Myers, 253

Nägelsbach, 178
Nash, 139
Needles, 177
Nelson, 139
Nesbit, 208
Nettleship, 384
Newman (B.), 378
Newman (H. W.), 252
Nicholson, 343
Niles, 98
Noel, 376
Nomland, 144
Noriskin, 403
Norris, 252

Ochs, 56, 376
Ochsner, 358
Odegaard, 274
Oldt, 293, 300
O'Leary, 163, 168, 170, 171, 181
Oleson, 322, 323
Oliver, 387
O'Malley, 266, 270, 273

Opie, 125, 126, 130, 131, 132, 133, 134, 143, 145, 146
Opie (E. L.), 217
Oppenheimer, 93
Oranje, 403
Ornstein, 134, 136
Osborn, 403
Osler, 179, 282, 299
Ossenfort, 71
Ottenberg, 82, 83, 84
Owing, 330

Pachman, 251
Pack, 343
Padgett, 139
Page, 6
Paisseau, 108
Pales, 89, 357
Pardo-Costello, 185, 381
Parker (A. J.), 80
Parker (S.), 396
Parker (S. L.), 7
Parounagian, 374
Parran, 163, 168, 170, 171, 181
Parson, 300
Parsons, 47
Paskind, 97
Pasternack, 179
Path, 97
Patterson, 247
Patton, 98
Paullin, 167
Paulsen, 25
Paulson, 191
Pautrier, 334
Payne, 134, 138
Pearce, 172
Pearl, 336, 340
Pearson, 41, 42, 47, 280, 384, 386
Peaslee, 330
Peckham, 366
Peery, 296, 297
Peiper, 104
Penrose (C. B.), 330

Penrose (L. S.), 385
Perret-Gentil, 200
Petersen, 262, 346
Peterson, 173
Pevaroff, 208
Pfuhl, 25
Phehn, 305
Phillips, 213
Pijper, 85, 96, 225
Pincus, 231, 232
Pinner, 134, 136, 141, 142, 144, 146, 148, 150
Pirie, 352
Planta, von, 396
Plazy, 349
Pöch, 74
Polak, 294
Poliakowa, 88
Pollock, 172, 274
Pool, 99, 325, 326
Poole, 254
Porter, 325
Powell (A.), 333
Powell (T. O.), 266
Poynter, 78, 81
Prates, 352
Preston, 363
Price (A. E.), 253
Price (W. A.), 404
Pride, 367
Prieur, 315
Prudhomme, 272
Pruett, 70
Pruner-Bey, 65
Puffer, 208
Pullman, 243
Pund, 390
Puntigam, 178
Pyle, 71

Quinland, 343, 345, 358

Racquet, 87
Ragins, 145

Raiford, 254
Ram, 349
Rambar, 278
Randall, 319
Rauschkolb, 389
Ray (H. H.), 356
Ray (J. M.), 394
Reason, 316
Reasoner, 162
Reece, 262
Reiche, 54
Reichenbach, 305
Reiman, 202
Remy, 209
Reyburn, 118
Rich, 244
Richter, 178
Ridgway, 33
Riggs, 363, 364
Riley, 256
Rippy, 2
Rivers (A. B.), 308, 311
Rivers (T. M.), 217
Rivoalen, 252
Roberts (J. R.), 309, 385
Roberts (M. H.), 356
Roberts (S. R.), 298
Robertson (H. F.), 145
Robertson (J. D.), 219
Robertson (S.), 66
Robertson (T. L.), 37
Robinow, 276
Robinson (H. M.), 189
Robinson (S.), 92
Robinson (S. C.), 307, 311
Rodgers, 139
Rodman, 307, 313, 324, 345
Rodriquez-Pastor, 143
Rogers, 134, 143
Rokitansky, 346
Rolfe, 2
Rolleston, 54
Rollin, 397
Rome, 188

Root, 221
Rose, 312
Rosenberg, 177
Rosenfeld, 231, 232
Rosenthal, 343
Ross (R.), 196
Ross (S.), 265
Rosser, 190, 306, 329
Roth, 137, 149
Roubier, 107
Routil, 397
Roy (J. N.), 393, 394, 398
Roy (P. S.), 223
Royster, 70
Ruelle, 360
Rufz, 373, 377
Rush, 117
Russell (H.), 237
Russell (J. H.), 3
Russell (W. K.), 95
Rutherford, 65
Ryerson, 238

Săbăreanu, 54
Sala, 145
Săleeby, 360
Salimbeni, 211
Sampson, 172
Sanderson, 390
Santo, 148
Sarasin, 64
Sasaki, 85
Sasano, 139
Saunders, 185
Sava, 348
Sawyer, 213
Schapiro (A), 88
Schapiro (L.), 256
Schenken, 190, 321
Schepegrell, 397
Scheult, 145, 314
Schiefferdecker, 58, 59
Schiff, 85
Schilder, 396

Schiller, 238
Schiller-Tietz, 36
Schilling, 232
Schlaginhaufen, 60
Schmidt, 57
Schminke, 148
Schnabel, 248
Schnitzer, 253
Schokking, 62
Schriver, 237
Schroedter, 165
Schüffner, 193
Schultz (A.), 145
Schultz (A. H.), 70, 74, 399
Schultze, 34
Schulze, 179, 290, 291, 293, 295, 298
Schurmeier, 360
Schwab, 179, 290, 291, 293, 295, 298
Schwartz (K.), 178
Schwartz (L.), 382, 387
Schwartz (L. S.), 238
Schwarzbach, 393
Schwertz, 399
Scott (E.), 145
Scott (H. H.), 263
Scott (J. F.), 389
Scott (L. C.), 264
Scott (R. B.), 279, 356
Scull, 391
Seale, 375
Seib, 74
Sellards, 213
Sequira, 349
Sézary, 176
Shabad, 353
Shapiro, 308
Sharp, 263
Shattuck, 222
Shaughnessy, 222
Shaw, 403
Shearburn, 325
Sheard, 35
Shelley, 275
Shelmire, 342

Shepherd, 254
Shivers, 345
Shore, 71
Sibley, 54
Sicomo, 360
Sights, 231, 233
Siler, 260, 262
Silva Lima, da, 378, 379
Simington, 139
Simon, 231, 233
Simond, 211
Simonot, 36
Simonton, 70
Singer, 239
Sklarek, 63, 381
Small, 217
Smillie, 255, 256·
Smith (C. A.), 300
Smith (D. C.), 179
Smith (D. N.), 92
Smith (E. C.), 200, 235, 237, 350, 351, 381
Smith (G. H.), 87
Smith (H. H.), 132, 133
Smith (K. J.), 319
Smith (O. N.), 145
Smythe (A. G.), 77
Smythe (M. G.), 208
Snyder, 83, 84
Sockrider, 208
Solente, 54
Sonne, 35
Soper, 213
Spencer, 265
Spiegler, 39
Spitzer, 333
Spitzka, 79, 80
Staley, 190
Stannus, 168, 188, 191, 262, 263, 384, 386, 388
Staub, 104
Staz, 401, 402, 403
Steffan, 83
Steggerda, 96, 406
Steigman, 307, 308, 311

Steinberg, 229, 236
Steiner (L.), 333
Steiner (W. R.), 251
Steinfeld, 238
Stelling, 276
Stelwagon, 164
Stewart (H. C.), 127
Stewart (W. B.), 230, 232, 233
Stickley, 181
Stitt, 139, 235, 237
Stockard, 24, 25
Stoddard, 14
Stokes, 163, 165, 168, 170, 171, 181, 212
Stoll, 256
Stone (C. T.), 179, 290, 291, 295
Stone (W.), 88, 265
Stones, 263, 301
Storck, 307
Stout, 380
Stowe, 14
Strachan, 180, 300, 351, 352
Straus, 71
Strauss, 376
Strong, 222
Studdiford, 341, 380
Sturtevant, 308
Suarers, 209
Suk, 400
Sullivan, 399
Sulzberger, 62, 168, 189
Surmont, 348
Sutton, 342, 343, 390
Sweet (L. K.), 277
Sweet (W. C.), 256
Swellengrebel, 193
Sydenstricker, 122, 231, 234, 235, 237, 238, 240, 242, 243, 247, 248, 262
Symmers, 155

Taliaferro, 192
Tally, 252
Tandy, 17
Tarayre, 161
Tauber, 342

Taylor (C. J. S. O.), 237
Taylor (T. G.), 25
Teague, 87
Templeton, 56
Terplan, 238
Terry, 71, 73
Testa, 396
Testut, 74
Theiler, 212, 213
Thibaut, 349
Thiroux, 370
Thomas (B. A.), 345
Thomas (E. A.), 74
Thomas (J. T.), 139
Thomas (W. L.), 390
Thompson (J. W.), 74
Thompson (L. O.), 161
Thompson (W. H.), 279
Thompson (W. S.), 6, 8, 12, 13
Thonnard-Neumann, 301
Thornton, 162
Thoroughman, 179, 291, 295
Tiffany, 341
Tildon, 179
Todd, 33, 34, 37, 38, 45, 68, 69, 70, 7 1, 72
Topinard, 30
Torpin, 189, 365
Torrence, 248
Traband, 107
Tracy, 69
Traut, 227
Trotter, 65, 66, 67, 71, 72, 73
Trowell, 253, 263
Trumpe, 139
Trumpeer, 277
Tucker (B. R.), 259
Tucker (W. B.), 128
Tulipan, 382
Tunick, 378, 379
Turner (G. A.), 265
Turner (K. B.), 295
Turner (T. B.), 162, 163, 167, 168, 169, 170, 171, 173, 176, 185, 186
Turner (W.), 74

Turnipseed, 77
Turpin, 390
Twine, 179

Ullery,
Ulnar, 136
Unger, 260
Usher, 384
Usilton, 158, 163, 168, 170, 171, 181

Van Cleve, 189
Vanderlehr, 158, 167, 173, 181
Vander Veer, 190
Van Gorder, 33, 34, 37
Van Milligen, 395
Vanzant, 179, 290, 291, 295
Vassalo, 310
Veal, 359
Vedder, 260
Vermooten, 317, 318
Verner, 27
Villaverde, 209
Vint, 81, 90, 96, 97, 310, 349, 353
Virchow, 74
Vogt, 241
Voorhies, 296
Vos Hug, 162

Wagner, 268, 271, 273, 274
Walker (H.), 325
Walker (K. M.), 265
Walker (P. H.), 321
Wallace, 231, 232, 235
Walraven, 397
Walsh, 99, 181, 325, 326
Ware, 236, 237, 238, 239, 242, 248
Waring, 323
Warren, 313, 387
Warring, 139
Warthin, 284
Washington, 6
Watkins, 220, 352
Watson, 275
Waugh, 237
Weatherford, 1

Weaver, 361
Webster, 323
Weidmann, 343, 388
Weiner (J. S.), 265
Weiner (L.), 122
Weiss, 293, 297, 299, 356
Weller, 186
Wellisch, 83
Wellman, 379
Wells (A. S.), 363
Wells (C. W.), 132, 133, 143
Wells (L. H.), 74
Welty, 145
Wender, 172
Wenger, 167, 173
West, 145
Westmoreland, 328
Westphal, 396
Whayne, 74
Wheeler (G. A.), 259
Wheeler (P.), 189, 190
Whelpton, 6, 7, 8, 12, 13, 15
Whipple, 260
White (P. D.), 287, 294
White (W. H.), 334
Whitman, 213
Whitney (C.), 71
Whitney (J. S.), 122, 129, 130
Wiener, 88
Wieser, 394
Wilcocks, 105, 115
Wilder, 61
Wile, 163, 168, 170, 171, 181
Willcox, 5, 6, 7
Williams (C. D.), 263
Williams (D. H.), 305
Williams (G. D.), 36, 74
Williams (J. R.), 92

Williams (J. W.), 363, 364
Williams (W. C.), 127
Willis (T.), 253
Willis (T. A.), 71
Willson, 27, 228
Wilson (D. B.), 193
Wilson (J. W.), 92
Wilson (M. E.), 193
Wilson (U. F.), 284
Wimp, 74
Wise, 62, 63, 168, 189, 376
Witherspoon, 331, 332
Wolf, 334
Wollstein, 235, 237, 238, 243
Wood (J. E.), 179, 290, 291, 295
Wood (R. H.), 167
Wood (W. B.), 253
Woodson, 1
Woofter, 5, 6, 7
Wooley, 333
Woringer, 334
Wright (A.), 205
Wright (C. S.), 374
Wright (R. R.), 2
Wyckoff, 179

Yampolsky, 181
Yandell, 341
Yater, 238, 242, 300
Yates, 237
Youmans, 265, 323

Zeisler, 161, 162
Ziemann, 63, 104, 373, 374, 377, 381
Zilboorg, 272, 273
Zimmermann, 161, 162, 163, 164, 165, 166, 167, 168, 172
Zingher, 202
Zschucke, 254, 265

SUBJECT INDEX

Abdominal crises in sickle cell anemia, 240–41
Abnormal pelves, 362–63, 364–67
Abolition of slavery, 3–4
Acne vulgaris, 377
Acute empyema, 358–59
Acute infectious diseases, 199–226
Acute intestinal obstruction, 357
Acute poliomyelitis, 219–23
Adamantinoma, 328
Adaptive features
  of anatomy, 18–19
  of the nostrils, 96
  of the skin, 26
Addison's disease, 145
Age changes in pigmentation, 36–37
Age composition of the population, 8–9
Agranulocytosis, 252
Ainhum, 378–79
Albinism, 384–86
Alcaptonuria, 286
Alcohol, toxicity of, 98
Allelomorphs
  for isohemagglutinins, 83
  for pigmentation, 43–45
  for sacral pigment spots, 51
Anatomy, 18–81
  adaptive features of, 18–19
  association of, with disease, 18
  body forms, 19–22
  external features of, 19–41
  internal organs, 75–77
  muscular system, 73–74
  sex organs, 76–77
  skeleton, 68–81
Anemia
  hemolytic, 252–53
  pernicious, 227–28
Aneurysm, 144, 179, 301
Angina pectoris, 294–99
Ankylostomiasis, 255–57

Anomalies of muscles, 73–74
Antigens in typhoid fever, 225
Apocrine sweat glands, 58–60
Appendicitis, 357–58
Appendix, anatomy of, 357–58
Arcus senilis, 396
Arteriosclerotic heart disease; see Heart, diseases of, arteriosclerotic
Athletes, limbs of, 73
Atropin, response to, 97

Bahr el Ghazal, tuberculosis in, 115
Basal metabolism, 96
Benign tumors; see Tumors, benign
Beriberi, 264–65
Biliary calculi, 313–15
Biliary disease, 359
Biochemical characteristics, 82–98
Biochemical index, 82–86
Birth rate, 11–13
Blood
  cells of, 96–97, 139–40, 253, 254
  chemical constituents of, 88–91
  diseases of, 227–54
  sedimentation rate of, 239, 254
"Blue gums," 51
Body
  distribution of pigment in, 37, 343
  forms, 19–22
  odors, race specific, 59, 93
Boeck's sarcoid, 144, 382
Bone
  changes in sickle cell anemia, 241–42, 244–46
  syphilitic lesions of, 162, 163, 164, 165, 167, 168, 169
Brachycephaly, 20
Brain
  anatomy of, 77–81
  frontal lobes of, 79, 80
  gyri of, 81

Brain—*continued*
  sulci of, 81
  tuberculoma of, 145
Breast milk, 92
Breasts, 77

Calculi
  gall-bladder, 313–15
  urinary, 316–18
Cancer, 335–55
Carcinogenic substances, 353
Carcinoma
  of the liver, 351, 352, 353, 354
  of the skin, 341
  of the stomach, 338, 339, 344, 348, 352
Cardioesophageal junction, 311–12
Cardiovascular syphilis, 178–80
Carotin, 40
Carotinemia, 38
Carriers
  diphtheria, 202
  typhoid, 225
Cataract, 395
Cathartic drugs, 97
Census, errors in, 4, 5
Charcot joint, 173
Chemical tests for race, 88
Childbirth, 362, 366
Childhood tuberculosis: *see* Tuberculosis,
  childhood infections in
Cholelithiasis, 313–15
Chondrodysplasia, 356
Clavicle, 71
Cleft foot, 360
Cleft lip and palate, 360
Climate, effects of, 96
Cocaine, response to, 97
Colloid goiter, 322–24
Color
  components of skin pigmentation, 31–34
  standards of pigmentation, 30–31
Color-blindness, 396
Color-top, use in skin-color measurements, 31–34
Condyloma, 163–64

Configuration of palms and soles, 60–61
Consecutive depigmentation, 387–88
Coronary arteries, diseases of, 294–99
Corpus callosum, 79–80
Correlation of hair and skin color, 48
Cortex, histology of, 81

Decennial population increases; *see* Population, decennial increases of
Decline in population increase rates; *see* Population, decline in increase rates of
Deficiency diseases, 258–65
Dental diseases, 399–407
  caries, 401–7
Depigmentation
  consecutive, 387–88
  by monobenzyl ether, 387
  by rubber, 387–88
  by skin bleaches, 41
Dermatosis
  papulosa nigra, 374–76
  venenata, 383
Dermotropic spirochetes, 175–76
Diabetes mellitus, 282–85
Diazo reaction, 92
Diet, 258–61, 262, 310–11, 313, 315, 317–18, 323, 353, 406–7
Diphtheria, 199–202
  carriers, 202
Dolichocephaly, 20
Dolichopododactylism, 360
Donovan bodies, 390–91
Drugs, response to, 97–98

Ear, diseases of, 397–98
Eclampsia, 366
Embryonal hematopoietic persistence, 252
Empyema, 358–59
Environmental factors in tuberculosis, 145, 146, 148, 149
Ephedrine, 97
Epithelioma of the skin, rarity of, 341
Errors in estimating syphilis prevalence, 157–58
Errors in the census, 4–5
Erythroblastosis, 252

Esthiomene, 188, 191

Euphthalmine, 97 .

Evanescent pigmentation, 48

Evisceration, postoperative, 361

Exocrine sweat glands, 58–59

Expectation of life, 15

External body features, 19–41

External skin irritants, 382–83

Extragenital chancre, 161–62

Eye
  diseases of, 393–97
  syphilitic lesions of, 163, 165, 168

Facial features, 20

Fair-skinned Africans, 28

Feet, anatomy of, 73

Female genital organs, 76, 77

Females, excess in the population, 9

Fetal mortality, 366

Fibroids, 329–32

Fibromyomata of the uterus, 329–32

Fingerprints, 60–61

Footprints, 60–61

Fractures, 360–61

Frei test, 188, 189, 190

Frontal lobes of the brain; see Brain, frontal lobes of

Fungi, skin diseases caused by, 392

Fusospirochetal angina, 398

Future populations, estimates of, 6–7

Gall-stones, 313–15

Gametic formulas
  for sacral pigment spots, 51
  for skin color, 43–45

Gastric analyses, 312

General paresis, 171, 172, 173, 174

Genital organs, 76, 77

Genotypes in skin-color inheritance, 43–45

Genotypic low resistance in tuberculosis, 146, 147, 149

Goiter, 322–26
  simple colloid, 322–24
  toxic, 324–26

Granuloma inguinale, 389–91

Growth of the population, 1–4

Gynecology, 367–68

Gyri of the brain; see Brain, gyri of

Hair, 61–68
  at birth, 64
  chemical analysis of, 65
  classification of, 65
  correlation of, with skin color, 48
  follicles, 66
  forms, 61–65
  inheritance of, 48, 61–62
  lanugo, 63
  microscopic shape of, 65–67
  "peppercorn," 21, 64, 65
  straighteners, 67–68

Handprints, 61

Head shapes, 20

Heart
  diseases of, 287–302
  arteriosclerotic, 291
  congenital, 249
  hypertensive, 291
  rheumatic, 299
  syphilitic, 178–80
  thyrotoxic, 299
  normal size of, 76

Heat rays, protection against, 94–95

Hemagglutinins, immune, 86

Hemolytic anemia, 252–53

Hemolytic icterus, congenital, 243

Hemophilia, 250–51

Hereditary multiple cartilaginous exostoses, 356

Hermaphroditism, 360

Hernia, 358

Hodgkin's disease, 351

Hookworm, 255–57

Hormones, 25

"Hottentot apron," 77

Household tuberculosis, 126, 130, 131, 132

Hyperestrinism, 331–32

Hypermorph, 24

Hyperpigmentation, acquired, 388

Hypertension, 292–94

Hypertensive heart disease; see Heart, diseases of, hypertensive

Hypertrophy of the prostate, 319–21

Hypomorph, 24

Icterus, hemolytic congenital, 243
Ilium, 71–72
Immunity
  in hookworm disease, 255–57
  in malaria, 192–95
Increase of pigmentation, congenital, 388
Indians, intermixture with, 28, 29
Infant mortality, 17
Infantile paralysis, 219–23
Infectional diseases, acute, 199–226
Influenza, 217–19
Inheritance
  of albinism, 385–86
  of hair form, 61–62
  of pigmentation, 41–48
  of sacral pigment spots, 50–51
  of sicklemia, 236
Inoculation tuberculosis, 140
Insanity in pellagra, 262
Internal organs, 75–81
  brain, 77–81
  genital, 76–77
  heart, normal size, 76
  intestines, normal length of, 76
  liver, normal size, 76
  spleen, normal size, 75–76
Intestinal obstruction, acute, 357
Intestines, normal length of, 76
Isohemagglutinins, 82–86, 139, 237–38
  abnormal, 86
  among African Negroes, 84
  allelomorphs for, 83
  among American Negroes, 84
  biochemical index of, 82–86
  effect of race intermixture on, 84
  in race classification, 82–86
  secretors of, 85
  in sicklemia, 237–38
  in tuberculosis, 139

Joint, Charcot, 173
Joints
  anatomy of, 73
  crises in sickle cell anemia, 240–41
  syphilitic lesions of, 162, 163, 165, 173

Keloid, 332–35, 382
Keratoses, 379–80
Kidney, diseases of, 303–4

Lanugo, 63
Leg ulcers in sickle cell anemia, 239
Leprosy, 197–98
Leukemia, 252
Leukoderma, secondary, 387–88
Light, trauma from, 383
Limbs, 72, 73
Liver, normal size of, 76
Lobar pneumonia, 202–7
Lupus erythematosis, 376–77
Lymph glands
  syphilitic lesions of, 162, 165, 168
  tuberculosis of, 107, 108, 113, 125, 129,
    141, 142, 147, 151
Lymphogranuloma venereum, 188–91

Malaria, 192–96
  and neurosyphilis, 175–78
  in the treatment of syphilis, 181
Male genital organs, 76–77
Malformations, 359–60
Malignant tumors; see Tumors, malignant
Massive infections in tuberculosis, 109,
  148
Measles, 215–16
Median age, 9
Medical diseases, 99–304
Melanin, 39–40, 343–44
Melanoma, 342–43, 347–48, 350, 355
Mendelian law in skin-color inheritance,
  41, 42, 46, 48
Meninges
  pigmentation of, 81
  syphilitic infection of, 170, 171, 174
Meningioma, 329
Mental diseases, 266–79
  etiology of, 273–75
  incidence of, 266–73, 275–76
  in leprosy, 198
  Mongoloid imbecility, 277–79
  in pellagra, 262
  pupillary changes in, 396–97
  qualitative features of, 273
  suicide and, 272–73
Mental foramen, 70
Mesaticephaly, 20
Mesomorph, 24

Metabolism, basal, 96
Mongolian blue spots, 48
Mongoloid imbecility, 277–79
Monobenzyl ether, action on skin pigment, 387
Mortality
  fetal, 366
  general, 13–17
  infant, 17
Mucous membrane, syphilitic lesions of, 163, 165, 166, 167, 169
Mulattoes, 10, 11, 42, 43
Mulberry-colored spots, 48
Munitions dermatitis, 383
Muscular dystrophy, 280–81
Muscular system
  anatomy of, 73–74
  anomalies of, 73–74

Nails, pigmentation of, 55–57
Natural history of tuberculosis; see Tuberculosis, natural history of
Natural selection in tuberculosis; see Tuberculosis, natural selection in
Neoplasms, 327–55
  benign, 327–35
  malignant, 335–55
Neurosyphilis, 170–78
Neurotrophic spirochetes, 175–76
Night vision, 394
Nose, diseases of, 397
Nostrils, adaptive features of, 96

Obesity and diabetes mellitus, 283–84
Obstetrics, 362–67
Octoroon, 10
Odors, body, 59, 93
Oral mucosa, pigmentation of, 51–55
Origin of the Negro population, 1–4
Orthognathism, 20

Pain, sensitivity to, 299
Palpebral fissure, 397
Parasitic diseases
  of the blood, 253
  of the skin, 391
Pediculosis, 391

Pellagra, 261–63
Pelvic infections, 331–32, 368
Pelvis
  abnormal, 362–67
  anatomy of, 71–72, 362–63
"Peppercorn hair," 21, 64, 65
Peptic ulcer, 307–12
Pernicious anemia, 227–28
Pertussis, 216
Photometry in skin-color measurements, 34–36
Physiological characteristics, 94–98
Piebald Negroes, 385
Pigmentation; see also Skin color
  action against heat rays, 94–95
  action of monobenzyl ether on, 387
  action of rubber on, 387–88
  age changes of, 36–37
  allelomorphs for, 43–45
  of American Negroes, 28
  anomalies of, 383–88
  of Bantus, 27
  at birth, 36–37
  body distribution of, 37, 343
  of Bushmen, 27
  changes of, in skin diseases, 370, 371
  diseases of, 383–88
  effect of, on action of ultraviolet light, 94–96
  effect of, on color of pediculi pubis, 391
  effect of vitamin C on, 388
  of fair-skinned Africans, 28
  gametic formulas for, 43–45
  of Hottentots, 27
  increase of
    acquired, 388
    congenital, 388
  inheritance of, 41–48
  measurements of, 29–38
  of meninges, 81
  of nails, 55–57
  of oral mucosa, 51–55
  protective action of, 94–96, 342
  relation to melanoma, 342, 343, 355
  relation to rickets, 264
  of the skin, 26–29
  of transplanted skin, 40, 41
  variation of, among African Negroes, 27–28
  of West Indian Negroes, 29

Pigments of skin, 38–41
Pilonidal sinus, 360
Pneumonia, 202–7
  and influenza, 217, 218, 219
Polycythemia vera, 254
Polydactylism, 359, 360
Population, 1–11
  age composition of, 8–9
  decennial increases of, 4–6
  decline in increase rates of, 5–6
  errors in the census of, 4–5
  estimates of future, 6–7
  excess of females in, 9
  growth of, 1–4
  median age of, 9
  mulattoes in, 10–11
  origin of, 1–4
  present, 4–7
  sex composition of, 9
  shifts of, 7
  trends of, 4–7
Pott's disease, 108
Prediction before birth of skin color, 46–47
Primary skin lesions, 369–71
Primary syphilitic lesion, 161–62
Primitive tuberculosis, 108
Prognathism, 20
Prostate, hypertrophy of, 319–21
Protective action of pigment; see Pigmentation, protective action of
Psoriasis, 373–74
Psychoneurogenic factors
  in hypertension, 293
  in peptic ulcer, 311
  in pylorospasm, 356–57
  in toxic goiter, 326
Pupil in psychoses, 396–97
Pylorospasm, 356–57

Quadroon, 10, 42

Race
  differentiation, 10, 42, 87, 88
    by chemical means, 88
    by serologic means, 87–88
  intermixture, 9–11, 28–29, 37, 38, 42, 43, 55, 84–85, 228
  degrees of, 10, 11, 42, 43
  effect of, on isohemagglutinins, 84–85

effect of, on pernicious anemia, 228
  general effects of, 10
  with Indians, 28–29
  tests for, 37–38, 55, 87–88
  with whites, 28–29
Racial odors, 59, 92–94,
von Recklinghausen's disease, 356
Rectal stricture, 167–68, 190
Rectum, syphilis of, 167–68
Red blood cells, 96–97, 253–54
Refractive errors, 393, 394, 395
Renal calculi, 316–18
  diseases of, 303–4
Resistant "ectoderm," 370
Respiratory tract, syphilitic lesions of, 167, 168, 169
Response to drugs, 97–98
"Reversion to black," 47
Rhabdomyoma, 328
Rheumatic fever, 223
Rheumatic heart disease, 299
Rickets, 263–64
Rubber, depigmenting action, 387
Rural birth rate, 12, 13

Sacral pigment spots, 48–51
  allelomorphs for, 51
  histology of, 48–50
  inheritance of, 50–51
  location of, 48
  significance of, 49–50
  size of, 48
  time of appearance of, 49
  time of disappearance of, 49
Sacrum, 72
Sarcoidosis, 144, 382
Scabies, 391
Scarlet fever, 207–10
Schick tests, 199, 200, 201
Scurvy, 265
Secondary syphilitic lesions, 162–65
Secretion of isohemagglutinins, 85
Sella turcica, 70
Senegalese, tuberculosis in, 105–9, 115
Sensitivity to pain; see Pain, sensitivity to
Sensitivity to tuberculin; see Tuberculin, sensitivity to

Serologic tests for race, 86–88
Sex composition of the population, 9
Sex organs, 76–77
Sexual significance of keloid, 334
Shape of hair section, 65–67
Shifts of population, 7
Shovel-shaped teeth, 400
Sickle cell anemia, 228–50
  abdominal crises in, 240-41
  active, 230
  anemia in, 238–39
  bone changes in, 241–42, 244-46
  incidence of, 233–34
  joint crises in, 240-41
  latent, 230
  leg ulcers in, 239
  pathology of, 243–47
  red cell sedimentation time in, 239
  relation to sicklemia, 235–36
  resemblance of, to congenital hemolytic
    icterus, 243
  spleen in, 240, 243, 244
  splenectomy in, 247–48
  treatment of, 247–49
  vascular phenomena in, 242, 246
Sicklemia
  isohemagglutinins in, 237-38
  rarity of, in whites, 230–33
  in tuberculosis, 139
Silicosis, 112, 113, 114
Skeleton, 68–73
  clavicle, 71
  feet, 73
  joints, 73
  limbs, 72
  pelvis, 71
  skull, 68–70
  synchondrosis of, 71
  synostosis of, 71
  vertebral column, 70
Skin
  adaptive features of, 26
  anatomy of, 26–41
  and its appendages, 26–41, 369–92
  bleaches, 41
    effect on, 41
  color; see also Pigmentation
    of African Negroes, 27–28
    of American Negroes, 28–29
    changes of, in skin diseases, 370–71

  classification of, 26
  components of, 31–34
  correlation of, with hair texture, 48
  deviation of, from color of parents, 46
  prenatal prediction of, 46
  range among offspring, 46–47
  standards of, 30–31
  tests for race intermixture, 37–38
  variation of, among African Negroes,
    27–28
  vitamin C, influence on, 388
  of West Indian Negroes, 29
  diseases of, 369–92
  functions, 94–96
  irritants, 382–83
  pigments, 38–41
  syphilitic lesions of, 164, 165, 166, 168,
    169
Skull, 68–70
Slave importations, 3–4
Slavery, 1–3
  abolition of, 3
  beginning of, 1–3
  effect of, on death rate, 13–15
  illicit trading during, 3
  prohibition of slave importation dur-
    ing, 3
  relation of, to smallpox, 214
  relation of, to yellow fever, 210
  slave ships during, 14, 210
  total slaves imported during, 4
  tuberculosis during, 117–18
Smallpox, 214–15
South Africa, tuberculosis in; see Tuberculosis, in South Africa
Spanish explorers, 2
Spasmogenic aptitude, 298, 356
Spleen
  normal size of, 75, 76
  in sickle cell anemia, 240, 243, 244, 246,
    247, 248
Splenectomy in sickle cell anemia, 247–
  48
Stature, 19, 20, 21
Steatopygy, 22–24
  among Bushmen, 22, 23
  among Hottentots, 22, 23
  internal secretions and, 23, 24
  among Negritos, 22
  theories concerning, 22–23

Stercoral appendix, 358
Subacute bacterial endocarditis, 299
Suicide, 272–73
Sulci of the brain; *see* Brain, sulci of
Surgical diseases, 305–61
Surgical risks, Negroes as, 305–6
Surveys for tuberculosis
  with tuberculin; *see* Tuberculin, surveys
  with x-ray; *see* Tuberculosis, x-ray surveys for
Surveys for yellow fever; *see* Yellow fever, surveys for
Susceptibility
  to pertussis, 216
  to rickets, 263
  to smallpox, 214
  to tuberculosis, 141–51
Suture closure, 70
Sweat glands, 57–60
Synchondrosis, 71
Syndactylism, 360
Synostosis, 71
Syphilis, 155–83
  cardiovascular, 178–80
  congenital, 174–75, 180
  diminishing severity of, 155
  errors in estimating prevalence of, 157–58
  extragenital chancre in, 161–62
  introduction into Africa of, 155–56
  latent, 169–70
  prevalence of, 156–61
  primary lesion in, 161–62
  respiratory tract, lesions in, 167, 168, 169
  secondary lesions in, 162–65
  tertiary lesions in 165–69
  treatment, 180–81
Syphilitic heart disease; *see* Heart, diseases of, syphilitic
Syphilitic meningitis; *see* Meninges, syphilitic infection of

Tabes dorsalis, 171, 172, 173, 174
Tanganyika, tuberculosis in, 115
Teeth, 399–407
Tertiary syphilitic lesions, 165–69

Tests for race, 88
Tests for race intermixture, 37–38, 55
Throat, diseases of, 397–98
Thromboangiitis obliterans, 299-300
Thyroid, diseases of, 322–26
Thyroidectomy, 325
Thyrotoxic heart disease; *see* Heart, diseases of, thyrotoxic
Thyrotoxicosis, 324–26
Tongue, pigmentation of, 52–53
Toxemias of pregnancy, 366–67
Toxic goiter, 324–26
Trachoma, 395–96
Transplanted skin, pigmentation of, 40–41
Trauma from light, 383
Trends of the population, 4–7
Tuberculin
  sensitivity to, 105–6, 135
  surveys, 103–5, 124–30
Tuberculoma of the brain, 145
Tuberculosis, 100–154
  in American Negroes, 116–54
  in Bahr el Ghazal, 115
  basis of susceptibility to, 141–51
  blood calcium in, 140
  case fatality in, 136–37
  childhood infections in, 124, 125, 127, 128, 129, 130, 133, 143, 145, 146, 147
  clinical course of, 133–36
  duration of, 136–37
  during slavery, 117–18
  in Dutch Guiana, 116
  environmental factors in, 145, 146, 148, 149
  epidemiology of, 126, 130–33
  genotypic low resistance in, 146, 147, 149
  hospital beds for, 137–38
  inoculated artificially, 140
  introduction into Africa, 101, 103
  isohemagglutinins in, 139
  in Jamaica, 132–33
  of lymph glands, 107, 108, 113, 125, 129, 141, 142, 147, 151
  massive infection with, 109, 148
  mortality from, 118–22

natural history of, 123
natural selection in, 150, 151
in the North, 120
pathological anatomy of, 140-45
Pott's disease in, 108
primitive, 108
resistance to, 146, 147, 149
in Senegalese, 106-9, 115
of the skin, 381-82
in the South, 120
in South Africa, 109-15
in Tanganyika, 115
treatment of, 137-38
x-ray surveys for, 127, 128, 129
in Zanzibar, 115
Tumors, 327-55
benign, 327-35
malignant, 335-55
Typhoid fever, 223-26
agglutinins in, 225
antigens of, 225
carriers, 225

Ultraviolet light, protection against, 94-96
Urban birth rate, 12, 13
Ureteral calculi, 316-18
Urolithiasis, 316-18

Vaccination
against pneumonia, 204-5
against smallpox, 214

Vascular phenomena in sickle cell anemia, 242, 246
Vasomotor reactions in hypertension, 294
Vertebral column, 70
"Virgin soil" tuberculosis, 106
Vision, acuity of, 393-94
Vital statistics, 11-17
birth rate, 11-13
expectation of life, 15
general mortality, 13-17
infant mortality, 17
Vitamin C and pigmentation, 388
Vitamin D and rickets, 264
Vitiligo, 386-87

Weights of organs, 75-77
White melanin, 39
Woolly hair
among whites, 62-63
protective action of, 96

Xanthism, 386
Xeroderma pigmentosum, 380-81
X-ray surveys for tuberculosis; see, Tuberculosis, x-ray surveys for

Yaws, 184-87
Yellow fever, 210-14
surveys for, 212, 213

Zanzibar, tuberculosis in, 115

Printed in the USA
CPSIA information can be obtained
at www.ICGtesting.com
LVHW071928271023
761758LV00103B/122